DATE DUE

AP 7 97

Culture and Development in Africa

RICLAC

RICLAC

Culture and Development in Africa

Edited by
Stephen H. Arnold and Andre Nitecki

Africa World Press, Inc.

P.O. Box 1892
Trenton, New Jersey 08607

Trenton, NJ 08607

Library of Congress Catalog Card Number: 89-81234

ISBN: 0-86543-145-0 Cloth
    0-86543-146-9 Paper

Cover Design: Cindy Bower

Comparative Studies in African/Caribbean Literature Series

Series Editor: Stephen H. Arnold
Associate Editor: George Lang

African and Caribbean Literature Section
Research Institute for Comparative Literature
The University of Alberta
Edmonton, Alberta
CANADA T6G 2E6

Contents

Preface

The plight of Africa derives not just from historical forces of exploitation, but from the ineffective efforts of many people of goodwill — Africans and non-Africans — who toil to reverse the results of imperialism, colonialism and neo-colonialism. Of the European legacy in Africa, balkanization is one of the most enduringly frustrating facts. Another kind of balkanization, however, and one which is remediable, has not been the subject of sufficient debate. As V.Y. Mudimbe has so potently and plentifully pointed out, African thought and language are thoroughly colonized by European thought and language. The mind-drawn boundaries of this thought system have balkanized intellectual and practical approaches to almost every problem or object/ subject of study and action, be it Africa or any other topic.

African Studies was once a broad, holistic superdiscipline, emphasizing language, culture and history. Sadly, like with other Area Studies traditions, African Studies have in recent decades been eclipsed by the rise of Development Studies in our institutions of higher education and in the halls of governments that occasionally find use for academics.

A degree in Development Studies is a ticket to development work "in the field" or a key to governmental and non-governmental offices concerned with a variety of preoccupations generally subsumed or masked under the rubric of development. A degree in Area Studies leads to museums or back into the classroom, away from the field and from concrete consideration of the plight of the living. Both approaches to our subject, Africa, have balkanized it so much that there no longer seems to be an avenue of intellectual preparation to grasp the whole.

Development Studies are technocratic in nature; they tend to treat humans as cyphers and often regard concrete problems as abstractions calling for technical solutions. They tend equally toward arid empiricism and brittle theoretical generzations. Area Studies are humanistic in nature; their practitioners fully accept the significance of human subjectivity in almost every event, but they have become so consumed with jargon envy of the non-humanists that they also have become balkanized within their own ranks, bifurcating far too often into impotent empiricists and theorists. Embodying subjective contradictions, they feel simultaneously that their work is irrelevant to the human dramas which grind relentlessly on across the African stage, or that their work, no matter how valuable, is inaccessible to the philistines they imagine to be in need of it.

The gulfs that divide Area and Development Studies professionals from themselves and from each other may be the result of profound, historical causes which have perverted much of the academy beyond their realms, but these gulfs can be bridged. Just as Africa is a splendid whole which transcends the sum of its parts, moreso ought to be the total of our fragmented knowledge about it. The missing link among parts and among peoples, scholars, government and aid workers, etc. is — to use a cliche that cannot be avoided — communication.

It was a concern about our technocratic balkanization and a desire to promote holistic views leading toward a healing, transcendent understanding of Africa which led colleagues at the University of Alberta to host a conference in 1987 which brought a focus on culture as a neglected, crucial factor in development work and study. From April 30 to May 10, 1987, the Canadian Association of African Studies and its guests met as "CAAS '87" to discuss two major, interlocked themes: "Crises in Africa: Successes and Failures of Governments, Aid and Academe," and "Cultural Aspects of African Development."

"CAAS '87" drew several hundred participants, from many countries and from many sectors, from the purely academic world to the worlds of business, labour and government. They participated in pre-conference work-shops on Music, Textiles, Storytelling, Agricultural Issues, Management Problems, Theatre for Development, Research Methodologies (stressing techniques of "participatory research"), etc. At the conference itself, about two hundred papers were presented. This present volume is only a sampling of the thoughtful offerings of so many Africanists. Many excellent papers from the conference can be read in a variety of periodicals, including the *Canadian Journal of African Studies/ Revue canadienne des études africaines.*

With so many papers to consider, your Editors had to rely on the advice of area panels headed by University of Alberta Africanists. Ironically, perhaps, we promoters of holistic approaches to Africa had to resort to our own balkanization and its attendant distortions in order to accomplish our task. Editorial sub-committees were headed by: Frances Adam (Social Sciences); Stephen Arnold (General Culture and Media); David Barnet

(Theatre); Ann McDougall (History and Agriculture — out of this latter area came a companion volume of proceedings: *Sustainable Agriculture in Africa*); Eloise Murray (Women in Development); Andre Nitecki (Education and Communications); Jane Ross (Health). (Among the many subcommittee members who did particularly valuable work were professors Fred Judson and Alain Noel of the University of Alberta in the social sciences group, and Rick Stewart of the University of Calgary in History.)

The criteria of selection were complicated. Quality, of course, was necessary. Relevance to either or both of the major conference themes was, as well. A spread across disciplines and some balance between area and development studies orientations were also sought. Finally, since the conference organizers had put special emphasis on participation by non-academics and graduate students, these groups had also to be represented in the final sample presented here.

Since by design the conference involved public admission and analysis of failures, we should explain why there are no papers here on one of the conference's central objects of scrutiny, Theatre for Development ("TD"). (There was, in fact, one paper accepted on this topic, by Oga Abah of Nigeria, but we regret that flawed communications prevented necessary editing from being done in time. Another paper here, by K. Bame, does touch on some experimentation with drama as a development tool, though that is not its major focus.) If any element of the conference was itself a success and a failure, it was the "TD" events. As Abah observed astutely, development practitioners were too impatient to see the value of this proven tool for promoting positive participation in development projects by people for whom development is being pursued. In a short period of time, and in a remote place like Canada, the *in vivo* effectiveness that TD practitioners have demonstrated in Africa could not be convincingly taught *in vitro*. However, the tool is not what failed. Nor was it the instruction, for that was provided by experienced and celebrated practitioners brought from Africa (Stephen Chifunyise, Hansel Ndumbe-Eyoh, Oga Abah and Mathilda Malamamfumu), as well as well known practitioners resident in Edmonton (David Barnet, Jan Selman, Kevin Burns, Tolo Mollel and others). The source of the failure was the mind-forged manacles that are cultivated in our development and even area studies students. Culture is not sufficiently important to them as a factor in development until they have actually tried to apply their abstract learning in the field.

The conference was billed as a hard look at failures and a welcoming of success stories. Both of these emphases encouraged case study presentations, which abound in the pages that follow here. In allocating the travel money at their disposal, organizers favored younger scholars and graduate students, those who had the most to learn from case studies and the most promise of being susceptible to the conference's biases. A large proportion of the papers in this volume, therefore, come from scholars who are still in the formative stages of their careers. Two such papers are "Conflicting Perceptions of Hazards in African Development: The Case of Floods and Drought" and "Women and Trees," by Saidou Jallow and Liz Osborn, both graduate students who shared the Fraser Taylor Prize for the best student papers at CAAS '87. These two papers express the vital heart of the conference themes, the issue of subjectivity as an objective factor in development problems.

There are hydrologists who do development work who are convinced that water is H_2O and nothing more, that it is the same everywhere. There are agroforestry experts who do development work who think that mangongos are *Ricinodendron rautanenii* and nothing more, that they are the same everywhere. These people forget that in all cultures — their own included — the *genus* of water or tree has subjective significance, and that the 'species' names (ice, fog, rain; oak, baobab, birch) are even more rife with connotative meanings. Water and trees are indeed palpable, manipulable, quantifiable, exploitable, material necessities for life. But they are also the stuff of poetry, reflections of the spiritual and cultural beings of the peoples who depend on them. As such they have qualities which developers must not ignore. Jallow and Osborn, as young representatives of our profession who grasp firmly the principles implicit here, give us hope for the achievement of holistic, transcendent, effective approaches to our common cause. In the pages that follow here they are joined by many other authors who put forward the same message.

For those who remain sceptical that culture is so significant in the development process, an anecdote to explain why Niyi Osundare's paper on poetry opens this volume may clinch the point. Dr. Osundare writes poems to newspaper readers. His unusual approach to his art and craft combines inspirational concerns with practical matters of the day. His poems motivate millions and threaten the status quo. If poets had no material importance, Dr. Osundare, winner of the 1986 Commonwealth Prize for Poetry, would have made it to CAAS '87 to be its banquet speaker. But he did not make it because shortly before he was to depart for Canada he was viciously attacked and left for dead, allegedly by thieves who did not bother to take his car, his watch and few other belongings available to them when they put an axe in his head at night on the University of Ibadan campus as he was leaving work late for home. Dr. Osundare survived, and we are most pleased to print here the text of the banquet address he could not give in person. (A funding residue brought him to campus in late 1988 to delight local crowds at the University and children in schools.)

The order of papers that follow Osundare's in these selections from CAAS '87 is somewhat inspired by Osundare's pointed whimsy. The reader should find here an oscillation between elucidation of practical particulars and less mundane studies of a more general, theoretical importance. It is the rhythm of this oscillation which should provoke in serious Africanist minds a dialectical balancing back and forth from culture and subjectivity to technological and "objective" matters, revealing how they are mutually interdependent and how they must be considered together.

Non-Canadians are often surprised to learn that Canada gives more dollars per capita of its own population to aid developing countries than any other nation, and that a very large percentage of this aid is concentrated on Africa. Given this investment, it is particularly laudatory that a main channel of this aid, the Canadian International Development Agency/ l'Agence canadienne de développement international, would be so generous as it was in order to ensure that a conference which might criticize it could be held. We are most grateful to CIDA and its Public Participation and Africa 2000 Programs for having the vision to provide substantial funding for a conference like CAAS '87 and we hope that the following pages will vindicate their trust. It is also through the generosity of CIDA that we are able to provide free copies of both volumes of these proceedings to research libraries in Africa.

Stephen H. Arnold
University of Alberta
July, 1989

Bard of the Tabloid Platform: A Personal Experience of Newspaper Poetry in Nigeria

Niyi Osundare
University of Ibadan

I

> Poetry matters because of the kind of poet who is more alive than other people, more alive in his own age. He is, as it were, at the most conscious point of the race in his time . . . . The potentialities of human experience in any age are realized only by a tiny minority, and the important poet is important because he belongs to this.[1]

Traditional, oral Africa thrives on the song; every occasion has its lyrics, even trivial incidents provoke a ballad. There are songs which mark the inexorable cycle of human existence — birth, puberty, marriage, age, and death. There are songs for praising, songs for cursing, songs of abuse; songs which wax purple in the King's palace, songs which josh and jolt in *buka*[2] banters. The towncrier talks in song, the food hawker chants panegyrics for his tasty wares, while in the marketplace haggling and hustling take place in rhythms of comical ditties. I have seen old people weep in poetry; I have also seen them wipe their eyes with a piece of rounded *alamo*.[3]

These are facts which establish themselves without the simplism of Mr. Senghor's I-dance-therefore-I-am, or the naive racism of others who only see the African as a singing swaying bunch forever trapped in the castle of his drum.

But the pressing question here is: if traditional Africa is so full of song, how do we explain the pitiable plight of written poetry in that part of the world? The hasty generalization that even in the developed, literate world poetry is a "dying genre" will not answer our question. The galloping popularity of dub poetry even in the West has shown that poetry could be made not only alive and well, but also to help keep society so. We must look farther, therefore, for the answers to our question. And our locus of operation is the Nigerian society.

The first bane of written poetry in Nigeria is, ironically, its medium. A colonial, alienating language, English is used with a more than average competence by less than 15 per cent of Nigerians. It is a language of incalculable power for the few lucky or privileged enough to master it, and the butt of scepticism, even hostility by the majority who are oppressed by it.

Pioneer Nigerian poets of English expression deepened this alienation by reaching out for a kind of literary dialect which set the tongue at variance with our ear. Borrowing a leaf from the cultivated stylistic arrogance of Eliot, Pound, and Dylan Thomas, our poets gave their audience a short shrift and commenced a private dialogue with their Muse(s). The taut, ruthlessly elliptical style of Soyinka, the lyrical though eccentrically eclectic style of Okigbo, the learnedly Latinate mode of Echeruo just could not have gone down well with a people still caught up in the painful transition from illiteracy.[4] As Margaret Schlauch has said about the poetic situation of another place, our audience could not share the idiom of their poets.[5]

The problem of alienation did not stop with form. The subject of these poets was so staid, so distant, so art-for-arts-sake. The problems of dehumanizing poverty, colonialism and neo-colonialism, political tyranny, class oppression and other such monsters which lay our spirit low are either ignored (as in the case of Echeruo), or broached in impenetrable idioms (Soyinka and Okigbo); J.P. Clark's poetry is relatively free of stylistic opaqueness, but a failure of clear social vision put him behind our times.

Generally, therefore, the first generation of Nigerian poets were poets of the ivory tower, literary cultists who monologued to each other. The people wanted to see their image; the poets' mirrors were too high above their heads.

A new generation of poets has risen in Nigeria; though mindful of the artistic prodigy of their forerunners, they are ready to match accessible, elegant style with relevant content.[6]

My experiment with newspaper poetry grew in this ferment of aesthetic revolution.

II

Let every mouth tell
A listening ear:
> We find in his many and varied songs
> Voices of his and other times[7]

Intrigued, indeed provoked, by the paradox mentioned earlier on between the astounding popularity of oral poetry in Nigeria and a relative nonchalance towards the written, I decided in March 1985 to attempt a popularization of written poetry through the medium of the newspaper. The Editor-in-chief of the Tribune[8] newspapers embraced the idea, and we both agreed that the *Sunday Tribune* would be a perfect forum for it. Thus began *Songs of the Season*, a column which has taken an average of two poems (about 35 to 40 lines each) every week.

But the "psychological" origin of *Songs of the Season* dates back to 1983. The blatant way the general elections of that year were rigged, and the widespread civil strife which ensued left many Nigerians perplexed and despondent. I felt the occasion called for satire and a poetry of indictment, and I wrote a few songs which the *Tribune* published on a full page in one of its daily issues. The tremendous response from my students and colleagues, and from the reading public generally, instantly opened my eyes to the possibilities of the newspaper as a platform for verse journalism. That awareness received concrete fulfillment in 1985.

Of course, it would be both erroneous and immodest to say that mine was the first poetry column in a Nigerian newspaper. Far from it. Before *Songs of the Season* there were "Poet's Corners" in some papers, but a poverty of expression and triviality of substance crippled many of these "corners" and turned them into a great disservice to genuine poetry in general. One of my first missions, therefore, was to create a genre which transcended these largely despised doggerels, but which steered clear of the alienating opaqueness of the so-called serious poetry.

And why the newspaper? Because it possesses enormous potential for reaching the people whose joys and sorrows, whose lives and deaths, whose triumphs and travails formed the crux of the *Songs*. My overriding mission is to create songs which jolt the slumbering, give hope to the despondent, open up the eyes of the blind. In a country of astonishing social inequalities, and pervasive ignorance, it is to show my people that the rich were not born so, and the poor need not die so. It is to stress the inevitability of change and the possible triumph of justice.

I discovered early enough that learned journals and poetry magazines lack the ease of expression, immediacy of purpose, and general accessibility needed to carry the weight of my social vision. To make matters worse, these publications are an endangered (if not yet extinct) species in Nigeria. Of all the creative writing journals of the sixties and seventies, only *Okike* has managed to break the *ogbanje* syndrome. Even *Black Orpheus*, that once robust outlet of creative tempests, now hangs on to life by intermittent gasps. The gruesome reality of our IMF-commanded economy has no mercy for humanistic ventures. As for published poetry collections, they are regarded as awesome pills prescribed only for those sick enough to study literature for their examinations.

The newspaper, therefore, presents a viable forum. It is accessible, relatively cheap, and widely distributed. It feedback is almost immediate: one can feel the pulse of those he is trying to touch. It is a good platform for wooing an audience for poetry, for making it possible for poetry-haters to "stumble upon" poems they will read and forever ask for more.

For this to happen, the poet's offering must be varied, he must render songs which pluck a chord in every throat. This condition rhymes in well with my intention to assail the myth that certain experiences, certain phenomena cannot (or should not) be captured in poetry and verse. My newspaper experiment is thus aimed at tapping the expressive potentialities of poetry so as to show that the genre need not trap itself in those lofty ideas which establishment critics proclaim as its only province. My subjects, therefore, have ranged from the local to the universal, from the national to the international. This has not only pushed forward the ideational possibilities of poetry, it has also confirmed for me and my readers that oft-cited oneness of humanity, from Tema to Tegucigalpha, from Soweto to Seoul, from the harmattan bush fire to nuclear armagedon, our world of manifold struggles yields abundant ingredients for the sensitive song.

But how can you do all this, I have been asked once by a curious friend, without boring your readers? How is it possible to have a subject or two every week about which poems could be written? My experience has shown that "poetic" subjects abound; the poet may even be in some difficulty choosing which one to sing about. The decidedly topical nature of my enterprise makes this all the more so: ours is a restless world where things are always happening. The hands of its clock never stay in a spot for too long.

The first step, therefore, was to understand my medium (the newspaper), to study the demands of its register, and master the psychology of its coverage. True to the title of the column as *Songs of the Season*, the first priority for the choice of the week's subject is its "newsiness," its topicality. Thus, poems like "Not Guilty," "Sacrifice," "Where Are the Millions Gone?," "Health for All by Year 2000," "IMF," "A Tongue in the Crypt" sprang straight from contemporary happenings and parlance. Closely tied to this is the social import of the subject. Generally, the theme of social conscientization permeates the poems, but to avoid monotony I have devised four modes of articulating the message:

through parables: "Crying Hyena," "The Pot and the Pan," "Slaves who Adore their Chains," "The Oppressor's Recipe," "The King and the Poet," etc.

through direct address: "A Song for Ajegunle," "Song of the Street Sweeper," "Retrenched," "Song of the Jobless Graduate," etc.

through dramatic exchange: "A Peasant Debates a Professor," "Olowo

Debates Talaka," etc.
through hymn-like lyric: "Our Land Is Rich, Our Mind Is Poor," "Song of
the Kangaroo," etc.

There are also eulogies and tributes: For Olaf Palme, Fela
Anikulapo-Kuti, Tai Solarin, Ayodele Awojobi, Dele Giwa, Esiri
Dafiewhare etc.; songs for local festivals: "A Song for Olosunta"; songs on
socio-philosophical issues: "Money," "Truth," etc.; songs of humour:
"Snaplines," "Buka Banter," etc.

Prominent at the back of my mind are the traditional roles of the oral
poet to whom I owe a lot: to entertain, to inform, to satirize, and to warn.
Thus, when hundreds of politicians detained for stealing government funds
were released in 1985, and they were welcomed back as if nothing had
happened, "Song of the Sudden Storm" raised a painful alarm:

Ah! the hyenas are back again
To thundering bugles of our crippled memory.

And the poem ended with an anxious fusion of warning and indictment:

Fickle like a fart
Forgetful like a tale-less tribe,
People of our land,
Our memory is a lazy dust
Washed easily off our head
By showers of arbitrary seasons.

The subjects are many, the possibilities vast and the challenge to put
them all in song lofty and often daunting. Too brazen factuality is injurious
to poetry, and that bane goes hand in hand with topicality, one of the prime
props of *Songs of the Season*. In a number of songs I have tried to tame fact
with fancy by using the parabolic mode. (See reference to parables above.)
The folktale technique has been enormously useful here. Casting new
happenings in old modes, couching the here-and-now in the form of
once-upon-a time, I have discovered that the poem could actually be an
everlasting proverb.

A very elastic proverb, too, whose mirror admits all kinds of seminal
contortions and aesthetic indirectness. To present current happenings in the
can and can't in which they come would be to court a certain kind of
photographism that would insult the audience's imagination. Where possible,
therefore, attempts are made to present the familiar in the style of the strange
and vice-versa. For I strongly believe that art thrives on recognition, but I
also believe there must a shock in that recognition.

Writing poetry (an "elevated genre") for a newspaper (a popular if not populist outfit) involves a considerable balancing act. The ropes are particularly precarious in a largely non-literate society trying to grapple with the problems of an alien language. A cautious simplicity comes in as some kind of solution. As much as possible, my vocabulary stays close to the marketplace, the public square, the crowded motor park, the festival crowd, the seething slum, the opulent districts, the sun, the moon, the rivers, the mountains, the green glory of the rain forest, the copper glow of harvested fields. The challenge has been to *mediate* all this for a newspaper audience without allowing the mode to dip into banality, the subject-matter into *kitsch*.

Response from this audience has been inspiring, which explains why I have been able to go for two years now without buckling. A few colleagues in the ivory tower consider the poems of *Songs of the Season* not tough and torturesome enough. Raised on the ascetic diet of Eliot and Pound, their clearest definition of poetry is enlightened masochism. They are hardly aware of the *purpose* of the songs, the *medium* of their articulation, and the *target* of their message.

But the response of the majority of readers has been robustly heartening. In its two years of existence the column has provoked many "letters to the editor," some of them poems written as feedback to poems published earlier on in the slot. I have also received many personal letters from places far and near, commenting on some of the songs. The most touching of these responses was that of a middle-aged man to the poem "Retrenched" (published in March 1985). Actually "retrenched" at a multinational company which he had served for over twenty years, with a wife and seven children and a long line of extended family dependents, he suddenly lost interest in living and was seriously contemplating suicide when on Sunday morning he stumbled upon the poem "Retrenched." As he told me when he came a few days later to see me at the university, what re-affirmed his faith in life was the last stanza:

> My wife is wan, my kids are cold
> the times are hard but so my heart
> I will never die on the rubbish heap
> I've sowed my sweat, I deserve to reap.

I had never met him before, and he travelled well over five hundred kilometres to make this meeting possible.

To sum up, *Songs of the Season* is a humble attempt to intrude upon the world, to create a "new aesthetic democracy"[9] locked in an historic, regenerative conflict with the protean monsters of our underdevelopment. It is a demonstration of my long-cherished belief in the transformative, emancipatory power of art, of poetry. For, as F. R. Leavis has very remarkably observed, "if poetry and the intelligence of the age lose touch with each other, poetry will cease to matter much, and the age will be lacking in finer awareness."[10]

TABLOID POEMS by Niyi Osundare

Retrenched

Sunday Tribune, 24 March, 1986, p. 13.
Once I had a job in hand
Menial though, I stuck to it
It put no beef in the cooking pot
But I shamed my hunger with oku Eko*

I worked and worked as a factory hand
I worked till my hands were rough like granite
At thirty and five I look like sixty
My frame is crouched like a bended bow

I worked and worked for a grateful boss
Who used me just the way he liked
And raised my wage once a dozen years
The priests have said he's a godly man.

I worked and worked, then the dizzying news:
The nation is broke and factories fail
the boss is licensed to suck the sack
And that is how I lost my job

The boss has said it's the nation's good
To lower our coffin and bike his profits
Sacrifice! sacrifice? for motherland
Time to starve for fatherland

Who wields the knife and who the lamb
Whose blood must flow like August rain
To wet the roots of the desert greed
Of those who think they own the earth?

Country broke? Who broke the country?

Who looted the millions of the oily boom?
Who stole the licence to import our needs
To swell their fortunes and shrink our own?
We work for the land they work it dry
Their private greed our public griefs
They borrow and borrow for us to pay
Who never know their Swiss escape

And so it was I lost my job
In a plant I've served with youth and strength
I know no trade besides the one
That's sapped my life for twenty years

My wife is wan, my kids are cold
the times are hard, but so my heart
I will never die on the rubbish heap
I've sowed my sweat, I deserve to reap
   *Oku Eko-the corpse of Lagos, i.e. frozen fish.

Poverty's Offence

Sunday Tribune, 24 March, 1986, p. 13.
"Where are your fees?"
The teacher asked,
his face one mask
of screaming bell;
"Where are your fees?"
the teacher asked again.

"I don't have them, Sir,"
Replied the trembling boy,
"Daddy lost his job a year ago,
We hardly have enough to eat,
And the landlord, Sir . . . ."

"Shut up your silly mouth!",
The teachers bellowed,
Growing more and more demonic,
"I ask for fees, not a tale of woe"

He snapped his finger
And in rolled a bundle of canes:

A dozen strokes on the boy's ragged butto
A dozen strokes, for owing a fee.

Come Home (a mother's plea)

Sunday Tribune, 27 April, 1986
Come home, Tanimola,
Come home

It is a long time now
Since your gentle feet last touched
The dust of our village road:
The egg hatched by the hen of your youth
Has grown through rain and sun
Into a crowing cock,
The tree on whose branches once
Hanged your puberty clothes
Has shot into the towering skies

Come home today,
For your childhood friends
Are wreaking wonders:
Alogbo just married his seventh wife —
The king's own daughter
Whose skin is smooth as glass
Whose eyes are eggs of a priceless bird;
Sapadl came back from Lagos
In the season of grating corns,
And three months later, a stunning mansion
Ate up the forest near the baobab
Its miserable dung;
Pagbon too is back, corpulent now
Like a fattened pig, a gold tooth
Or two peeping out of his fleshy jaws;
Some call him rogue, some call him robber,
Some even say his wealth came
From the spirits of night
The village tongue borrows a wag
From the tail of its favourite dog.
but everyone knows Pagbon's father
Now has a leg of wheels,
His mother has a wardrobe more ample
Than a corncob's in the apogee
Of the season of thundering rains.
And yet my soles are sore
My temples crack under unmerciful burdens
My powder is ash, my raiment rags
With widening windows;
When will this darkness see

The gleaming of your dawn?
When will my first dream drop
From the spring of your golden pot?

Come home, Tanimola,
Come home, son of the rumbling elephant;
Yesterday's butterflies are soaring .
Now like eagles
Those who couldn't count their fingers
Book or money
Gongosu who carried one dumb rock
Between his ears
Now owns a streetful of houses
He came back last year —
In khaki and buttons
With a swagger stick in his glistening hand
And a golden swagger in his piglike mouth;
His orixi fills every mouth like dry meat,
The Oba swears by his powerful frame.
And yet, there you are, son,
Obscure like a hidden coin.

Come home, son
Come save me
From this heap of darkening shame;
They say your books fill up
A whole house
They say you can even hold the pen
With your bare toes;
Your certificate is large, my son,
But my wrappa is small.
 I am tired of simpering glances
 I am tired of poisonous whispers
 I am tired of sniggering jeers
 I am tired of pinching prattles
(To be continued next week)

Come Home

Sunday Tribune, 4 May, 1986, p. 5.
(Cont'd from last week)
Come home, son
Carry your pot to the river
Where others have fetched that water
Which now blooms their ancient deserts.
Or are you that fool, son

Who lives in the sea
but washes his hands with spittle?

Fools have prospered;
Why suffer, wise man?

Come home, Tanimola
Come home, son of the water buffalo
With a thousand horns,
Come home, TODAY

You were born in the fold of lions
Do not graze with a flock of sheep

women
(watch out for the son's reply)

A song for human rights day

Sunday Tribune, 15 Dec., 1986, p. 6.
My heart goes to you today
You buried alive in dreary dungeons
Where darkness looms like an iron cloud
And TERROR rules every chip
In the stony silence of windowless walls

My heart goes to you today
You whose flesh lies broken in the wake
Of the TORTURER'S orgy
My ears attend your groans, you
Whose skulls crack under
The practiced clatter of IRON HEELS

My heart goes to you today
You toiling antelopes stalked daily
by the greed of prowling lions
I remember the snail
Whose shell suddenly turns furnace

In the blinding fires of eating chiefs
My heart goes to you today
Comrades with ankles eaten pale
By the crocodile teeth of Apartheid chains
I remember Mandela caged up
For the soaring banners of a billion dreams
    And the millions who stagger down

the jaws of Jo'burg
Without a shadow, without a name
Brutally interned in the prison of their skin.

I remember Moloise
I remember Biko
I remember Ruth, ever First
I remember Sharpville
I remember Soweto
I remember Langa

I remember our deathless heroes
Rising and falling, falling and rising
Finally torching the pyre which melts
The chains of a thousand years

My heart goes to you today
Embattled Nicaragua stiffly striving
To save Sandino's dreams
My heart goes to Angola
Where a stubborn valour fights back
The hosts of Sunset killers
I remember Sabra and El Salvador
And Chile and Guatamala
I remember Liberia where a boy-king
Daily soaks his stolen throne in brimming blood
And Zaïre where a blackened leopard
Holds us in leash for Sunset cheatahs

My heart goes to you today
You ceaselessly donkeyed by the slaver's burden
My heart goes to you
Too hungry, too ill, too ignorant
To know your trampled names

I shout those names
In the silent alleys
Of hurrying ears
I shout those names
In the urgent baptism
Of coming thunder

Health for all by year 2000

Sunday Tribune, 5 Jan., 1986
Though rubbish builds skyscrapers in our
streets
And malaria struts the lanes like a conquering
demon
> HEALTH FOR ALL BY YEAR 2000

Though poxes tattoo our skins
And cholera mines the pit of every stomach
> HEALTH FOR ALL BY YEAR 2000

Though a dog(ed) living harasses our nerves
And tension snuffs out our hearts like
OGUSO flames
> HEALTH FOR ALL BY YEAR 2000

Though our young age at a score and ten
And the old die hungry deaths in dingy hovels
> HEALTH FOR ALL BY YEAR 2000

Though kwashiorkor decimates our brood
And our children so obese with needless hunger
> HEALTH FOR ALL BY YEAR 2000

Though medicine merchants murder with
unnatural prices
> HEALTH FOR ALL BY YEAR 2000

And DEATH sells at a thousand for ten kobo
> HEALTH FOR ALL BY YEAR 2000

Though hospitals are horse-spittles
And theatre doors open into crowded
mortuaries
> HEALTH FOR ALL BY YEAR 2000

Health for all by year two thousand
Health so plenty like Sahara sand
In Geneva the WHO has set the game
In Lagos our rulers have echoed the same
Health for all by year two thousand
Bring the drum and pluck the sound

Snaplines (3)

Sunday Tribune, 5 Jan., 1986
Disquieting like a reluctant gun
Disastrous like a failed coup

Tell me, people of our land,
In what school do African rulers learn
The craft of graft?

The antelope which plays
Near the lion's den
Let it tread with mortal care

The thief
   is not one who steals
   but
one powerless enough to be caught

Take your choice:
IMF plus Conditionalities
IMF minus Conditionalities
Conditionalities minus IMF

There were ten casualties
In yesterday's riot . . .
One PERSON
and
Nine Blacks

In my dear beloved country
DEATH is cheaper than Sahara sand
You need no queue to get your share.

Song of the sudden storm

Sunday Tribune, 13 Oct., 1985, p. 6.
A sudden storm ripped through
The jungle of torture
Where chamber-pots held the prisoner's dinner
And men, packed like alligator-pepper seeds,
Scrambled animally for scanty air,
A sudden storm
Where steel-headed monsters once relished
gory shrieks from dungeons of death

A sudden storm which threw open
The doors of anguish
And, alas, out trooped animals
Of unspeakable colours,
Their claws still cunning as ever
Their fangs ever so fatal . . .

Ah the hyenas are back again
    thundering bugles of our crippled memory
The people hailed the triumphant freedom
Of the gazelle whose beauty is sun
    to our brooding streets,
The dazzling antelope whose lithesome legs
Play carrier to speedy hopes,
Even the parrot whose stubborn beak
Is question mark for a thousand answers . . .

BUT
We also saw the hyena with paws still dripping
The blood of our recent hopes,
We also saw the lion who gobbled us for lunch
And sprawled out our children
For his evening banquet . . .

Ah the hyenas are back again
To thundering bugles of our crippled memory

We saw the monkey, we saw the mongoose
We saw the hare, we saw the hound
We saw the earthworm, we saw the serpent
We saw the wolf who covered his thieving track
With quenchless infernos in our treasure houses
We saw them all . . .
Galloping through the crests of our merciful madness

Ah the hyenas are back again
To thundering bugles of our crippled memory

We saw them all . . .
Their cheeks still so robust, their claws uncanny,
We saw them all . . .
Talkathief like a waterfall
Cocky like cockatoos
We saw them all . . .
Wondering what frantic fiat has heroed thus
These carrionsters of our yester corpses . . .

Ah the hyenas are back again
To thundering bugles of our crippled memory

Fickle like a fart
Forgetful like a tale-less tribe,
People of our land,
Our memory is a lazy dust
Washed easily off our head
By showers of arbitrary season

Diverscope

Sunday Tribune, 24 Feb., 1985, p. 14.
Serves him right the fool
He was sacked - summarily
For sauntering so confidently
Into the senior staff toilet
A bulging bladder blinded his eyes
To the SENIOR STAFF ONLY
Which stood guard like a silent sentry
On the forbidding door
And so, he got the sack for criminal "jay-pissing."

The Surgeon-General won a medal
And copious panegyrics cursived in gold and silver
A man of unmatchable feats
Just last week he sent a fortunate patient
On a blissful voyage:
He sewed him up with the surgical knife
In his bleeding belly
Our patient went into everlasting night
Sir surgeon into everprospering knighthood

"Chase him out of town," shouted the crowd,
Raging like a swindled storm,
"Twist his neck till he sees his ears."
But a quieter look shows the innocent man
Merely pocketed (didn't even steal)
A few millions . . .
And that, on ALL OF US's behalf.
Chase him out of town?

Whatever has become of African hospitality?
Next time a saaji sculpts your back
With patriotic koboko
Bend one knee and thank the god of WAI

IMF

Sunday Tribune, 24 Feb., 1985, p. 14
I am the deathly belt
    swallowed hastily by the mindless rat

I am the brazen bandit
    garnering global loot into sunset peonage

I am, indeed, the doctor
    who heals by killing the patient

Echoes from the rural abyss

Sunday Tribune, 9 March, 1986, p. 5.
OUR water comes from the brook
which swells with the cholera floods of August
and, in December, dries up
like a shy droplet on a sizzling rock

OUR electricity comes from OGUSO
and the old merciful moon
which lends a milky flicker
to our long and lingering nights

OUR roofs are thatch
our eaves dog-eared like forsaken rags
our mansions are mud
wearing bamboo belts like staggering sentry

OUR school is the farmland
where hoes scribble juicy yams for city tables
our children are the unlettered legion
with blank diplomas from the jungle college

OUR expressway is the footpath
only wide enough for our thorn-harassed soles
our bridge is a fallen mahogany
spanning the risky breadth of roaring rivers

So
Next time the taxman comes in his hel(i)copter
let him come like an iron hawk:
he will find us waiting
a flock of iron chicks.

The pot and the pan

Sunday Tribune, 9 March, 1986, p. 5.
THE pot once said to the pan:
"I deserve the crown of the fireplace
I have shamed so many flames
And farted on heaps of conquered ash"

"You have no head to put a crown "
The pan answered in fiery anger,
   "Thick-bottomed, heavy footed piece
Of hollowed earth, You
You cook one rat and a few morsels
Of soft yam
Then shout: Oh! see how I feed the world;
What do you want me to say
Who reign in harvest seasons
And bear the heat of festive hearths?"

   And so they bragged
   So they quarreled
But neither said a word
About the EATERS
Of what they cooked.

Money

Sunday Tribune, 16 March, 1986, p. 5
you who behead without a sword
you who speak without a mouth

you who fool the sage and sage the fool
you who are the aroma of the strutting skunk

you who plant a squint in the eyes of the Law
you who hawk justice at ten for half kobo

you who walk naked through a crowded market
robed in rustles and ogling glitter

"When I am not at home," you once declared.
"let no dreams rise above their lowly beds
let no pestles fight their matron mortars
for I am
        the monster in the millionaire's paunch
        the gorging glitter in the gold-digger's
        eyes
        the undying smile on the strumpet's lips
        the fanciest feather in the wing of
        angels

Verily verily I am
        the grass of the open sky
        the blood of rolling stones
        tears of sobbing stars

am
        the God of all gods

Our land is rich our mind is poor

Sunday Tribune, 16 March, 1986, p. 5.
Why grow it here
If available there?
We have the cash
They have the brain

Our land is rich our mind is poor
We hang the hoe and hug the drum
A barrel of oil is all we need
To get our food without delay

A barrel of oil will till the land
In USA or Thailand
The whole wide world is our pastureland
They know the nurture of our oily guts

Yes, the sweating back in Prairieland
Labouring hard to milk our thirst
They sapped our sweat in days of yore
And now the sea has changed its course

Hail Black Gold our sweet Messiah
Our liquid pride will bow the sky
The proud white world must know its place
A king now lives in Nigerland

Opel Toyota Jaguar and Benz
Our roads are paved to ply the world
Make them quick and send to us
Our thanks are full to the brim with cash

You think, we pay, you make, we take
Exchange, they say, is not a theft
Unending just like the mighty sea
Our oil will last and last and last

Unending, yes, our liquid gold

We shake the banks in Switzerland
From dawn to dusk we count our cash
Then go to bed like Arab sheiks

Very soon in our oily land
We'll ship in air and Tundra snow
The belles of Europe for our royal beds
We have the cash to buy the world.

Slave market, 1986

Sunday Tribune, Feb., 1986, p. 5
The sun this day
is an early bloomer:

crashing through the crimson womb
of January's clouds,
it stands, one ball of fire
in the furnace of the sky

Sweating even so early
they converge on the familiar spot
where intersecting roads douse waiting heads
in cloudy rains of dirt and dust
at this cannibal crossroads
they are the voiceless sacrifice
abandoned to vultures of greed

a motley crowd, remnant majority,
their faces one long map of uncharted anguish,
their tattered garments held together
by a stitch of lice
their coverless heads, their shoeless soles
their eyes burning distant like stubborn fires
in old, forgotten caves

a motley crowd
of desperate men and daring women
their children clothed by the morning mist,
pregnant with misery

Then
glides in a glittering Benz
glossy like a giant dolphin;
a fattened baron steps out
of the "owner's corner"
and the crowd becomes a babel of pleas:

> "Take me, massa, me, massa,
> I get pawa, pawa,
> I fit pull, I fit push
> Even self, if you put elephant for
> ground
> I fit carry am one time
> Look, massa, look massa,
> My arm complete, my finger

Take me, massa, take me, massa,
I don carry pounpoun for Chief Gbadodo
I don work plenty year for construction site
They know my work good; sir, they . . . .

The baron rummages the yelling crowd
like a cautious buyer in a used goods shed;
checking their biceps, inspecting their mouths,
examining their balding temples for hidden
cracks
and, without a word, without a whimper,
he lumbers back to his waiting monster
galloping on to another joint

the yelling crowd freezes back
to their welting perch
with the sun now so high
in the baking skies
and their brows one streak
of breadless beads.

Slaves who adore their chains

Sunday Tribune, 2 Feb., 1986, p. 5
Drudging donkeys
from the jungle of night
they plod silent lanes
beneath their voiceless burdens:

harried by history
ridden lame by mountains
of accumulated insults;
on they plod
at peace with their yoke

Restless ball
in the game of giants
they are kicked from pole to pole
crushed countless times
in the battering pit of iron heels
they leak from every vein
neither grumbling, neither kicking

Faggot in the raging fire of power
burning wearily from end to end
neither crackling, neither stirring
they borrow the deadening hush
of rain-afflicted hearths

Other-cheek-turners they are
who cherish the servile thunder
of wrongful slaps;
they are slaves
who adore their chains.

Wrestling from America

Sunday Tribune, 2 Feb., 1986, p. 5.
Their legs are baobab
their arms throbbing mortars
of frantic elephants
their necks are caryatids
for weighty heads
their mouths boastful
like a rainless thunder:

      words were sent to fight
      the first dual
      in the lingering alleys
      of captive ears;
      with vowels battling consonants,

and the field heavy with the grunt
of windy swagger . . .

Then the brawl:

And the one lifted the other
past knee, past chest, past head,
spinned him round and round
like a ponderous dummy
then slammed him like a bad burden
on the wailing canvas

the yelling crowd swept the thrower
off his winning feet,
the thrown lay (alone)
like a fallen mountain.

They say all this is called
WRESTLING FROM AMERICA

A song for Olosunta

Sunday Tribune, 4 Aug., 1985, p. 6.
You have counted twelve moons
On the fingers of time
Oh rock with the winkless eye;
You have broken another year
Like a seasoned kola
Oh rock too heavy for the pupil
Of the looking eye;
You who master Ikere's ancient sky
As the elephant rules the rump
O giant forests:
Mountain of mountains
Which tries the patience of the haughty leg

You have come in this prodigy of seasons
When thunder daunts the earth
And the sky is one shuddering jungle
Of lightning serpents
You have come, again,

When the season's promise ripens
In the womb of earth
And practiced hands midwife the advent
Of bouncing roots

Yours are fingers of grains, toes of tubers
Your eyelashes are pumpkin leaves
Begging the tasty fancy of the homing basket
Waters of your roots are mellow wines
In sagely skins
Your teeth are the healthy beads
On the corn's crispy cob.

Yours is the season of easeful laughters
Of heady pestles and merciful mortars
Of sudden rains and scanty suns
Yours is the season when iyan
Wrestles the agile throat
Laying him flat on his gobbling back
Yours is the season of songs
Of streets throbbing under
The frenzy of pounding feet

KEREREKE GIRODO
KERE RE KE KE GIRODO

So let AGBA hail the season
With accents of dawn:
Wonder drum whose leather is
Hide off the back of the gleaming sky,
Drum of distant depths which woes the choicest wood
In the forest beyond the eye

KEREREKE KE GIRODO

Let the sticks plunge their hoary heads
Into the leather's unfathomable belly,
Prompting ageless idioms

And proverbs with a thousand tongues

KEREREKE KE GIRODO

Gathered here, again,
Are feet which have broken
Twelve earthworms on the road
Of another season
Gathered here
to do your timeless bidding.
Rise, oh ancient drum,
Rise
And
    Take possession.
        *Olosunta is a huge rock in Ikere-Ekiti, also essence of the harvest spirit.
        *AGBA is a man-size drum beaten during the Olosunta festival.

Shout of the People

Sunday Tribune, 8 Sept., 1985, p. 6
We have heard so many dawn crows
And brave pledges from cocky throats
But their rooster has never laid an egg
And our brood waits, bereft
Of hatched hopes
    And shout the PEOPLE:
    Behold we starve

We have heard booming guns
Seen stern faces
And armoured monsters galloping
Like giant caterpillars

Down the spine of our creaking streets
We have seen neophytes crashing in
From History's unwritten books
Getting bloated with power
Breathing manacles and iron cudgels
    And shout the PEOPLE:
    Behold we starve

We have seen flimsy flames of dawn
Licked up by the sun of turbulent noons
We have seen seeds sown
In the compost of cheering crowds
Wither in the steel chambers
Of iron laws
     And shout the PEOPLE:
     Behold we starve

We have seen earthworms
Twirl into seething serpents
We have seen the dove
Swoop down like practiced hawks
We have seen a matronly moon
Suddenly turn a matriarch of mayhem
     And shout the PEOPLE:
     Behold we starve

We have seen a flowing tribe of
Agbada, kente, and babariga
We have seen caucuses of khaki
We have seen the shooter shot
And the shot rising into a convoy
Of haunting demons
We have seen smokes without fire
We have seen fires without smokes
     And shout the PEOPLE:
     Behold we starve

We have been trampled
Like peeny carpets
Spat upon
Like a dunghill
Chewed, then spat out
Like a hapless root

And shout the PEOPLE:
Break these chains!
For we bleed.

A song for my land (1) (for Nigeria at 25)

Sunday Tribune, 29 Sept., 1985, p. 6.
A pondering pilgrim
I have journeyed across my land,
A stubborn needle in her ample shreds . . .

My eyes have swum the brackish waters
Of coastal swamps,
Read the slippery lips of the Atlantic;
Through shoals, through shells
Through reefs which drill shy ships
Like hidden bombs,
And in shacks of zinc which bathe their kneeless stilts
In the copper basins of generous waters.
I have fed my fill on the sheer aroma
Of fishes coiled up like teasing hoops
Around the charmed circle of roadside fires
       * * *

Bearing leafy letters scribbled
By the mangrove fingers of slush regions,
I have knocked on the woody door
Of the rain forest,
Evergreen, dark, densely dark, even darker
Than Conrad's unpolished heart.
I have seen creepers belly-down like serpents
And climbers wrestling zealously
With the biceps of towering trees:
Iroko, obeche, mahogany . . .
Their teeming tribes blunting the boastful blade
Of seasoned matchets.
I have heard the earth quaking
Under the elephant's impassive mortars
And the monkey messaging countless grunts
From the telegraph of pylon branches
       * * *

Then the savannah grass
In the orchestra of the wind
Dancing, dancing, like straw stilts,
The elephant grass, having borrowed

Its elephantine height from the rain,
Sways loftily to the wearisome sadness
Of the hoeing framer.
And yet this the colony of lordly yams
Strutting out of earth's sandy belly.

This the colony of the capering cassava
Whose swollen foot is healthy news in hungry season
I see the grasscutter daring the smoking gun
The gazelle dazzling every shrub with maidenly beat
But the leopard it is which drives me
Up the desert fringes
      * * *

Whistling winds, daring dunes
Which have an eye in every sand,
The sun plants burning arrows in labouring heads,
Its own brow glowing with blue barrels of sheabutt ...
The baobab stands like a sitting giant
Its massive fruit swinging juicily
Like breasts of a thousand dreams
Here is the house of the millet,
The soybean, the guinea corn,
Their green fingers in the morning wind
Waiting for the golden promise of the rising sun,
Here once the pyramids of plenty
Since denied their feet
By storms of petroleum madness

A song for my land (2)

Sunday Tribune, 6 Oct., 1985, p. 6.
The milkmaid's anthem,
Mellow like a morning moon,
Rises above the horns
Whetting the thirst of waking ears,
Then fastening its timbre
Round the udders of meagre clouds,
Oh milkmaids of generous breasts!
Oh fairies of capacious smiles ! ...

A shortish snake springs from the belly of the sand,
Dirty, unapologetically dirty,
Taking a clean club on its veno(r)mous head.

Through hills, through mountains
Through Kudero plateaux spreading eternally
Like a patient mat for the sitting sky;
Through the Udi stretching undulating hands
To the sugar-loaf humps of the Kukuruku
I have mounted Mandara tops
And see one land, one people, one future,
Sliced into pockets
By the glistening blade of political tongues

Through cracks, through rivers,
Through young heady streams
Still throbbing with upland pride,
I have seen Osun flash a solid smile
To the gongola, the Cross throwing open
Her teeming banks to the precious waters of the Imo
I have seen the Shari rising bravely from the Cameroons
Traversing tribes, traversing tongues,
Keeping the ultimate tryst with the waiting Chad;
I have witnessed the supple marriage
Of the Niger and the Benue
And watched them lay their alluvial burden
At the feet of the demanding sea.
I have seen rivers and hills
Crossing Europe-implanted borders
Without pallid passports or stamp-heralded visas
I have seen the Degema fisherman
Struggling tirelessly with his wholesome net,
The Uruala farmer offering ceaseless sweat
To his dwindling soil
I have seen the weather-beaten cowherd
Leaner than his herding stick.

Through crumbling villages
And hamlets with lampless nights
Through hordes of aging children
With our black hopes yellowing
In their starving eyes,
Through glittering mansions,
And a clanging convoy of bastard Benzes . . .

Through fields heavy with harvest promise

Through palms busy with singing birds
Through dreams hovering so teasingly
Around our sleeping eyes
Through a sun springing lustily
From a colony of clouds

I pluck this flower
From the tree of my land.

A Peasant Debates A Professor

Sunday Tribune, 1 Dec., 1985, p. 6.

PROFESSOR:

> Our streets swarm with vagrants
> And hands longing desperately
> For a paying job
> Firms falter, factories fail
> Yet our colleges turn out their stuff
> In dizzying thousands

PEASANT:

> What do we do then, wizard of books?
> If our children go to college
> How can we prevent their coming out?

PROFESSOR

> A very long question, Sir,
> Which seeks a short answer:
> I have plodded through the jungle of books,
> Ruffled undergrowths of wisdom,
> And turned every leaf
> Around its knowing spine.
> A desperate ailment deserves
> A desperate cure:
> Shut down all colleges
> And order universities to prune down
> Their crazy crowds.

PEASANT:

It is a desperate cure
Which fathers a desperate ailment,
Wizard of books,
You have told us to burn our heads
To kill a nagging louse;
Because a fledgeling flood
Disturbs our farm,
We should ask the sky
To seize the rain,
But tell me,
Where shall we go
When a savage drought cracks up
　　Our patches of folly?
　　If you shut the schools
　　Who will bring the jobs?

PROFESSOR:

You need no school to till the land
You need no school to man the factories

PEASANT:

What eternal truths!
But tell us, wizard of books,
How come this coat and your noose of a tie?
Son of Tanimola, remember:
Our village sold its barn to buy your books,
Your ship sailed to the white man's land
On the oceans of our sweat.
Remember
Or has the cock grown so big
It has forgotten the fragile shell?
Must they so rudely destroy the ladder,
Who conquered the top
By its millipede rungs?

(To be continued next week)

A Peasant Debates A Professor

Sunday Tribune, 8 Dec., 1985, p. 6.

PROFESSOR:

Your memory gives voice
To long-forgotten tales,
But the times now are different
Now there are more schools than factories
And I say we ought to stem the tide.

PEASANT:

Even without school, the teaming hands
Must not be idle
Wizard of books.
How is this to be?

PROFESSOR:

The school, if you care to know,
Is what puts crazy ideas in humble heads
Any trade would do for simple folks:
Our country boasts countless chances
For labourers and house servants.

PEASANT:

Will the tongue which utters this
Go back into its brutish mouth?
Wizard of books,
You feast that others may starve
Your surplus joys foster on the grave
Of sorrowed millions

PROFESSOR:

Not by any means my peculiar fault:
Remember: fingers are not equal.

PEASANT:

How true your words, wizard of books,
But you preach that sermon
From a tribe of thumbs;

The fifth finger knows the distance
From the juicy morsel.
Shut the schools and sack the pupils,
But make sure your children
Are listed too
In the army of labourers and sweating servants.

The oppressor's recipe

Sunday Tribune, 8 Dec., 1985, p. 6.
The elephant mounts the deer
like a monstrous warrior
rides him through hills and mountains
through swampy thickets
and paths of thorny pebbles;
and when the deer frantically groans
about a breaking back,
the elephant retorts with grave concern:

> "I pity your plight and mourn your pain
> How I wish I weighed a little less!
> But since ride I must and you must bear
> A thought or two will lessen your burden:
> Fancy yourself a horse with an iron mettle
> A dream like this will kill your pain."

Millions Gone?

Sunday Tribune, 19 Jan., 1986, p. 5.
Now that we are being asked again
to hug needless hunger
and die silent deaths
in the dingy corners of our rickety huts
          Asks the village wag:
          Where are the millions gone?
Now that budget baggers have tied
basic prices to soaring kites
and flown them out of the reach
of our shortening hands
          Asks the village wag:
          Where are the millions gone?
Now that the naira has shrunk
like petrified paper
and unverified debts gobble up
the core of our national harvest
          Asks the village wag:

Where are the millions gone?
What happened to those millions
Patriotically stowed away by our eating chiefs
What happened to those fortunes
which made ours once "the land of gold"
where kings dined and dallied
knowing not what to do
with our bursting banks?
  Asks the village wag:
  Where are the millions gone?
How did yesterday's ragged upstarts
suddenly turn the doyens
of golden circles?
How did they mass up their countless mansions
who just last season squatted in borrowed huts
where did they strike their fortunes
those warriors, who tiring so early,
now shoot idle guns at bags
of accumulated gold?
  Asks the village wag:
  Where are the millions gone?
Elephants have passed through
in the kangaroo cabal
of our darkling jungle,
elephants too monstrous
for the feline sheriff
of our trampled shrubs:
the antelope starves near the rumps
while giraffes munch their loot
on forest tops
  Asks the village wag:
  Where are the millions gone?
Where are the millions gone
Oh where have all the millions gone?
Now that SACRIFICE rules the roost
of every tongue
and corpulent priests
shout shivering shibboleths
in altars of fiery knives
where have all the millions gone?
In this season of blinding immolations
who wields the knife,
and who is the LAMB?
  Asks the village wag:
  Where are the millions gone?

Not Guilty

Sunday Tribune, 26 Jan., 1986, p. 5.
THE saintly bird hated excreta
Like incurable poison:
It only ate the maggots
Which fed on this forbidden stuff;
Who, just who, can then say
Our sinless bird ever had a whiff
Of our wrecked and reeking roost?
Just who says he ever saw its hoofprints
In the dunghills of our seething streets?

And the jury hurried down a deafening verdict:
NOT GUILTY!

OUR kings hated dogmeat so much
They couldn't lend out their knives
to cut that unwholesome mess;
Instead, they sliced the loathsome cur
With their golden teeth;
Who still says the offensive flesh
Ever moved near their righteous mouths?

And the jury hurried down a deafening verdict:
NOT GUILTY!

The Headman presided over our brimming barns
And open-eyed, he watched
While eating chiefs stormed the land
With greedy knives -
Reaping, raping, squeezing, squandering
They kept the Headman's share in distant
caves,
Fattening, while hunger flattened our toiling
brood;
they met a land of bounteous harvests
They left a desert of rattling bones.
Who says the Headman ever saw those
Wily hands with a thousand fingers?
Who, just who, still says

The Headman it is
Who touched our stolen yam?

And the jury hurried down a deafening verdict:
NOT GUILTY!

Ghost poachers, proxy plunderers
They who looted our barn
Have covered their tracks
With sands of complicated cant
We sent track tracers
We sent thief catchers;
but they came back, all,
With empty eyes
They came back, all,
With prostrate pleas;
Oh! what infinite folly
Sending leopards to catch the other leopards

And the jury hurried down a deafening verdict:
NOT GUILTY!

Not guilty! Not guilty!
Leaves heard it and told the trees
Not guilty! Not guilty!
the pigeon heard and told the partridge
Not guilty! Not guilty!
Even the dickering duck squawked menacingly
Scrawling doubting ripples.
On the lake's unwinking face
Not guilty! Not guilty!
The sun heard it mid-noon
And moaned like a swindled orphan
Not guilty! Not guilty!
the Atlantic heard it in its distant depths
Dispatching an army of stubborn weeds
to choke those offending shores.

And the jury hurried down a deafening verdict:
NOT GUILTY!

The thief is not one who steals,
No, the thief is one powerless
Enough to be caught:
Elephants have passed once more
Through the eye of our needle
Elephants with mortars still drenched
In floods of our yesterblood;
A venal blindness assaults our land
A blindness, venal, awaiting the piercing look
Or our coming eyes.

And the jury hurried down a deafening verdict:
NOT GUILTY!

For Olof Palme

Sunday Tribune, 23 March, 1986, p. 5.
Let no birds sing
In the forest of Noorland
No prancing mackerels
In the placid waters of the Vanern:
Keepers of the crimson gate
Sound your horns;
Olof Palme has hit the pall
   Rest, spirit of the stirring wind

Your Heart was generous as the rain
Your eyes clear as a sunful sky
You were the thumb who halted the feast,
Urging other fingers to share
The dodging morsel.
   Rest, spirit of the stirring wind

Elephant who sought the peace
Of the deer
Arogidigba* who tended the cradle
Of struggling minnows
You went briskly up the slippery hill,
Ever so mindful of its toilsome foot
   Rest, spirit of the stirring wind

You knew why

The North was north
The South so south
You knew who sowed the fields.

And the one who came to reap
With a blind whip in his dripping hand;
Yours was the ear
Which heeded tomorrow's whisper
From the running rubble of cannibal chaos.
     Rest, spirit of the stirring wind

Fingers of bread
Heart of dogged doves
Palm of maps
Maps, of borderless lands
And seas of wedding waters:
Your world was ONE.
One, like the moon
Which milks the thirst of sweaty nights
One, like the sun which ripens
the sky of its hurrying days.
     Rest, spirit of the stirring wind

Oh cruel times!
How could the spirit who mastered
The peace of dawn
Meet twilight so suddenly
In the alley of a smoking gun?
     Rest, spirit of the stirring wind

Rest, Olof,
Rest, music of running rivers
Rest, canary of swinging forests
Rest, oh palm with a frond
From every clime.
     Rest, spirit of the stirring wind

Sing now,
Forests of Svealand,
Blow your horns

You bards of Gotaland
Shout these tidings
to the Scandinavian winds:
Olof Palme is NOT dead.

   *Arogidigba - a big, graceful fish.

Crying hyena

Sunday Tribune, 30 March, 1986, p. 5.
Once upon a time
When ears were far from the head
And the eye stood below the knees
Once upon this amazing time
A king there was who owned a thousand thrones
And slaves numbering all the sands
Of a crowded beach;
He cherished crimson stars
In the noon of day
And lone rainbows in inky nights
His hands were thick like hippo skin
He had more jewels than sense
Sitting on his baobab neck.

A tribe of hyenas broke loose
On his terrified kingdom,
Tearing fathers up at noon
And eating their children
With twilight rage.
Moon after moon, season after season
Bereavement spread like a plague
And no household escaped
Without a missing child.

Harried, hungry, and cruelly shaken,
the people trooped to the palace.
May you reign for long
The spokesman began the urgent tale.

"Your Majesty, a tribe of hyenas
There is in this land, which threatens
The future of our fold."

His head glittering with assorted stones,
The king sat up in his crimson throne,
A volley of anger pouring
down his capacious jaws.
"Hyenas! hyenas! Why must you people
Always find something to fret about?
I have never seen a hyena in this land
And my royal hunters have never caught
Sight of any such offending cat"

Dejected, surprised,
But more surprised than dejected,
the people trooped back again
Each into their trembling huts.

Exactly one moon later
A cock crowed in the height of noon
Royal hunters ran amock
In their crimson skirts
Streets were silent, markets deserted.

The king's only son had just disappeared
Into the spotted beast's capacious stomach.

Snaplines (4)

Sunday Tribune, 30 March, 1986, p. 5.
Whoever cannot wonder
Is as good as dead
Whoever can only wonder
Is an eternal child

the moon is the mother
Of the sun

And the sunset Horseman strutted
Down the streets of Grenada
Savouring the democratic aroma
Of the recent raid

Debtors of the world
Unite!

In Pretoria
The sprawling black body
Is a grafitto
On the long white wall

The cross against the Crescent
the Crescent against the Cross
Our land adin with holy wars
While HUNGER routs our lowly roots

"Confederation is the answer!"
Alright, but what is the question?

A Song for Ajegunle

Sunday Tribune, n.d.
You stretched out your calloused hands
Switched on your week infested smile
And spread your battled history
Like a tattered mat for my calling feet

I, who like a curious bird,
Have seen you sprawled out
Like an empty bag on the threshold
Of Ikoyi's bursting barns
       * * *

Through roads potholed by callous rains
Through hovels eaves-deep in swelling pools,
Through gutters heavy with burdens
Of cholera bowels
Through the feverish orchestra
Of milling mosquitoes

I saw you sprawled out

Like the daub of a prentice painter

Here evenings are pale smokes
Making out of idle kitchens
The toothless swagger of beer pallors
....
The battering clamour of weeping wives
The salaaming clamor of manacling mosques

I saw you sprawled out
Like a sheath with an absent cutlass

And night, ah night, when it comes.
The shadowy thunder of hurrying feet
The hooded stench of nightsoil pads
the brooding brow of starless pangs
The sweaty stupor of crowded mats
The gutsy blasts of angry guns

I saw you sprawled out
Like a stream without a bed

Morning here is a crow without a cock
Taps without water, tables without bread
Children without schools, schools without children
And shoeless hordes drifting
Drifting, dreamily to Ikoyi chores
On Victoria's own Island where lawns
Are green with sweat
And Senior Service brats murder the peace
Of tired nannies

I saw you sprawled out
Like a cat with hidden claws

Ajegunle
Oh dreg of our foaming wine
Graveyard of our truant conscience
Cesspool of brewing rage

      I saw you sprawled out
      Like a wounded snake.

A tongue in the crypt

Sunday Tribune, n.d.
Patriots
      Thinkers
            Countrymen.
Behold your tongue
Sealed up in this iron cage
For public safety
And national interest

For permission to use,
Apply to:

The Minister of Whispering Affairs
Dept. of Patriotic Silence,
53 Graveyard Avenue,
DUMBERIA.

Song For Children's Day

Sunday Tribune, 9 June, 1985, p. 6.
If you don't see me in the parade today
Don't think I love my country less

I have asked daddy for the new shoes
We have to wear
And those white stockings
And belts of glittering leather
Daddy merely shook his head
But a manly tear betrayed his empty purse:
He hasn't gone to work for several months
Since a retrenchment letter
Scribbled away his job

And a ravaging hunger took permanent shelter
In our crowded shack.

If you don't see me in the parade today
Don't think I love my country less

I asked mummy for those green shorts
And lovely shirt we have to wear;
Without which the teacher's cane
Would carve painful patterns
In my bony buttocks,
      * * *

If you don't see me in the parade today
Don't think I love my country less

Our line will be short at the stadium today
Short, very short, like a stunted millipede:
Umaru left the school roll some weeks ago,
After throwing his satchel in an angry stream
One unhappy morning;
Akanni now haunts parks and marketplaces,
Alternating petty trading with petty thieving;
Ngozi left one noon without a word,
Cruelly drafted into the harem of a man
Whose youngest daughter is about her own age;
The teacher says our names are all in pencil
Waiting for hampering fees to ink our fate;
The blackboard suddenly sprouted a million thorns
The school gate sprang a door of iron padlocks.

If you don't see me in the parade today
Don't think I love my country less

We eat once a day — and that's a rare feast
When there's nothing to eat
We sprawl on our crowded mat,
Counting stars through our leaking roof;

My legs are straws of want
My belly an arena for warring worms;
So if I stumble through the anthem

....

Where every gate tells the world to
BEWARE OF THE DOG.
Where fathers are company bosses
And Mothers hoarders of "essential goods,"
Where cats fatten from silver bowls
While we starve like a forgotten race.
Oh what a wonder seeing the children
Scampering out of those Mercedes Benzes
Glistening like new coins,
Filing up, marching, singing, saluting
Oh what a wonder shaking our nation's hands
With such unequal fingers.

If you don't see me in the parade today
Don't think I love my country less

NOTES

1. F. R. Leavis, *New Bearings in English Poetry* (Pelican, 1979), p. 16.
2. An earthy, inexpensive eating place popularly patronized by the poor.
3. A long, extraordinarily rich Yoruba-Ekiti song which involves a skillful variation of tone; its subject matter is episodic and occasionally satirical.
4. See W. Soyinka, *Idanre and Other Poems* (London: Methuen, 1969), and *A Shuttle in the Crypt*. (London: Rex Collins, 1972); C. Okigbo, *Labyrinths* (London and Ibadan: Heinemann, 1971);and M. Echeruo, *Morality*. (Nairobi: Longman, 1968). It must be stressed, however, that the later poems of Soyinka are much more relevant and immediate in terms of subject matter, and less forbidding in form. *Ogun Abibiman* (London: Rex Collins, 1976) is an accomplished instance of this development. Nor is everything written by Okigbo equally opaque. "Paths of Thunder," the last sequence of *Labyrinths*, signalled a new tone of accessibility and relevance which, unfortunately, the poet's untimely death prevented him from developing.

For more on all this, see, O. J. Chinweizu and I. Madubuike, "Towards the Decolonization of African Literature," *Transition* Vol.9 no.48 (1975), pp. 29-37, 54-57. Soyinka's response, "Neo-Tarzanism: the Poetics of Pseudo-Traditionalism," is in the same issue, pp. 38-44. Chinweizu and others later expanded their idea into a book: *Towards the Decolonization of African Literature* (Enugu: Fourth Dimension Publishers, 1980).

5. M. Schlauch, *Modern English and American Poetry*. (London: Watts, 1956).
6. See F. Aiyehina, "Recent Nigerian Poetry in English: An alternative Tradition," *The Guardian* (April 27, 1985), p. 9; (May 4, 1985), p. 9; (May 11, 1985), p. 9; and (May 18,

1985), p. 9.

7. Last four lines of one of my poems, "A Song for All Times."

8. The Editor-in-chief of the Tribune newspapers, Mr. Felix Adenaike, and the editor of *Sunday Tribune*, Mr. Folu Olamiti, and all their staff were not only willing to give the experiment a try, but did everything to ensure its success.

9. M. Dash, *Literature and Ideology in Haiti, 1915-1961.* (London: Macmillan, 1981), p. 94.

10. Leavis, p. 9.

Women and Trees: Indigenous Relations and Agroforestry Development

Liz Osborn
University of California, Berkeley

Introduction

Many agroforestry projects aimed at meeting local needs for fuelwood, fodder, building materials and other tree products, fail to benefit women (Wood et al., 1980). Women and men in African societies often have separate domains in the use, management and ownership of trees and tree products. Only men's needs are met by tree establishment projects which lack consideration of women's special role. To guide the design of forestry projects which more equitably fulfill household needs, a better understanding is required of indigenous gender-based responsibilities and rights.

A possible starting point for understanding gender roles are the detailed ethnographic accounts already recorded for many cultural groups. Presented here is a summary of the literature from several subSaharan countries describing the allocation of labor, and rights, regarding trees.[1] Where possible, data are pulled together to provide a cross-cultural analysis identifying commonalities and determining factors in tree use and management. The survey also provides an opportunity to assess what is known about women and trees, and suggests which information gaps, when filled, will be useful in guiding the design of agroforestry projects.

Early Ethnographic References

Tucked away in the records of colonial administrators and ethnographers is a wealth of detail about the diversity of lifestyles found on the African continent. A survey of hundreds of articles and books discussing resource use in Africa published between 1940 and 1970 uncovered fewer than fifty mentioning anything about tree use or tree tending by women, and rarely does the description comprehensively cover the roles and rights of men and women. Heizer (1963) has noted that few ethnographers give firewood collecting more than passing mention; consequently, it is difficult to obtain a precise and detailed picture of indigenous forestry practices from ethnographic data.

Nevertheless, some clear patterns emerge from the information accumulated, especially regarding the use of tree products. The most ubiquitous division of labor among African ethnic groups occurs in the collection of fuelwood. Of 18 references to this, all reported fuelwood collecting to be the exclusive domain of women. In only one case, among the Nyamwezi cultivators of Tanzania, men cut the trees for women to gather and carry home (Abrahams, 1967). The predominance of women as the primary, if not sole, providers of fuelwood is confirmed with data analyzed by Murdock and White (1969), and Williams (1982). Based on a coding of ethnographic records for 38 subSaharan cultures, fuelwood was collected predominantly or exclusively by women in 84 percent of these. In only four societies, the Luguru, Fon, Mende and Maasai, was fuelwood collected exclusively by men. Matching these findings with cross-cultural data on the general characteristics of the subsistence economy (Murdock and White, 1969), sheds some light on the circumstances under which women are more likely to collect firewood than men. Women were found to perform the task exclusively under all types of subsistence economies: intensive agriculture, shifting agriculture, pastoral, and hunting-gathering societies. However, three of the four cultures where men had responsibility for firewood collection (the Luguru, Fon and Mende) practiced shifting cultivation. Those same groups also had permanent settlements; whereas, the range of transhumance societies was represented among female gatherers of fuel. The fourth ethnic group for which firewood collection is an exclusively male activity is the Maasai, nomadic pastoralists of East Africa. It has been noted elsewhere, however, that married Maasai women do collect fuelwood (Wood et al., 1980). In summary, those societies where men, exclusively, collect wood for fuel, are more likely to be permanently located, slash-and-burn cultivators, while female firewood collectors are likely to be found within subsistence patterns.

No general correlations link features of community organization with gender responsibilities for fuelwood collection. A range of community sizes, population densities, family form and household arrangements, were associated with all combinations of gender responsibilities for fuelwood procurement (Murdock and Wilson, 1972).

Nevertheless, the usefulness of Murdock's data is limited for current agroforestry design purposes. Not only is the sample size rather small for discerning correlations, but most of the enthnographies from which the data has been retrieved were published before 1950.

While Murdock and colleagues do not go into detail about other activities involving trees, several anthropological accounts do provide information. Generally, though not exclusively, housebuilding and clearing land for agricultural crops is the domain of men.[2] Otherwise, there is considerable variation in the roles of gathering forest products. Both sexes may gather plant material for medicines. Women usually are responsible for collecting any available wild fruits, leafy vegetables and tree insects whether these supplement crops or are a dietary mainstay.[3] Men may help, and in some cases also collect bark for rope making (Dupire, 1963). Among the Ibo in Nigeria, men are the sole gatherers of palm nuts for commercial oil processing (Ardener, 1953).

Rights to trees can be intricate and quite separate from land tenure, yet few authors give full details as to how tree rights are acquired or transferred. Typical scenarios do, however, emerge from the sketchy descriptions. Generally tree tenure is shaped by whether the tree was planted, by whether it has economic value, and by who has the rights to the land it grows on. Free access to most tree products prevails in many regions. Where individual rights to trees do exist, they frequently lie with the planter and are inherited, as with the Luguru of Tanzania (Beidelman, 1967). Tree planting itself may not only establish ownership of the trees, but the land upon which they are planted. This is true for Sukuma men and women of Tanzania (Malcolm, 1953) and Akan men of the Gold Coast (Manoukian, 1950). The economic benefits from bee-keeping shaped tenure rules for the Tanzanian Ngindo whose men earned money selling beeswax. Any man placing a hive in a tree secured control over the tree as well as the hive (Crosse-Upcott, 1956).

A rare insight into the complex nature of resource and land tenure existing in some societies is provided by Obi (1963). Among the Nigerian Ibo, naturally sown trees of economic value become the land owner's property. Otherwise, a tree is owned by its planter, regardless of who's land it grows on. Generally, only men possess timber trees and although women may own food trees some, such as pear, citrus, coconut and kola nut trees, are always exclusive male property. Obi elaborates on women's direct rights to trees, and those rights they derive through their husbands, and describes the rules surrounding transfer of tree tenure through sale, pledge and lease.

Information regarding indigenous practices of tree management is extremely sparse. Little is revealed except that where trees are key sources of cash income, they are often tended only by men, as among the Ibo (Morgan, 1955), Tiv (Bohannan and Bohannan, 1969) and the Yako (Forde, 1964).

The limited usefulness of these records in understanding gender roles involving trees reflects the interests and awareness of the ethnographers at the time. Until recently, the distinct role of women in communities was generally overlooked. Furthermore, colonial administrators focused on economic development; their descriptions of tree use and management were often limited to cash crops: palm oil, copra, cocoa and gum. Uses such as fuelwood, housing material and fodder, essential to subsistence existence, were seldom elaborated upon. Where the information does exist, there is no indication as to its comprehensiveness.

Recognition of Women and Trees

Indeed, much of the paucity of data on women's roles with respect to trees is due to lack of conscious recognition of the distinct role of women and the significance of tree products in African communities. Not until the 1970s was the need to recognize women separately as participants in rural society widely acknowledged. Much has been published since in an attempt to understand the dynamics within subsistence household economies. Still, that literature concerns mostly women's economic positions under the influx of market conditions and their agricultural roles in household farm management. Tree cultivation as a means of benefiting the rural poor was only recognized even more recently. Consequently, the majority of literature on village tree management in rural Africa has been produced in the last half dozen years. When descriptions of indigenous management systems are published, they do not always specify who does what. Typical is Ohler's (1985) report of tree farming practices among the Kagoros and Bambara in Mali which refers ambiguously to the androgenous "farmer" who keeps trees. Where the attention to women and interest in trees coincide, it largely centers around the labor women expend collecting fuelwood.

The Fuelwood Complex

The focus on fuelwood is sparked by its salient role as an energy source in rural households; wood supplies over 90 percent of domestic energy in many African nations (Eckholm, 1984). Adding a sense of urgency to fuelwood studies is the estimate that fifty million Africans experienced acute fuelwood scarcity in 1980 and that supplies are still dwindling (FAO, 1985). Intensive time-labor studies and interviews have uncovered considerable detail concerning the nature of fuelwood procurement. Several publications presenting compilations of these findings (for instance, Barnes et al. (1984), Cecelski (1985) and Wood´ et al. (1980)) have enabled some general principles to emerge.

The amount of time spent collecting enough fuelwood for a household's weekly needs varies from 21 hours in Ethiopia to one hour in Nigerian forests. During that time, women carry loads weighting 15 to 35 kilograms as far as ten kilometers (Cecelski, 1985). Naturally, the volume of wood used depends on the amount of cooking the diet requires: pastoralists primarily living off milk consume forty percent less fuel per person than a maize and tea diet, as discovered in a comparison of nomadic with settled Galole by Ensminger (1984). Heating is another reason for burning wood during tropical wet seasons, and temperate winters. An additional principle determining fuelwood consumption is the availability of wood and energy substitutes. As wood becomes scarce, women expend more time gathering and carrying it to their homes until they resort to alternatives, such as dung or crop residues. Those who can afford it purchase charcoal for some or all of their cooking and heating. During the late 1960s at Bara, Sudan women obtained fuelwood after a fifteen to thirty minute walk. Ten years later, when distance to the nearest supply had increased to one to two hours of walking, few women still collected wood; most bought it, or charcoal instead, from local sellers (Hammer, 1983). On the other hand, if alternate sources are not readily available, women may begin to adopt strategies to save cooking time and conserve wood supplies (Cecelski, 1985; Engelhard, et al., 1986; Hoskins, 1983).

The definition of a tree varies considerably, and local interpretation can have impact on what women harvest for fuelwood. For instance, among the Luhya, women are not allowed to cut planted trees, but may take small indigenous woody species growing wild, such as *Sesbania sesban*, because these are not considered trees (Engelhard et al., 1986). The actual species women are permitted to use differs among Luhya clans.

The way in which women use tree resources can also be dictated by their economic position. Those with sufficient income are more likely to opt to purchase their energy supplies. In Tanzania, it is the poorer women who make charcoal to sell (Fleuret and Fleuret, 1978).

Husbands are not completely removed from the fuelwood domain, but they participate in ways distinct from women. Among the Embu in Kenya, men will cut wood, but use an ox-cart to bring it home, while their wives carry loads (Haugerud, 1984). In Bara, Sudan, men become involved when there is opportunity to make money through fuelwood or charcoal sales (Hammer, 1983).

Studies are also revealing that the dimensions of fuelwood in people's lives are not static; traditional roles are shifting. Whereas women were often accompanied by their daughters, some as young as five years old (Cecelski, 1985), but with higher proportions of girls attending school, the burden of gathering is falling more heavily on adult women (Barnes, 1984). A recent decline in Ghana's market economy created heavier dependence upon subsistence means of production, resulting in men taking on women's traditional duties, including carrying wood (Cecelski, 1985). In Embu regions of Kenya which are experiencing fuelwood scarcities, boys and sometime men help with collecting. Fuelwood procurement as the exclusive domain of women is breaking down under changes in economic circumstances and resource availability.

Planting Trees

Fuelwood scarcities have also prompted investigations into the social factors affecting forestation programs. A few examine ways to involve women in tree planting (Fortmann and Rocheleau, 1985; Hoskins, 1979; Hoskins, 1983), yet seldom is there elaboration on indigenous tree management tasks and roles. The dirth of information on tree management may be because it is not traditionally practiced. When asked why he did not attempt growing *Ricinodendron rautanenii*, a !Kung San man replied "Why should we plant when there are so many mangongos in the world?" (Lee, 1979; 204). Even among the Chagga and Nyakyusa of Tanzania, who include trees in their intensive agriculture systems, tree planting only began in response to colonial programs initiated in the 1950s (Skutsch, 1985).

Isolated references do give an indication of the range of factors influencing women's involvement in tree management, especially planting. In areas experiencing fuelwood scarcities, women do recognize the need to plant more trees (Barnes, 1984; Haugerud, 1984). Yet where planting trees is regarded as men's responsibility, women's genuine interest in tree planting may be dismissed by men, as Williams (1985) noted in Burkina Faso. Gender roles, especially associated with tree planting, may be reinforced with taboos which deter women's involvement. In Burkina Faso, some believe that tree planters will die young (Williams, 1985). Women who raise fruit trees in Senegal fear becoming barren (Hoskins, 1983). Unfortunately, for neither of these examples is the context of tree tenure and use in which these taboos operate described.

From Skutsch's (1985) data, collected in 18 Tanzanian villages, inferences can be made about gender roles in tree planting. Nearly two-thirds of the households she surveyed planted trees privately and 30 percent participated in communal woodlots; yet in only 29 percent of the village households did women plant trees either privately or communally. Again, however, not enough background is provided to understand fully why women are considerably less involved in tree planting than men.

Whether different species are planted by men and women is seldom specified, yet can constitute a critical factor in the design of tree planting programs. A survey of Siaya, Kenya revealed that men and women wanted different species planted on their farmlands. Men preferred fodder trees, while their wives voted for fuelwood trees (Rocheleau et al., 1987). The economic importance of the tree may determine, more than anything else, under who's domain it rests. When cocoa trees were introduced as a cash crop to the Yoruba of Nigeria and the Beti of Cameroun, in both cases, cultivation of the crop became men's responsibility, although wives helped with harvesting for compensation (Guyer, 1978). This division of labor occurred despite the differing allocation of tasks within the two hoe agriculture societies. Men farmed among the Yoruba while Beti agriculture was women's work.

The domains of women and their husbands in tree management can be so separate that spouses are unaware of their mate's activities. Hoskins (1979) relates an incident in Senegal where a forestry officer insisted that women could not plant trees, then later learned that the trees in his courtyard were planted by his wife. Significant divergences have been documented in the range of men's and women's knowledge of tree species and uses. In some instances, women are better informed about tree species and products than their husbands or forestry extension workers (Fortmann and Rocheleau, 1985). On average, Ghanaian women can list 57 tree products, whereas men can only list 14 (Owusu-Bempah, 1986).

The relationship of women to the resource is clearly multi-dimensional, and each of the many interwoven facets are critical in the design of agroforestry projects which affect women. Unfortunately, many accounts contain only isolated details of tree management, without the entire context. Too little has been recorded to determine to what extent women care for trees, especially beyond planting, and under what circumstances.

An indication of the complexities surrounding gender-based domains in the rights, use and management of trees, and the consequences for forestry project design comes from a rare, detailed description of Luhya men's and women's roles in the Kakamega District of Kenya (Engelhard et al., 1986). Women there have so much difficulty finding enough fuelwood, they are resorting to crop residues, buying wood in the market, and cooking sparingly. Yet family farms are abundant in woody biomass growing in woodlots, windrows, along pathways, around houses, and as hedges. Most farmers plant their own trees and maintain them by pruning branches. Luhya women's predicament lies in their lack of rights to harvesting planted trees, even when their husbands are mostly absent from the farm. Tree planting is confined to men, and reinforced with taboos against women's involvement. They fear infertility or their husband's death as a consequence of planting trees. This division of labor reinforces women's position of having no property rights since tree planting, by customary law, establishes land ownership.

The trees men plant are destined for sale to the local sawmill, for providing firewood for their funerals, and produce wood for house repair and tool making. Men have no interest in growing fuelwood trees, since they believe these survive on wild bushlands and do not require management. But at the same time, much of the bushland has been converted to cropland, eliminating women's fuelwood supplies.

Traditions in Flux

Social sanctions delimiting gender roles in tree management may not be fixed, as illustrated by an incident at Kathama in the Machakos District of Kenya. Although taboos prevented women there from planting fruit trees, after the women organized as a group and fruit tree seedlings were made available, the taboo broke down (Dianne Rocheleau, personal communication).

Clearly, any number of outside conditions can change the roles of men and women regarding trees. The salient influences seem to be resource abundance, economic importance, and the availability of substitutes. How these factors affect the allocation of rights and labor, Guyer (1978) suggests, is shaped by two conditions. One is the prevailing investment of each sex in particular skills and the ease with which new tasks combine with existing routines. Second, the reallocation of labor within those broad categories is influenced crucially be relative returns to labor — men adopt those tasks with higher economic yields. The complexities of these conditions may require detailed task allocation for tree cultivation. For example, in a Senegal forestry project men dug holes in which women planted seedlings and watered them, then afterwards, both maintained the trees (Hoskins, 1983).

Deciding What to Plant

How well agroforestry projects address women's needs is often influenced by women's position in community decision-making. At the village level, women are usually underrepresented in mixed community organization. Village woodlot programs in Tanzania, for instance, are administered by the Forestry Division, which deals directly with the local government, a body comprised mainly of me (Skutsch, 1985). When women are included in forestry planning meetings, they typically are not equally involved in leadership or decision-making. At group meetings, taboos may cause women to be silent, even when a discussion is directly relevant to their particular needs (Fortmann and Rocheleau, 1985; Williams, 1985).

In societies where women are not publicly vocal in community decision-making, and given low profile and prominence in community forestry programs, agroforestry projects only meet men's requirement (Wood et al., 1980). But at the same time, overlooking women's involvement often leads to the failure of the project (Hoskins, 1979). Indeed, in Tanzanian villages which had successfully begun communal woodlots, proportionally twice as many women were involved in tree planting than in villages which had not begun woodlots (Skutsch, 1985). But it must also be noted that where women's organizations do serve as a vehicle for women to exercise power in community affairs (March and Taqqu, 1986), these may only represent a segment of the women in a given community. In Kenya, for instance, group members tend to be the older, wealthier and married women (Feldman, 1984).

A Framework for Agroforestry Project Design

The findings collected so far on women and trees suggest a framework for the analysis of gender roles to guide the design of agroforestry projects. Identification of the factors which may affect women's involvement in, and benefits from, forestry activities must begin by describing the position of individual women within the community. A woman's economic status, age, marital status, caste, and whether she belongs to a polygynous marriage or heads a household, may affect the activities she is interested in and her decision-making power within the household or village. Accepted mechanisms for women's involvement in decision-making may influence such things as whether their input into forestry project planning is most effectively presented as a group.

The compatibility of an individual's tasks in the household economy with forestry activities, will determine what additional forestry activities they are willing to enter into. Prevailing perceptions of the use, rights and responsibilities allotted to men and women for each tree species will also influence women's involvement in projects and benefits. A key variable in this regard is whether the tree products are distributed in a market or subsistence economy.

Differences between husbands and wives in their access to productive resources, especially money, land and transportation can also be critical factors. At the same time, property rights in both land and trees, and mechanisms by which these are acquired, need to be identified and taken into account in the planning process.

The importance of each of these factors will depend upon the local circumstances. Conditions vary considerably among ethnic groups, and possibly even with societies. It is crucial, though, to obtain a complete picture of the influences determining women's involvement in tree management and benefits, and how these might change.

Conclusion

Two overriding findings result from this survey of African women's traditional rights and practices in tree use and management. One, the roles of women and men in tree management can change, shifting under a variety of environmental, economic and cultural influences. The dynamic nature of resource conditions and the economic and social patterns governing tree use necessitate relying on current information for project design. However, existing interactions are likely only to be understood fully when placed in an historical, environmental and social context. Some early ethnographies may provide this background, especially for the circumstances peripheral to tree management. In a few cases, little has changed from earlier records and details recorded decades ago are still relevant. For instance, Richard's' (1939) detailed observations on Bemba farming techniques in the 1930s were largely still accurate in 1983 (Kakeya and Sugiyama, 1985).

A second observation derived from this ethnographic survey concerns the scope of knowledge which has been recorded. The information most commonly generated concerning women and trees in subSaharan Africa is focused on selected aspects. Many considerations vital to agroforestry design have not been recorded by ethnographers or agroforestry practitioners. We have little information about the role of women from different strata of society (Barnes et al., 1984). It is not clear whether a woman's economic position, caste, age, and status within her family affect her rights and activities regarding trees and if so, to what extent. The level of analysis needs to be more finely tuned; research must go beyond fuelwood and tree planting and ask for the range of uses, rights and management: "which women?" and "which trees?"

NOTES

1. Some reviews of ethnographic literature published before 1970 were generously provided by Julia Verney, Jennifer Dudley and Gill Sheperd of the Overseas Development Institute.

2. Among the Baraguyu of Tanzania (Beidelman, 1968) women build houses of wood, whereas in nine other reported cases, men were housebuilders. In three of fourteen references to land clearing, both sexes share the task, otherwise it is described as men's work.

3. As is the case among hunter-gatherers such as the Kindiga (Cooper, 1949; Woodburn, 1958).

BIBLIOGRAPHY

Abrahams, R.G. *The Peoples of Greater Unyamwezi, Tanzania*. London: International African Institute, 1967.

Ardener, E.W.R. "A Rural Oil-Palm Industry: 1. Ownership and Processing:" *West Africa* Sept. 26, 1953: p. 900.

Barnes, Carolyn. "The Historical Context of the Fuelwood Situation in Kisii District" in Carolyn Barnes, Jean Ensminger and Phil O'Keefe, eds. *Wood, Energy and Households, Perspectives on Rural Kenya* Stockholm and Uppsala, Sweden: The Beijer Institute and the Scandanavian Institute of African Studies, 1984, pp. 61-78.

Barnes, Carolyn; Ensminger, Jean and O'Keefe, Phil eds. *Wood, Energy and Households, Perspectives on Rural Kenya*. Stockholm and Uppsala, Sweden: The Beijer Institute and the Scandanavian Institute of African Studies, 1984.

Beidelman, Thomas. "The Baraguyu" *Tanganyika Notes and Records* 55: 245-278, 1960.

Beidelman, Thomas. *The Matrilineal Peoples of Eastern Tanzania, Ethnographic Survey of East*

Central Africa Part XVI. London: International African Institute. 1967.

Bohannan, P. and L. Bohannan, *Tiv Economy* London: Longmans, 1969.

Cecelski, Elizabeth. *The Rural Energy Crisis, Women's Work and Basic Needs: Perspectives and Approaches to Action* Geneva: International Labour Office. 1985.

Cooper, B. "The Kindiga" *Tanganyika Notes and Records* 27: 8-15, 1949.

Crosse-Upcott, A.R.W. "Social Aspects of Ngindo Bee-Keeping" *Journal of the Royal Anthropological Institute* 86 (2): 81-99, 1956.

Dupire, Marguerite. "The Position of Women in a Pastoral Society" in Denise Paulme, ed., *Women of Tropical Africa* Berkeley CA: University of California Press, 1963.

Eckholm, Erik; Foley, Gerald; Barnard, Geoffrey; Timberlake, Lloyd. *Fuelwood: The Energy Crisis That Won't Go Away* London: International Institute for Environment and Development, 1984.

Engelhard, Rutger; Bradley, Phil and Shuma, Boaz. "The Paradox of Abundant On-Farm Woody Biomass Yet Critical Fuelwood Shortage. A Case Study of Kakamega District" Nairobi, Kenya: The Beijer Institute. 1986.

Ensminger, Jean. "Monetization of the Galole Orma Economy: Changes in the Use of Fuel and Woodstock" in Carolyn Barnes, Jean Ensminger and Phil O'Keefe, eds. *Wood, Energy and Households, Perspectives on Rural Kenya* Stockholm and Uppsala, Sweden: The Beijer Institute and the Scandanavian Institute of African Studies, pp. 124-140, 1984.

FAO Committee on Forest Development in the Tropics. *Tropical Forest Action Plan* Rome: FAO. 1985.

Feldman, Rayah. "Women's Groups and Women's Subordination: An Analysis of Policies Towards Rural Women in Kenya" *Review of African Political Economy* 27/28: 67-85, 1984.

Fleuret, Patrick and Anne Fleuret. "Fuelwood Use in a Peasant Community: A Tanzanian Case Study" *Journal of Developing Areas* 12(3): 315-322, 1978.

Forde, C.D. *Yako Studies* London: Oxford University Press, 1964.

Fortmann, Louise and Dianne Rocheleau. "Women and Agroforestry: Four Myths and Three Case Studies" *Agroforestry Systems* 2(4): 253-272, 1985.

Guyer, Jane. "Women's Work in the Food Economy of the Cocoa Belt: A Comparison" Working Paper No. 7. Boston, MA: African Studies Center, Boston University. 1978.

Hammer, Turi. *Wood for Fuel, Energy Crisis Implying Desertification. The case of Bara, the Sudan* DERAP Publication No. 160. Bergen: CHR Nichelsen Institute. 1983.

Haugerud, Angelique. "Economy, Ecology and the Unequal Impact of Woodfuel Scarcity in Embu, Kenya" in Carolyn Barnes, Jean Ensminger and Phil O'Keefe, eds. *Wood, Energy and Households, Perspectives on Rural Kenya* Stockholm and Uppsala, Sweden: The Beijer Institute and the Scandanavian Institute of African Studies, pp. 79-101, 1984.

Heizer, Robert. "Domestic Fuel in Primitive Society" *Journal of the Royal Anthropological Institute* 93 (2): 186-194, 1963.

Hoskins, Marilyn. *Women in Forestry For Local Community Development: A Programming Guide* Washington, DC: USAID. 1979.

Hoskins, Marilyn. "Rural Women, Forest Outputs and Forestry Projects" discussion draft. Rome: FAO, 1983.

Kakeya, Makoto and Yuko Sugiyamako. "Citemene, Finger Millet and Bemba Culture: A Socio-ecological Study of Slash-and-burn Cultivation in Northeastern Zambia" *African Study Monographs* Supplementary Issue 4: 1-24. 1985.

Lee, Richard. *The !Kung San: Men, Women and Work in a Foraging Society* Cambridge: Cambridge University Press. 1979.

Malcolm, D.W. *Sukumaland An African People and Their Country. A Study of Land Use in Tanganyika* London: International African Institute and Oxford University Press. 1953.

Manoukian, Madelaine. "Akan and Ga-Adangme Peoples of the Gold Coast, Ethnographic Survey of Africa" in G. Forde, ed. *Western Africa, Part 1* London: International African Institute and Oxford University Press. 1950.

March, Kathryn and Rachelle Taqqu. *Women's Informal Associations in Developing Countries* Boulder CO: Westview. 1986.

Morgan, W.B. "Farming Practice, Settlement Pattern and Population Density in South-Eastern Nigeria" *Geographical Journal* 121: 320-333, 1955.

Murdock, George and Douglas White. "Standard Cross-Cultural Sample" *Ethnology* 8(4): 329-369, 1969.

Murdock, George and Suzanne Wilson. "Settlement Patterns and Community Organization: Cross-Cultural Codes 3" *Ethnology* 11 (3): 254-295, 1972.

Ohler, F.M.J. "The Fuelwood Production of Wooded Savanna Fallows in the Sudan Zone of Mali" *Agroforestry Systems* 3 (1): 5-23, 1985.

Obi, S.N. Chinwuba. *The Ibo Law of Property* London: Butterworths. 1963.

Owusu-Bempah, Kofi. "The Role of Women Farmers in the Choosing os Species for Agroforestry Farming Systems in Rural Areas of Ghana" paper prepared for the International Conference on Women and Development, University of Florida, Gainesville, Florida, Feb. 26 to March 1, 1986. 1986.

Richards, Audrey. *Land, Labour and Diet in Northern Rhodesia* London: Oxford University Press. 1939.

Rocheleau, Dianne, Louise Buck, and Hilary Feldstein. "Intrahousehold Dynamics and Farming Systems Case Studies Project" manuscript, 1987.

Skutsch, Margaret. "Forestry by the People for the People — Some Major Problems in Tanzania's Village Afforestation Programme" *International Tree Crops Journal* 3: 147-170, 1985.

Williams, Paula. "Women and Forest Resources: A Theoretical Perspective" in Molly Stock, Jo Ellen Force and Dixie Ehrenreich, eds. *Women and Natural Resources: An International Perspective* Moscow, Idaho: Forest, Wildlife and Range Experiment Station, University of Idaho, pp. 93-130, 1982.

Williams, Paula. "Women's Participation in Forestry Activities in Burkina Faso" Hanover, NH:

Institute of Current World Affairs. 1985.

Wood, Dennis et al. *The Socio-Economic Context of Fuelwood Use in Small Rural Communities* AID Evaluation Special Study No. 1. Washington DC: USAID, 1980.

Woodburn, J.C. "The Hadza: First Impressions" *East Africa Institute of Social Research* conference papers 1-10, 1958.

Conflicting Perceptions of Hazards in African Development: The Case of Floods and Drought

Saidou S. Jallow
Gambia College

An Indian's attitude towards clouds and rain remains fundamentally different from that of the Westerner. To the one, clouds symbolize hope; to other, they suggest despair. The Indian scans the heavens and if cumulus clouds blot out the sun his heart fills with joy. The Westerner looks up and if there is no silver lining edging the clouds his depression deepens.

Khushwant Singh

Introduction

The quotation overleaf, by Singh, an Indian, is especially appropriate as an opener for this presentation, because although the context is different it succinctly expresses the central them of this paper — the fundamental difference in the Western and traditional African perceptions of natural phenomena.

The introduction of the African continent into the international market economy in the late 19 and early 20th centuries ushered in fundamental changes in the sociocultural and economic lives of the people. These changes were to later have, among other things, major land use implications, and today they may be responsible for the profound change in outlook (at least among policy makers) towards the environment.

In many instances the leadership of African countries have uncritically adopted the Western philosophy of economic, social, and political organization of society. The African continent is rife with models derived in and designed for Western societies. African policy makers with help from Western governments and agencies have been able to impose these models, albeit with differing levels of success. Most, if not all of the models have indeed failed to effect the anticipated elevation of living standards of rural people, by far the majority, after over 25 years. Economic and social indicators for African states attest to this unfortunate fact as most of Subsaharan Africa is found in the World Bank's lowest income bracket category (World Bank Reports 1980-1986).

63

Nevertheless, recently there has been an obvious proliferation of the Western notion of hazards and its inextricable response model in Africa. But with the experience of African countries with Western models in general, the inevitable question is whether this is the best way to deal with hazards and simultaneously raise the standard of living of the people. I must, however, from the onset point out that I am not against Western models, but that great caution should be exercised with them. Indeed, numerous questions must be answered first before adopting Western or any other foreign model for that matter. The object of this paper is to raise some pertinent questions which require critical examination before adopting any particular model to deal with hazards. In doing so, the Western and traditional perceptions of hazards will be briefly examined to see how these influence response models; in addition, the implications of adopting the Western approach to hazards in development in Africa will also be discussed.

1. The Notion of "Hazards"

All societies at one time or another have experienced extreme geophysical events, be they floods, droughts, earthquakes, hurricanes, snowstorms, or frost. Accordingly over time, adaptive practices have been evolved to soften the impact of such events. The nature of the response techniques adopted are generally influenced by the people's perception of the hazard, as well as the type of technology available. In effect, markedly different perceptions of a "hazard" and response technology may obtain in different societies. In traditional societies experiences with geophysical events have produced interesting perceptions of hazards. Land use patterns, social and religious practices associated with some of these extreme events, for instance, floods among the Lozi of Western Zambia, preclude them from the category of "hazard" or "disaster" (Prins 1980). These societies have been able to live within the cycles of extreme events and have interwoven their cultural practices into the annual or periodic occurrence of these "hazards." On the other hand, Western societies characterized by capital-intensive modes of production, capital investment is required to make hazard-prone environments productive. These may be in the form of structures to protect the environment, and financial insurance schemes designed to cover damages by hazards. The capital investment and cost of maintaining these protective structures would qualify the events as "hazards." We will now take a brief look at the perception of hazards from the Western and traditional African viewpoints.

1.1 the Western Perception of Hazards

Although natural hazards study began in North America in the mid-1950s by Gilbert white (then at the University of Chicago) working on flood hazard, it became formalized during the following decade with the teaming up of White with Ian Burton at the University of Toronto, and Robert Katz at Clark University. Other geographers including Saarinen studied the perception of drought and other natural hazards. The modern perception of flood hazard, indeed the Western attitude towards water could be partly traced back to the Dutch experience with water in the 17th century. To cut a long story short, the Dutch experience with water over the centuries developed a national perception in which water is seen as an enemy which has to be controlled for reasons of self-preservation. The Dutch approach therefore, has predominantly been "of a defensive or offensive character" (Harris 1957, p. 301). To the Dutch, the battle with the sea and other waterlogged areas required the building of dykes, pipes, and dams, an essentially hydraulic problem. These massive structures however, could only be undertaken by governments and few private organizations which therefore determine the allocation and use of the reclaimed land. Very often recovery of the invested capital with substantial profit is foremost in mind when it comes to land distribution (Namafe, 1986). The Dutch technology and its inherent philosophy of land use was utilized in Britain to drain the english fens, and subsequently diffused to other parts of Europe. Over time, the same antagonistic attitude towards water pervaded the North American continent wherever floodplains were occupied by people. This ushered in a flood control technology which is very expensive involving substantial capital and other inputs.

Similarly, following the systematic study of drought in North America after the experiences of the 1930s and 1950s, and perhaps taking their cue from the ancient Egyptians, the Americans saw the issue of water shortage again as mainly a hydraulic problem. Given the broad spectrum of alternatives, the most reliable and economically feasible technical solution was water transfer for irrigation from regions of surplus to those with deficits through the construction of dams, canals, reservoirs, and other infrastructures. These no doubt called for the investment of enormous amounts of capital, sophisticated technology, materials and expertise, which were by and large present in Western industrialized societies. This perception of hazards seem to be essentially different from that of traditional communities in Africa.

1.2 Traditional Perceptions of Hazards

It is stated that riverine ecosystems have supported the densest rural populations in African savanna environments, and that droughts and floods had been adequately contained by different adaptive practices (Burnham, 1980; Scudder, 1980). But no unlike other societies however, the traditional African communities also had their experiences with hazards which by and large caused famines and loss of life. The interesting thing, however, is that these extreme geophysical events were seen as naturally recurrent phenomena, and over time adaptive practices evolved which enabled the people to coexist with them. They were able to live within the cycles of these hazards, indeed, their cultural practices were closely integrated with the seasonal occurrence of some of these geophysical events (Prins, 1980; Scudder, 1980; Burnham, 1980; Massing, 1979). It is said of the Lozi people of Western Zambia that their food production system, annual ceremonial trans-human movements, and the societal calendar as a whole, were intimately related to the annual flooding of the Bulozi floodplain (Namafe, 1986; Prins, 1980). According to Prins who has repeatedly studied the Lozi at first hand, an agricultural system such as that of the Lozi, the occurrence of abnormally high or low floods is not indicative of "disaster," but rather of an event which results in a dramatically strengthened society. In effect, in spite of the fact that the Lozi dwellings periodically stood in water when most of them would move to the drier uplands, they had no concept of "hazard" (Namafe, 1986). Similarly, the Tonga people of the Zambezi, the multi-ethnic inhabitants of the Inland Niger delta in West Africa, and other occupants of riverine environments also developed cultural practices which were closely integrated with the annual flooding of their lands. Thus floods were seen as naturally occurring phenomena which they had adapted to and were able to contain.

Perceiving drought, which is basically a condition of water deficit capable of disrupting normal human activity, as a "non-hazard" is perhaps more difficult to explain. However, the issue in this case is not one of nomenclature, rather, it is one of effective adjustment to a natural hazard, and the exacerbation of the impact of the hazard resulting from a change in land use patterns. Several instances have been cited in the drought literature where land use practices and societal organizations have enabled traditional societies to effectively cope with droughts (Kirkby, 1974; Hankins, 1974; Dupree and Roder, 1974; Burnham, 1980; and many others). To these traditional societies, solutions to floods or droughts were not seen purely as hydraulic or technical problems. Rather they were seen as the efficient utilization of *ethno-scientific information* on crops and livestocks (resistance to drought, to flooding, crop mixing, etc); on *land* use (recessional cultivation, the use of uplands and flood plain at different times of the year); and *societal organization* which ensures the accumulation and redistribution of community resources to all during times of need. In effect, in traditional societies, intimacy with nature and sensitivity to its cycles was the order of the day, and this helped them tremendously to survive extreme environmental events. Some of these practices are still common in some rural communities in Africa, but as we shall see later, they are increasingly threatened.

2. Response Models to Hazards

The Western and traditional models of response to hazards are different in nature. The Western style of response is basically a high-cost, capital-intensive system which in many cases involves the extensive manipulation of the environment. This is achieved through the construction of sophisticated infrastructures which are supposed to produce profitable returns on the capital invested. On its polar opposite is the traditional model of response which is characterized by a low-cost, labour-intensive system. This system involves minimum manipulation of the environment based on the cycles of natural events. Both models nevertheless, have been able to contain hazards, albeit in different environments. We will now briefly take a look at the requisites and characteristics of the two models before examining the implications of adopting the Western approach for development in Africa.

2.1. The Western Approach — Capital Intensive

As indicated earlier and graphically illustrated in Fig. 1 below, the Western approach to hazards is capital-intensive. The approach is rooted in the manipulation of the natural environment by the application of inputs in the form of massive doses of capital, sophisticated technology, expertise, and materials (derived from research), and legislation. It can also be seen from Fig. 1 that the financial and environmental costs of the approach are very high, indeed they could by staggering. The short-term success of this approach and its consequent contribution to local and regional economies in the West has justified the undertaking of hydroengineering projects that might be called megaprojects to control hazards notably, floods and droughts.

THE TRADITIONAL RESPONSE MODEL — LABOUR INTENSIVE

Input	Mechanism	Goal	Environmental and Financial Costs
Labour, Technology, Materials, Ethno-Scientific information, Legislation	Seasonal movement, Crop selection and mixing, Social organization, Supplemental activities (hunting, fishing, etc.)	Adjustment	Very Low

Fig 2. Showing the Inputs, Mechanisms, and Costs of Adjustment to Hazards using the traditional model.

Water deficits have thus been controlled by weather modification, water transfer, the introduction of drought tolerant cropsand breeds of livestock among other techniques; and floods by damming, floodwalls, and flood insurance schemes for compensation. These evidently require an enormous amount of capital, not to mention the other requisites of the approach. It is important to note however, that all the above prerequisites for the approach are available in Western societies either in the hands of governments, private organizations, or both.

The question at this point is whether African states can afford the costs of the approach not to mention the accompanying by-products. A couple of examples may illustrate the magnitude of some of these schemes. Although by no means typical, the examples referred to here serve to illustrate the nature and magnitude of inputs, and the financial and environmental costs required. The proposed N.A.W.A.P.A. and Soviet Arctic schemes involve the transfer of massive amounts of water through the diversion of rivers, the construction of networks of huge dams, thousands of kilometers of canals, and gigantic reservoirs for water in transit to irrigate water deficient regions in Canada, the U.S., and Mexico; and in the case of the Soviet Scheme, the arid lands of Kazakhstan (Barr, 1975; Hannell and Harshman, 1980; Drew, 1983). The impacts of these megaprojects on local environments and global climate cannot yet be determined, and unfortunately, experiences with much smaller dams on the Volga, Nile, and other rivers, and over-irrigation in the states of California, Nevada, and Nebraska can only give us a flavour of the impact of such schemes on the global environment and human life. Examples of the impact of the Western approach to floods and droughts abound all over the world, and Africa is no exception. A question worth reconsidering at this point is whether this model (Western) is the best approach to deal with hazards in Africa. We will now shift our focus to the traditional model of response to hazards to bring out the contrast in approaches.

2.2. The Traditional Approach — Labour Intensive

THE WESTERN RESPONSE MODEL — CAPITAL INTENSIVE

Input	Mechanism	Goal	Environmental and Financial Costs
Capital, Technology, Expertise, Materials, Scientific information (research), Legislation	Dams, Reservoirs Weather modifications, Crops and livestock hybrids, Floodwalls, Insurance (Banks)	Adjustment	Very High

Fig 1. Showing the Inputs, Mechanisms, and Costs of Adjustment to Hazards using the Western model.

The traditional approach is basically a labour-intensive model requiring limited manipulation of the environment. As illustrated in fig. 2, the inputs include the labour provided by the family or community, and technology which in this case refers to the cultural techniques associated with the use of crops and animals which have been tested by time and proved effective (ethnoscientific information). Legislation as an input here refers to the use of communal land, storage and distribution of surplus food. The mechanisms are simple, involving seasonal movements between wet and dry lands for cultivation or livestock grazing, crop selection, mixing, and matching of crops with deficient or excess water, societal organizations, and supplemental activities such as fishing, hunting, and gathering. Unlike its Western counterpart, the environmental and financial costs of the model are very low because the profit motive is not foremost in mind, nor is the natural environment extensively altered.

It might be argued or implied by some people that population pressure in these societies must have warranted a shift in technology and more extensive use of land resulting to its misuse, and that the arrival of the Western approach was really a blessing (Stebbing, 1935; Glantz, 1977; Le Houerou, 1977; Exkholm, 1977; and in most of the literature). Quite the contrary, West African cultivators never needed a major shift in technology to meet increasing population or contain hazards. A writer on changing agricultural and pastoral systems in West Africa asserts that agricultural intensification in West Africa was seldom based on major technological innovation. Rather, intensification was achieved by more extensive and labourious application of such well known techniques as crop rotation, and manuring with compound manure (Burnham, 1980: 67). Scudder (1980) also makes reference to mixed farming among the Western Dinka people in the Sudan as a response to population pressure. He further maintains that "the type of reverine food-production systems (farming, livestock rearing, and fishing) have supported millions of people for thousands of years in Africa without adverse ecological effects" (Scudder, 1980: 390). Indeed, contrary to the generally published view in the literature, the traditional African societies have been able not only to maintain a reasonable level of ecological balance through their land use practices, but were also able to adjust to and live with natural hazards for thousands of years. Some of these practices which are still common in some rural communities are now threatened by the adoption of the Western approach to hazards.

3. Implications of Adopting the Western Approach to Hazards in African Development

In spite of the experiences of other countries with the Western approach to development in general, and hazards in particular, most African governments still embrace the approach. This approach is supposedly the best way to raise the living standards of the African people through increased agricultural production and improved health services. These, it is argued could be realized by draining riverine environments and putting them under production, and sinking boreholes and irrigation canals to provide water for drought-prone regions. However, despite the apparently good intentions associated with projects of this nature, it is cash crop production which is invariably increased usually at the expense of food crops. And the health and welfare of the former inhabitants of these areas are seldom incorporated in the overall plan. I am inclined at this point to agree with the view that capital intensive, large-scale irrigation projects for instance, are not the best way to raise rural living standards because in Africa such projects tend to involve a relatively small number of tenants and labourers whose standard of living is not raised as high as previously thought (Barnett, 1979; Scudder, 1980).

The proliferation of the Western approach to hazards in Africa has developed a general notion among policy makers that the best and perhaps the only solution to floods and droughts is the Western hydraulic (technical) model. Simply put, this translates into moving the people from the floodplains and swamps (the fertile lands) to build dams to control flooding and irrigate the dry areas, or sinking boreholes in the Sahel to provide drinking water for people and livestock, their living standards will rise. This so far has not been the case in Africa. As in other tropical environments, these technical solutions are often implemented without adequate understanding of their impact on the biophysical and human components of the environment. The meagre amount of literature available on tropical environments abound with admissions of the relative paucity of knowledge about tropical ecosystems. Indeed, very few studies if any, have been carried out on the sociocultural and economic systems of people living close to major water courses and wetlands in the African savanna (Scudder, 1980: 385).

The building of large-scale dams in Western and Southern Africa to control hazards and increase agricultural production has caused major disruptions in the socioeconomic and cultural lives of the floodplain occupants. There is no need to itemize the number of people affected, but in the construction of only 4 dams, about 200,000 people have been forced to move from future lake basins. The most distressing aspect of such projects is that the interests of the local lake- and river-basin populations are not considered, and very often the area is used for cash crops or for the generation of electrical power.

Similarly, the sinking of boreholes and expansion of irrigation in the Sahel to control drought also failed to elevate the standard of living of the rural populations. It is becoming increasingly apparent that the Western solutions to drought succeeded in pressuring local farmers and not only into cultivation of marginal lands (since the fertile lands are under the control of a partnership of government and Western investors), but also into cultivating cash crops for export on most of their marginal lands. This has created an unbalanced relation between people and resources which has increased the vulnerability of the Sahel people to naturally recurrent rainfall fluctuations which had been effectively contained in the past. Under such circumstances, the slightest variation in rainfall could spell famine and disaster. Some writers including Moran, have observed that

> in many areas of Africa where sorghum and millet once dominated are now planted in corn or cash crops like cotton, coffee, and sugar cane. In many of these areas that adopted corn, farmers gave up the cultivation of sorghums and millets despite the uncertainty of local rainfall. The result has been greater susceptibility to (hazards) and a less stable relation between population and resources.

> (Moran, 1979, p. 8-9)

The socioeconomic and cultural implications of these changes in land use patterns are tremendous, but putting aside the impact on people for the moment, may we pause first to figure out the impact the Western approach to hazards has on African economies. The adoption of the latter model has succeeded in exerting excessive strain on the economies of African states and made it very difficult for these countries to make headway in the process of raising the standard of living of its people.

Firstly, the technology, materials, and expertise which are some of the prerequisites for the use of the approach have to be imported from the Western countries at rapidly escalating costs. In the process, other sectors notably health, education, and social welfare, are denied much needed capital.

Secondly, in most cases, bilateral or multilateral loans or both have to be secured from the industrialized countries to effect the projects. This invariably places a burden on the economy as urgently needed foreign exchange earnings are used to service and repay the loans.

Thirdly, it is common knowledge in environmental circles that the occurrence of large, permanent, freshwater bodies (reservoirs) in tropical environments signal the presence of freshwater diseases such as schistosomiasis, bilharzia, malaria, and so on. And without enough resources allocated to the health sector, the limited facilities are easily overwhelmed and disease reigns supreme. Human beings, by any means the major agent in development is in this case a victim of "development."

Finally, and perhaps one of the most saddening things about the use of the Western approach to hazards in Africa is the marginalization of the food-producing small farmer. Drained, fertile floodplains and complex irrigation systems favour the most 'economically profitable' land use system which invariably amounts to the large-scale cultivation of cash crops destined for the export market. As a result of the small farmer's weak financial position he cannot effectively compete for the fertile lands, and is therefore relegated to lands of marginal fertility for food production (hence most African states including former food exporters like Egypt are now net food importers).

The net effect of the Western approach to hazards currently in use in Africa has been to generate the following conditions:

1. Inadequate capital for development programmes, hence substantial proportions of development or investment capital is secured from foreign donors.

2. Less healthy populations to carry out development efforts combined with exces sive pressure on health facilities.

3. Low food production, hence most African states are net food importers.

4. Disillusionment in rural populations dispossessed of their homelands result in massive rural-urban migration increasing social and health problems in urban centers.

5. Relatively enormous external debts which have to be serviced and repaid.

One might wonder at this point how development or standards of living could be raised in such an environment. However, the present situation is certainly not a hopeless one. This is not merely intended to sound optimistic, but if positive development in African states is to be a reality, then policy makers must ask aloud previously whispered questions regarding the suitability of the Western approach to hazards vis-a-vis the traditional approach. These may include the following:

1. Which mode of response to hazards is *best* for *African* development?

2. Is the Western approach to Hazards (floods and droughts) appropriate for *African* states?

3. Can *African states* afford *Western-style* remedy for hazards?

4. How does using the *Western* approach as opposed to the *traditional* approach affect the desire to improve the living standards of Africans?

5. How can the efficiency of the traditional approach be enhanced to meet present day drive for national development?

6. How do the *financial* and *environmental* costs of the Western model compare with those of the traditional model?

7. Is it possible to integrate the positive features of both approaches for the sake of mutual benefit?

These are some of the questions which African policy makers, scholars, and their Western counterparts must ponder upon if genuine development in Africa is to be realized.

Conclusion

The Western and traditional perceptions of hazards are fundamentally different. One is capital-intensive and the other is labour-intensive. Consequently, the response models that were evolved are different in nature. Despite their differences they have both been effective in dealing with hazards in their respective societies. However, the anticipated contribution of the Western approach to hazards in the development of African states has not been forthcoming. The approach has been unable to uplift the standard of living of the people in general, and the rural population in particular. One might wonder whether this is an indication that the Western approach is not appropriate for development in African states. The answer to this question notwithstanding, a note of caution has been sounded regarding the whole-hearted embrace of Western or any other foreign model without its critical examination. Of special significance are the questions related to the traditional approach which hopefully imply that the approach is not to be ruled out as a medium for development.

BIBLIOGRAPHY

Burnham, P. "Changing Agricultural and Pastoral Ecologies in the West African Savanna Regions," in *Human Ecology in Savanna Environments*. D.R. Harris (Ed). London: Academic Press Inc., pp. 147-70.

de Wilde, J. *Experiences in Agricultural Development in Tropical Africa*. Baltimore: John Hopkins University Press, 1967.

Glantz, M.H. "Climate and Weather Modification in and around Arid Lands in Africa," in *Desertification: Environmental Degradation in and around Arid Lands*. M.H. Glantz (Ed). Boulder, CO: Westview Press, 1977, pp. 306-37.

Hughes, J.D. *Ecology in Ancient Civilizations* Albuquerque: University of New Mexico Press, 1975.

Katz, R.W., and M.H. Glantz. "Rainfall Statistics, Droughts, and Desertification in the Sahel," in *Desertification: Environmental Degradation in and around Arid Lands.* M.H. Glantz (Ed). Boulder, CO: Westview Press, 1977, pp. 81-102.

Le Houerou, H.N. "The Nature and Causes of Desertization," in *Desertification: Environmental Degradation in and around Arid Lands.* M.H. Glantz (Ed). Boulder: Westview Press, 1977, pp. 17-38.

Leiss, W. *The Domination of Nature.* Brazillier, N.Y.: 1972.

Moran, E.F. "An Introduction to African Agriculture," in *Changing Agricultural Systems in Africa.* M.D. Zamora and others. (Studies in third World Societies #8) Williamsburg, VA: College of William and Mary Press, 1979, pp. 1-4.

Namefe, C.M. *Environmental Education: A Comparative Study of Modern and Traditional Systems in Zambia* Unpublished M. Ed. Monograph, McGill University, Montréal, Québec, Canada, 1986.

Prins, G. *The Hidden Hippopotamus: Reappraisal in African History: the Early Colonial Experience in Western Zambia.* London: Cambridge University Press, 1980.

Scudder, T. "River-Basin Development and Local Initiative in African Savanna Environments," in *Human Ecology in Savanna Environments.* D.R. Harris (Ed). London: Academic Press, 1980, pp. 383-405.

Stebbing, E.P. "The Encroaching Desert: Threat to the West African Colonies," *Geographical Journal.* Vol. 85, No. 6, 1935 (June), pp. 506-24.

Waddell, E. "The Hazards of Scientism: A Review Article," *Human Ecology.* Vol. 5, No. 1, 1977, pp. 69-76.

Ware, H. "Desertification and Population: Sub-Saharan Africa," in *Desertification: Environmental Degradation in and around Arid Lands.* M.H. Glantz (Ed). Boulder, CO: Westview Press, 1977.

World Bank. *World Bank Reports.* 1980-86.

The Yoruba Village: Cultural Perspectives

Jack Lieber
Institute for Development Education Through the Arts —
Toronto

There is an apocryphal story about Pablo Picasso who relates an incident involving an American GI who met him in Paris and told Picasso that he didn't like his paintings because they weren't realistic. Picasso made no reply. However, when a few minutes later the soldier showed him a snapshot of his girl friend, Picasso exclaimed, "My word! Is she really as small as that?" It is clear that neither the GI nor Picasso was comfortable within the other's perceptions of reality.

The unnerving fact is that most of us are like that GI: we are not aware of our own insensibilities, although we appear to be experts at discerning other people's patterns of selectivity. Personal experience sets up one grid between us and reality. Our culture adds another one. Our language and our media system tighten the mesh, so that for most of us, it takes a conscious and protracted effort to extend our cultural awareness beyond the parameters of our own immediate experience. This becomes painfully obvious when we try to relate to a Third World society with an unfamiliar category of cultural symbols. Let me give you an illustration.

On my first field trip to Nigeria over twenty years ago, driving an automobile, I was shaken at the frequency with which I encountered the carcasses of dogs littering the roads, victims of hit-and-run drivers. Later I learned that these animals were actually considered to be sacrifices to the divinity Ogun, the god of iron, to whom the dog is sacred. I was informed that automobile drivers who were devotees of Ogun, were advised, as soon as they had obtained a driving permit, to purposely seek out a dog to run over, as this act would ensure that the divinity would protect them from running over a human being. However rational the explanation, it still offended my ethnocentric conviction that dogs are household pets, rather than cultic sacrifices.

The Institute for Development Education through the Arts, or IDEA, as it is usually called, is an agency that attempts to address this type of cultural misperception. The Institute is predicated on the assumption that the arts of a people offer the most illuminating and unobstructed view of their culture and hence of their thought processes, traditions, attitudes, and values. Further, IDEA believes that any governmental or non-governmental agency which ignores the arts in their dealings with indigenous communities, runs the risk of a communications breakdown and hence of functional misperceptions in bilateral relations. The art of a particular culture can reveal ever-changing human images and attitudes, so that an awareness of a people's indigenous art and cultural symbols can become an important instrument for cross-cultural understanding. And since most indigenous art has its genesis in village culture, it is essential that we recognize and reaffirm the simple fact that, next to the extended family or lineage, the village is the basic operational unit of Third World society.

In general, the morphology of the village constitutes the limits to the activities of daily life. The village acts as a social haven of familiar custom to which the individual adheres as a bulwark against an invasive technology which he interprets as a threat to established tradition, the link between his material and spiritual identities. Indeed, these two aspects of tribal man's psycho/social makeup, the material and the spiritual, are so inextricably conjoined as to constitute the basic substance of his beliefs, and nowhere is this more aptly demonstrated than in the organizational details of the Yoruba village. [1]

In most Yoruba villages there is a variety of privilege groups and associations which reflect both modern and traditional economic, political, social, recreational, and religious interests. These are interactive associations, and it would be impossible at this time to do much more than hint at the traditional importance of this complex grid of interlinking affiliations. Today these associations no longer function as effectively as they did in the past because their traditional role is being constantly usurped by technology and the inroads of the electronic media. Nevertheless, their impact on villagers' daily lives is still considerable and should never be underestimated, particularly those associations with a powerful religious bias and dedicated to the reaffirmation of the unity of man's personal, social, and spiritual realities.

Two of these associations which have somehow managed to withstand technological change, and which still continue to function in many Yoruba villages are the exclusively male *Ogboni* and the female dominated *Gèlèdé* associations. Both societies have maintained a strong symbolic hold on the Yoruba imagination, the *Gèlèdé* particularly, still being regularly celebrated in spectacular pageant and masquerade. Both associations have been responsible for the creation of an immense regalia of ritualistic imagery, mostly in bronze and wood, as well as of an infinite variety of masks and related costuming. Before proceeding toward an examination of some of these extraordinary objects, which will, hopefully, help explain the meaning of the culture which has produced them, I would like briefly to review a few ethnological notes relating to both the *Ogboni* and the *Gèlèdé* societies, which through their impact on the history of the Yoruba people have given their culture and their art its particular richness, colour, and complexity.

The origin of the *Ogboni* tradition is obscure,[2] but some of the brass images sacred to the cult could be as old as the 10th century. Some writers date the *Ogboni* to the 15th. Today *Ogboni* still functions as a secret society open only to men recruited partly by hereditary right or by invitation from *Ogboni* priests, on the basis of age, wealth, presumed wisdom, and prominence in secular or religious life.

The primary function of *Ogboni* society members is to judge. Thus they are proficient in matters dealing with traditional law and some modern legal practices. During precolonial days, *Ogboni* checked the power of the king. But is was the earth which was the bulwark of morality. *Ogboni* members were forbidden to shed blood upon the earth,[3] and this then became a compact of peace between litigants. Two men who swear to each other to embark jointly upon a serious matter, touch the earth to make their contract binding. This gesture is also related to a belief that a maternal force constantly watches humanity from the depths of the earth.

The main sculptural form is the *edan*,[4] twinned brass images, male and female, chained together and usually worn about the neck. Many have sharp iron pegs at the base, so that they can be stuck into the earth. In this way the sexual and the agricultural symbolism are combined. The most important element is the chain which unites male and female, thus transforming two into three with the binding force of the earth. The importance of the left hand is indicated by the typical *Ogboni* greeting: left fist over right with the thumb hidden. The *onile* or kneeling figures, are particularly delicate specimens of the art of the *Ogboni* brass caster, many of them dating from the early nineteenth century.

Today, with their religious aspects frowned upon by both Islam and Christianity, and their political functions diminished or entirely taken over by modern local government, the old *Ogboni* organizations have retreated, but a new form of the cult has arisen, now know as the *Reformed Ogboni Fraternity*. It constitutes an economic elite, and has taken root in the larger urban centres as a social club, somewhat in the tradition of Freemasonry, with lodges almost everywhere in Yorubaland. It is interesting to note how the old talismans have also evolved to show a surprisingly modern style of brass casting.

Whereas *Ogboni* rituals are always celebrated behind closed doors and observed only by a select group of powerful male functionaries, *Gèlèdé* is just the opposite.[5] The *Gèlèdé* society and associated masquerades represent a highly visible artistic expression of the Yoruba belief that women, primarily elderly women, possess certain extraordinary powers equal to or greater than that of the gods and the ancestors, a view that is reflected in lavish spectacle which features dancing, drumming, and elaborate costuming.

Mothers are believed to possess a life force that they can use for either the benefit or detriment of the individual or the village community. Regular propitiation of this negative propensity is therefore necessary to ensure that the destructive force of the mothers, or witches representing them, is deflected. Their recurrent pacification is the *raison d'être* for the *Gèlèdé* ritual.

Central to the celebration are the masks, which are among the most imaginative in the entire corpus of African art. They owe their variety to motifs abstracted from practically every aspect of Yoruba life and thought. the subject categories of these masks include fashion modes, social roles, animals, foreign elements — in brief, a glossary of the external environment. As well, the masks suggest broader categories of meaning, and embrace such concepts as the recognition of the hierarchical structure of Yoruba society; satiric commentary relating to personal foibles and political indiscretions; commemorative functions such as funeral rites, or celebrations in honour of mythic personages.

One may almost assert that a sensitive examination of *Gèlèdé* masks could generate a deeper insight into Yoruba life and values than, say, consulting the literature of statistics, demographics, population density figures, and other variant readings, important though they may appear in the light of the disciplines involved. There seems to be a gray area, a sort of vacuum between anthropology, sociology, and art history, which has never been properly addressed, and it yet it may very well be precisely that area from which a holistic view of a village community can be observed, from the perspective of its symbols, rituals, and art.

Many Yoruba masks have snakes in their iconography, which are generally depicted in combination with other animals, usually birds, and their interaction becomes either a metaphor for various types of personalities in Yoruba society, or an illustration of a moral lesson. One example illustrates a Yoruba proverb 'In a struggle to the death there is no victor.' This mask represents a seemingly unresolvable struggle between a cock and a snake. Each seems to have the other in a mortal death grip: the cock has the snake firmly grasped in its jaws, whereas the snake's tail and jaws seize the cock's legs in an unbreakable hold. The symbolism of the two waiting alligators below them now becomes clear: it is they who will reap the spoils once the struggle between the snake and the cock is resolved in mutual destruction.

A much more complex iconography is evident in a "mammy wagon" mask which is probably familiar to anyone who has travelled in West Africa. Mammy wagons are lorries with wooden benches for travellers to perch upon while the lorry lurches through the swirling dust of laterite roads, teetering precariously on the edges of open sewers as the driver weaves past the chickens and goats who nonchalantly share the roads and somehow miraculously survive the wheels. The mask is an imaginative representation of what appears to be a lorry crowed with passengers. The fenders are two snakes, the tails of which are held by the driver and his helper who is sitting beside him. The eyes of the snakes are the rear lights; the motor mimics the head below it. Holding the door closed at the back is the fare collector. The remaining figures are passengers sitting quietly and amiably observing the passing landscape.

It can be seen therefore that the imagery in *Gèlèdé* subject matter is extremely diverse and frequently shows a concern with humanity. Here we see how a mechanical object like a lorry is sculpturally transfigured by a snake metaphor to illuminate the symbolic correlation between the two. A significant number of *Gèlèdé* masks are also mediums of satire: anyone familiar with the automotive habits of Yoruba lorry drivers will at once be reminded of their predeliction of serpentine weaving in and out of traffic. The analogy with the convolutionary progress of a reptile through the tall savannah grass is inescapable.

Another dramatic mask demonstrating the skill of the Yoruba carver shows a mosque framed within the arc of a rainbow, the symbol of the divinity Osumare, as exemplified by a python coiled around the base of the mosque. According to one authority, the python is the great snake of the underworld who comes up to drink the sky. An extension of the rainbow framing the bearded facial features is subtly metamorphosed into a striped turban worn by Hausa to protect against the swirling desert sand. Although the beard typifies the Muslim Hausa stereotype, it is interesting to consider that a beard also defines an elderly woman, with all the connotations of knowledge and wisdom that such status implies.[6]

It might be noted that the snake or python figures prominently on these three *Gèlèdé* masks. In the first, the snake and the cock are a symbol of aggressive violence; in the second, the snake becomes a metaphor for an intrusive technology doubling as a satiric comment about Yoruba truck drivers; and in the third *Gèlèdé* mask, the python is transformed into a mythological creature potentiating an Islamic icon.

To summarize: The well springs of Yoruba art are its villages, and a careful examination of that art may reveal more about the processes of Yoruba life and thought than has been previously suspected. This idea has been articulated most eloquently by Wole Soyinka, the Nigerian poet, novelist, dramatist, critic, and present laureate of the Nobel Prize in Literature, in the first volume of his autobiography *Ake: The Years of Childhood*, wherein he reconstructs the magical ambiance of the little village near Abeokuta where he was born: "A time capsule . . . an archine space fringed by the watchful luminous eyeballs of petrified ancients and deities . . . a humane succession of bookshop, church, cenotaph, sewing academies, bicycle repair shops, barbers' shops, petty trader stalls, stray goats, noisy hawkers, kneeling priestesses, sacrificial scenes, royal processions, denizens of the ancestral world." This is the cosmology of the Yoruba village.

NOTES

1. See G.J. Afolabi Ojo. *Yoruba Culture.* (Ife: University of Ife Press, 1966). A useful text which deals with the relations between Yoruba culture and the ecology of village communities.

2. In *Black Gods and Kings.* (Bloomington: Indiana University Press, 1971), R.F. Thompson suggests that the mature period for *Ogboni* brasses is 1640-1830.

3. William Bascom, *The Yoruba of Southwestern Nigeria.* (New York: Holt, Rinehart and Winston, 1969), p. 37. A more comprehensive account of the legal role of *Ogboni* among the Yoruba is Peter Morton-Williams' "The Yoruba *Ogboni* Cult in Oyo," *Africa* 1960, pp. 362-374.

4. Th. A.H.M. Dobbelmann's *Der Ogboni-Geheimbund* (Berg En Dal: Netherlands, Afrika Museum,1976), is one of the most comprehensive analyses of the aesthetics of Ogboni art and of the extraordinary variety of its forms.

5. John and Margaret Drewal's monumental study of the cult, *Gèlèdé: Art and Female Power among the Yoruba* (Bloomington: Indiana University Press, 1983), places the cult in a dominant historical position in respect to Yoruba culture generally.

6. Drewal and Drewal, *op cit.*

BIBLIOGRAPHY

Armstrong, R.P. *The Affecting Presence.* Urbana, Illinois: University of Illinois Press, 1971.

-----. *The Powers of Presence.* Philadelphia: University of Pennsylvania Press, 1981.

Bascom, William. *The Yoruba of Southwestern Nigeria.* New York: Holt, Rinehart and Winston, 1969.

Dobbelman, Th. A.H.M. *Der Ogboni-Geheimbund.* Berg En Dal, Netherlands: Afrika Museum, 1976.

Drewal, Henry John and Margaret Thompson Drewal. *Gèlèdé: Art and Female Power among the Yoruba.* Bloomington: Indiana University Press, 1983.

Fadipe, N.A. *The Sociology of the Yoruba.* Ibadan:Ibadan University Press, 1970.

Fagg, William and John Pemberton. *Yoruba Sculpture of West Africa.* New York: Alfred A. Knopf, 1982.

Forde, Daryll. *The Yoruba-Speaking Peoples of South-Western Nigeria.* London: International African Institute, 1951.

Morton-Williams, Peter. "The Yoruba Ogboni Cult in Oyo," *Africa.* 1960.

Ojo, G.J. Afolabi. *Yoruba Culture.* Ife: Universityof Ife Press, 1966.

Soyinka, Wole. *Ake The Years of Childhood.* New York: Random House, 1981.

Thompson, R.F. *Flash of the Spirit.* New York: Random House, 1982.

-----. *Black Gods and Kings.* Bloomington: Indiana University Press, 1976.

Trowell, Margaret. *Classical African Sculpture.* London: Faber & Faber, 1970.

Wassing, R.S. *L'Art de l'Afrique Noire.* Paris: Bibliothèque des Arts, 1969.

Effects of Cultural and Linguistic Diversity on Development Project Implementation in the Gambia, West Africa

Regna Darnell
University of Alberta

This paper might well be subtitled "The Saga of the Three Murdered Donkeys — with observations on unforeseen consequences of cultural and linguistic diversity." That is, I will use the style of a non-western storyteller to make some very serious points about the often tragi-comic results of well-intentioned projects geared toward the progress of third world countries into the modern, presumably civilized, world. First, as is always necessary when one speaks to strangers, I will set forth my credentials as narrator. The story I offer as parable is a true one, in which I was a participant — though unable to affect the outcome. (The powerlessness of the social scientist is perhaps a subsidiary point of some note.) Second, I will set forth a basic profile of The Gambia and its population which provides the context within which it will at last be possible to tell the story. Finally, there are some generalizations which emerge by implication. Indeed, what Kenneth Burke has called "the representative anecdote" is often the most effective way to draw attention to a claim about the nature of the real world and how its denizens deal with its complexity. I would even go so far as to claim that the trouble with much of the development literature is its abstraction from the consequences of the particular.

I am an anthropologist with a specialization in American Indian language and culture. My acquaintance with international development projects in The Gambia results from marriage to the manager of an international technical project there. I offer no apology for lack of expertise specific to Africa. My discipline is one in which observation of human behavior leads to interpretation, to an effort to make everyday behavior intelligible rather than exotic. I and my four children have spent nine months in The Gambia over three summers. It is clear to all of us that — at least some of the time — it has been our home.

The Gambia is a small country constituted by the former British water rights over the river of the same name, surrounded on three sides by francophone Senegal. Its population of ca. 800,000 is linguistically and culturally diverse. The largest group is the Mandinka, dominant in national politics since Independence in the early 1960's. Substantial local minorities speaking Jola and Serahuli are also found in rural villages; in the capital, Banjul, these minorities stick together and are cautious in public behavior. In the capital, Wolof, largely from Senegal, form a substantial segment of the population; they are middlemen in trade with Senegal and tend to be more urbanized, richer, and more widely multilingual than any other indigenous group. A Fula minority is active in trade with the interior of Africa. Particularly in the urban area, it is not unusual for individuals to speak two, three or more of these African languages, as well as one or more European languages. Urbanity and multilingualism are felt by all groups to increase life opportunities and personal status.

Three foreign languages are also fairly widely spoken by segments of the native population. English is the official language of the country but is still not learned automatically, even in the capital. French is widely known, particularly by the Wolof, many of whom have had some formal education in French in Senegal. The country is 90% Muslim and Arabic is learned by rote in a religious context. Arabic letters are occasionally applied phonetically to African tribal languages. Literacy is not widespread in any language and multilingual speaking skills are acquired through interaction rather than academic study.

Oratorical skill is highly valued in all languages. There is no feeling that only a native speaker can speak a language well. Moreover, multilingualism is one kind of oratorical skill, which politicians and traders are at particularly pains to acquire. Translation is viewed not as an interruption of the flow of communication, but as a dignified, preferably ponderous, aesthetically-pleasing elaboration of any proceeding. Translators are spirited, and often perform (as opposed to simply quote) the speech for which they are the responsible spokesman. There is considerable commentary from members of the audience who understand both languages. The meeting of persons who do not share a language is an occasion for everyone to show off their oratorical skills and convince others of their arguments in front of an appreciative audience. Stylistic elaboration is, therefore, a necessary part of referential meaning, within local understanding of communication. There is no expectation that translation will necessitate simplification of either content or style.

The Gambia has been severely affected by Sahel drought conditions over the past decade, although there is water to be tapped. The quality of the water, however, is questionable at many places because of its high salt content (the Gambia River is tidal and there are some saline groundwater spots). In drought years, wells have to be deeper than traditional methods can construct; even with modern technology, such wells are expensive.

Moreover, groundwater level fluctuates seasonally; annual rainfall is restricted to the two to three month rainy season. Rainfall records in The Gambia are sporadic, but the annual precipitation is generally comparable to eleven-year sunspot cycles. A twenty-two year low-point in 1984 was the culmination of four years of drought; local resources were already severely strained by that time. Many traditional wells, in some areas all, were dry in 1984. A government emergency team deepened 1000 traditional wells and about 100 of the semi-modern wells (sides were secured but not entirely lined). During the previous decade, various international programmes dug or drilled a number of modern wells and boreholes.

Local water supply is, thus, high on the agenda of rural villages. Villagers were forced to utilize one or two wells in a village which were not dry or to impose on nearby villages. In area of the country where virtually all wells were dry, government trucks transported water. The situation was disastrous in some parts of the country, especially to cattle. Cattle were sent elsewhere for water, but their grazing needs created mini-deserts around the wells. A system was devised of rotation between three wells in a triangle, thus spreading out the grazing, to which ten to fifteen villages had common access. Although villages were generous in sharing available water, the effect on local resources in some areas was devastating.

All petroleum products must be imported; like most other African countries, The Gambia has a negative balance of trade. Dependence on imported fuel which has to be purchased on hard currency for local water supply thus places considerable hardship upon local communities and considerable pressure upon the Gambian government. The few windmill- and solar-powered wells are among the country's show-projects. They have not been popular, however, with external granting agencies (whose personnel are almost invariably unaware of local conditions) because of the higher cost of initial installation (this attitude now appears to be changing). Solar-powered water systems are particularly attractive because they require little maintenance. Windmills, on the other hand, require trained maintenance and considerable small-scale replacement of parts. Most of the development contracts, however, stipulate that the Gambian government will provide local personnel and maintenance. In spite of training programs for local personnel, including maintenance, the superstructures of some of the expatriate-constructed wells are sufficiently complex to require the regular services of an engineer. In spite of the obvious impracticalities, efficiency of water systems is generally evaluated by western technological criteria alone.

The Gambia has no codified central water law. In the villages, it is understood that everyone has access to water. Each village has several traditional wells, though not every family has one. Wells may be located in private compounds as well as on public land or land that is claimed but unfenced. The supplier of water does not charge for access to it, but nonetheless becomes a patron of those who use it. Modern wells, which are much more expensive, are understood to be for public use — but there is no definition of the public in question. The new wells, moreover, involve structures (some sort of building, and a pump to extract the water) as well as the water itself. And, they need maintenance. Someone has to be responsible for the continued functioning of the modern well.

After the decision is made that a given village will receive a new well, the village headman is consulted about a suitable site. The headman, however, is never above criticism from other factions (or lineages) in the village. The construction is done by an external agency on contract, with the village formally taking over the completed well. Public attitudes are unchanged by the increasing complexity of wells. When damages arise, therefore, the question of responsibility — for which there is no precedent in custom — inevitably arises. The headman, who is the only identifiable individual at the local level, is unable to repair the well himself. Outsiders must, therefore, be involved.

But outsiders are not interested in negotiating ownership of the well or access to its water. Those who build the wells are told that access will be public but not who owns the land. In spite of public access, there is considerable local prestige to the person who owns the land or lives nearest to the well site. Moreover, status within a village is a delicate balance. For example, if the well is placed on elevated ground belonging to Mr. X, which is already valued, the counterbalancing wealth in sheep of his neighbor Mr. Y will have less status than it did before the building of the well. Mr. X may then counter that the well is a great inconvenience, with people always coming and going, and explain that he puts up with the inconvenience because of his magnanimity. Since generosity is highly valued, Mr. Y can only counter by detracting from the importance of Mr. X's actions. These sorts of issues are as important, at the local level, as the new water supply itself.

The national political system distributes perks among the various districts or villages in informal rotation, with local political representatives getting credit for the innovations. The President (who has held office since Independence) travels frequently with his ministers, listening to local problems and asking the appropriate minister for information as needed to solve a particular problem. Although this method does not add up to a systematic bureaucratic policy, local people feel that "the country has an owner." The wise man is expected to come up with compromises and external input which couldn't be achieved with village resources alone.

The "Saga" of concern to us involves the most isolated of the wind-powered wells, located on the north bank of the Gambia River, some distance upriver from the capital. Several weeks before a scheduled presidential visit to the village in question (involving a political rally in anticipation of an upcoming election year), a delegation of several men from this village mounted an expedition to the capital to the office of their local representative, who was their access to the highest ranks of the government, to seek indemnity for lost property and to insure the continued safety and prosperity of their village. They reported that a blade had fallen from the windmill, in the process killing three donkeys which were grazing beneath it. The representative, whose legitimate concern was political rather than scientific, took this report quite literally and requested that the agency which had installed the windmill investigate and repair the damage. Any compensation to the villagers for their donkeys presumably remained a government issue. Politically, of course, blaming the external agency was the easiest course of action.

Upon investigation, it emerged that the windmill had been installed over a year previously, during an earlier phase of the same project, and had received no recorded maintenance since. Nor was there any budget for or scheduling of maintenance. The expatriate personnel considered the likelihood of the literal demise of three donkeys to be highly unlikely at best. Some exaggeration of the literal facts, however, lent seriousness to the complaint and was probably taken for granted by all African parties to the negotiation. Although these social facts were seen as irrelevant by the project personnel, there was clearly a problem with the equipment — which did fall within the project's domain and required an official expedition to "the field."

The personnel of this expedition included the project manager (whose authority as an observer conferred considerable prestige to the village in local interpretation, the more so because he did nothing but observe), the project engineer, a second engineer borrowed from another international project, a Gambian mechanic (who declined conversation with any of the expatriate personnel during the entire half-day journey), a Gambian driver (who happened to be a native speaker of Mandinka, the language of the village in question), and the observing anthropologist (having no visible function in anyone's eyes).

In addition to its personnel, the expedition was rendered impressive as a response to a local crisis by its oversize jeep with paradiplomatic license plates. Among other things, this insured that the vehicle could pass some 50 cars and trucks lined up waiting for the ferry across the Gambia River.

On the other hand, even crisis response has to proceed alongside other priorities. The various personnel had to be picked up at their residences. A minor crisis at the project training center where the mechanic was picked up had to be settled. And a brief stop to inspect another project water system was considered in order given the rarity of en masse trips to the field by senior project personnel.

Even with preferential status in the queue, the wait at the ferry dock was 90 minutes. In order to catch the last ferry back to the south side of the river in the afternoon, the expedition team had approximately 90 minutes to deal with whatever might be found in the village.

The jeep was greeted at the north bank of the river by a man from the village who had presumably waited all week at the ferry dock. He had been a member of the delegation to the capital and considered himself in charge of the response, a highly prestigious political coup for him. The project engineer had met this individual before. However, he spoke no English (the language of the project though by no means the native language of all its personnel) and was therefore able to communicate only with the mechanic and the driver. The mechanic immediately became animatedly talkative, though his reports to the two engineers remained laconic.

Life around the village appeared to be proceeding without any particular disruption. The village women were diligently doing their laundry, immediately under the blades so as to save carrying distance of water. Several had infants on their backs; various additional infants were playing near their mothers. A number of donkeys were happily grazing. The ladies paid no overt attention to any of the ensuing proceedings, avoiding eye contact with both project personnel and their own menfolk. Small children stared at both when considering themselves unobserved.

Several blades were missing from the windmill, although only one was apparently reported to have caused difficulty. Indeed the villagers appeared not to have noticed that others were missing. The mechanic and project engineer climbed the windmill structure to tighten all bolts and remove one blade for examination back in the capital to decide why it had been sheered under wear. Neither seemed surprised or upset by what they found. There was a repair job to be done and they proceeded matter-of-factly.

Meanwhile, perhaps 20 men had gathered, clustered in three groups, observing and talking quietly among themselves. No one paid any attention to them until the two engineers decided that the issue of danger to the village was not the windmill blades but the potential contamination of groundwater supply by soap from washing too close to the well itself in the absence of a tiled run-off drain. Realizing that it would be impossible to persuade the women to move, they decided among themselves that it would be possible to deliver tiles to line a drainage trench in time for the President's upcoming visit. The only remaining detail was to explain to the men of the village (who, after all, were already present) that they must dig a drainage trench to line with the forthcoming tiles.

By default, the translator was the Mandinka driver. It had apparently not occurred to anyone that it might be necessary to communicate with the villagers. The project engineer made the bald statement that he wanted a trench here, dug this way. He offered no explanation as to why it was needed (or certainly of whether or how it was related to the falling windmill blades). The driver took the initiative and delivered a lengthy discourse which he did not translate for the engineer, who appeared to notice no anomaly.

After the driver's speech (and we should note that he knew nothing about ground water, wells or the notion of sanitation encouraged by all expatriate-run projects), the milling groups of men coalesced into clear factions, each with a leader who proceeded to harrangue his constituency. Both speakers and their supporters aligned themselves away from the project personnel to mid-space in the direction of the windmill (well above the heads of the women bent over their washing, who incidentally showed no inclination either to move their washing back from the water tap or to listen overtly to the three simultaneous speeches of the local faction leaders). It was immediately obvious that the man who had met the expedition had a considerable advantage thereby.

In local terms, then, the issue was not groundwater contamination or reimbursement for donkeys. Rather, the problem of local concern was which faction or factions would have control over the well. When the only issue was the falling blades, the success of the delegates to the capital in obtaining attention, both political and technological, to their problem was the focus of village discussion. The new issue, however, offered even more potential for local political advantage because those who dug the trench could lay special claim to the water supply itself.

This discussion was barely underway and certainly far from resolution when the engineer observed that it was time to leave. His position, when queried later, was that delivering the tiles was all that anyone could legitimately expect of the project. It was someone else's problem whether they were installed. At least the President would be able to see that the tiles had been delivered. What the President would make of a pile of tiles beside the village windmill was not the engineer's concern. Certainly, no one present would be able to explain the potential sanitary problem to the President. (In fact, however unlikely it appeared at the time, the trench was dug and the tiles were installed by the time of the President's arrival.)

Now then, the meaning of the parable: Importantly, no one acted in ill will. Unfortunately, poor communication often occurs with the best of intentions. The engineer is a diligent man, committed to doing his job well and to training local men to install and maintain equipment. He assumes, however, that the goals of local communities are the same as his own and his agency's. For him, the problems are those of engineering and must be solved at the level of engineering.

Urban politicians may be of the same tribal background as their constituents in the villages but they are more concerned with political realities than with either donkeys or wells. The Gambia has a hierarchical social structure, in which urban politicians have higher status than villagers. Nonetheless, urban political life is locally-based, and villages, if not individuals, have a hearing before their elected representatives. Although the actual event precipitating the repair expedition may have been no more complex than a blade falling in a place where donkeys normally graze and being interpreted as a danger to the donkeys of the village, the purported demise of three donkeys lent credence to the grievance and provided bargaining chips in negotiation of monetary and political compensation. Moreover, politicians are in the position of granting favors to villagers and their status is reinforced thereby. (The same thing, of course, occurs at the village level when leaders of various factions attempt to manipulate the relative fortunes of their constituents.) It does not occur to any of these parties that any other parties, i.e. the expatriates, might not behave with similar motices.

Nor does it occur to local people that they have a right to communicate effectively with outsiders who presumably enter their lives to respond to their perceived needs, i.e. for a reliable clean water supply. The opportunity to learn English has been sporadic in most villages, in spite of national efforts to improve the school system. Traditionally in The Gambia, multilingualism (indeed, any kind of lingua franca) has involved the individual of lower status learning the new language and the individual of higher status merely listening in his own language or listening to a translation produced for his benefit. The higher the status, the more likely the individual to be, or at least behave as if, monolingual.

And it is indeed the case that expatriate personnel in The Gambia rarely learn any native language. The higher the rank, the more this is true. The few exceptions tend to be themselves from the Third World, leading to various speculations about why people may be willing to learn another language and how that means they feel about the people who speak it natively. Many other Africans, however, tend to stick to English and to look down on Gambians as less sophisticated. Whites frequently offer the rationalization that they can't decide with language they ought to learn and so do not learn any. Surprisingly, most of these same whites are extensively multilingual in various European languages. It does not seem to occur to them that learning an African language is not different in principle from learning French, German or English. Even in the absence of multilingualism, moreover, African custom allows for the exchange of information through translation; yet translators are not considered necessary to project field inspections.

There are attitudes here, individual and cultural, which need to be examined further.

I'd like to close with some comments on the place of social science expertise alongside that of engineering in effective implementation. Effective expatriate projects must communicate with their clientele, both in terms of the priorities, means and implementation of projects and of the mutual respect of parties to any program involving changes in people's ways of life. The project personnel are outsiders and must behave like civilized persons in local terms. If that means patiently listening to elaborate translated speeches involving concerns about donkeys rather than groundwater contamination, so be it. Innovations not understood by the local users will not work. Effective explanation will have to be culturally as well as technologically appropriate.

The process of political negotiation in West Africa is often laborious to westerners, particularly those whose expertise is primarily technological. But effective projects are those that learn to deal with local ways of getting things done. A brief summary of a project visit with a more positive outcome (from the local point of view) may highlight the effective strategies. In this case, the Vice-President responded to a complaint about a well system built by a private contractor. He visited the village with a large entourage of foreign experts and a few politicians. It quickly became obvious that the contractor had fulfilled its obligations. The difficulty arose in that two watering troughs for "small animals" had been thrown in as a gift for the village. The villagers now complained that the cattle were endangered by coming to a well located on the main road through the village; moreover, the nearby mosque (a flimsy structure of bamboo and palm leaves) might by damaged by the cattle. The builder countered that the well was contracted for human consumption only and that it was in the center of the village to make it easier for the women to carry water. A local man burst out with the statement: "Never mind the women, what about the cattle?" The contractor noted that the site was approved by the headman, whose detractors suggested that he was a fool for not realizing people would bring their cattle to the well. The Vice-President, in an apparent non sequitur, asked the contractor if he believed in God, implying that a devout believer (even a Christian) would not build near a mosque. The contractor, however, was a veteran of African construction disputes and assured the assembled company that he thought the village wanted the well near the mosque to facilitate their ceremonial ablutions. Moreover, the well would not run during Friday services, because the operator was undoubtedly a devout Muslim who would be inside the mosque. Villagers were much impressed by this logic. Discussion soon settled down to the cost of extending the water system to allow for watering troughs in a more secluded place. The Vice-President and the contractor agreed on the terms and returned to the capital to prepare the necessary paper work. The Vice-President gained in prestige because he solved the local problem, leaving the village with two watering sites rather than the original one. Local factions were left to dispute who got credit for the happy outcome. And more business was provided for the outside contractor.

Both the style, in the sense of oratorical skill, and the cultural relativity of these negotiations pose a sharp contrast to almost all of the project implementation meetings conducted by expatriates. The Vice-President required translators in the village he visited, but these were easily available. The meeting was followed by social and political discussions which enhanced both local and government prestige. There is no real necessity for project implementation to be as bland and insensitive as it is usually perceived by Gambians (and, I assume, by other Africans as well). Outside technological advisors could certainly devote more attention to communication processes, both linguistic and cultural, which influence acceptance of their work and enhance the sense of goals for development shared by recipients and donors.

Adult Literacy for Development in Zimbabwe: The Third Phase of the Revolution Examined

H.S. Bhola
Indiana University

Political independence came to Zimbabwe on April 18, 1980. That day marked the end of the first phase of the revolutionary struggle. The second phase of the revolution would be economic independence. But there was also to be the third phase of the revolution that would seek the emancipation of the mind. The *Transitional National Development Plan* of the Republic of Zimbabwe published in November 1982 clearly saw literacy to be the instrument for the emancipation of the mind as it said:

> A large proportion of adult Zimbabweans are illiterate or semi-literate. Past administrations showed little interest in eradicating illiteracy. Voluntary groups, notably the Adult Literacy Organization, have made heroic efforts under difficult circumstances to alleviate the problem. As government views literacy as a right as well as an important instrument for effecting economic and social development, government-sponsored programmes of adult education will relate literacy to work experience and production activities as well as to household concerns such as hygiene and child care. They will be designed to create an awareness among adults of the role they can play for the benefit of society as a whole.[1]

The Plan document promised a massive *campaign* to liquidate illiteracy from among the 2.5 million adult illiterates and semi-literates out of the estimated population of some 7.5 million people at the time of independence.

A Campaign is Launched

The National Literacy Campaign of Zimbabwe was launched by Comrade Prime Minister Robert G. Mugabe on July 16, 1983 as what has come to be known as the Mudzi Declaration on "Literacy for All in Five Years." The Prime Minister called it a historic day. He called the literacy campaign a campaign "to set the mind free." Freedom, he asserted, meant little unless the people were mentally emancipated; and their mind is not free if it is illiterate and inumerate.

He declared that Zimbabwean adults had the "right to be taught to read, write and calculate." To passion, he added reason:

> The skills to read, write and calculate enable us to participate in the world of thought and innovation, thus availing to us, through the written word, the ideas of others near and far, dead and alive. Through the intellectual interaction, we learn new ideas and become better thinkers and operators in our own time and localities.
>
> . . . .
>
> Literacy and numeracy are the first conditions which must be satisfied before real political, economic and cultural emancipation can be attained . . . . If the adults of the nation are illiterate and inumerate then any hopes the nation has for socio-economic emancipation will take longer to be realized.

The objectives of the campaign as laid down in the Prime Minister's speech were stated simply but elegantly. These were to enable adults:

1. to understand information about themselves, their localities and their country; and

2. to become effective leaders and productive members of their co-operatives, village committees, management committees and any other organizations to which they might belong.

The Prime Minister promised that it would be a true national literacy campaign, "not aiming at some illiterate adults, or many illiterate adults, or most adult illiterates, but at all illiterate people outside the formal school."

He promised new infrastructures that would mobilize the state and the people for the implementation of the literacy campaign: a national coordinating council at the center, followed by provincial coordinating committees, district coordinating committees, and village development committees. At the village level, there would be village development centers where literacy groups would meet. The Prime Minister had conceptualized a literacy campaign for the people, by the people. "Every government Ministry, nonGovernment organization, the private sector and indeed all literate people should organize themselves into brigades to fight illiteracy and to wipe it out within the next five years," he exhorted. It is significant to note that much of the work for the campaign was to be "voluntary."

The Ideology and the Technology of the Zimbabwean National Literacy Campaign

The available theory of the literacy campaign identifies two dimensions of ideology and technology as determinants of the success or failure of literacy campaigns.[2] The Zimbabwean National Literacy Campaign started on the right ideological foot as the above-quoted pronouncements from the Prime Minister should indicate. What happened to the ideological fortunes of the National Literacy Campaign over the years 1983-87 will be discussed later in the paper. We will first talk of the technology of the campaign and of the results achieved by the campaign.

The Technology of the Literacy Campaign

Along the technological dimension, the Zimbabwean National Literacy Campaign was undoubtedly well planned.[3] A great fund of knowledge and experience in literacy promotion in different socio-economic settings had in fact become available during the 1960s and the 1970s. The planners of the Zimbabwean National Literacy Campaign were able to visit literacy campaigns and programs of many different countries in Asia and Africa for some first-hand experience. The head of the reputedly successful adult literacy campaign in Tanzania, Z.P. Mpogolo, spent six months in Harare helping Zimbabwean colleagues in the development and design of strategies for implementation of the campaign to be launched in Zimbabwe.

The Planning and Administration of the National Literacy Campaign

In 1981, when the idea of literacy promotion for development was first mooted in Zimbabwe, the government decided to assign the task of delivering literacy to adult learners to the national Ministry of Education and Culture. Later, in July 1982, the task was divided between the Ministry of Education and Culture and the Ministry of Community Development and Women's Affairs. The Ministry of Education and Culture was to make technical contributions through production of materials, training of District Literacy coordinators (DLC's), and evaluation. The Ministry of Community Development and Women's Affairs, with its community development workers in the field, would be responsible for the training of field-level staff such as Voluntary Literacy Teachers (VLT's) and for the delivery of literacy instruction to the 2.5 million illiterates and semi-literates in the urban and rural areas of the country. This division of work between the two ministries would be found later to have fragmented the government's literacy effort and to have seriously hurt the literacy initiative.

The Two Main Agents for the Delivery of Services

Under the plan, the two main agents for the delivery of services came to be the DLC's and the VLT's. Great hopes were invested particularly in the role of the DLC's. These DLC's were to be recruited from the pool of ex-combatants who will now be asked to exchange their guns and grenades from the days of the struggle for pens and primers to now fight for victories of peace. Those of the ex-combatants who had at least five O-level passes were selected as DLC's. These DLC's would mobilize the illiterate adults to come to learn and to enthuse the literate volunteers to offer themselves as VLT's and come to teach. It has turned out that the politicians and development planners themselves sank deep into complacency, leaving the campaign to the mobilizational capacities of the DLC's and voluntarism of the VLT's.

The Structures for People's Participation

The Prime Minister in his speech had already promised an infrastructure of councils and committees going from the center to the village. During 1985 and later, as part of decentralization of politics and development, there were further structures established that were vertically integrated. However, these structures have not done much by way of literacy promotion.

The Language of Literacy

The Mashona constitute 71 percent and the Matebele 16 percent of the total Black population of Zimbabwe. In the earlier stages of the National Literacy Campaign, decisions were made to teach literacy in two vernacular languages — Shona, and Ndebele. Literacy in English was to be taught in the last stage of the learning cycle. Later in the years, other languages such as Tonga, Venda, Kalanga, and Shangani have been added.

Curriculum and Instructional Materials

The curricular objectives include the essential triangle of literacy, functionality and awareness. Scientific analysis of cause and effect, new economic skills, history of political independence, awareness of the exploitation of women, national consciousness, patriotism and commitment to a socialist and egalitarian society are supposed to form the specific content of the curriculum. The instructional materials are an adaptation of Paulo Freire's approach. A set of forty-four posters provide themes for discussion by adult learners. These posters carry key words both in Shona and Ndebele and are meant to be used in a different sequence for each of the two languages. Most of the themes included in the posters are on the subject of struggle against the white minority regime overthrown through a successful struggle by the people. The instructional kit includes: a primer (in Shona or Ndebele), a numeracy workbook (in Shona or Ndebele), a tutor's guide (in Shona or Ndebele) and a numeracy tutor's guide (only in English). Primers are distributed free to learners, but they must buy their own exercise books and pencils. These materials are supposed to be followed by functional books some of which have already been written but not yet published.

Training of DLC's and VLT's

The training of DLC's is conducted by the Ministry of Education. It is of four week duration and is essentially technical in nature, discussing methods of teaching and class organization. The training of VLT's is the responsibility of the Ministry of Community Development and Women's Affairs. The training for VLT's is supposed to be two weeks but exigencies of time and resources have often reduced it to two or three days. Supervision of VLT's by DLC's is inhibited by the fact that travel by DLC's on their motor bikes is limited to 500 kilometers a month and no more than 50 Zimbabwe dollars can be granted as halting allowance each month to a DLC.

The Teaching-Learning Encounter

Classes are taught in whatever places are available from elementary school buildings to under the trees. Classes typically meet 3 times a week for 2 hours each time. There is no pattern to when classes begin and when they end. Adult learners are known to stay anywhere between 6 to 18 months in their learning groups. Three somewhat distinct stages have been talked about: stage 1 of 24 weeks when vernacular literacy and numeracy are introduced; stage 2 of 24 weeks when skills in vernacular literacy and numeracy are strengthened; and stage 3 of 16 weeks when English is introduced as well as some history, geography, hygiene and science are taught to bring the adult learner to a level of skills aquisition equivalent to the VII grader. It is not clear if in practice VIIth grade skills are learned by anyone at all.

Support Materials and Institutions

There is very little available by way of support materials in print or other media. Follow-up books and reading materials are scarce. Extension materials produced by other development ministries such as the Ministry of Agriculture, Health or Labor are not directed to the new literate and an excellent opportunity is missed. The government's *Peoples Weekly* may be the only reasonable reading material in print. Radio 4, which is wholly dedicated to education provides some useful information to adult learners. The Zimbabwe Foundation for Education with Production has the possibility of becoming a useful support institution for new literates but its role is thus far minimal.

Coverage by the Campaign During 1983-86

One of the plans for national coverage considered during the earliest period of the campaign had, rather optimistically, developed the following projections:

Year

| 1983-84 | 1984-85 | 1985-86 | 1986-87 |

Participants to be covered

| 200,000 | 500,000 | 1,000,000 | 1,000,000 |

Literacy instructors to be mobilized

| 10,000 | 25,000 | 50,000 | 50,000 |

In reality, the figures recently released by the Government of Zimbabwe are as follows:

Year	Total Learners Enrolled	Male	Female	Male/Female Ratio
1983	90,052	13,775	76,277	1:5
1984	117,461	17,423	100,038	1:6
1985	105,203	15,676	89,527	1:6
1986	82,138	13,435	68,703	1:5
TOTAL	394,854	60,309	334,545	1:5

The table below presents figures of tutors trained, retrained and those who withdrew:

Year	Trained	Retrained	Withdrew
1983	5,765	4,429	584
1984	7,536	3,250	1,117
1985	10,135	5,867	1,824
1986	6,942	2,199	1,434

Understandably, all those concerned with the campaign are talking about the "loss of momentum" in the campaign and of the need for its revitalization.

Some Evaluations of the Campaign

Some evaluations of the Zimbabwean National Literacy Campaign have since become available and are summarized below.

An evaluation of learners achievement was conducted by the Ministry of Education during May-June 1985. The Ministry of Education invited all learners who had participated in the campaign to come to be tested during a pre-determined week. Only 35,000 (about 11 per cent of the total cumulative enrollment during 1983-85) showed up. This low level of showing is explained by the fact that the national test competed with the agricultural cycle and a national election. Of those who took the test, 27,000 (some 77 per cent) were declared successful. Learners needed to score 50 per cent marks to be declared successful and most of the 27,000 who passed may have been semi-literate rather than fully literate. Unlike Tanzania, whose national literacy tests provided the model, the Zimbabwe testing failed to make any mobilizational use of the testing event. The Party took no interest in the testing nor did the local leadership. Indeed, the testing may have spread frustration among those who did take the tests, by sending their certificates late and many to the wrong addresses. Another nation-wide test is planned for 1988.

A study conducted by Ines Grainger[4], found potential for reorientation in both the objectives and processes of the campaign. Literacy, she suggested, had become an affair for women. Men preferred to drink beer rather than attend classes. The program did not seem to meet learners' objectives which were to acquire academic knowledge to enter the formal economy. They did not want functional literacy. Perhaps they could be convinced otherwise but the program as presently run taught neither functionality nor academic literacy effectively. Tutors failed to inspire their learners since they were themselves seen as social and economic failures.

In a deeper political analysis of adult literacy in Zimbabwe, Davison[5] suggests that the regime may have indeed abandoned its policy of "growth with equity" promulgated in the first few years of independence. Naturally, therefore, universalization of adult literacy was no more on its agenda. She suspects also that the power elite in Zimbabwe may not be willing to release women from the cultural (and legal) bondage in which they live and since women are the main beneficiaries of the campaign, the male power establishment may not be too serious in making literacy succeed.

The Ideology of the Literacy Campaign

It is quite clear from the forgoing description and evaluations that the National Literacy Campaign of Zimbabwe has lost momentum and is indeed in need of revitalization, lest it should peter out completely. It can also be asserted that the cause for the present condition of the campaign does not lie in its technology which is more than adequate, but in its ideology which today is less than stimulating. The campaign when it was first launched in July of 1983, did seem to have had the right ideological roots. The language of justification for literacy promotion used in the Prime Minister's speech sounded right for a political elite committed to developing a socialist and egalitarian society. However, the ideological drift from revolution to reform was already there for the perceptive to see. From the advantage of hindsight, the ideological drift should be clear to anyone willing to ponder.

Political Culture and Literacy Strategy: Positing a Theoretical Relationship

Elsewhere, I have proposed a political theory of literacy promotion.[6] I have suggested that there is a discernible dialectical relationship between a nation's political culture and the literacy promotion strategy that a nation would normally choose. The following graphic representation of the model delineates these relationships:

Motivational-Developmental Model		Planned Development Model		Structural-Developmental Model
<> _____	...	<> _____	...	<>
Gradualist Organic Growth	... ..	Reformist Growth with Efficiency	... ..	Revolutionary Growth with Equity
Project Approach to Literacy	...	Program Approach to Literacy	...	Campaign Approach to Literacy

The categories along each continuum in the model above are not discrete but should be seen as interpenetrating into each other. Again, the various points on the parallel continua are not meant to be seen in perfect vertical integration. The model should, nonetheless, help us understand how political cultures, and strategies of development and literacy promotion stand in dialectical relationships among each other, with particular partialities and propensities.

As ideal types, the nations following the motivational-developmental model are basically conservative, even reactionary. They look at growth and change as an organic process, expecting the individual to aspire, get motivated, and to achieve to obtain his or her own share of social goods. Structures, if not neutral, are seen as amenable to change under emergent pressure from the newly motivated. Nations following this model are in no hurry to change their socio-political realities. They believe in gradual social transformations without social disruptions. Literacy is seldom a governmental priority. When it is given a consideration, justifications for literacy promotion are found in religion, patriotism and productivity. Literacy initiatives typically end up supporting professionalization of labor in the context of functional literacy projects tied to small- and medium-scale economic projects.

At the other end of the continuum are the nations following the structural-developmental model. These are revolutionary societies which may draw strength from varied sources of nationalism, populism or marxism. The focus is on changing structures which determine the rules of the political and economic game. Within the newly established structures citizens are motivated to participate in the new political, social and economic institutions. Typically, these societies claim egalitarian and democratic ideologies of some sort. Their developmental agenda is growth with equity. Literacy is central to their plans for both modernization and democratization and the strategy of literacy promotion is almost always the campaign involving high political passion, and popular mobilization.

Somewhere in the middle of this continuum are societies that can be seen as following the planned development model. These societies as ideal types do want to change structures but wish to keep the dynamics of change under the planners' control. The masses are invited to participate in the implementation of the outcomes planned by the power elite. These societies can be best described as reformist. Growth and equity are sought to be kept in an efficient balance so as not to create economic malaise or social conflict. Both formal education and nonformal education are seen as necessary for promoting modernization and democratization. The favourite strategy of literacy promotion of such societies seems to be a national literacy program, which may be nation-wide but which is often under bureaucratic control and is lacking in the crusading and combatative spirit of a literacy campaign.

The above model should help us understand the nature and path of the ideological drift in Zimbabwe from the structural-developmental model to the planned development model. With this drift, the concern for growth with equity may have begun to change into growth with efficiency and, quite obviously, the literacy campaign has become a literacy program at best and may be in the danger of fragmenting into a multiplicity of small projects.

The context and history of the ideological drift that we have talked about is sketched below in bare details:

The Politics of Paradoxical Partnership

The elite who came to govern Zimbabwe after their long negotiation sessions at the constitutional conference at Lancaster House during September 10 to December 15, 1979 had in fact surrendered the revolutionary option. They were not doctrinaire but pragmatists. They had agreed not to dispossess the white settlers and industrialists who then owned more than half of the gross investment in development. These property owners were allowed the time necessary to sell their properties or to keep them as long as they wished. Thus, there developed vested interests on both sides. The white settlers kept their properties and the new governing elite were assured that economic life of the nation will not be disrupted. Whether it was good or bad is not the question for us. The new leaders of Zimbabwe had to practice the art of the possible. What must be realized, however, is that history is a tough master and that the political compromise brought with it a series of constraints.

The Driving Forces Behind the Campaign

In spite of what the formal pronouncements may have said, adult literacy was not, therefore, central to the development strategy of the nation. The leadership was not dealing with a revolutionary situation any more. They may have reasoned thus: The property relations would not be possible to change for a long time. The changes in the superstructure that would have followed were also not in the immediate future. Distributive justice will have to wait. Why then prepare people for a future that did not exist. In reading between the lines, one finds that the justification for literacy presented in the *Transitional Development Plan (TDP)* is somewhat cold and passionless. More significantly, the development strategy of the TDP is not rooted in the assumption of universal literacy.

There is thus a discontinuity between the language of the TDP and the Prime Minister's speech of July 1983. It could perhaps be suggested that the driving force for the launching of the campaign may not have been endogenous at all — the national planners were not really convinced about the usefulness of adult literacy. The motivation may have come from outside, from the Regional Conference of Ministers of Education and Those Responsible for Economic Planning in African Member States held in Harare, Zimbabwe from June 28 to July 3, 1982 and organized by Unesco with the cooperation of the Economic Commission for Africa (ECA) and the Organization of African Unity (OAU). The Harare Declaration made at the end of the Conference had challenged the African nations:

> to eliminate illiteracy through a vigorous, sustained two-pronged campaign to universalize primary schooling for children and to promote literacy among young people and adults on massive scale.[7]

The declaration of the national literacy campaign by Zimbabwe may have been an attempt at being a good host to the Conference and to live up to the expectations of the Declaration that was named after the nation's capital city. It is important to note that the campaign was to be a completely voluntary effort and the Party was spared the responsibility to mobilize the people.

Mobilization in the Context of Demobilization

There is nothing inherently wrong with a campaign being voluntary, if voluntarism can be elicited and then sustained through non-monetary incentives and rewards. Indeed, the national literacy crusade in Nicaragua provides an example of how the mobilization to overthrow the Somoza regime was redirected into a new mobilization for the eradication of illiteracy from the country.[8] Nothing of the kind was done in Zimbabwe. ZANU(PF) was and remains a spectator to the campaign. The Prime Minister has not spoken again about literacy since his speech that launched the campaign in July 1983.

An interesting and significant fact is often missed by analysts of the Zimbabwe literacy initiative. It is the fact that mobilization for literacy was planned in the general context of a *de*mobilization of the nation. The mobilization for the literacy campaign, basically through DLC's who were all excombatants, might have succeeded, except that there were opposite and stronger pulls in operation at the same time. While mobilization for literacy was to begin, the nation had been through a successful demobilization of the armies that had fought the white Rhodesian regime. The incentives were for change from the underground to the establishment, from the cadre to the functionary, from the guerilla to the career oriented wage earner or shop keeper. No wonder the DLC's failed to generate a literacy movement and the VLT's kept on asking for honoraria for the work done.

The Nature of the Present Political Culture

Zimbabwe today is caught in the paradox of socialism in partnership with capitalism. There is a duality in the society and the economy and, therefore, in the development strategy. Interest in literacy has fallen between the cracks of the dual strategy of the new Five Year Plan which shows little interest in literacy promotion.[9] Understandably — and here there is no paradox — the orientation of the national system of education is toward manpower development for the formal economic sector. Nonformal education and adult literacy are seen as mere frills.

The existing plans, actions, incentives and rewards have socialized the present generation of the young as entrepreneurs and competitors, not as egalitarian cooperators. The recent draught, failure in the Unity talks with John Nkomo, the uncertainties on the border with South Africa all suggest that revolutionary gambles should be avoided.

From Ideological Drift to Political Design

Are their possibilities of going from the ideological drift to serious self-conscious political design for development and literacy promotion? Our answer is in the affirmative. Possibilities can be discussed at two levels: theoretical possibilities and practical possibilities. At the theoretical level, it is possible to develop a mix of socialism and capitalism. The Swedish experience should tell us that it can be done. In Zimbabwe today, it is a practical possibility as well in spite of the fact that the political economy of the country is confounded by racial considerations. It will not be easy considering that a class committed to comfort and consumption has perhaps already emerged. But it can be done.

Coming to the question of campaigning for literacy, the policy makers and planners in Zimbabwe should not let go of the hopes and aspirations of the Mudzi Declaration. Again, it is theoretically possible to run a literacy campaign in a culture which is no more revolutionary but has demobilized and accepted a mix of capitalism and socialism. As we have indicated in our discussion of the model of literacy promotion above, the relationship between political culture, development orientations and choice of literacy strategies is neither uni-directional nor deterministic. It is dialectical and, therefore, mutually definitional. The tail can wag the dog. By conducting a successful adult literacy campaign, the ethos of the political culture can be changed and, within limits, also the social and economic relationships.

It remains a practical possibility for Zimbabwe to conduct a successful national literacy campaign if the political elite at the highest level show interest and come out openly in favor of the campaign. There is no reason why the Prime Minister can not demand that the Party take the responsibility to mobilize the learners to learn and the teachers to teach. There is no reason why the 320,000 secondary school students and over 100,000 primary and secondary school teachers in full employment of the government can not be sent to the villages and asked to teach literacy. There is no reason why resources can not be made available to the Ministry of Education and to the Ministry of Community Development and Women's Affairs to implement a national initiative and show results. There is no reason why instructional materials used in the program can not serve multiple functional purposes to change the lives of farmers, workers and housewives in the formal and in *the informal* sectors of economic development.

Literacy is needed in Zimbabwe. If the bulk of the population which is outside the formal economy have to be more productive, they have to be provided education and this education will have to be nonformal education *with* adult literacy. How else will the country move out of the economic dualism in which it finds itself? How else will the farmers learn to produce more, drink less, have fewer children, eat nutritious food and follow health education? How else will they learn to be cooperators? How else will they move into politics from outside politics where they are now?

Lessons for Zimbabwe and Elsewhere

Political power in Zimbabwe is in the hands of a group of intelligent, and committed people who have been hardened first by the armed struggle and then by the designs of the enemy within and the enemy without. Their policies remain pro-people. They are seriously committed to creating a society of fairness and freedom. But they have to face up to the fact that the historical compromise made at Lancaster House, has removed some important options. Distributive justice has to wait because what is to be distributed is not immediately available. The continued use of revolutionary rhetoric may mystify people in the short run but can not for ever hide the reformist mode of social transformation. An appropriate change in the language of discourse may indeed clarify development discussion.

The politicians and policy makers in Zimbabwe also need to learn that political will does not grow in a vacuum. It has to be planted in the proper ideological soil and has to be continuously nurtured to be sustained. Related with it is the idea that mobilization is a political process lead by political actors; it is more than bureaucratization and inter-departmental coordination.

What needs to be further understood is the fact that Zimbabwe planners may be making the "conventional error" in regard to the role of literacy in development. Literacy is a deprivation that is not directly and immediately felt. The illiterate can not attribute the experience of pain and disadvantage directly to their illiteracy. But that does not mean that the planners themselves should succumb to the social demand for formal education and forget about literacy which is not part of the social demand but definitely remains a co-requisite of development. Reform needs literacy as much as the revolution. Literacy must yet play an important role within the development planning model. If about half the population works within the informal sector of the economy, they need nonformal education with literacy now. That is the only way for them to become participants in the transformation of their culture and their technology and that is the best justification for literacy in Zimbabwe and in all societies in a similar set of conditions.

Those unsympathetic to the cause of literacy may be tempted to say: "I told you so!" But it really ain't so. The conclusion is not that literacy is not needed, but that literacy can be neglected even by those who are otherwise well intentioned. We can not, as some have done, bury the issue by saying that literacy is a "cultural phenomenon", implying that some day culture will need it and demand it. But that is mystifying the issue and surrendering responsibility as leaders. Aren't agriculture, family health, fertility, nutrition all cultural phenomena? In all these development sectors, we are under the moral burden to act. We need to work to create new cultural phenomena in which literacy has given all citizens opportunity and independence to act in their own behalf.

NOTES

1. *Transitional National Development Plan (1982/83 - 1984/85)*. Harare: Government Printer, Vol. 1 (November), 1982, p. 92.

2. Bhola, H.S. "The Theory of the Mass Literacy Campaign," paper presented to the Seventh Annual Henry Lester Smith Conference on Research in Education, Bloomington, Indiana, February 1-2, 1982.

3. There is little available on the Zimbabwean National Literacy Campaign in literature. The description of the ideology and the technology of the campaign has been built on the basis of newspaper stories and papers, reports and related materials made public by the Ministry of Community Development and Women's Affairs, and the Ministry of Education and Culture of the Government of Zimbabwe.

4. Grainger, I.P. *Literacy Participation in Zimbabwe*. Harare: University of Zimbabwe, 1986.

5. Davison, J. "Adult Literacy Training as a Volunteer Enterprise in Zimbabwe," paper presented at the annual meeting of the Comparative and International Education Society, March, 1987.

6. The political model of literacy promotion first presented in H.S. Bhola. *Campaigning for Literacy*. Paris: Unesco, 1984 was later expanded in its present form in a paper, entitled "Literacy in Revolution and Reform: Experiences in the SADCC Region of Southern Africa," presented to the International Conference on the Future of Literacy in a Changing World, Literacy Research Center, University of Pennsylvania, Philadelphia, May 9-12, 1985. ERIC Document No. ED 260 208.

7. Unesco. Regional Office for Education in Africa. *Regional Programme for the Eradication of Illiteracy in Africa*. Dakar: [Unesco ?], 1984.

8. Miller, V. *Between Struggle and Hope: The Nicaraguan Literacy Crusade*. Boulder, CO: Westview Press, 1985.

9. *First Five-year National Development Plan, 1986-1990*. Harare: Government Printer, Vol. 1 (April), 1986.

Nigerian Television and the Problems of Urban African Women

Harriet D. Lyons
Wilfrid Laurier University

> Ugly people are accused of being witches;
> beautiful ones are accused of being prostitutes.
>> Ivie Erhahon
>> Benin City woman,
>> 18 in 1983;
>> research assistant to the author

Critics of television drama in the West, particularly critics of situation comedies, have frequently noted the tendency of such productions to trivialize the problems of daily life by the use of artificially happy endings. Feminist critics have been especially concerned with the impressions conveyed by such programs, that family problems can be brought to a humorous and satisfactory conclusion in half-an-hour or an hour, often as a result of the calm wisdom of a husband and father.[1] If the male hero of a situation comedy is not calm and wise, he is likely to be a good-natured, but silly or gullible poseur, easily manipulated by his wife and children, and gracious in acknowledging the defeat which he meets at the conclusion of each episode. Since women's role in the family ensures that real life domestic difficulties are, overwhelmingly, women's problems, it has been argued that such trivialization denies the social realities which shape women's lives. Women whose problems are not so easily solved are made to feel somehow inadequate, and serious family issues — domestic violence, severe poverty, alcoholism, abandonment, and incest — tend to be avoided in programs whose main intention is to entertain. Where they are not avoided, solutions may be made to seem easier and more available than is really the case. The shelter for battered wives has spaces when the abused heroine finally decides to call, and her husband makes great strides in a support group. A country house with a garden is found for a bag lady by a dedicated young social worker; alcoholics join AA in record numbers. Those problems which cannot be solved must be small enough to be laughed at; tyrannical husbands and fathers can be humiliated by their wives and children in a spirit of good, clean fun. In such circumstances they can be counted upon not to leave or take revenge with their fists. In almost all cases, even in those instances where happy outcomes are not provided, the impression is given that family problems (and their solutions) are individual matters. Failures are individual failures, and good families, like good people, can be strengthened by adversity. Love, hard work, and a sense of humour can keep a family together, so that hard times become good times. Ethnic and class differences contribute little to plot development beyond local color. Poor blacks in Chicago, rich blacks in New York, and poor whites on Walton's Mountain experience many of the same problems and approach them in much the same way.[2] Those who can't pull a lesson out of every obstacle life throws in their paths have only themselves to blame, and women, watching the shows, blame themselves in huge numbers.

In this paper, I will argue that Nigerian television drama, despite low budgets and other constraints, manages to avoid both individualization and trivialization of the domestic problems of women, without sacrificing the ability of programs to entertain. I will argue, further, that locally produced comedy and drama, viewed during two studies in Benin City, Nigeria, provide both visibility and social context for many of the problems faced by women in contemporary African cities. It will be noted, nonetheless, that a number of the programs demonstrate a tendency to blame women for the problems of modern men, portraying women as supernaturally threatening, greedy for money, or both. In some instances, most notably where plots revolve around the issues related to polygamy, the acknowledged hardships of women become men's undoing.

The research on which this paper was based was carried out during a brief pilot study in the summer of 1976 and a six month investigation of the impact of mass communications on a Nigerian city, undertaken during the academic year 1983-84. Both studies were conducted jointly with my husband, Andrew P. Lyons. In the course of our study we watched a great deal of television, listened to the radio, examined print media, talked with media producers, and conducted 354 interviews with consumers of media products. These consumers included men and women of all ages and social classes, and children of both sexes. When we could, we watched television in company, so that we could gauge audience reaction directly. The following remarks represent one part of our findings.

Although cultural imperialism and the "dumping" of Western videotapes on third world markets are a major concern of students of mass communications in developing countries, our study revealed a strong preference for local drama and comedy when it was available. In particular, in Benin City, when our informants were asked to name their favorite programs, two locally produced series emerged among the most popular programs on television. The NTA, Benin, comedy series "Hotel de Jordan" was the most popular program by a wide margin; eighty three out of 354 informants named it as their favorite program. The drama series, "Bendel Playhouse"," was fourth in our survey, with televised wrestling and the British crime show, "The Professionals," coming in between.

"Hotel de Jordan," in some ways, incorporates the typical sitcom plot structure, in which a pompous and foolish, but beloved man is made to seem ridiculous by the actions of his family and friends. The man in question is the wealthy and corrupt, but uncultured and none-too-intelligent Chief Ajas. Those who regularly bring him low include his servant, Idemudia, his servant's friend, Kokori, and a series of wives and girlfriends, to whom he is rendered vulnerable by a combination of lust, available wealth, and lack of personal attractiveness.

For example, in one episode Chief Ajas, normally a womanizer and in this episode a polygnist, has worked out a new system for winning the football pools, but one of his three wives burns what turns out to have been a winning coupon because of her resentment of the attention Chief Ajas devotes to the pools. While Ajas lies on the sofa in a state of shock, after discovering his loss, his wives have a heated altercation with each other. Ajas recovers his sangfroid sufficiently to enable him to concentrate on the reinvention of his pools system. He wins again, but his joy is quickly dampened as his wives wrangle over the division of the spoils. The general buffoonery of the situation is heightened by the fact that two of the wives are played by male actors in female dress, actors who normally play Idemudia, Ajas's servant and Kokori, Idemudia's ally in various plots to thwart Ajas.

In another episode, Idemudia and Kokori, in their normal male roles, attempt to seduce a beautiful and wealthy young woman, upon whom the middle-aged Ajas has his own designs. In the end, the girl is rescued (and won) by a handsome young journalist after a scuffle between the other contenders for her favours.

In a scene from yet another episode,[3] Ajas boasts to his girlfriend, whom he has just ordered to serve drinks, about a large share of the produce of his land which he intends to allot to her mother and sister. She asks him for a share of her own, which he attempts to refuse by appeals to their spiritual unity, saying that they are like a snail and its shell, and that their property should be inseparable. In the end, the girl holds out, and Ajas relents.

In each of these episodes, Ajas is portrayed as acquisitive of both money and women, and exploitative in his pursuit of both. His wife burns the pools ticket because she is angry at his gambling the family money without consulting her; he has kept his win a secret because he doesn't want to share his windfall. The young girl he pursues in the second episode described above is as rich as she is beautiful. She is the child of a wealthy relative of Ajas, resident in Hong Kong, who has sent his daughter on a visit to her homeland after her graduation from college. Ajas is at least as attracted by her money as by her pulchritude. In the third episode I have mentioned, Ajas' speeches on the subject of the produce grown on his land, or otherwise available for him to sell, make it clear that he has come by this property through corruption and hoarding.[4] Polygyny, in a real-life urban Nigerian context, is not merely characterized by quarrels erupting from emotional and material jealousy, it is an inordinately expensive operation in a city economy, where people live on wages and profits, rather than crops grown by women. Polygamy, in the minds of many contemporary Nigerians, contributes to corruption by increasing man's need for money. Women are said to suffer because there is not enough money to go round; it is in this context that the jealousy and suspicion of Ajas and his "wives" is played out. Sexual and financial indiscipline are kindred weaknesses; Ajas, in all three episodes discussed, is shown as suffering from both. It is worth noting that the programs were aired at the time when the Buhari government was just unveiling the "War Against Indiscipline." A number of techniques used in the staging of these programs, however, make them into something more than jokes about an individual's foibles and the amusing scrapes into which they lead him. The casting of actors who normally play Ajas's servants as his "wives" provides more than burlesque; it is a convenient device for equating the struggle between men and women with class struggle, a stratagem brilliant in its economy. The producer of "Hotel de Jordan," Jonathan Ihonde, was president of the Nigerian Labour Congress in Bendel State.

One crucial way in which Chief Ajas (and other big men) portrayed on "Hotel de Jordan" differ from the pompous, selfish (but lovable) daddies shown on imported situation comedies is that characters like Ajas do not have hearts of gold. Unlike George Jefferson, who learns a lesson about humility and family values at the end of every show, and who paid a heartrending visit to his Harlem birthplace during one Christmas episode, Ajas and his kind are portrayed without sentiment.

If Ajas is popular with audiences (and he is), it is because he is perfectly predictable: the comic distillation of all that people believe to be wrong in contemporary urban Nigeria. If watching his antics cheers, rather than depresses, it is not because he is shown as possessing a finer side. It is, rather, because he is regularly defeated, and defeated by just those qualities which make him a danger to the poor and the weak: lust, greed, ignorance, and lack of scruples.

The lack of sentiment in "Hotel de Jordan's" portrayal of Ajas extends to the program's depiction of Ajas's "class enemies," women and servants. Kokori and Idemudia are as interested in girls and money as is Ajas; they are simply barred from acquiring any, at least on a permanent basis. Ajas's women either are members of his own class or aspire to be; their situation is realistically portrayed, insofar as they are dependent upon men's whims if they are to achieve and retain class privilege. In this sense, they may be seen as exemplifying a genuine dilemma of women under capitalism. However, the program's very denial of personal solutions to political problems ensures that the women in Ajas's life are portrayed as parasites. Unlike traditional African women (and unlike Ajas's servants) they perform no real labour, make no real economic contribution. The absence of psychological mystification denies Ajas's wives and mistresses even the therapeutic functions of a Louise Jefferson, who may lead a life of relative leisure, but who possesses the power to humanize her husband, to mitigate some of his self-aggrandizing tendencies. If unhappy wives, watching "Hotel de Jordan," are spared the burden of comparing themselves unfavorably with women depicted as possessing unrealistically noble qualities as wives and mothers, their husbands may be offered an opportunity to view women as grasping and dangerous. The image of women in "Hotel de Jordan" is, in some ways, reminiscent of the Onitsha market pamphlet warning "Never Trust Money-Monger Girls" (Okonkwo, n.d.). For all its drawbacks, it is at least superficially an empowering image, which may help explain why women enjoy "Hotel de Jordan" as much as men.

Jonathan Ihonde has said that the main subject of "Hotel de Jordan" is class struggle (Programme Notes, NTA Benin Benefit Concert: April, 1984): if women's issues form part of the show's subject matter, they do so as a subtext of the discourse of class. "Bendel Playhouse" is another popular production of NTA Benin, in which women are often seen as central characters and in which the family and its problems provide the main focus of most of the plots. The families whose lives are dramatized on "Bendel Playhouse", however, are not, as is often true of families on Western television drama, enclosed in a world in which their emotions provide the only motivation and meaning for their actions; rather, their passions are portrayed as a product of the difficult times in which they live. "Bendel Playhouse" is neither a situation comedy nor a soap opera; it offers original, serious, hour long plays, often with unhappy endings.

I shall discuss three "Bendel Playhouse" dramas, one broadcast in August, 1976, and the others during our 1983-84 study. In these discussions I shall attempt to identify salient themes in the program's treatment of women's role in the contemporary Nigerian family. These themes include the stresses placed on the family by modern ideals of individual achievement and romantic love, the impact of economic and social competitiveness on women's lives, and the dangers surrounding sexuality and reproduction in the contemporary environment. One characteristic feature of "Bendel Playhouse" is its unselfconscious use of witchcraft and magic as elements in plot development, despite the very contemporary dilemmas faced by its characters; another is the frequency with which wrongly motivated choices lead to extreme consequences. On all three of the programs to be discussed someone dies as a result of a woman's manipulations; once by murder, once by witchcraft, and once through a botched abortion.

In August of 1976, during our pilot study, I monitored an episode of "Bendel Playhouse", in which the entire plot structure seemed in large measure, to be a modern African resetting of Hamlet, leading, with total appropriateness, to a climactic scene in which the ghost of the hero's father utters the tag line, "As for your mother, leave her to heaven."

This excellent example of televison drama dealt, as does much of contemporary West African literature and theatre, with the clash between traditional concepts of filial piety and the demands and opportunities presented by an individualistic urban culture. Significantly, the Shakespearean elements in the play seemed entirely at home in the author's world.

The episode opened with a soft focus portrayal of a vision, which appeared to a traditional healer called upon to treat the wife of a city-dwelling polygynist. In the vision, a man attempts to carry a coffin, bearing the remains of the patient, down a hill to a river. The doctor/priest interprets this vision as a warning that the woman will die if she does not confess an injury she has done to some man in the past, provoking in her victim a desire for supernatural retaliation. In the discussion that ensues, between the woman, her husband, and her twenty-three year old son, it becomes clear that the son is both more modern than the father, and angry at him for the pain his mother has suffered as a co-wife in a polygynous household. The mother is clearly reluctant to confess, but fear eventually drives her to do so.

In television's equivalent of Shakespeare's play within-a-play, the scene then shifts to a flashback of a wealthy building contractor, making corrupt business deals over the telephone. The woman who figures in the priest's vision enters the office, some twenty-three years younger then we have previously seen her. The man hurriedly hangs up the phone, and the woman, who turns out to be his mistress, tells him that she is pregnant, and needs money for an abortion; she is certain the child is his, and not her husband's. He refuses her the money, and offers to marry her, if she will leave her husband. He reminds her that he loves her, and that her husband has recently taken another wife, much to her dismay. She says that she cannot bear the shame of leaving her husband, and being publicly branded an adulteress. The contractor threatens to expose her to her husband. The woman is next shown having a whispered conversation with one of her lover's workers. In the next scene, the contractor, while inspecting a high-rise building under construction, is jostled by the worker in question, and falls to his death.

The scene shifts back to the present, where for a moment, son, mother, and pater stare at each other in shocked silence. "You are not my father," the son finally exclaims in a hoarse whisper. "And you are not my son," the erstwhile father replies, as it visibly dawns on both men that they are now free of each other. The priest departs, and the family is left to readjust its internal relations.

The mother disappears upstairs; her husband pursues her, shouting, and we shortly see her clothes being thrown down the stairs. She follows them, only to be chased around the room by her son, who is brandishing a machete, and crying, "You have killed my father; you have killed my father." At that moment, the ghost of the murdered father is heard to speak: "As for your mother, leave her to heaven." The son throws down his weapon and leaves, to seek his new life in the city outside. The mother sits alone in the living room. The play ends.

The slightly misquoted line from Shakespeare[5] is appropriate here, because the world inhabited by this contemporary Nigerian family has much in common with Shakespeare's world. Witchcraft and magic are still important forces for many people, but more earthbound causes are frequently cited for personal misfortune. As in Shakespeare's England, individual ambition is recognized as a valid motivation for action, but people are acutely conscious of the potential for such ambition to conflict with traditional family duties and loyalties. Indeed, such loyalties, in the guise of "ethnicity" and "tribalism" may even be perceived as being against the national interest, yet there are few, if any, Nigerians who would advocate complete disregard for filial piety. What our play does, among other things, is to provide its young male protagonist with moral permission for individualism; his pater is not his father, and his mother is a murderess, who would have aborted him had she the opportunity. His dead genitor was corrupt, as well as being an adulterer and a blackmailer, so he need do little for him beyond refraining from killing his mother. For women, the conflict between self and family is more likely to concern the actual or potential family of procreation than the natal lineage. A woman must choose between attempting to advance her interests on her own or linking her fortunes to those of a man. Should she choose the former, she must contend with lesser opportunities than would, in all likelihood, be available to a man. Should she select the latter course, she risks abandonment, widowhood, polygamy, and her man's failure in the economic ratrace. The mother in our "Bendel Playhouse" drama chooses to make her way in the world through men, and finds herself doubly disappointed: her husband insists that she share his favours (and material goods) with other women; her lover turns out to be as much of a bully to her as to everyone else. Despite the living man's telephone and modern office furnishings, his ghost appears capable of wreaking some very old-fashioned vengeance, although our modern woman is sufficiently uncertain of this to suffer agonizing doubt over whether to heed the priest's warning to confess and risk whatever gratifications her marriage brings her. This woman may be a murderess, but her conflicts are ones which could be faced by many modern, urban Nigerian woman. No easy solutions are offered her, least of all any personal ones, and no one in the family learns any homiletic moral truths from the episode. The audience may learn that if this woman is a danger to men, it is a danger they have, in part, brought on themselves, by both their sexual and economic maneuverings. And it is a danger in which their country shares.

The two other "Bendel Playhouse" episodes I wish to discuss, monitored during 1983/84, both concern women whose full destructive potential has been unleashed by the ambition and competitiveness which characterizes modern life. In one of them, a woman is married to a man whose first wife has died, leaving a daughter of about the same age as the wife's own daughter. The stepdaughter is brilliant at school and well behaved in all ways. The woman's daughter is disobedient, poor at her studies, and delinquent. The man loves his daughter, but is systematically turned against her by his wife. When the woman's daughter does so badly at school that the husband threatens to remove her next term, the wife curses the good sister, who dies in a road accident, leaving her stepmother to suffer guilt and vilification. The anti-heroine of this play seems to combine the least appealing elements of Goneril and Regan, Cinderella's wicked stepmother, and a traditional African witch. The most that one can say in her defense is that she seems quite startled when her curses actually work; of course, to a traditionalist, her surprise would merely serve to add lack of respect for the supernatural to her list of transgressions.

In addition to providing the catharsis of pity and terror which Aristotle thought to be the hallmark of tragedy, this melodrama attempts to ground the evil it portrays in the pathogenic conditions of development gone wrong. There are roads, and cars, and education; women and girls are free to take advantage of those things. The roads and cars, however, are notoriously lethal, and schooling has become an arena where competition among students and their parents is more important than learning. The mother must attempt to train her child to live in a world she, the parent, does not understand. In this world, moreover, men still retain the ultimate power; by withholding school fees, a woman's husband can seal her daughter's doom. In traditional African cosmology, nefarious spiritual power often intruded where formal, temporal power was denied. Fear of such power may continue to be great in an urban setting where competition and jealousy are intensified, while traditional controls are relaxed. In such a setting, the apparently powerless may be suspected of seeking unpredictable revenge. The gentle, understanding, and subtly manipulative mothers of foreign television dramas have, in this domestic production, been replaced by a Fury, an ambiguous creature who may inspire fear and loathing, but who certainly must be taken seriously.

In the final "Bendel Playhouse" episode to be discussed, political ambition, greed, and social climbing lead a woman to bring about her own daughter's death. This play opens with a pretty and refined young student telling her boyfriend she is pregnant; it ends with her death during an abortion. Most of the action of the play consists of a conversation between the parents of the couple.

The boy, it seems, is willing, indeed eager, to marry the girl; his parents, a rural schoolteacher and his wife, give the match their blessing. The girl's father, a successful politician, opposes the marriage. Poor and unsophisticated in-laws would be a social hindrance; he had hoped to use his daughter's marriage to further his career. After concluding this uninspiring interview, the girl's mother talks her into agreeing to an abortion; in the last scene, word is brought to the expensively furnished waiting room, where the mother is sitting, that her daughter has died.

In this play, the connection between personal and political ills is not symbolic, but direct. The girl's father is one of the very same corrupt politicians widely blamed for Nigeria's difficulties; the girl's mother is both the victim of his ill-conceived ambition and a conspirator in it. The boy's parents, on the other hand, might be described as heroes of development, having dedicated their lives to rural education. It is their own and their country's tragedy when they are snubbed and denied their first grandchild by one of the ruling élite.

Although the programs we have mentioned take women and their problems seriously, they do not provide sustained images of women (or men) actively taking positive action against private or public difficulties. One NTA program which attempts to do so was being aired nationally during our 1983/84 study. This weekly serial, about rural development in the Jos Plateau, did not sacrifice popularity in its attempt to provide some positive images; it rated ninth in our audience survey, well behind the locally-produced "Hotel de Jordan" and "Bendel Playhouse," but ahead of most of the slick, foreign imports.

The popularity of "Cock Crow at Dawn" may be attested by the fact that it was one of very few NTA programs to have a regular commercial sponsor during the 1983/84 broadcast season.

The central characters in "Cock Crow at Dawn" are a family of former urban residents, who are trying to run a poultry farm in a village which is, itself, trying to modernize. While the program does not ignore the jealousy and personal ambition which can affect rural life and hinder development, its protagonists are serious people, engaged, albeit sometimes reluctantly, in productive labour. When disputes arise in the village over local elections or the use of a tractor, settlements are reached after the appropriate number of minutes of comic maneuvering. These settlements differ from the mystifying "happy endings" of American sitcoms, in that they do not promise personal happiness, only a chance to get on with the daunting job at hand.

It is significant that the only episode we saw in which the village faces real tragedy involved a rare contact of villagers with bureaucracy and city life. It is also an episode which portrays the destruction of an admirable women's rural development project. In this segment, the woman of the village pool their savings in the hope of establishing a small pharmacy in the village, dispensing basic drugs: vitamins, Paracetamol, topical antiseptics. When the representative of the women's group goes to the city to obtain permission for this undertaking, she encounters a sleeping receptionist at the Ministry of Health, who finally permits her to see an officious bureaucrat, who refuses the proposal on the grounds that none of the women is a trained pharmacist. Outside in the street, the woman flings down her handbag in anger and loses the roll of money which represents her colleagues' hard-earned savings.

The contrast between the village woman and the urban receptionist portrayed in this episode of "Cock Crow at Dawn" is significant, insofar as it encapsulates a number of oppositions which form part of contemporary Nigerian collective representations. The village woman is relatively uneducated but is dedicated to development. She is not "sexy," but enjoys a genuinely cooperative relationship with her husband, who accompanies her to the city, despite having joined the other men in teasing the women about their project. She is hard-working and does her work outside the sphere of official interest. Indeed, when she manages to momentarily attract such interest, it is only to be thwarted in her efforts. The city woman works in a government office. She is both lazy and sexually attractive; she may well be sleeping with her boss. The boss himself is arrogant and, in his insistence on formal qualifications, shows himself to be dedicated to the maintenance of existing power relationships, even at the expense of the goals his Ministry is supposed to achieve.

While "Cock Crow at Dawn" succeeds in presenting positive and popular images of the role of women in development, this picture of rural women forms part of a dichotomy in which urban women, like other city dwellers, are seen as obstacles to progress. Inhabitants of Benin may pay lip service to the need for rural development, but like city dwellers everywhere, they are more excited by the urban scene than by admirable rural examples. They may have a certain interest in a program like "Cock Crow at Dawn," but they are more deeply affected by the satirical farce of "Hotel de Jordan" and the urban tragedies of ""Bendel Playhouse"." As of the time of our study, they had yet to be offered a program, local or foreign, good or bad, truly produced from a woman's perspective. The same could be said of the television audience in most Western countries, so further imports are not the answer to this problem. Indeed, the Nigerian television industry has offered employment, and an opportunity to influence program development, to a relatively high proportion of women.

One must not, however, assume that urban dwellers in Nigeria, like recent migrants to North American cities, do not yearn for the real or imagined simplicity of an earlier existence, even at the expense of personal liberation. At the NTA Benin benefit concert mentioned earlier, more than 500 people, at least half of them women, were brought to their feet by an admittedly powerful rendition of Tammy Wynette's "Stand By Your Man," sung by a female producer at NTA Benin, who possesses a Master's degree in mass communications from the University of Ibadan. The question which must now be answered is whether mass communications in Nigeria can continue to entertain, avoid mimicking Western mystification, and present choices for urban women other than simply standing by their men or seeking to destroy them.

NOTES

The research on which this article was based was supported by a Social Science and Humanities Research Council of Canada Strategic Grant on the Human Impact of Science and Technology.

    1.   Gaye Tuchman, in a classic study of the image of women in the media, has argued that while traditional sociology sees men as instrumental in the public arena and women in the management of personal, domestic problems, television has tended to expand the male leadership role to encompass both spheres (Tuchman 1978: 14).

    2.   Todd Gitlin (1986: 520-521) has provided a highly cogent discussion of these issues.

    3.   For an extended discussion of this episode, and "Hotel de Jordan" generally, see Lyons and Lyons: 1985.

    4.   The reference is to the Ghost's speech in Act I, Scene v, 1, 84-86, in which Hamlet is advised not to extend his father's vengeance to Gertrude:

> Taint not thy mind nor let thy soul contrive
> Against thy mother ought. Leave her to heaven...
> (Kittredge 1936: 1156).

Emmanuel Obiechina has commented (1973: 72-75) upon a tendency of the authors of the famous Onitsha market pamphlets to insert quotations and paraphrases from Shakespeare at relevant points, in order to underscore moral messages, affirm the author's erudition, and give members of the audience, many of whom have studied a standard school curriculum, the pleasure of recognition.

BIBLIOGRAPHY

Gittlin, Todd (1987). "Prime Time Ideology: The Hegemonic Process in Television Entertainment." In *Television: The Critical View*, Fourth Edition, edited by H. Newcomb. 506-531. New York: Oxford University Press.

Kittredge, G., ed. (1936). *The Complete Works of William Shakespeare*. Boston and New York: Ginn and Company.

Lyons, A. and H. Lyons (1985). "Return of the Ikoi-Koi: Manifestations of Liminality on Nigerian Television." In *Anthrolpologica*, N.S., XXVII: 1-2. 55-78.

Obiechina, E. (1973). *An African Popular Literature: A Study of Onitsha Market Pamphlets*. Cambridge: Cambridge University Press.

Okonkwo, R. (n.d.). "Why Boys Never Trust Money Girls." Extracted in *Onitsha Market Literature* by E. Obiechina. 130-131. New York: Africana Publishing Corporation.

Tuchman, G. (1978). "Introduction: The Symbolic Annihilation of Women by the Mass Media." In *Hearth and Home: Images of Women in the Mass Media*, edited by G. Tuchman, A.K. Daniels, and J. Benét. 3-38. New York: Oxford University Press.

FESPACO 1987: African Cinema and Cultural Identity

J. R. Rayfield
York University, Toronto

FESPACO, the biennial Festival Panafricain du Cinéma, epitomises the aims and activities of African film-makers and all who are involved in the arts of Africa. This paper[1] will therefore make it the focus of a discussion of the state of the contemporary African cinema and its role in the promotion and expression of African cultures and societies. FESPACO, the Festival Panafricain du Cinéma de Ouagadougou,[2] was held for the tenth time in February 1987. It has been held every other year since 1969. The idea that some action must be taken to promote the African cinema was mooted as long ago as 1959 at the eleventh Congress of Black Writers and Artists held in Rome. FESPACO was inaugurated in 1969 as the outcome of the First Festival of Black Arts held in Dakar in 1969. It was supported by the Journées cinématographiques de Carthage, a film festival held in Tunis every other year, which had shown mostly North African and Middle Eastern films, but which was opened to sub-Saharan African films in 1966; and also by the ACCT (Agence de Coopération Culturelle et Technique) which was founded in Paris in 1970, with the aim of promoting cultural communication among francophone countries. It was decided that FESPACO should be held biennially, alternating with the journées cinématographiques de Carthage, FESPACO also cooperates with the Festival du film africain de Montreal, the Journées cinématographiques de Québec, and the Festival International du film d'Amiens, (Meda 1987: 8-11).

The 1987 Festival lasted for a week. It began with an elaborate opening ceremony at the sports stadium, the unveiling of a statue of a film camera and the renaming of a square in downtown Ouagadougou "Place des Cinéastes." Three days were occupied by a colloquium on oral tradition and the African cinema. All the films entered for the competition and many others (only two films could be entered by each participating country) were shown. Most of the screenings were in the evening, and each morning began with a forum at which the makers of the films shown the previous evening could be questioned and the films could be discussed. There was also a film market at which videotapes and films in videotape form were shown and inquiries could be made about their distribution.

The theme of FESPACO 1987 was "the African cinema and cultural identity"; three mornings were devoted to a colloquium on oral tradition and the African cinema. Its most prominent slogans, displayed all over the city, were "Il faut décoloniser nos écrans" (we must decolonise our screens) and "Qui tient la distribution tient le cinéma" (Control of distribution means control of the cinema). These basic concerns: (1) rejection of colonialism and its aftermath, and the continued pervasion of colonial values in the non-African cinema; and (2) the use of the African cinema for this purpose, and to promote and validate African cultures and values — were the theme of every activity of the Festival, of every lecture and discussion and of most of the films. The theme implies solidarity with all oppressed and colonized people. Films from other third world countries were shown, and also Afro-American films. Many Afro-American film-makers and writers were present, and a whole morning was devoted to a colloquium on Paul Robeson. The Harlem Third World Trade Institute arranged travel to FESPACO for Afro-Americans, and devoted a special edition (March-April 1987) of its journal, *Trade Winds*, to it.

Most of these concerns of African film-makers and governments and intellectuals are not new.

They were expressed, not for the first time but most extensively, in a seminar on "the role of the African Film-Maker in Rousing an Awareness of Black Civilization" held in Ouagadougou in April, 1974 and reported at length in the 90th issue of the quarterly journal *Présence Africaine*. The points for examination were:

how the cinema can inspire a feeling of cultural and historical solidarity between black communities and *rouse an awareness of a common civilization*;

how the cinema can present the human, social and cultural realities of Africa and make Africans think about their destiny;

how the cinema can work for African independence and cultural authority;

how and why the African cinema should use African languages;

the problem of an original cinématographique language freed from certain Western models, criteria and myths (e.g., the individualistic hero myth, the all-pervading power of money, unbridled sex, violence, false luxury, etc.).

African films should deal with African history and legend as well as contemporary situations. Contemporary social realities include "the condition of the African woman, youth, racism, migrations, emigration, duality between town and country, industrial development, the living conditions of different categories of people, etc." (Société Africaine de culture, 1974).

The cooperation of African writers should be sought. African languages should be used. Large budgets are not necessary — in any case they are not available.

Despite the seriousness of purpose, films should be entertaining and humorous where appropriate.

Since 1984, and even before then, many African films have been produced which fulfill all these aims. But their numbers are disappointingly few. FESPACO was deeply concerned with this; there was much discussion in both formal and informal situations of the problems which hamper the production of African films, and which are not much nearer solution than they were in 1974.

In many ways the plight of the African film-maker parallels that of the African writer. Until fairly recently, in order to be published the writer had to aim at a readership of non-African francophones and anglophones. This meant that he had to use one of the colonial languages and to adapt his style and content to the non-African public. African content had to be cast into non-African forms, such as the novel and the printed story, and the narrative often had to be interrupted with ethnographic information. Even so, the financial situation was impossible: with very few exceptions even eminent and prolific African writers cannot make a living by their work as writers.

For the film-maker the situation is even worse. True, he does not depend on a literate audience: Africans enjoy the cinema and attend it as often as they can. But there are still very few cinemas outside the capital cities. And the tastes of audiences have been corrupted by trashy American and Asian films — ancient Westerns, "Hindu" musicals, films of violence made by the thousands in Singapore and Hong Kong. Even without the use of studios, and even though most of the actors are unpaid or paid very little the costs of production are enormous. Footage has to be taken to London or Paris to be developed and printed at great expense; I was told that it would be uneconomic to set up laboratories in Africa because there would not be enough work for them, and there cannot be enough work because of the expense of shooting films. There is one editing facility in Ouagadougou.[3] Almost every film-maker I talked to had unfinished films waiting for funds to enable him to complete them. At the Festival screening schedules had constantly to be rearranged as film-makers arrived at the last minute carrying the only print of their work which they had been afraid to entrust to postal systems.

A few film-makers are helped financially by their governments or by French and other cultural organizations[4] but most find their own financing.[5] They use the takings from one film to finance the next, they save from their salaries (like African writers, most of them cannot make a living from practicing their art and must work at various occupations), they beg or borrow from their friends.

Some of the films shown at the Festival were in an unfinished state — in working prints, on videotape or in African languages without subtitles.

Most film-makers are unwilling to compromise their ethical or artistic principles for the sake of getting finance or for the opportunity of showing their films outside Africa (Ascofare, 1975). (A few African films, including some which were shown at the Festival, have been shown in Paris with considerable success, but these are a minority.) Although all the films are directed at African audiences, many of them would be successful in the international market and many film-makers would appreciate access to a non-African audience. But marketing mechanisms are poorly developed. There exist organizations such as CIDC and CIPROFILM, which were founded to distribute and finance African films and to act as agents for non-African films to be shown in Africa (Rayfield, 1985), but for various reasons, mostly to do with financial problems, the failure of governments and agencies to meet their commitments, they have recently been almost inactive; there was much discussion at FESPACO about the possibility of revitalizing these organizations (Tapsoba, 1987).[6]

Although FESPACO activities included a "marché des films," it was not easy for a possible customer to find out how to buy or rent African films. Many films exist only in the form of a few prints or videotapes, and the film-maker makes individual arrangements to show them.

The concern for liberation from colonialism and the development of African cultural identity is expressed not only in the politics and economics of the financing and distribution of films, but even more in the content of the films. It is not surprising that the main prize was won by *Sarraounia*, which tells of how a warrior princess of a pagan people defeated a barbarously cruel French military expedition which was slaughtering its way from Dakar to Rabat. At the forum, the film-maker was asked whether he had not exaggerated the atrocities committed by the French soldiers, such as playing polo with the decapitated heads of Africans. He replied that he had drawn his information from respected French historians, including Suret-Canale.

Conversely, an Algerian film, *Le moulin* was criticized by Sub-Saharan Africans because it made fun of a socialist government's attempts to bring socialism to a small, backward town. The hero of the film is an old Frenchman, whose mill must be nationalized before a great official visits the town. A wall is built to hide a slum. A mischievous telephone operator sabotages everybody's efforts to prepare a suitable reception for the bigwig, who never turns up. Resistance to a progressive government and affection for a colonial, it was felt, are not suitable topics for an African film, even when treated humorously.

It is not surprising that many films dealt with anticolonialism, and that the prize winning film, *Sarraounia* was the most vehemently anti-colonial of all.

The valuation of traditional African cultures was, of course, the theme of the colloquium on oral tradition and the cinema, which showed many ways in which films relate to oral poetry and narrative. The discussion dealt with films based on folk tales, films with the temporal and thematic structure of folk tales, films in which everyday life is presented realistically yet permeated with poetry. The films themselves provided examples of all these kinds of relationships.

Sarraouina begins almost like a myth. We see the twelve-year-old princess entrusted by her father to a wise man to be trained as warrior queen. Wearing only a loincloth, she practices horsemanship, archery and other martial arts, including magic. When her tutor finds her trying on beautiful fabrics, he tells her she must expose her body to the sun and the wind; she must forgo all feminine pursuits and devote herself to leading her people in war. However, the mythical element disappears after the first ten minutes of the film. We are told that Sarraouina derives her power from her fetishes, but we never see her performing any magical rituals; her victories seem to be the result of superior guerilla tactics.

An interesting example of the modernization of a popular folk tale is a videotape of *Tipoko*; the traditional story goes as follows: The heroine refuses to speak except to her parents. Her father promises her hand in marriage to the first man who can make her speak. Many suitors failed. But at last came a cloth merchant, who also never spoke. But every evening he visited the girl and tore up and then burned a beautiful silk cloth. At last, when he was about to destroy a particularly costly and splendid piece of fabric, the girl suddenly exclaimed: "Don't do it!" the triumphant suitor rode off with his bride. Then a butcher, one of the unsuccessful suitors, stopped him and offered to buy his horse for an enormous price. The girl spoke for the second time, saying, "You can sell it to him." But the butcher insisted that the bride was included in the bargain, and, supported by the village chief, took her home with him. The husband finally won her back with the help of a leper, who "used the same trick as the butcher," and took her home to live happily ever after.

The story was used for a television film by the Burkinabe film-maker Emmanuel Sanon. He chose it partly because it could be produced economically, but mainly because of its "important themes: injustice, feudal power, the situation of women, etc."

Especially interesting are the changes made in the story. The seven suitors represent various social classes; the successful cloth merchant is about the middle status. The horse is replaced by a bicycle, for which the butcher offers about ten times its value. The leper is replaced by a venerable beggar to whom the merchant has been generous. The silk cloths are replaced by cloths produced by the Burkino Faso National Textile Factory. ("I wanted to make people appreciate Faso cloths" explained the film-maker.") The very special cloth which provoked the girl into speaking was printed with the symbols of the National Council of the Revolution; it would be sacrilegeous to destroy it. The film fleshed out the story with scenes of everyday life and a *griot* who acted as commentator. It stressed modern, relevant values: the quality of local manufactures, the struggle against injustice, the fight against false mystics, the freedom of women to choose their husbands (Kam, 1987).

Two films which treat of everyday problems in poetic, though not mystical style, are *Desebagato* and *Nyamanton*. The former contrasts the difficulties of the underpaid labourer, threatened with dismissal when he tries to organize a protest against working conditions, and the luxurious life of the entrepreneur who, however, is also threatened with ruin if he cannot satisfy his French clients. There is a recurrent scene of the foreman walking round the work site, saying, almost chanting, "Anybody who does not want to work is free to leave." Photographed from above, the scene looks like a ritual dance. *Nyamanton* depicts the efforts of an eleven-year-old girl and a nine-year-old boy to earn the money to attend school, which they see as the only way of escaping the lot of their mother, an underpaid servant and their father, a chauffeur who has not received his salary for months. After each defeat, they repeat, "I shall be like our father, you will be like our mother." (The title means "garbage" and refers to a proverb: "Anything can be hidden beneath a heap of garbage, but garbage itself cannot be hidden.")

Many of the films are poetic, but there is little mysticism or supernatural intervention. Magic is sometimes practiced, but it is treated in a matter-of-fact way; an example is the traditional healer in *Le Médecin de Gafiré*, whose treatments depend on communication with spiritual powers, but whose methods can be taught and learned by anybody whom the healer will accept as apprentice.

Le *Médecin de Gafiré* is also an example of the treatment of the relationship between traditional and modern forms of culture. A Paris-trained physician goes to practice in a remote village. His treatments are less successful than those of a traditional healer. The physician apprentices himself to the healer and practices both kinds of medicine. But the healer is very angry when he discovers that the physician is writing a book about his methods, for secrecy is essential to the effectiveness of his powers. The physician becomes dangerously ill; it is suggested that the healer has poisoned him. But he recovers. The ending is ambiguous. Perhaps the film-maker is not sure whether traditional and modern cultures can co-exist.

In the several films in which an individual or a family leaves the village and goes to the city to escape poverty or famine, it is not implied that the migrants would have done better to stay at home. In *Desebagato* there is a flashback in which the hero takes leave of his father. The father is sad to see his son go, and concerned about his future, but does not try to persuade him to stay. The Burkinabe film *Yam Dabo* (the choice) shows a family deciding to migrate from their drought-stricken village rather than wait for international aid.

Economic problems are the keynote of most of the films. There is much emphasis on the struggle to escape from poverty or even to survive. Inequality and injustice are condemned, but, except in the films dealing with colonialism, there is little blaming. In *Desebagato*, the foreman who bullies the workmen is intimidated by the owner of the enterprise, who, in turn, is afraid of failing to satisfy his wealthy client. In *Nymanton* the employer who does not pay his chauffeur, the hospital personnel who let their patient die of neglect are referred to with bitterness, but they do not appear in the film. In *Ablakon*, the wealthy businessman who returns to the village and cheats his kinsfolk and corrupts the young girls is ridiculed, but one is left feeling that he is just one effect of rapid social change and can be coped with. The village chief in *Juju* who uses public funds to build himself a magnificent villa is shown as an absurd, small-time crook, and the village deals with him appropriately. There is no major protest about governments; all corruption seems to be on a manageable scale. Of course, the film-makers are in such a precarious position that they cannot afford to offend possible patrons; the films *were* being shown in a country with a fairly new revolutionary government, benevolent and apparently popular, but, still, a military government.

Although few of the films shown at FESPACO were made by women (though there are several eminent African women film-makers), many of them are very feminist in outlook. This was pointed out by Thomas Sankara, President of Burkina Faso; the promotion of women's interests is an important item in the programme of his government. The prize for the film competition is a bronze statuette (a picture of it adorns posters and programmes for the Festival) of the warior princess Yennenga riding a stallion and brandishing a sword.

Many of the documentary films showed women participating in various development projects, and one was about a long distance motor-cycle race across difficult terrain, in which all the participants were women.

Several films concerned women who refused arranged marriages and insisted on marrying the man of their choice. Orikia in the film of that name poisoned her unwanted fiancé. The heroine of *Duel sur les Falaises* left her husband and went to live with her lover. The husband attempted to kill the lover, but was himself killed. In *Love Brewed in an African Pot* the educated daughter of a civil servant refuses to marry a lawyer and marries a mechanic.

Though women are often shown as being deeply in love with their men, sexuality is downplayed in most African films. In *Desebagato* the tycoon is shown romping with his mistresses and making a pass at his secretary, but the scenes between the working-class couple are much more muted. At the Festival the audiences were very critical of the sexual scenes in *Visages de Femmes*; the film-maker said that he wanted to show all aspects of women's lives, but the audience still looked disapproving.[7] President Sankara mentioned "pornographic" foreign films among those he refuses to have shown in Burkina Faso. He associates sexual modesty with African dignity and sexual exhibitionism with Western decadence.

In the documentary films the most important theme is modernization and development.

Most of these are didactic in style, and many of them are in the form of television programmes. Several speakers emphasized the importance of television in the social and technical education of African populations; it can help to bypass the obstacle of mass illiteracy.

Individual ownership of television sets is of course not envisaged. Television receivers are seen as mini-cinemas to be set up in schools and village community centres. Videotapes are easier and cheaper to make than films. They will become increasingly important in the implementation of development programmes.

One problem which African film-makers seem to be no nearer to solving is that of language. All film-makers insist that for authenticity the characters in a film should speak in their own language, an African language for most people, some form of French or English for the elite. Some African languages are widely used, such as Bambara, but others are local. The films are subtitled in French (there are very few English-language films), which makes the films understandable to the European or educated African, but does not help the ordinary African, who is not likely to be sufficiently literate to read transitory subtitles. The film-makers try to tell their story in action more than in dialogue, but I for one found it difficult to follow a Bambara-language film which was shown without subtitles because its maker had not had time or money enough to finish the film. When I inquired about the possibility of obtaining a film with English subtitles instead of French, I was told that the expense would be prohibitive. Language makes many African films difficult to distribute, inside as well as outside Africa.

At the last session of FESPACO, Thomas Sankara, President of Burkina Faso, gave a press conference at which he answered all questions frankly, and spoke movingly about his government's policy of helping all oppressed peoples to liberate themselves. He rejoiced at the spirit of international cooperation manifested at FESPACO. "We fought against Hitler," he said, "and we continue to fight against all oppressors." He praised Olaf Palme and Breytenbach for their struggle against oppression.

In an interview with Serge Daney of the left-wing French newspaper *Libération* he spoke of the Festival as promoting friendship and understanding between not only film makers and their audiences but between people of many different cultures. "This proves that we may have political attitudes opposed to the governments of various countries, but still sincerely love the peoples of those countries."

He justified his protection of African film-makers and their audiences by refusing to permit the showing of films which promote unethical practices or might tempt people to aspire to Euro-american styles of life which they could never attain.

He agreed that it was important to develop television as a means of education and communication.

In answer to Daney's last question: "What has not yet been shown of Africa and the African soul, by the cinema?" Sankara replied: "Dignity has not been presented enough. The cry from the heart, justice, too, the nobility and the necessity for struggle in Africa, that has not been shown enough. Sometimes one has the impression that Africans are striving in vain in a world of evil men. What we have experienced, what we have suffered, what we are now experiencing, what we are still suffering — this has not been publicized enough and we also know that the media elsewhere in the world are efficacious in preventing people in other countries from understanding the struggle which we are waging here."

This, I think, is a good note on which to end a discussion on the African cinema and cultural identity.

Some Reviews of Films Shown at FESPACO 1987

I have included only those in periodicals reasonably accessible in North America. For further reviews see more recent issues of the periodicals cited; for films issued earlier than 1986, see Nancy Schmidt's bibliography.

ABLAKON
Biloa, Marie-Roger
    "Ablakon, de Gnoan M'Bala" *Jeune Afrique* Magazine no. 32, December 1986.
Biloa, Marie-Roger
    "Sacré Charlemagne" *Jeune Afrique* no. 1349, 2 November, 1986.
Batala, Michel
    "L'art africain et son message" *Afrique Réalité*, January, 1987.

G. B.
    "Ablakon: Maudit Charlemagne" *Télérama* no. 1923, 22-28, November, 1986.
Watrigant, R.
    "Ablakon" *Afrique Réalité* January, 1987.

JOM
Paranagua, Paulo-Antonio
    "Afrique noire" *Positif,* 257-8, July-August, 1982.

LE MEDECIN DE GAFIRE
    D'Allones, Fabrice Revault
    "Le Médecin de Gafiré" *Cinéma,* 336-8, 14 January, 1986.

NYAMANTON
Hamou, Salima
    "Pauvres mais beaux" *Jeune Afrique,* no. 1351, 26 November, 1986.
Diawara, Manthia
    "Images of Children" *West Africa* no. 3599, 25 August, 1986.

SARRAOUNIA
Balogun, Françoise
    "A hymn to dignity" *West Africa,* 17 November, 1986.
Chevalier, Jacques
    "*Sarraounia:* Le mouvement de l'histoire" *La Revue du Cinéma* no. 422, December, 1986.
Nicolini, Elisabeth
    "Sarraounia de Med Hondo" *Jeune Afrique Magazine* no. 32, Decembre, 1986.
Vieyra, Paulin S.
    "Le Med Honda nouveau est arrivé!" *Africa International* no. 197, October, 1986.

TOUKI BOUKI
Vieyra, Paulin
    "Le cinéma africain des origines à 1973" *Présence Africaine* 1975.

WEND KUNI
Jeancolas, Jean-Pierre
    "Autour du cinéma" *Positif,* May, 1984.

BIBLIOGRAPHY

Information for which no bibliographic reference was given was obtained orally in formal or informal situations at FESPACO.
Carrefour is the official weekly news journal of Burkina Faso.

AGECOP Liaison. Notes on African film organizations. AGECOP Liaison 1/2, 1982.

Ascofare, A. "Cinéma Africain: Espoirs," *Septième Art.* Année 22, No. 55 (Septembre), 1985, pp. 12-21.

Bachy, V. "La Distribution Cinématographique en Afrique Noire," *Film Echange.* No. 15 (Summer), 1981, pp. 31-44.

Bellow, L. "Du Nouveau au FESPACO," *Jeune Afrique.* No. 1364 (February 18), 1987.

Boughedir, F. "FESPACO: Cap sur l'an 2000," *Jeune Afrique*. No. 1364 (February 26), 1987.

Dabia, A. "Pour une Production Africaine Rentable," *Film Echange*. No. 33 (Summer), 1983, pp. 45-54.

Daney, S. "Sankara: le Cinéma, un Bon Pretexte," *Libération*. (March 5), 1987.

Haffner, P. "Les Films de la Différence à Ouagadougou," *Peuples Noirs, Peuples Africains*. No. 48 (November-December), 1985, pp. 97-131.

Haffner, P. "Quatre Entretiens avec Paulin Soumanou Vieyra," *Peuples Noirs, Peuples Africains*. No. 37 (January-February), 1984, pp. 14-29 and No. 38 (March-April), 1984, pp. 27-49.

Jeune Afrique Plus. Special Issue on African cinéma. Nos. 1941 and 6 (April), 1984.

Kam. "Trois Exemples D'exploitation Medistique (cinéma) de Textes de Tradition Orale Burkinabé," Contribution to colloquium on oral tradition and African cinema, FESPACO, 1987.

Meda, Y. "FESPACO et Autres Festivals," *Carrefour*. (February 20), 1987.

N'Gosso, G.S., and C. Ruelle. *Cinéma et Télévision en Afrique: de la Dependence à l'independence*. (Communication et Société #8), Unesco, 1983.

Obenga, T. "Le CICIBA et le Devenir Culturel," *Afrique Réalité*. (January), 1987.

Rayfield, J.R. "The Use of Films in Teaching about Africa," *Film Librarians Quarterly*. (March), 1985.

Rouge, J.F. "Ouaga, le Star de son Festival," *Libération*. (March 5), 1987.

Sankara, T. "The Political Orientation of Burkina Faso," *Review of African Political Economy*. 1984.

Swadogo, E. "A Quand la Décolonization de Nos Ecrans," *Carefour africain*. (September 27), 1985.

Schmidt, N. *Sub-Saharan African Films and Film-makers: Preliminary Bibliography*. African Studies Program, Indiana University, Bloomington, 1984.

Société Africaine de Culture. "Texte de Base, Séminaire sur le Role du Cinéaste Africain dans L'eveil," *Présence Africaine*. No. 90, 1974.

Soyer, C. "Afrique Noire: Un Cinéma Etranger à Son Propre Monde," *Filmaction*. No. 2 (February-March), 1982, pp. 10-11.

Tapsoba, C. "Le Burkina sur la Co-production," *Afrique Nouvelle*. No. 1960 (February 11), 1987.

Tapsoba, C. "CIDC et CIPROFILM: La Conférence de la Dernière Chance," *Carrefour* (February 20), 1987.

Vokouma, F. "Traditions Orals et Nouveaux Médias: Du Role de nos Cinéastes pour Perpétuer nos Valeurs," *Carrefour*. (February 20), 1987.

Waintrop, E. "Souleymane Cissé, les Années Lumière," *Libération*. (March 6), 1987.

NOTES

1. Research for this paper was made possible by a Small Research Grant from York University, which financed attendance at FESPACO and preliminary research in Paris.

2. Ouagadougou is the capital of Burkina Faso, formerly called Upper Volta.

3. Congo has a laboratory for 16mm, black and white, dependent on the Ministry of Information Ivory Coast has a 16 and 35mm black and white laboratory, run by the Société Ivorienne du Cinéma. Guinea also has a 16 and 35 mm laboratory run by the Société d'Etat Silly Cinéma.

Madagascar has a 16mm black and white laboratory run directly by the television nationale malagache under the Ministry of Information and Culture.

Togo has a complex consisting of a 16 and 35 mm black and white and colour laboratory, editing rooms, etc., since 1977.

4. I was present at an informal conversation between Haile Gerima, the Ethiopian film-maker who has also made films in the United States, Lionel Ngakane, the Black South African film-maker living in London, and Tewfik Saleh, the Egyptian film-maker who is a member of the jury for FESPACO 1987. All complained of the great expense of film-making, and discussed their attempts to economise. Ngakane said he takes four shots of each scene, selects the two best and then decides between them, but Saleh said he could afford only one shot. Only once did he have to repeat a shooting because of a mistake in the laboratory. Then they discussed means of obtaining money. Ngakane recommended France is a good source of aid. Saleh has not made a film for several years. He won't take money with strings attached and cannot get it otherwise. Gerima has no patience with prospective backers who ask to see a script, say they like it but must get the approval of other possible backers, and then lose interest. The French are bad in this way; Germans are better, they say yes or no. Ngakane likes to bounce ideas around and does not mind changing his script. As for their present situation; Gerima is working on a film which he cannot afford to complete, Saleh does administrative work in connection with films, Ngakane is not at present working at film-making.

5. The Senegalese delegation to FESPACO distributed a booklet mentioning two organizations: SIDEC (Société Sénégalaise d'Importation de Distribution et d'Exploitation Cinématographique) created in 1973 whose title is self-explanatory, and SNPC (Société Nouvelle de Promotion Cinématographique), which seek partners to finance two Senegalese equipment and offers to make films for Senegalese and other West African institutions. Haffner 1984 gives further information about problems of financing and distribution. Soyer 1982 also deals with this problem.

6. The prudish audience at FESPACO consisted mainly of people connected with film and television, journalists, academics, government officials and other intellectuals. I do not know whether ordinary African film-goers would appreciate efforts to protect them from foreign "pornography." I was present at the showing in a local cinema in Abidjan of a very bad French film called "Les Folles Nuits de la Bovary," based roughly on Flaubert's novel. The sound was turned up so loud that the dialogue was incomprehensible and the operator put on the reels in the wrong order. But the audience, mostly young men loved it. They shouted with laughter at the erotic scenes.

Djibril's *Touki Bouki*, a Fellini-like fantasy set in Dakar, was shown at FESPACO 1987, although it was made in 1972. Nobody raised any objection to one scene where the heroine takes off her jacket and kneels naked and ecstatic in the blood shed by a slaughtered bull (though she is seen only from the waist up) or another in which the hero stands naked in a jeep being driven into Dakar (though he is seen only from the back).

7. Most sexual encounters in the films shown at FESPACO resemble those in Victorian novels, where the heroine becomes pregnant after a kiss and a row of asterisks.

Some Strategies for Effective Utilization of Research Information in Africa: Some Ghanaian and Other African Experience

K. N. Bame
University of Ghana

Introduction

It is common knowledge that in both developed and developing countries, but especially in third world countries in Africa, such as Ghana, piles of research data gathered with valuable human resources and public funds remain in academic theses and reports and files of scholars. The picture is the same with those data delivered to sponsoring agents. They remain in office cabinets and shelves of administrators all unutilized. Quite often the results that emerge from those data that are utilized, at best, turn out to be moderately effective.

Several reasons may be adduced to explain the prevalence of this situation. But for our present purpose let us look at a couple of them. One reason for non-effective utilization of research information is the tendency of African policy makers or politicians to ignore research information or recommendations that do not serve their parochial interests. In other words, they have a tendency to ignore research data or recommendations unless the data could be used to serve their political purpose. For example, if research findings indicate that a health post or center needs to be cited at a particular area, this might be ignored by politicians who would site it at a different place to fulfill an election promise.

This point about politicians ignoring expert and research recommendations has been noted by other observers of the African scene. Ng'weno in a recent book on *Development Options For Africa* (1985) does not mince words on the issue. In his view "Politicians usually refuse to admit that they are not experts on everything. In the field of economics they persist in commissioning bodies of experts to give them options for action and then proceed to ignore the options proposed and to substitute others of their own choosing which have either not been discussed or have been shown to be impracticable" (Ndegwa *et al.* (eds.), 1985: 172).

The second reason in most cases is that researchers usually report their findings in scholastic jargon with a theoretical slant. Such data are not easily understood by administrators who are often called upon to implement the recommendations. A third reason which partly explains the lack of utilization of research information is that researchers in the social sciences conscious of the limitations of their data often do not provide what the potential users of their data regard as viable solutions to the social problems which plague them. We should hasten to point out that this is certainly not in any way a condemnation of social researchers. Their reticence in this respect is a realization on their part of the limitations of their data and the answers they can suggest at the present stage of the development of their science. Moreover, research findings from say, survey data, often point to problem areas and not to specific solutions which policy-makers and administrators may be looking for. Our fourth and final reason we would like to indicate for non-effective utilization of research data in African and other third world countries and to some extent even in developed countries, is that people who implement the recommendations often *fail to involve* all people who are to be affected by the change being sought actively and continuously in the implementation. This point and others indicated above are further developed in our discussion on the strategies.

Policy Options and Strategies

As it is apparent from the title, the aim of this paper is to make a modest attempt to suggest some strategies for effective utilization of research and development information in Africa. The points raised in the preceding introductory section suggest two broad problem areas which should receive attention. They are (1) administrative and/or organizational and (2) dissemination.

With regard to the first problem area, namely organization, an institutional arrangement readily comes to mind. The strategy which would seem to recommend itself here is for each African government to establish a Research Data Implementation Bureau. Such a bureau may have two categories of personnel. One category may be headed by an executive secretary in charge of the supporting staff of the bureau. The other category may be a board of planners membership of which may comprise policy-makers, administrators, university lecturers and action programme officer as well as occasionally co-opted members with needed expertise. The bureau may be charged with among other things the responsibility of first compiling all available research data relevant for the country's development projects and translating them, where necessary, into simple and easily understandable language(s) for field implementation; secondly, it should be charged with the responsibility of working out a field implementation strategy. For example, it should work out a programme of educating the public, including members of the governing body and politicians, of course, about the relevance and importance of research-based action programmes and the dangers and frustrations that attend any attempt at social change that ignores research information and relies solely on hunches and political expediencies.

Like all experiments in social change, field implementation of research information may proceed in a number of ways but one component of any strategy which would seem to make way for success is the active involvement [1] of the people or the opinion leaders of the people to beaffected by the change being initiated. Active involvement here implies that all people concerned — policy-makers, administrators, field action programme officers and members of the target population should endeavour to make the implementation a joint enterprise. This also means that the authorities and action programme officers should, where possible, hold discussions with members of the target population concerning the goals and objectives, the necessity and importance of the desired change expected.

The participants should be made aware of the possible new roles that they may have to assume or new ways of living they may have to adopt as a result of the implementation and the restructuring of relationships necessary to accommodate the change. They should also participate fully in the discussion of the problems which may be encountered in the implementation and how best such problems can be efficiently solved. In short, to achieve success in the implementation of research recommendations those initiating the change should make it meaningful, desirable and achievable to all people affected as well as making members of the target population actively involved in the implementation.

Moreover, as we indicated above, research findings from survey data often point to problem areas without providing specific solutions. Adopting a strategy of involving all people concerned, may lead to some policy evolving from their discussions of the specific meanings of the findings.

This involvement of members of the target population we have been stressing should however not take place in a social vacuum. It should take into account the social milieu, education, reference groups or opinion leaders and the cultural norms, beliefs and values of the people. For without that any attempt at social change seems doomed to failure.

Turning to the second problem area, namely, dissemination of new ideas or research findings in the field which basically boils down to the complex problem of communication of development ideas, we rely on empirical studies conducted in Ghana and elsewhere in Africa.

One strategy which has been the focus of experimental studies is the use of folk media or traditional channels of communication.

Concert Party Plays and Development

In line with the folk media approach, the present writer attempted to tailor the message of modern family planning to suit the rural and largely illiterate population of Ghana by resorting to traditional mode of communication in presenting the ideas to them. We conducted an experimental study on the communication of family planning through traditional media. The study was funded by the Population Dynamics Programme of University of Ghana, Legon-Accra.

Before the study, the channels of communication which had been used in the communication of family planning in Ghana had been radio and television broadcasts, mobile cinema shows, newspaper articles and handouts written in English and local languages and individual personal contacts by family planning workers. Traditional modes of communication such as folk drama, folk tales or story-telling, folk singing and dancing activities had not been used.

The Study

In our experimental study we chose two traditional media of communication — Concert Party Plays and town or village group discussions to communicate family planning. We chose the Concert Party Plays because they not only effectively combine visual and oral effects in driving home their message but they are also familiar to, and highly popular among Ghanaians of all walks of life but especially among the rural and illiterate folks who were our target population.

Methodology of the Study

The study was oriented to diffusion of innovation theory and the field techniques used in collecting its data were observation and interview using questionnaires. The respondents were a probability sample selected by means of systematic sampling procedure using as a population universe listed houses in six Ghanaian communities (Adabraka, G.A.R.; Tsito, V.R.; Essarkyir, C.R.; Effiduase and Kuronum, A.R.; Badu, B.A.), with the married people in the sampled houses as respondents. The study was carried out in two phases: (i) the field experiment and (ii) the survey.

The first part of the study covering a period of four months involved the exposure of the would-be respondents in three of the six communities to the experimental treatments — the performance of a concert party play based on family planning ideas in the form of a story, and group discussion (also in three of the selected communities), led in each case by two trained members of the staff of the Planned Parenthood Association of Ghana in the regions concerned.

In the first month of the first phase, the concert party play was performed once in each of the communities and the family planning discussion group in each community began its fortnightly and guided discussions a couple of days after the performance of the play in the community.

The second phase of the study, which lasted for about a month, was a survey of respondents in the six communities.

The play which was performed by Kakaiku's concert Party depicted the contrasting life style of well-planned, well-organized and well-disciplined family on one hand and that of disorganized, impoverished unplanned family on the other (see Appendix for summary of the story).

Summary of Findings

The findings which emerged from our four confirmed hypotheses are that (i) literate respondents as well as respondents living in urban communities tended to indicate more often modern mass media items as the source of their family planning information; conversely, illiterate respondents and respondents living in rural communities tended to indicate more often traditional or folk media items as their source of family planning information; (ii) literate respondents and respondents who perceived modern family planning as being good or of advantage to them tended to have adopted it more than illiterate respondents and respondents who did not perceive it as good or of advantage to them.

Further analysis of other aspects of the data yielded the following results. Indicating the media that had helped them most to become committed to family planning, the respondents gave the following ranking: first, radio; second, concert party play; third, cinema; fourth, group discussions with family planning workers; fifth, individual discussion with family planning workers; sixth, discussion with a spouse, a friend or relative; seventh, television; and eighth, family planning handouts. However, respondents who actually saw the concert party play ranked it first.

With respect to their effectiveness in conveying family planning messages to the people studied, the two folk media items: the concert party play and the village or town group discussions compared favourably well with the items of modern mass media; they were surpassed only by radio and mobile cinema respectively. Thus, whereas the concert party play proved to be specially suitable for disseminating family planning ideas to rural dwellers, the group discussion seemed to be suitable for both urban and rural dwellers but even slightly favoured by urban dwellers. Further research is needed here to get the explanation. However, the general pattern is that urban respondents tended to rank high folk media items with respect to their influence on their attitude change in connection with family planning.

The respondents in the experimental communities, that is, those who received the experimental treatment showed more favourable attitude and seemed to be more committed to family planning than those in control communities, that is, those who did not receive any treatment.

I have deliberately left out a detailed description of the research methodology and the statistical analysis of the data and the testing of my hypotheses. These can be found in a paper published in the Spring 1975 issue of *Rural Africana* No. 27, specifically devoted to "Communication For Rural Development" in Africa, or in my unpublished report on the study.

Village Drama and Development

Another example of this strategy of using traditional modes of communication to disseminate ideas of development is what Pickering terms "Village Drama" (Pickering, 1957) which was one of the most effective audio-visual aids used by mass education teams in Ghana during the fifties.

In giving as one of the reasons for the use of this medium of communication, Pickering rightly asserts that "village drama is the most truly Ghanaian audio-visual aid, depending as it does upon a nationwide aptitude and liking for drama and by its intimate relation to local custom and tradition" (Pickering, 1957: 178).

Operating within the framework of traditional drama, the village drama uses as its "stage" any open space between two trees, a village square or a "clearing in the crowd." As to be expected in such a situation no elaborate lighting system is employed; simple kerosene lamps are used to light the stage.

Stories of the village drama like those of concert parties were unwritten — members of the teams discussed the plot line and action of the drama, allocated parts to the actors and let them free to "do their own thing" or place individual interpretation on their roles during the performance.

Mass education teams used village drama in their campaigns on literacy, child-care, co-operation, village health and sanitation and rate-collection or the raising and expenditure of local council revenues in the fifties.

The following skits show how village drama was used to motivate people to participate in rural development.

A chief and his elders sell a 20-acre plot of stool land to a prospector and put their thumb-prints on a document sealing the bargain. They subsequently discover they have sold him 200 acres which a large diamond concern is trying to acquire. The case is sent to court and justice prevails and the play concludes with the chief and his elders undergoing literacy training by attending mass education classes.

A second play which we shall examine in detail deals with rate-collection in a very difficult area where the people did not want to pay their rates or levies, where the people complained that their rates were higher than people in other areas and that they did not have pipe-borne water supply as people in a nearby village had. The first part of the play dealt with the importance of rate payment. As Pickering reports it:

> The play was a simple story of one Kofi Basake, a forthright man who whilst loudly condemning the local council to friends in his compound is called upon by the rate-collector to pay his rate. In indignation he throws the intruder out and in pursuing him into the street he falls into the gutter gashing his leg in the process. About this he makes an enormous fuss, is very frightened at the sight of his own blood (red ink) and suffers his friends to bear him to the clinic. There, attended to by a spotlessly uniformed nurse, with brisk efficiency and assurance that there is no cause for alarm, he is moved to ask who provided the clinic.
>
> The answer (of course) is the local authority and so it is to his further questions about the nurse's salary, her uniform, and the equipment of the clinic. Asked if she herself has to pay rates the nurse produces her receipt (previously obtained from the council's treasury). The play ends with a chastened Kofi swathed in bandages making his peace with the rate-collector and dutifully acquiring his own receipt (Pickering, 1957: 181).

In the same area, there prevailed an unfounded belief that people who collected and disbursed rates were free from controls. Thus it was necessary to make the people aware of three important facts: (1) first, rate-collectors in the district bonded themselves for a large sum of money on appointment, (2) secondly, the council meetings during which the decisions on the disbursement of revenues and other matters were taken were open to the public and (3) thirdly, some council expenditure unsanctioned by the Ministry of Local Government could be recovered from the individual councilors themselves.

Owing to the fact that the play about Kofi Basake commanded great interest, the plot was adapted to include the three points. The first point was made in the opening scene where Kofi quarrels with the rate-collector and the second is made in a scene in which a member of his ward persuades Kofi Basake to attend a council meeting and the third is made in a scene showing the actual council meeting. "The three points were again emphasized when a converted and thoughtful Kofi Basake returns to his village and taxes his former co-belligerents with their ignorance and teaches them his new lessons" (Pickering, 1957:181).

This use of village drama was so successful and effective that according to Pickering statistical records showed considerable increase in rates paid in 1953 and 1954 in the areas concerned.

In a Nigerian study (Fiofori, 1975) an experiment was carried out by incorporating information on modern family planning in familiar oral narratives to see their effect on listeners' behaviour with regard to family planning practices. The audience was comprised of husbands and wives with similar traditional outlook. A knowledge, attitude and practice (K.A.P.) survey conducted before and after the experiment revealed that the messages had definite changes in both attitude and behaviour of the participants who were exposed to the experimental treatment in contrast to very little of such changes in those participants who were not exposed to the experiment.

Similarly, in Botswana, for some years, adult educators have been harnessing the creative energies of the people for development through popular theatre. In these innovative experiments they combine popular theatre and extension work to facilitate development. Ross Kidd and Martin Byram (1977) in a case study of the experiment, describe how it was conducted in the northern Bokalaka region of Botswana. Here extension workers and community leaders organize annual one-week programme of popular theatre activities such as drama, puppetry, music and others in which they incorporate development ideas and problems. The main objective of this "community-awakening" festival known as Laedza Batanani ("the sun is already up", "It's time to come and work together" is "to promote participation and self-reliance in development by bringing people together to discuss their problems (reflected in the performance) agree on changes that need to be made and take action" (R. Kidd and M. Byram, 1977: 1). In their preliminary assessment of the festival the authors confirm that it has had effect on the community. This is evidenced by the fact that it has led to a decline in cattle theft and also led to an increase in the number of people who have been reporting cases of venereal diseases and receiving proper medical treatment.

Implications For Policy and Practice

The main findings of the studies summarized above convey a number of practical implications for development action programmes for African and other third world countries. But one general implication which seems immediately apparent is the need for varied and multi-source approach in the presentation of development messages to suit the different areas of African and any third world countries as well as different sections of the target populations. This implies that the whole array of both modern mass and folk media items analyzed in the studies and others which may not have been mentioned must be employed. The multi-source approach will not only take account of the rural-urban and literate-illiterate variabilities with respect to people's attitude toward acceptance of different development projects which have been empirically substantiated in our analysis, but also it will take account of a possible variability between persons living in the same community.

The practical implication deducible from the general ranking of the various media items in the family planning study, is that the radio, the concert party play (or folk drama in general), the mobile cinema and group discussions stand out as the four most effective media for communicating family planning in Ghana and other African countries. Thus if people in charge of family planning or other development programmes for any reasons have to select only four media for their communication and motivation campaigns then the findings of the study suggest that the four indicated above are to be recommended. On the other hand, if bearing in mind the rural-urban dichotomy they decide to divide the four media channels between rural and urban areas, then the two most effective media channel for urban communities are the radio and group discussions in that order whereas the two most effective channels for rural communities are concert party play or folk drama and the mobile cinema also in that order.

The village drama study and indeed other studies conducted in the area elsewhere all convey similar messages for policy and practice. They all confirm that folk drama or folk entertainments, in general, have a great potential in the field of community development in Africa. They can be effectively used to convey messages or ideas concerning development activities, such as literacy campaign, child care, family planning, payment of taxes, constructing village latrines, oral rehydration therapy and may other to rural African folks and motivate them to accept and participate in the action programmes designed to achieve the desired objectives.

These policy implications call for one of the two or both action programme approaches. First, African governments may from time to time commission a couple of drama groups such as concert parties in Ghana to promote development projects, by performing dramas about the projects. Secondly, and better still, the governments or the ministries of information may establish in each district in each country a folk theatre or "cultural group" for the same purpose. The district groups may, in turn, establish drama groups in towns and villages in the districts to promote development by developing and performing dramas about development projects and issues at the grassroot levels.

Modern Media

Another strategy which recommends itself for use especially in urban areas in Africa is a more extensive and efficient use of modern media channels (especially radio, television, newspapers and posters) than before in the propagation and popularization of research and development-oriented information among African population. The research data implementation bureau or some such agency will, of course, first have to translate the information, where necessary, into simple language(s) that can easily be understood by the mass communicators to enable them to convey their messages to the masses or members of the target population and thereby mobilize them to achieve the desired end for which the information is presented.

If the information is development-oriented then of course the mass media communicators must be given even greater encouragement and necessary financial or material resources and freedom to pass their messages on to the people. In so doing the communicators will heighten the awareness of the target groups and make them participate in the process of development. The role of the mass media communicators should not be a one-way process. When they have conveyed the information or messages to the target population, they should keep the channels of communication open in the other direction too. They should carry feed-back to researchers who gather the information or the political decision-makers who make development policies.

Mobile Cinemas

From the findings of the writer's "Study of Traditional and Modern Media for Communicating Family Planning in Ghana" referred to above, the mobile cinema emerged as extremely effective channel for conveying family planning messages to rural Ghanaians. It was surpassed only by the radio and the concert party play. Thus the film as an extension of folk entertainments which will be shown in rural Africa by mobile cinema vans would seem to recommend itself as a third communication strategy which should be adopted to disseminate development research information. Such films could depict entertaining but educative stories concerning development projects and issues encouraging people to accept and get involved in the projects.

Radio Forums

A fourth and our final category of communication strategy for reaching rural African people with new ideas and persuading them to utilize them in their every day living is a combination of media and oral system in the form of radio forums. Radio forums combine mass media with interpersonal channels of communication.

These media forums, which originally developed in Canada among farm families and later spread to developing countries like India, Nigeria, Malawi, Costa Rica and Brazil, have been found to be most effective channels for disseminating innovations among rural people.

"Media forums are simply organized small groups of individuals who meet regularly to receive a mass media programme and discuss its contents."

The most-often used mass media linked to the forum is radio, and is thus termed radio forum. It has been extensively used in India and tried in Ghana.

The central hypothesis which is the basis of media forum is that: "The effects of mass media channels, especially among peasants in less developed countries are greater when these media are coupled with inter-personal channels in media forums" (Roger and Shoemaker, 1971). Radio forums should form a component of the systems of communication in Africa.

These are some communication strategies which seem specifically effective for disseminating new ideas to African population especially the rural folks. But in emphasizing them we are not in any way suggesting that they only must be used to the exclusion of any other mass media channels such as magazines, handouts and others which may be used to supplement those mentioned in this paper.

In conclusion then, when administrative and/or organizational problems have been taken care of by the Bureau for Research Data Implementation, all efforts should be made to involve people to whom the information is being presented to generate social change in the decision-making as well as in the development process. As regards communication, multi-source or multi-channel approach should be adopted in the dissemination of research and development-oriented ideas. It is an approach which will ensure maximum results from all development efforts.

APPENDIX

A Summary of The Story

The first part of the play depicted a couple who had planned their family, had two sons and a daughter and had given them good educations. One is a medical doctor, the other a lawyer and the girl a professionally qualified nurse. All three live abroad in Britain and they have come home to visit their parents. The life style of this family is enviable; they wear good clothes, eat good food and punctuate their merry-making with intelligent discussions about the welfare of their town and family. Before the children return to Britain they decide to build a better house for their parents. They each contribute his or her quota towards the construction of the house. Just before their departure each of them including even the youngest, the nurse, gives their parents some pocket money. Delighted and almost overwhelmed by the kind gesture of their children, the enthralled couple says bon voyage to their happy children.

In contrast, the second part of the play depicts another couple who have not planned their family according to their means. They have ill-fed and ill-clothed eight children with the mother expecting another baby. The scenes for this family begin with one in which a guardian of one of the eight children apprenticed to learn fitting work reporting to the father, Kofi Ataapim, that his son has made a secondary school girl pregnant and the father of the pregnant girl has been threatening to take the case to court. Kofi Ataapim should accompany him, the guardian, to go and settle the case. Money is needed for this but Ataapim does not have it and so he tells his friend to go back and expect him in a few days' time, hoping he will then have secured a loan from a friend for the settlement of the case. Just then another son of Ataapim apprenticed to learn carpentry comes to tell his father that he has mastered his trade and his master wants Ataapim to pay the apprenticeship fees.

This money too will have to be borrowed by Ataapim from a friend. While Ataapim is informing his son, the carpenter apprentice, about his financial problems, the only educated child of his, a daughter, attending teacher training college arrives with yet another unwelcome news that she too has been sent home to collect her fees before she will be allowed to sit for her teachers' certificate examination. Ataapim now inundated with demands for money does not know what to do.

As if these do not constitute enough and disturbing financial problems for Ataapim, his educated daughter who has gone to see her expectant mother at the hospital returns with the news that Ataapim has yet another mouth to feed: her mother has a new baby and the hospital authorities want him to go and pay the hospital bills before his wife and newly-born baby will be allowed to go home.

Ataapim now fumes with anger for the situation which he has created for himself by not planning his family and bluntly refuses to go and pay the hospital fees, saying that his wife and the new baby could remain in the hospital: "when the doctor becomes fed up with their presence he will send them home."

Meanwhile Ataapim's friend visits him and Ataapim recounts his financial problems to him. The friend advises Ataapim to stop producing any more children. He could obtain help in that respect from the family planning workers. Ataapim invites his friend to share his kenkey meal with him. While they eat, all the eight children come in turns peeping in search of some of the kenkey to eat. Both Ataapim and his guest friend are embarrassed and the friend stops eating and Ataapim also stops eating. As if by some pre-arranged signal or order, all the eight children, most of them in thread-bare clothes, storm the eating place to struggle for the left-overs of the kenkey and literally fight to obtain some of the food to eat.

The embarrassed friend of Ataapim leaves and another friend comes to enquire about what is happening amidst such shouts and noise over food. He too advises Ataapim to stop producing any more children because all his problems are the consequence of the unplanning of his family.

BIBLIOGRAPHY

Bame, K.N. "Comic Plays in Ghana: An Indigenous Art Form for Rural Social Change," *Rural Africana*. African Studies Center, University of Michigan, Ann Arbor, No. 27 (Spring), 1975.

Fiofori, F.O. "Traditional Media, Modern Messages: A Nigerian Study," *Rural Africana*. African Studies Center, Michigan State University, East Lansing, (Spring), 1975.

Kidd, E. and M. Byram. "Popular Theatre and Development: A Botswana Case Study,"

Convergence. Vol. 10, No. 2, 1977.

Ng'weno, N. "The Role of the Mass Media in African Development," in *Development Options for Africa in the 1980s and Beyond.* Ndegwa and others (Eds). Nairobi, Kenya: Oxford University Press, 1985.

Pickering, A.K. "Village Drama in Ghana," *Fundamental and Adult Education.* Paris: UNESCO, 1980.

Ranganath, H.K. *Using Folk Entertainments to Promote National Development.* Paris: UNESCO, 1980.

Rogers, E.M. *Diffusion of Innovation.* New York: Free Press, 1962.

Rogers, E.M., and F.F. Shoemaker. *Communication of Innovation: A Cross-Cultural Approach* (2nd ed). New York: Free Press, 1971.

Wignaraja, P. "Towards a Theory and Practice of Rural Development," *Development.* Vol. 2, 1984, pp. 3-11.

Zibardo, P. and others. *Influencing Attitudes and Changing Behavior.* London: Addison-Wesley Publishing Company, 1969.

NOTE

1. For a discussion of why educational innovations have failed in the past in North America and what can be done to make future ones succeed see Michael Fullan, "The Problem of School Change and Implications for Organizational Futures," a paper presented at the annual meeting of the Canadian Sociology and Anthropology Association, and the Canadian Association of Professors in Education, Montreal, May, 1972. See also R. Chin and K.D. Benne, "General strategies for effecting changes in human systems" pp. 32-59 in W. Bennis, K. Benne and R. Chin (eds.), *the Planning of Change* (2nd ed.) Toronto: Holt, Rinchart and Winston.

Canadian Development Assistance to Sub-Sahara Africa

Sontwa Sinkala
University of Manitoba

Introduction

In Canada, foreign policy with regard to the developing countries tends to be mainly identified with aid. Wood calls it an "air fixation" (1982, p. 99). It is true that such a fixation may or may not be justified when other issues between developed and developing countries are compared, but of course the role played by development assistance is itself understandable. The delivery of Canadian aid with a total net of government to government involving $816.21 million is a sizable amount. Of this amount $335.69 million went to Africa (CIDA, 1986, pp. 15-23). While this aid will not by itself work miracles in the development process of these developing countries as a whole, it can, if properly directed and utilized have some positive impact on the countries that receive such assistance.

It is, however, interesting to note that despite this sizable amount of foreign assistance to developing countries, there is still some confusion about the true objectives and motives of Canadian development assistance, or the reasons why those particular objectives and motives have been important. This paper is an attempt to understand Canadian development assistance policy and its contribution to the development process of developing countries in sub-Saharan Africa. The paper will mainly focus on an analysis of the geographical distribution of bilateral aid flows in an effort to see whether or not aid goes to countries that need it the most, based on their low levels of development.

Canadian Development Assistance Policy

The potential contribution for Canada's development assistance to the development of the developing countries will very much depend on the objectives and the policy pursued by Canada when choosing the recipients and selecting and/or approving sectors and projects to concentrate on. The designing of aid policy may be perceived as being a result of the determinants of aid which have a direct impact on the objectives of foreign assistance on one hand, and on the choice of some particular policy responses to the needs of the developing countries on the other. It is possible to see the objectives as determinants of the foreign assistance policy pursued, but these objectives are in turn understood in relation with other primary factors. These factors may either be national or international in nature.

There are essentially four categories of factors that help to shape Canadian policy for development assistance. These categories are:

economic factors such as how well the national economy is doing and/or how much help the developing countries need;

political factors which may be expressed by public opinion, current political leadership and sometimes even the influence of some special interests and bureaucratic politics;

foreign policy considerations, especially those related to some international agreements in matters related to foreign assistance; and

social values and ideology, especially those concerning public opinion about the feelings of Canadians in relation to the developing countries.

The model is, however, more complex than this as most foreign assistance policies are usually changed and adjusted over time and in response to both national and international circumstances. Policies also change in response to their own effectiveness as seen from their own results. Some policies pursued may at times even lack any rationale other than political.

The criteria outlined in the government's *Strategy for International Development 1975-1980* still remain the most comprehensive policy statement and guidelines for the allocation of Canada's bilateral development assistance. This statement committed Canadian aid to support a basic needs strategy in its policy. It also called for a greater geographical concentration, giving more assistance to the least developed among the developing countries with priority being given to measures that would help in meeting the basic needs of the people of the recipient countries. However, with the changing international economic situation, the crisis in Africa and the different needs among the recipient countries, attention is given to some particular criteria among the general guidelines and in accordance with the prevailing economic situation in the country. For example, after the 1987 budget speech in which foreign aid was cut, the *Winnipeg Free Press* commented that, "This is not a broken promise but a reflection of current Canadian financial reality" (*WFP*, Feb. 20, 1987, p. 6).

Methodology

A total number of seventeen countries in sub-Sahara Africa which receive Canadian bilateral assistance were chosen. Amongst these eight are from Anglophone Africa and nine are from Francophone Africa. For each country, data were obtained from the World Bank Development reports and World Population Data Sheet on ten variables. These were then grouped into five development indices for each country (Table 1).

Table 1
Variables used to measure levels of development in
17 Sub-Sahara African countries

Development Index	Variables
1. Health services	1. Life expectancy at birth
	2. Population per physician*
	3. Population per nursing person*
	4. Infant mortality rate
2. Education facilities	1. Number enrolled in primary schools as % of age group.
	2. Number of secondary schools
3. Economic	1. GNP per capita
4. Agriculture	1. Food production per capita index
5. Labour force growth	1. Labour force growth in industrial sector
	2. Labour force growth in service sector

* For these two variables, it was not possible to use the formula below because population is already included in them; therefore, using the formula could have meant subjecting the variables to population twice.

For each variable, the share of each country relative to all the seventeen countries was computed using Isard's Location Quotient (LQ) (Isard, 1960, p. 24):

$$LQ = \frac{Si/S}{Ni/N}$$

Where: Si is the number of the variable in country i;
S is the total number of the same variable in all the seventeen countries;
Ni is the population in country i; and
N is the total population in all the seventeen countries.

Since the study is concerned with welfare conditions and with equitable per capita distribution of development assistance and its allocation according to need, population size rather than a real extent of the countries, was chosen as the most appropriate base for analysis.

An LQ greater than one indicates that, at the present level of development of that variable throughout sub-Saharan Africa, the particular country has more than its "fair" share of that facility or service. A LQ of less than one suggests that the country has less than its "fair" share of the facility or service. The LQ for each development index of each country was obtained by adding the LQs for all variables in that index and then finding the mean. Thus for the health index for each country four LQs were calculated for life expectancy at birth, population per physician, population per nursing person and infant mortality rate. The mean of the four LQs then gave the health index for the particular country (Table 2). The mean value measures the overall level of development of facilities and services in each country relative to all the other countries in sub-Saharan Africa. The variables chosen comprise a reasonable spectrum of facilities and services that are likely to have a direct effect on the quality of life of the population and even on their income.

Although the use of the location quotient gives a measure of the development of certain services and facilities in a particular country, two limitations should be noted. First, equal weight is given to all the variables. No account is taken of differences in the quality of the facilities and the differential impact which quality may have on the living standards and prospects for overall development. For example, many rural schools in Africa are still poorly equipped, are without properly trained and qualified staff and do not have enough books. Likewise most rural clinics and hospitals are generally understaffed, lack the necessary equipment and are usually overcrowded. Secondly, statistics averaging the economic and social activities of people in seventeen countries almost for a decade are sure to conceal more than reveal. They however, provide some comparative burdens carried by these countries on their harsh road to economic self-reliance.

Africa South of the Sahara: The Setting and General Economic Performance

Africa south of the Sahara is a region of great diversity. On one hand, it encompasses Nigeria, a country of over eighty million people (approximately one quarter of the total regional population) (I.B.R.D., 1981). On the other hand, it includes a number of small countries, such as Swaziland. There are countries rich in mineral resources like Botswana, Zaïre, Zambia and Zimbabwe, as well as those that depend entirely on agriculture like Malawi and Kenya. There are those countries located in the Tropical rain forests and those located in the semi-arid interior. Some of them are land locked and others have an ocean coast.

Within sub-Saharan Africa, there are countries where agricultural output grew by over three percent a year during the late 1970s and early 1980s (e.g. Kenya, Malawi and Ivory Coast) and others where agricultural output remained unchanged or actually declined during the same period. Countries in this group included Angola, Ghana, Mozambique and Uganda (O.E.C.D., 1983).

The general economic performance during the same period varied widely among the sub-Saharan African countries. There were countries of a very poor economic performance, for example, Ghana, Sudan and Zaïre. Other countries had a stagnated economic performance. These countries included Burkina Faso and Senegal. Elsewhere, liberation and civil wars and domestic strife lowered growth rates in countries like Angola, Mozambique, Uganda and Zimbabwe. The collapse of most mineral prices on the world market during the late 1970s onwards hit several economies very hard, notably that of Zambia which had depended solely on copper exports for over ninety-five percent and forty-five per cent of its foreign exchange and government revenue respectively (Mwananshiku L., 1986). Despite this bad picture, some countries maintained annual growth rates of over five per cent or above during the same period. Countries in this group included Botswana, Ivory Coast, Kenya, and Malawi (O.E.C.D., 1984).

Despite such diversity, there is, nevertheless, considerable homogeneity within the region. Most countries in this region have small economies (in economic terms), a result of low average incomes and small populations. Most economies in this region are open with foreign trade accounting for about a quarter of the GNP (World Bank, 1984). They have mainly specialized economies in that most of them rely heavily on agriculture and depend on the export of one or two primary commodities. Even in the mineral exporting countries, the bulk of the population, usually as high as over seventy per cent works in agriculture with subsistence related production accounting for half or more of total agricultural output (I.B.R.D., 1982). Modern urban-based wage employment absorbs a small proportion of the total labour force.

In addition to these similarities in the economic structure, other common characteristics at least since the late 1970s can be noted. It is said that sub-Saharan Africa is currently in a grip of an economic crisis. Of all regions, sub-Saharan Africa has been hit hardest by the 1978-1983 world recession. Deterioration in terms of trade ranged between 1976 and 1982. The situation has deteriorated further rather than improved during the 1982 to 1986 period. Many countries have also experienced severe droughts making a bad situation even worse. The 1979 to 1983 recession was particularly bade because many countries had no easy access to soft credits and Oil Facility credits (O.E.C.D., 1984). This led many of these countries to rely on supplier credits and Commercial Bank loans to bridge what they assumed to be a short slump. Unfortunately, the slump continued longer than expected and meanwhile, interest rates (both nominal and real) rose drastically, leading to unmanageable external debt service situations.

The unexpectedly long duration of what was assumed to be a short slump and the cut-backs in imports forced by the poor performance of the economy, combined with increasing debt service costs drastically reduced governments' revenue bases. Some governments reacted by imposing real cuts in spending, but recurrent budget deficits became unbearable even in countries like Tanzania and Malawi which had surpluses previously (I.B.R.D., 1984). These deficits coupled with deteriorating terms of trade resulted in far more significant currency overvaluations than had been experienced by any country before.

When Anglophone and Francophone countries are analyzed to see whether Anglophone or Francophone Africa did better than the other economically, it is apparent that they both seem to be facing the same problems and at the same magnitude. Much of course depends on the indicators chosen for analysis. Generally speaking however, Botswana had a better record when compared to Gabon, while Cameroon performed better than Nigeria in the early 1980s. Kenya was seen to have done better than Ivory Coast, especially considering the latter's debt situation. Senegal despite its near stagnation for the most part of the last two decades has however, done less badly than Ghana (O.E.C.D., 1979-1985).

Table 2
Location quotients for five development indices 1984

Country	Health index	Education index	GNP index	Food prod. /capita index	Labour force index	Overall mean
1. Zambia	1.52	2.89	2.97	1.92	2.96	2.45
2. Zimbabwe	0.98	2.78	2.83	1.67	2.93	2.22
3. Senegal	1.60	1.56	2.39	1.63	2.04	1.84
4. Guinea	2.22	1.63	1.76	1.80	1.69	1.82
5. I. Coast	#	1.19	2.75	2.24	1.03	1.80
6. Malawi	2.30	0.98	0.76	1.95	1.02	1.40
7. B. Faso	2.71	0.54	0.68	1.91	0.96	1.36
8. Cameroon	0.89	1.74	1.96	1.07	0.90	1.31
9. Rwanda	2.79	1.04	0.98	1.06	0.64	1.30
10. Ghana	0.82	1.89	0.93	0.79	1.98	1.28
11. Niger	2.03	0.69	1.09	1.58	0.77	1.23
12. Mali	1.76	0.78	0.60	0.67	1.80	1.12
13. Kenya	0.47	0.88	0.63	1.09	0.69	0.75
14. Uganda	0.93	0.62	0.64	0.61	0.63	0.69
15. Sudan	data not available					
16. Tanzania	0.54	0.45	0.36	0.59	0.40	0.47
17. Zaïre	0.28	0.55	0.19	0.37	0.43	0.36

Data not available.

Source: Calculated from 10 variables obtained from World Bank Development Reports and World Population Data Sheets 1979 - 1985.

Table 3
Top 17 recipients of Canadian bilateral aid flows 1970-1985.
(Shown in millions of $ and percentages).

Country	Overall mean dev. index**	Development Assistance Received in years 1970-85				
		70/75	76/79	80/85	%	TOTAL
1. Zambia	2.45	8.84	36.84	83.72	7.78	129.40
2. Zimbabwe	2.22	0.18	0.09	34.66	3.22	34.93
3. Senegal	1.82	19.34	26.27	69.77	6.48	115.38
4. Guinea	1.69	0.54	1.01	18.87	1.75	20.42
5. I. Coast	1.61	16.4	28.77	45.24	4.20	90.41
6. Malawi	1.40	10.47	38.02	48.44	4.50	96.93
7. B. Faso	1.36	6.48	7.18	51.15	4.75	64.81
8. Cameroon	1.35	16.34	35.38	86.46	8.04	138.18
9. Rwanda	1.31	9.77	22.45	52.07	4.84	84.29
10. Ghana	1.27	39.05	44.45	66.03	6.14	149.53
11. Niger	1.23	35.12	17.47	44.74	4.16	97.33
12. Mali	1.10	9.06	12.60	50.51	4.69	72.17
13. Kenya	0.75	15.70	25.47	149.15	13.86	190.32
14. Uganda	0.69	5.01	1.42	11.23	1.04	17.66
15. Sudan	0.54	*	1.36	51.01	4.74	52.37
16. Tanzania	0.46	65.35	72.72	154.56	14.36	292.63
17. Zaïre	0.41	11.90	15.31	58.36	5.42	85.57

* Data not available.

Source: ** Table 2 above and CIDA *Annual Reports* 1970-1985.

Geographical Distribution of Bilateral Aid Flows to Sub-Sahara Africa

The way development assistance is distributed across a region to recipients is one of the most revealing dimensions of a donor's development policy. One would expect different aid disbursement patterns depending on whether or not development assistance is given basically for political, economic and/or humanitarian grounds. Table 3 shows the major sub-Saharan Africa recipients of Canadian bilateral aid.

The main assumption is that if Canada chooses its aid recipient countries on humanitarian grounds, then it should be expected that most of that aid will go to the poorest countries within this region. There is of course one factor working in the opposite direction for such an assumption, and that is, the limited capacity of very poor countries to manage and absorb large amounts of aid (Gillis, M. *et al.*, 1983). Even with this limitation, however, it should be expected that the poorest countries will receive large amounts of aid relative to how much they can absorb, but lower amounts than other countries on a per capita basis.

The LQs for the five development indices and the mean LQs are shown in Table 2. A variety of reasons including political, historical, economic and geographic factors and even the effect of the ruling governments, explain the pattern of development across the continent. The results in Table 2 suggest that there are small, but fairly significant differences in the levels of development, particularly between the best and the least served amongst the seventeen countries analyzed. The five countries with the highest LQ (those with LQ greater than 1.50) generally have scores well above unity on at least four of the five indices, and are particularly well served with the education index. Their high LQs on the education index are mainly due to the greater emphasis placed on this by almost every newly independent country. Often, people complement government efforts by building what are usually referred to as "self-help" schools. Eight countries scored below one on this index. The methodology used, however, does not take regional disparities within individual countries into account. There are considerable rural/urban disparities in most countries in Africa.

Zaïre, located in the Tropical rain forests scored a mean index of 0.36, and is the least developed among the seventeen countries analyzed. It scored ratings of less than 0.5 in four variable. It scored 0.28 in health, 0.55 in education, 0.19 in GNP, 0.37 in food production per capita and 0.43 in labour force growth. Tanzania on the eastern coast compiled a mean index of 0.47 and was the second most needy country amongst those analyzed. Tanzania scored 0.54 in health services, 0.45 in education, 0.36 in GNP, 0.59 in food production per capita and 0.40 in labour force growth. It is, however, said that Tanzania is one country in Africa that has made great strides in basic health and education for its citizens. The emphasis has been on basic training in health care and learning to read and write. Such efforts are unfortunately not well noted by the sources of the data used in this study. There were two other countries with an overall mean index of less than one. These were Kenya and Uganda, Kenya, however, is seen to be one of the most economically advanced countries in the region. The possible reasons for it appearing in the category of the worst countries is probably due to the indicators used here which might not be the best developed in the country and also because of the large population which was taken into account in the calculations.

At the top of the scale, Zambia was given an overall mean of 2.45. Zimbabwe came second with an index of 2.22. Senegal and Guinea were the third and forth with 1.84 and 1.82 respectively. The development measuring index therefore places Zambia, Zimbabwe, Senegal, Guinea and Ivory Coast as the top five, with Zaïre, Tanzania and Uganda as the least developed of the seventeen countries analyzed and, therefore, the most needy.

Table 3 compares levels of development for the various countries with the amount of aid received. This should support or discredit Canada's claim that its aid goes to the poorest countries. It is seen that the top five countries got 22 per cent of the total aid from 1970-1985, with Zambia and Senegal getting 7.5 and 6.5 per cent respectively, whereas the bottom five got 36 per cent. Of this percentage, however, 27 per cent went to two major recipients of Canadian aid — Tanzania and Kenya — which received 16 and 11 per cent respectively from 1870-1985. There is a steady increase of aid to all the recipients, but more goes to middle income countries, except for Tanzania which is in the lower group and which has been a particular beneficiary of Canadian development assistance.

The question of whether our aid goes to the most needy countries is one on which results are difficult to generalize. There is some proof that one of the largest recipients, Tanzania is also one of the most needy. The picture is, however, spoilt by analyzing the amount of aid that went to the top five middle income countries which is quite substantial.

The distribution of Canadian aid to sub-Saharan Africa has of course been political. Under this category, one finds that Canadian aid has been used to provide a special measure of assistance to newly independent countries in their early years of nationhood. A good example of this is Zimbabwe which became independent in 1980, and whose aid has been rising steadily. Another trend has been the increase of aid to Francophone Africa in the mid-1970s which reflected the politics of Canada generally and the province of Quebec in particular.

CIDA in Sub-Sahara Africa

In the late 1960s and the beginning of the 1970s, political and developmental considerations were primary in Canada's development programmes in Africa (Freeman, L., 1982). However, in the years that followed, economic considerations as seen by aid tying by procurement have become paramount in shaping Canadian aid policy. Starting right at the beginning of Canada's involvement in official development assistance issues, it had stringent tying conditions. There were some changes in the late 1970s especially after the Government publication of its most comprehensive policy statement on Canadian development assistance policy, the *Strategy for International Development Cooperation, 1975 - 1980*. This statement committed Canada to a basic needs approach in its development assistance policy. The statement did not make changes in the underlying goals of Canadian development assistance, what it did was to elaborate and make them more specific in an effort to make it more effective. Some of the recommendations included a greater degree of untying, more geographic concentration and the giving of more development assistance to the least developed of the developing countries. More emphasis was also to be given to meeting the basic needs of the population in these countries.

Most of the recommendations contained in the 1975-1980 CIDA Strategy were never carried out. There is more stringent aid tying now as about 80 per cent of bilateral programme is used to buy Canadian goods and services. When all DAC member countries' bilateral development assistance to developing countries is analyzed, Canada has the highest tying record, excluding only Austria. Canada's tying percentage is also seen to be over what is considered as acceptable by ORCD (OECD, 1981; 1982; 1983; 1984). The priority that was supposed to be given to the least developed of the developing countries has not worked that well since most of Canada's development assistance now goes to middle income countries which have some political and commercial relationship with Ottawa. This is very apparent in Table 3 where it is seen that some middle income countries are getting more development assistance than some very poor countries. A good example of such countries include Zambia which is considered to be one of the middle income countries in sub-Sahara Africa. This clearly shows that aid easily flows to middle income countries as a means to secure export markets.

In the sub-Sahara African region therefore, Canadian development programmes have been the major means through which Canadian products and services have found their way there mainly through tying. It is doubtful that this business could have accrued to Canada with CIDA programmes and its development assistance tying requirement. It is often argued that Canada's competitiveness on the international market is not very strong (Freeman, L., 1985). Probably the distance to sub-Sahara Africa is another factor that makes it cheaper for countries in this region to obtain goods from elsewhere like Europe.

Conclusion

Development assistance has become a major component in the development programmes of many countries in sub-Sahara Africa. This is mainly a consequence of the current economic crisis that most of them are currently facing. Many African countries, both Anglophone and Francophone are particular beneficiaries of the Canadian bilateral development programme. The growth in aid at a time when various governments' expenditures are constrained has produced a lot of flexibility into many recipient countries' acceptance and use of aid which would not have existed otherwise. However, the opportunity of development aid has not been fully used by the recipients because instead of aid being utilized and directed by the respective governments' initiatives, the countries have become subjected to considerable influences by the donors.

Canadian development assistance does not flow to the most needy countries of the developing countries in sub-Saharan Africa, instead much of it goes to countries considered as middle income. This is a major contradiction to the laid down development policy which stresses more aid to the most needy of the needy. The question of whether or not Canadian development assistance goes to the least developed of the developing countries in sub-Saharan Africa, is one on which it is difficult to generalize. On one hand, there are some major recipients which are in the middle income group, on the other there are some from the least developed in the region. It is, however, difficult to tell whether this trend is by design or just by chance.

BIBLIOGRAPHY

Belshaw, D.G.R. "An Evaluation of Foreign Planning Assistance to Tanzania's Decentralized Regional Planning Programme, 1972-1981," *Applied Geography*. Vol. 2, 1982, pp. 291-302.

Carty, R. "Giving for Gain, Foreign Aid and CIDA," in *The Ties that Bind: Canada and the Third World*. R. Clark and R. Swift, (Eds). Toronto: Alger, 1982.

Canadian International Development Agency (CIDA). *Strategy for International Development Cooperation 1975-1980*. Ottawa: Information Services, 1975.

Canadian International Development Agency (CIDA). *Annual Reports*. Hull: CIDA, 1970-1985.

Freeman, L. "The Effect of World Crisis on Canada's Involvement in Africa," *Studies in Political Economy*. Vol. 17, 1985, pp. 107-139.

Freeman, L. "CIDA, Wheat and Rural Development in Tanzania," *Canadian Journal of African Studies*. Vol. 16, No. 3, 1982, pp. 479-504.

Gillis, M. and others. *Economics of Development*. New York: W.W. Norton and Company, 1983.

Hirschman, A.O. and R.M. Bird. *Foreign Aid — A Critique and a Proposal*. Essays in International Finance No. 69. New Jersey: Princeton University, Department of Economics, Finance Section, 1968.

International Bank for Reconstruction and Development (I.B.R.D.). *Accelerated Development for Sub-Saharan Africa: An Agenda for Action*. Washington: World Bank, 1981.

International Bank for Reconstruction and Development (I.B.R.D.). *World Development Reports*. Washington: World Bank, 1980-1985.

Mwananshiku, L.J. "From Reform to Recovery," *Africa Report*. Vol. 31, No. 3, 1986, pp. 33-36.

Organization for Economic Cooperation and Development (O.E.C.D.). *Review Development Cooperation*. Paris: Development Cooperation Committee, OECD, 1978-1985.

Todaro, M.P. *Economic Development in the Third World*. New York: Longman, 1981.

Wood, B. "Canada and Third World Development: Testing Mutual Interests," in *Rich Country Interests and Third World Development*. R. Cassen and others (Eds). London: Croom

156 · Sinkala

Heim, 1982, pp. 94-127.

Winnipeg Free Press. February 20, 1987, p. 6.

World Bank. *Developmental Reports*. 1984.

World Population Bank (WPB). *World Population Data Sheet 1979-1985*. Population Bureau
Inc. Washington.

Aid and Academe: Lessons to Be Learned from the Saskatoon-Somalia Linkage

John S. Owen
University of Saskatchewan

Background

In 1980, the University of Saskatchewan (U of S) was asked by the International Development Office (IDO) in Ottawa to assist the Somali National University (SNU) in strengthening its graduate programs in Agriculture, Education, Medicine and Veterinary Medicine. The genesis of the request lay in recommendations for postgraduate training and research made by Dr. J.W. Greig, University of Toronto and Dr. G. Rangaswami, Tamil Nadu Agricultural University who had visited Somalia in August 1978 to advise on these matters.[1] Only one Canadian Institution, namely the U of S, had the capability to respond positively to the IDO's request. No other anglophone university had the required complement of colleges.

In October 1980, a U of S team representative of the four colleges, led by a former Dean of Veterinary Medicine, made a three-week visit to Somalia to determine if appropriate assistance could be provided to the SNU in establishing graduate programs. Their report was favorable and in May 1982 a joint memorandum of understanding was signed by the two universities. The Canadian International Development Agency (CIDA) undertook to support the project with a contribution of $2,161,995.[2]

Nature of the Linkage

The memorandum of understanding provided for up to eight junior faculty from the SNU to be accepted as special students for study at the U of S in each of three consecutive years. After 12 months study, they would return to Somalia and pursue field research to fulfill the requirements for a masters degree awarded by their own university. U of S faculty would visit Somalia to work with the returned fellows and assist in the development of academic programs. A small number of SNU trained technicians would also be accepted for six months training in their respective fields at the U of S.

Additional features of the memorandum were the provision of library and laboratory materials and equipment, the assignment of a librarian to upgrade library resources and skills, and opportunities for SNU faculty to visit Saskatoon and familiarize themselves with the University's teaching and research.

A management committee consisting of representatives of the four colleges, the International Student Adviser and a senior person from the Comptroller's office, was appointed to administer the project. This committee perceived the linkage as challenging because of certain innovative characteristics. First, it represented the University's first formal linkage with an education institution in Somalia.[3] Second, the involvement of four colleges, with the potential that this created for interdisciplinary research, was unique in Canadian assistance programs. Third, the Somali fellows were to receive SNU masters degrees, an arrangement which recognized the impossibility of fulfilling University of Saskatchewan degree requirements in the time-frame allowed and which, it was believed, would ensure their remaining in Somalia following graduation.

Difficulties Encountered

From the outset, the Management Committee recognized that the University, indeed the Canadian government, was breaking new ground in contributing to the development of higher education in Somalia. This was a part of Africa that, in the past, had been influenced by both the Arab and western worlds. Whilst Islam dominated the religious and cultural scene, marks of the former colonial powers, Britain and Italy, remained. More recently, two superpowers, the USSR and the United States, had entered the scene, primarily at the political level. The former assisted Somalia in its invasion of the Ogaden in 1977, a move marked by considerable initial success. The Russians, however, switched their support to Ethiopia forcing the withdrawal of Somali forces and leaving the door open for the United States entrée to the Horn. This complex web of influences and alliances was further complicated by Somalia's extreme poverty. Had she not been designated one of the world's least developed countries?

It was within this framework of cultural diversity, economic deprivation and changing political alignments that the U of S undertook to work. Some account of specific difficulties experienced in the linkage follows. Those occurring at the U of S will be presented first.

Language

Both prior to and following the creation of the Somali Democratic Republic in 1960, Italian influence, particularly in the southern part of the country had dominated the educational scene. With the establishment of the SNU in 1969, it was only to be expected the Italian Universities would supply much of the professional manpower.[4] Funding through the European

Economic community assisted this process. Moreover, Italian became the language of instruction throughout the SNU apart from the College of Education.[5]

It was recognized that Somali fellows coming to Canada would experience language difficulties. For most, English would be their third or fourth language.[6] All were required to pass the Test of English as a Foreign Language (TOEFL) prior to leaving Somalia but it was deemed necessary for them to follow a two-month course at the Centre for Second Language Instruction on arrival in Saskatoon prior to starting academic work. Even so, most of the fellows required a lot of assistance from their supervisors in written assignments, particularly thesis preparation.

Culture

For most of the Somali fellows, studying in North America was a new experience involving not only the learning of a new language but adaptation to conditions as variable as an unfriendly climate and unfamiliar work habits. Not all U of S supervisors fully understood these cultural differences and experienced a good deal of frustration when problems arose, for example, how to handle what seemed to them an unending series of demands for more books and equipment. It was not easy to remain patient and communicative whilst overcoming these difficulties. In a few cases, fellows and supervisors were clearly mismatched.

Academic Standing

Initially, it was assumed that the Somali fellows would be enrolled in graduate level courses at the U of S. This belief was reinforced by the glowing transcripts they produced from the SNU attesting the high marks they had been awarded during their undergraduate years. Supervisors very soon discovered that these attestations were no indicators of ability to cope with class assignments. Graduate level work demands problem-solving ability and stresses independent study, neither of which had been fostered at the SNU. Much of their knowledge had been acquired through memorization of lecture notes and lacked a practical dimension. After floundering in graduate courses, the fellows were advised to include some at the undergraduate level. Following these experiences with the first batch of fellows who arrived in Canada in the summer of 1982, it was apparent they needed more study time to attain a satisfactory level of performance. An application was made to CIDA for additional funding to extend the training period in Canada. This was subsequently approved and enabled future batches of fellows to spend an extra semester at the U of S.

Faculty Commitment

Because of the poor initial academic standing of the fellows and their difficulty in adjusting to an alien educational system, supervisors were required to spend more time helping them to clear the hurdles than they would have devoted to Canadian students. Additional demands were also made on the supervisors when they were asked to spend some weeks in Somalia assisting fellows with their field work and thesis preparation.

No provision existed in the CIDA contract to pay for a replacement during a faculty member's absence at the SNU. Hence, it was difficult to identify experienced persons able and willing to spend prolonged periods in Somalia and provide the continuity which the linkage required. Recent changes in CIDA funding policy now provide for faculty replacements.[7]

Defections

the realization that Somalis possessing higher degrees from Canadian Universities would be attracted to better paid employment in neighbouring Arab speaking countries influenced the terms of the memorandum of understanding. These terms provided for the award of SNU masters degrees to successful fellows. It was not realized how attractive north American life would be to some of the fellows even though they lacked the qualifications and experience required to settle in Canada and find employment. Nor was it realized how sympathetic the Canadian government is to persons from overseas who claim refugee status on the grounds of persecution — a strange and untenable reason advanced by Somalis wishing to remain in Canada. Had they not been chosen by their own University with the support of the Somali government to study overseas?

Table 1 shows that four fellows of the 27 who studied at the U of S remained in Canada. Four others who returned to Somalia have now left the country and are regarded as lost to the project.[8] In addition, one of the three technicians who trained in Saskatoon is still in Canada.

TABLE 1
LOCATION OF SNU FELLOWS

	Somalia	Canada	USA	UK	Sweden	
Agriculture	8	1	–	–	1	10
Education	7	–	1	–	–	8
Medicine	4	2	–	–	–	6
Veterinary Medicine	–	1	–	1	1	3
TOTAL	19	4	1	1	2	27

The difficulties so far described pertain essentially to those arising in Canada involving the fellows and university faculty. Additional problems that merit description were encountered in Mogadishu.

Establishing a Canadian Presence

Initially this posed problems. The memorandum of understanding assigned to the SNU responsibility for providing office space and housing for visiting faculty. Location of these facilities at the new university site in Mogadishu was envisaged and would have immediately established a Canadian presence. It soon transpired that the SNU was unable to fulfill this commitment and sub-standard hotel accommodation had to be used until the terms of the lease on a privately owned property, designated "Canada House" were negotiated.[9]

Canada has no consular representative in Somalia and, although a senior member of the embassy staff in Jeddah proved helpful on his occasional visits to Mogadishu, the lack of a resident official delayed the creation of a sound, credible base from which U of S staff could operate.

Adjusting to Local Conditions

It is greatly to the credit of U of S visiting faculty, some of whom had had no previous Third World experience, that they quickly adjusted to a working environment very different from that of North America. African institutions function very differently from North American ones. Less attention is paid to time schedules, keeping appointments and meeting deadlines. The rapid turnover in staff, particularly those holding senior positions, adds to the problem of maintaining good communication. Government departments, in particular, are known for their bureaucracy. Visiting U of S staff quickly discovered that much of their time and energy was devoted to routine tasks which, given a sounder infrastructure, would have been performed by less highly qualified persons.

The scattered location of SNU Colleges dictated the need for readily available, reliable transport. Much time was spent in travel, obtaining fuel for vehicles and keeping them in running order.[10] Also, " Canada House" had no telephone. This meant the constant deployment of drivers and vehicles in delivering messages.

Another major problem, one causing much frustration, was the time and effort required to clear goods through customs. The U of S would have been well advised to assign this responsibility to the SNU. However, there would always have been uncertainty about the successful completion of the operation.

Acceptance by Italian Faculty

An Italian presence at the SNU had been firmly established by the time U of S faculty started to arrive in Mogadishu. This led to speculation as to how a Canadian presence would be perceived. Would the newcomers find themselves in a similar position to McGill professors and residents who contributed to the development of the University of Nairobi's Medical School in the decade 1968-78?[11]

Superficially, relationships with the Italians appeared to be cordial but, deep down, one could not help feeling that the U of S was seen as an intruder on territory regarded as an Italian preserve. Language barriers which reduced opportunities for both professional and social intercourse probably acted as a safety valve by limiting opportunities for potentially flammable face-to-face encounters.

Arrangements for Returning Fellows

Stipends paid to full-time SNU faculty are unrealistically low, with the result that additional work outside the University is eagerly sought and obtained. This limits the time for research and is one reason why so few original investigations are carried out. Returning fellows discovered that the small allowances they had received from the Italians prior to going to Canada were not reinstated during phase 2 of the project. It was obvious to the Management Committee that unless they received financial assistance, the chances of their carrying out field research were slim. Accordingly, a decision was made to provide them with modest stipends. Another factor limiting research was the absence of laboratory materials. Arrangements were therefore made to cover the cost of essential supplies.[12] These expenditures had not been foreseen at the time the budget for the linkage was being worked out. Fortunately, the supplementary funds provided by CIDA to maintain the fellows for an additional six months in Canada could be stretched to meet these commitments.

Another problem, one incapable of rapid solution, came to light on the return of the Somali fellows to Mogadishu. This concerned their status and the possibilities of promotion within the SNU system. Traditionally, junior faculty had been accorded minimal responsibility for teaching by the Italian professors and received little help or encouragement with research. If the enthusiasm of the fellows to make use of their newly acquired knowledge was to be sustained, it was imperative that Saskatoon faculty be on hand to boost morale and ensure that their energies were not directed into other channels.

College of Graduate Studies

A matter of growing concern to the U of S was the seeming reluctance of the SNU to establish a mechanism for granting higher degrees. It was also a cause for concern amongst the fellows. They had never been enthusiastic about receiving higher degrees from their Alma Mater; now, they wondered whether they would receive any official recognition for their course work and research.

Eventually, in June 1985, the Council of Ministers gave approval to the SNU's request to establish a College of Graduate Studies. Since then, there has been no move to appoint a director or allocate space. In the meantime, fellows who have completed and successfully defended their theses were issued with written statements confirming that they had studied at the U of S and also satisfied the requirements for a SNU graduate degree.

Evaluating the Linkage

The third and final batch of fellows returned to Somalia in December 1985. Since it seemed unlikely that CIDA would continue to support the project, there was urgency in ensuring that they completed their field research and defended their theses prior to the closing of "Canada House" in October 1986 and the withdrawal of U of S staff in November of that year.

Had the linkage been successful? Members of the Management Committee who had visited somalia in May 1985 to evaluate the project felt that, in spite of many difficulties, several important objectives had been accomplished. At the same time, others had only been partially met. Reservations about the ability of the SNU to maintain the impetus to scholarship provided by returning fellows when the U of S staff withdrew were expressed.

A listing of the accomplishments of the linkage is presented in the belief that it will serve as a basis for evaluation. Much of the information has been abstracted from the final report on the project submitted to CIDA.[13]

Twenty-seven SNU junior faculty pursued 12 to 18 months of course work at the U of S. In aggregate, this amounted to 38.5 person-years of study.

Three technicians completed 6-month periods of training at the U of S.

Sixteen fellows completed their theses with a further three in preparation (see Table 2).

Two senior SNU faculty — a Dean of Agriculture and a senior lecturer in the College of Education — spent four to six weeks at the U of S under the sponsorship of the project.

Library services at SNU were organized by a U of S Veterinary Librarian who also trained librarians during two work periods in Somalia.

The libraries of the four colleges involved in the linkage received numerous books and journals purchased from project funds. Some items were donated by faculty.

A substantial amount of equipment and laboratory supplies was purchased for use by fellows returning to Somalia.

The project was completed within the budget approved by CIDA.

TABLE 2
STATUS OF THESES

	Completed	In Preparation	Not Completed	
Agriculture	5	3	2	10
Education	6	–	2	8
Medicine	3	–	3*	6
Veterinary Medicine	2	–	1	3
TOTAL	16	3	8	27

* One fellow required to discontinue.

These accomplishments were achieved with the assistance of 17 U of S faculty who worked with their respective students at SNU for an aggregate of 11.3 person-years (See Table 3).

TABLE 3
VISITS OF U OF S FACULTY TO SOMALIA

	Number of Faculty	Months spent at SNU (aggregated)
Agriculture	7	41.5
Education	3	34.5
Medicine	3	18.5
Veterinary Medicine	2	2.5
Library	2	38.0
TOTAL	17	135.0 (11.3 years)

Against these accomplishments must be listed certain negative features of the linkage which caused concern.

A high defection rate (30 percent) amongst fellows and technicians trained at the U of S.

Failure of the SNU to proceed with the establishment of a College of Graduate Studies following government approval of the proposal.

Uncertainty about the SNU's ability or willingness to recognize the valuable contributions which returned fellows could make to teaching and research.

Having identified positive and negative features of the linkage it is pertinent to ask if expectations of the respective universities were met.

Looking at it from the SNU's point of view, Deans and the Rector have attested to the improved knowledge and skills displayed by returned fellows. They also recognize the benefits that have accrued to the four colleges from shipments of equipment, laboratory supplies and library materials. Demand for these acquisitions, however, seemed insatiable!

Not too much concern has been expressed by SNU officials about defections from the project. This has been a common feature of assistance programs mounted by other countries in Somalia. In this regard, the 30 percent defector rate experienced by the linkage, although seemingly high, is not so when compared with other projects. The Somali attitude is that sooner or later the defectors will return home. One wonders if their view is realistic.[14]

So far as the fellows are concerned, they have never accepted the fact that their graduate degrees would be awarded by the SNU rather than the U of S. All along, they maintained that what appeared to them to be a less internationally recognized qualification would place them at a disadvantage vis-à-vis their colleagues who had acquired degrees from overseas universities. From a practical point of view, to have brought the fellows to the required standard to obtain masters degrees from the U of S would have necessitated at least two years additional study.

The Rector was bitterly disappointed to learn that the linkage would not be continued beyond the time stated in the memorandum of understanding. Clearly, he had assumed that an extension together with appropriate funding would be approved by the Canadian government. From the time of the issue of the UNESCO Technical Report[15] containing recommendations about the development of graduate programs, SNU officials had attached importance to forging links with an English-speaking country. Almost certainly, they saw the link with Canada as an important step in the evolution of their university and a means of counteracting the strong Italian influences which prevailed.

From the point of view of the U of S, opinions vary on the degree of success achieved and whether expectations were met. Some faculty felt that the linkage should never have been undertaken, arguing that graduate work could not be satisfactorily grafted onto a fragile undergraduate base. Inability of many of the fellows to cope with graduate level courses on arrival in Saskatoon lent credence to the belief that they lacked basic knowledge in some subject areas. Their poorly developed practical skills and problem solving ability was rightly perceived as a function of Italian-style pedagogy and provided further evidence of the weak undergraduate base.

Communication difficulties experienced by some supervisors and fellows tended to be magnified. Invariably, they came to the attention of departmental heads and deans who developed negative attitudes towards the project. These attitudes were reinforced by the failure of some fellows to return to Somalia on completing their studies. As the project drew to a close and the question of extending it arose, the deans of three of the colleges failed to register their support. The College of Education wished to continue its involvement in Somalia and submitted a proposal to CIDA to maintain the link with its SNU counterpart. The request was turned down — a great pity since, of all the SNU colleges, Education was the one receiving no Italian support.

Although opinions about the success of the project among present and past members of the Management Committee are not unanimous, there is a general feeling that both the SNU and the U of S have benefited. Benefits to the former have already been listed. What of the latter?

The presence on campus of relatively large numbers of Somalis throughout the years 1982-86 added a new dimension to the U of S's international activities. The fellows were distributed throughout four major colleges and had dealings with many faculty members. As a result, greater understanding by faculty of the culture, hopes and aspirations of Somali peoples emerged. Hitherto, only the occasional student from Somalia had registered at the U of S. Little was know about the complexities of life experienced by inhabitants of the Horn of Africa. The fellows were at some pains to remedy this lack of knowledge.

Considerable benefit was derived by the 17 faculty members who spent varying lengths of time in Somalia. They all felt that exposure to a different cultural and socio-economic environment had broadened their educational experience. They also agreed that the project had been of benefit to the SNU fellows who had studied in Canada and returned to Somalia.

Some U of S personnel, whilst travelling to and from Mogadishu, availed themselves of the opportunity to visit other African countries and renew acquaintance with former students. Several faculty who had spent six months or longer in Somalia developed a real feeling for the country and its people and were unhappy to see the project terminated. These individuals, in particular, have given some thought as to how the link might be maintained, possibly through an intermediary such as the University of Nairobi.

It is pertinent to ask if some of the difficulties experienced in the linkage could have been avoided. Would, for example, a more detailed feasibility study prior to signing the memorandum of understanding have pinpointed likely problems. It is debatable whether the three weeks spent by the exploratory team in Somalia in October 1980 was sufficiently long to make a valid assessment. Little attempt was made to pick the brains of nationals from other countries supplying various forms of assistance to the country. Language differences, undoubtedly, limited the possibility of fruitful discussion with a key group — the Italians.

One of the bugbears of working in a developing country is the difficulty of maintaining equipment in working order and seeing that it is properly used. A good deal of equipment at the College of Education, supplied as part of a former United States assistance project, had never been used and had deteriorated because of poor storage. At any one time, most of the X-ray machines at the teaching hospital are out of order. Had the significance of these deficiencies been fully appreciated in 1980, the project could have been modified to ensure that more emphasis was placed on the training of technicians.

Another limiting factor was the poor standard of English possessed by many fellows selected for training in Canada. Mandatory courses of instruction in the language could usefully have been instituted in Mogadishu prior to departure. Also, the U of S should have had direct input to the selection process.

Other matters which had a bearing on the functioning of the linkage and could, with benefit, have received more attention include the disadvantage of Canada having no ambassador in Somalia; the necessity of requiring fellows to sign agreements that they would return to the SNU following completion of their studies at the U of S[16] and insistence that costs for replacement faculty be included in the CIDA allocation.

The Medical Component of the Linkage

Since this paper is being presented at one of the health science sessions of the CAAS Conference, it is appropriate to refer specifically to experiences with the medical component of the linkage. Only a few points will be highlighted since the subject has been dealt with in a previous paper.[17]

The SNU's initial request was to train junior faculty in clinical disciplines. The first two fellows were from Pediatrics and Anesthesia, the former, a man with several years experience of his specialty, the latter, a woman with minimal experience. The second batch of fellows comprised a man with some radiological experience and a recently qualified young man assigned to the Department of Anatomy. The third batch included two fellows who had graduated the previous year; the male was assigned to Physiology, the female to Anatomy. A female technician was also accepted for six months training in 1983.

The switch from clinical disciplines to basic science ones was dictated by the Somali Dean of Medicine's awareness that his College was very poorly staffed in the pre-clinical departments. Young graduates were, therefore, often against their will, directed into these departments.

The performance of these seven Somalis whilst at the U of S was variable, although the four who returned to Somalia have acquitted themselves well and demonstrated potential for further training. Details are as follows:

PERFORMANCE

Specialty	At U of S	At SNU	Present Location
Pediatrics (male	Poor	Very good	Somalia
Anesthesia (female)	Satisfactory	Good	Somalia
Radiology (male)	Satisfactory	–	Canada
Anatomy (male)	Poor	–	Canada
Physiology (male)	Poor	*	Somalia
Anatomy (female)	Good	Very good	Somalia
Microbiology (female)	Good	**	Somalia

* Assumed satisfactory since he is still working at the SNU.
** The fellow completed further training in Sweden and has returned to the SNU.

Two fellows carried out epidemiological surveys, one on the immunization status of young children in Mogadishu, the other a screening of Somali women for cervical cancer. Data from these surveys will be of value in determining the future evolution of Somalia's health services. The fellow trained in anaesthesia has learned techniques and skills appropriate to a developing country and is practising them with the aid of equipment supplied to the teaching hospital.

What Lessons Have Been Learnt from the Linkage?

Language Barriers

The Institutional Cooperation and Development Services Division (ICDS) of CIDA is promoting an increasing number of linkages between Canadian universities and institutions for higher education in developing countries. The majority of these linkages are with universities where either French or English is the language of instruction. This ensures effective communication and the maintenance of satisfactory pedagogic standards. Difficulties are likely to arise if the host university operates in a less widely understood language such as Italian. Such was the case with the Saskatoon-Somalia linkage. Although the SNU was committed to the use of English in its graduate, as distinct from its undergraduate programs, many of the fellows and some senior administrators possessed a poor understanding of the language. This was particularly noticeable in their writing and probably accounted for the reluctance of SNU officials to communicate in a language in which they lacked proficiency. During the five years that the author was associated with the linkage, he did not receive a single reply to letters sent to senior members of the SNU's Faculty of Medicine!

Canadian universities should think twice before undertaking to assist academic institutions where language differences can mar the success of projects. CIDA, likewise, should be circumspect in funding such linkages.

Italian Pedagogic Influences

Linked to the poorly developed use of the English language at the SNU was the type of educational system which the fellows had grown up in. Italian pedagogy follows a traditional pattern using didactic methods of instruction which favour learning by rote. Graduate programs demand problem solving abilities; grafting them onto this rigid undergraduate base was not easy. It was also difficult convincing the fellows that the glowing transcripts they had received at the conclusion of their undergraduate studies were not passports to automatic success in graduate work at the U of S.

Differing approaches to higher education, particularly those encountered outside the North American system, can adversely affect the outcome of university linkages. This again, is something which Canadian universities and funding agencies such as CIDA need to be aware of when evaluating requests for assistance from overseas governments.

Reciprocal Benefits

The signing of a memorandum of understanding presupposes that each partner to the agreement has a number of expectations which it hopes will be met. Only in this way can true reciprocity be said to exist. Did the signatories know enough about each institution's resources before putting pen to paper? Only minimal exchanges had taken place between the two sides. The three-week visit of the U of S team to Mogadishu in 1980 was hardly sufficient to assess the SNU's resources. Moreover, CIDA's lack of knowledge and experience of Somalia's higher education system proved a drawback. Inevitably, team members had to rely on their own somewhat brief observations. The visit to Saskatoon of the SNU Rector and deans in May, 1982 was even shorter and afforded little opportunity for getting to know one's future colleagues.[18]

Following the return of the first batch of fellows to the SNU in 1983, the paucity of its infrastructure was revealed. Not only did the fellows have to be provided with every piece of equipment required for their field work, but it was necessary to ship basic laboratory supplies to Somalia. Inadequate library resources necessitated the purchase of standard texts and journals.

One detected a lack of interest on the part of SNU faculty in assisting returning fellows with their field work. This reluctance to become involved probably stemmed from their own lack of research training. But it was also related to lack of time — many Somali faculty have to moonlight to augment their meagre academic stipends.

Lack of resources and indifference on the part of SNU faculty put an extra strain on U of S personnel who spent varying periods of time in Mogadishu. They might have expected to satisfy some of their own research interests whilst in Somalia. The involvement of four colleges in the linkage provided unparalleled opportunities for interdisciplinary research. Sadly, their waking hours were entirely devoted to establishing and maintaining a productive working environment for their protégés.

For their part, the Somalis may well have anticipated the presence of a larger number of senior U of S faculty for longer periods of time at SNU. Difficulties in maintaining core personnel at Canada House and ensuring a regular flow of supervisors to Somalia are described in the next section of the paper.

In retrospect, one has to question the wisdom of the SNU's decision to embark on graduate studies in the early 1980s when there was a clear need to strengthen the undergraduate programs. Such a move, however, might have been construed by the Italians as encroaching on their preserves and underming in their influence. An alternative would have been for the U of S to concentrate all its resources on providing assistance to the badly rundown College of Education. This College had been ignored by the Italians because of a wish to retain English as the language of instruction for its undergraduates. Such a move would have provided better opportunities for improving the knowledge and skills of students destined to teach in Somalia's school system. It was singularly unfortunate that the application to CIDA for funding to continue the linkage through the respective Colleges of Education was turned down. At the time of termination of the project, evidence of deteriorating standards of preparedness amongst Somali applicants to SNU was coming to light. This further justified strengthening the College of Education's programs.

U of S Commitment

No insuperable problems occurred in absorbing SNU fellows into U of S educational programmes. Admittedly, many fellows were insufficiently prepared to benefit from graduate courses and showed reluctance in pursuing undergraduate courses but, with patience and persistence, their needs were gradually met.

What proved difficult was sustaining a sufficient number of U of S faculty supervisors in Somalia for more than a few weeks at a time. This was a particular problem with senior staff for whom no budgetary provision for replacement had been made. Moreover, Canada was virtually starting from scratch in Somalia. She had no resident diplomatic staff in Mogadishu; SNU failed to live up to its commitment of provide housing; and educational and social amenities were not well developed — hardly an inducement for married faculty with children to opt for a year in the Horn.

A unique feature of the Saskatoon-Somalia linkage was its involvement of four colleges. One wonders how many Canadian universities possess the resources to operate on such a wide front in a developing African country. Would a consortium have made more sense? As it was, the U of S had to look outside the ranks of its regular faculty to sustain the linkage.[19]

At no time was a very senior U of S academic present in Somalia for more than a few weeks at a time. This tended to lessen the importance of the linkage in the eyes of the University community. Neither did it escape the notice of SNU officials. Stronger support for the project might have been shown by the colleges had a few of their senior faculty been willing to spend a year or two in Mogadishu. As it was, a good deal of continuity in the linkage was supplied by people peripheral to the mainstream of the university activity. It is greatly to the tribute of these temporary employees that the project was sustained.

Immigration Practices

Four fellows and one technician failed to return to Somalia on completing their training at the U of S. This matter was of great concern to the Management Committee whose members felt that the Department of Immigration was accepting at face value claims made by the fellows to be accorded refugee status.[20] Because of defections amongst the first and second batches of fellows, the third group had been required by Canadian embassy officials in Riyadh to sign an undertaking to return to Somalia. This assurance appears to have been ignored by immigration officials handling the case of a veterinary medicine fellow. Once an application for refugee status has been made to the Department of Immigration, it seems impossible for university representatives to enter into any type of communication with its officials.

Length of CIDA Contracts

With the signing of the memorandum of understanding between the U of S and the SNU in 1982, CIDA support for the linkage was assured for three years. There was reasonable expectation that, on expiry, the contract would be renewed for a further period. This did not happen and raises the question of what benefits can accrue to each institution in such a short time frame. The question is even more relevant when the underdeveloped infrastructure at the SNU is recognized. A 10-year linkage would have been more realistic.

It is worth noting that one of Canada's most successful Third World assistance programs — the Ghana-Guelph linkage was funded by CIDA for eight years.[21] And, in this case, the University of Legon was much better organized and equipped than the SNU to receive Guelph faculty and send well-prepared students, fluent in English, to Canada for graduate studies.

There are recent signs of a growing awareness in CIDA for the need to limit Canada's assistance to a smaller number of countries. This could result in longer periods of funding for institutional linkages and increased benefits to both donor and recipient universities.

Conclusion

The Saskatoon-Somalia linkage has added a new dimension to the University of Saskatchewan's international activities. Although receiving the support of the majority of faculty closely associated with the project, it failed to meet certain expectations. The deans of three colleges perceived it neither as a priority nor a success story. In retrospect the deans, none of whom had had significant Third World experience, should have been encouraged to visit Somalia and see for themselves the difficulties and achievements. This might have modified their attitudes.

CIDA's decision not to extend support for the project was a disappointment. There is a limit to what can be accomplished in three years to strengthen a university's graduate programs when the infrastructure is poorly developed and the undergraduate base weak.

CIDA recently received the Management Committee's final report on the linkage describing its accomplishments and the benefits accruing to each university. One hopes that this branch of External Affairs will carry out its own evaluation.[22] Whatever the result, however, it is known that Somalia is not on Canada's priority list of African countries for receiving assistance. So, a revival of CIDA support for developing graduate education at SNU is unlikely in the foreseeable future.

The Italian presence at the SNU is destined to continue for some years. It is not certain whether a Canadian presence was enthusiastically endorsed by senior Italian government officials. Relations at faculty level were reasonably cordial although somewhat limited by language differences. There is some reason to believe that the Canadian presence stimulated the Italian universities involved in assisting the SNU to rethink their contribution to graduate training.[23]

Some U of S faculty, particularly those who spent large blocks of time in Somalia, are keen to retain a link with the SNU. Ways of accomplishing this are being explored. It would be unfortunate if their skills and experiences remained unutilized in the future.

NOTES

1.   J. W. Greig and G. Rangaswami. *Post Graduate Training and Research Program at the Somali National University.* UNESCO Technical Report RP/1977-78/1.176.6, Paris, 1979, Mimeo, p. 9.

2.   A supplementary contribution of $170,400 was subsequently approved by CIDA to cover the costs of maintaining Somali fellows in Saskatoon for an additional six months after it had been determined they needed extra study time.

3.   Although the U of S had had no previous experience of assisting universities in the Horn of Africa, linkages with other African countries such as Uganda, Tanzania, Zambia and Swaziland had occurred form the early 1970s onwards.

4.   The principal Italian universities involved in helping to staff the SNU are Rome (Medicine), Florence (Agriculture) and Pisa (Veterinary Medicine).

5.   The College of Education grew out of the Lafole Teacher Training Centre established in 1954. English had always been the medium of instruction at this College, a tradition which was maintained when the SNU was formed. The Italians were unwilling to support any part of the university which did not employ Italian. Although the College of Education had received some assistance during the 1970's from English-speaking countries such as the United States, its status vis-à-vis other SNU colleges was low and hence its need for the injection of trained staff and equipment paramount.

6.   Since 1972, Somali has been the language of instruction in the school system. Some Somalis also speak Arabic. All entrants to the SNU are required to take a six-month course in Italian. Although English is beginning to assume importance in Somalia, only fellows with roots in the northern part of the country previously under British trusteeship demonstrated fluency in the language.

7.   On projects for which the CIDA contribution is $500,000 or more, an overhead of 40 percent to cover on-campus payroll costs is allowed: 25 percent is allowed for off-campus payroll costs. For projects of up to $500,000 overheads are 30 and 15 percent respectively.

8.   Since preparing this paper, it has been learnt that one of the fellows in agriculture who returned to Somalia died as the result of an automobile accident.

9.   Yearly rental of "Canada House" amounting to $32,000 US, payable in advance, proved a costly outlay. It also demonstrates the considerable assets owned by a small section of the population in one of the world's poorest countries.

10.   The Colleges of Agriculture and Education located at Afgoi and Lafole respectively are some 20 miles from Mogadishu. Regular commuting of staff and fellows engaged in research at these institutions created heavy transportation demands.

11.   For an evaluation of the McGill-Nairobi linkage, see Eva-Maria Rathgeber, *The Movement of Paradigms of Medical Knowledge and Research between Canada and Kenya: An Investigation into the Sociology of Knowledge Transfers*, Ph.D. thesis, State University of New York, Buffalo, 1982. During the 10-year linkage, 39 McGill faculty and senior residents staffed the department of paediatrics and assisted the University of Glasgow in staffing the department of medicine. A strong Glaswegian presence had been established at the University of Nairobi prior to the arrival of McGill staff. The author points out that the Canadians, although able to

make a useful contribution to the new medical school, nevertheless felt constrained by having to operate within a framework developed by a non-Canadian University. They would have appreciated more freedom in "doing their own thing."

12. Fellows received $250 a month for six months on their return to Somalia. A seventh payment was made when their thesis was handed in. At the supervisor's discretion, disbursements of up to $5,000 could be authorized for purchase of equipment and supplies required for field research.

13. University of Saskatchewan, *Final Report (#7) on linkage Agreement Between Somali National University and the University of Saskatchewan*, CIDA Project 338-90/31-7 covering the period February 1, 1986, to January 3, 1987, undated.

14. Recent events in Somalia as reported in *The New Yorker*, August 22, 1988, pp. 17-18, cast grave doubts about the willingness of defectors whose roots are in the northern part of the country to return to SNU. In May, 1988, a group calling itself the Somali National Movement consisting largely of the Isaq, a northern clan, launched attacks against supporters of Muhammad Siad Barre's government. Several thousand people have been killed and serious human rights abuses on both sides have been reported. Some 245,000 somalis have fled to Ethiopia reversing the flow of refugees from the Ogaden to Somalia which had occurred for more than a decade prior to the signing of a peace treaty between the two countries in April, 1988.

15. As pointed out in the paper, Canadian immigration officials have been too lenient with Somali fellows claiming refugee status. The availability of documentary evidence showing that a fellow planned to return to Somalia would have made it difficult to sustain a claim of persecution.

16. John Owen, "Graduate Medical Programmes at the Somali National University: Do They Meet Somalia's Needs?", Paper presented at the 13th Annual Conference, Canadian Association of African Studies, University of Laval, May 15-19, 1983.

17. During the life of the project, the original deans were replaced and other changes occurred amongst senior SNU administrative personnel. This lack of staff continuity did nothing to facilitate communication. Only the Rector retained his position during the four years that U of S faculty were in Somalia.

18. Three of the four Canadians who resided at Canada House or in local hotels for the longest periods did not hold faculty appointments at the time of hiring. They provided agricultural, medical and library science skills and played a major role in assisting returning fellows with their field work and thesis preparation.

19. Since presenting this paper, new regulations came into force on January 1, 1989, tightening immigration procedures. Had these regulations been in place in 1983, it would have been much more difficult for SNU fellows to justify remaining in Canada.

20. The Ghana/Guelph linkage involving four departments in the Faculty of Agriculture at Legon and one in the faculty of Science, covered the period 1970-1978. Guelph's assistance included supplying two department heads. Three faculty from the University of Saskatchewan's College of Home Economics were also seconded to the project. The linkage is well covered in eight annual reports and a final report compiled by Dr. J.C.M. Shute, Project Director. See also his article "Cooperation for Development," *Overseas Universities*, No. 20, 27-29, November, 1973.

21. In 1987, CIDA commissioned an Ottawa firm to evaluate a number of projects in East and central Africa. A consultant spent two days in Somalia during which time he interviewed senior SNU administrative and academic staff. Inspection of the notes he made of the interviews adds very little to the University of Saskatchewan's own evaluations.

22. Although some Somali faculty have undertaken graduate work at Italian universities, the programs have not been well structured. No formal degrees or diplomas have

been conferred at the conclusion of their studies. It now seems that a four-year program leading to a doctoral degree will be available in the future.

Consensual Politics and Development Aid in Africa

Kofi Ermeleh Agovi
University of Ghana

Since Independence, post-war Africa has experienced various forms of aid. These have been mostly concentrated on *select* areas of the African economy. Aid meant to develop agriculture, for example, has often been designed to promote efficiency in the production of cash crops and raw materials for industrial purposes. Technical advisers and equipment are normally provided to strengthen the mining industry so as to ensure continuity on the production lines of industrialized countries.[1] Even in the seemingly innocuous sector of local manpower training and development, educational exchange programmes, short-term travel grants and study tours, there has been a calculated objective to use it as avenues for political influence in the award of public contracts and projects of great financial value. Loan agreements have released foreign exchange components that have encouraged the consumer orientations of urban populations in Africa to the extent that nowadays part of Africa's political heritage is for each successive government to renegotiate its debt burdens.[2] In all these designs, the initiative for such forms of aid has quite often not originated from African countries themselves.

Although, admittedly there was a lot of goodwill towards African states during the Independence period, and this was reflected in both the number and variety of aid at the time, Independence also created a certain atmosphere of competitiveness and anxiety in trade and diplomatic circles in accordance with the cold war situation of post-war geo-politics. Consequently, one can say with a fair amount of certainty that goodwill as a *political* expression of aid was obviously hopelessly outweighed by the calculated motive of gain and self-interest in aid components to Africa before the Eighties.

The consequences of such aid initiatives have since become part of the fixed image of Africa in international relations. The political instability, intractable corruption, increasing involvement of multi-national corporations and banks, debts, a picture of abject poverty and helplessness. A people unable to salvage their economies let alone possess the will to live. In a world accustomed to value judgements and fixed images of other cultures in their international protocol arrangements, dealings and debates, a further proof of Africa's loss to world civilization and development was provided in the Eighties with the onset of draught, famine and dessertification. Once again, Africa was treated to the historical bout of Western humanitarian Band Aid, and the new civilizing "imperialism" of the World Bank and the International Monetary Fund, who insist on the moral discipline of Economic Recovery Programs.[3]

But, African states have consistently, since Independence, sought to change their economic relations with Europe. They have consistently sought to change the character of aid to Africa. They have sought to complement political nationalism with economic nationalism.[4]

They have always sought to create a condition where political nationalism and economic nationalism will be *fused* as complementary forces to meaningful development on the Continent.[5] If African nationalism had the immediate aim to liberate African colonies from political and economic exploitation, it also had definite aspirations towards modernization. There was the need to create new socio-political institutions, expand educational establishments and diversify the horizons of the national economy in order to take into account the quality of life of African citizens. On the eve of Independence therefore, Africa ushered in a new determination — in the words of Dr. Kwame Nkrumah in 1957 — that the African *given the chance* (emphasis mine) will "prove to the world that he is capable of managing his own affairs."[6] For some inexplicable reason, Western nations have never been willing to understand or support the *aggregate* character of the post-war nationalism in Africa. In their anxiety to maintain the colonial status of African economies at Independence — as suppliers of raw materials and industrial inputs — Western countries have never demonstrated the political will to come to terms with the political and economic implications of African nationalism in its drive towards modernization. Moreover, unfortunately handicapped as African countries were in terms of technical expertise and finance capital, they were compelled to make hard economic bargains and painful political compromises in order to embark on their modernization process. In such a context, the industrial countries used the factor of development aid to neutralize African economic nationalism. Independence of mind and initiative — two basic factors in any drive towards modernization — were completely eroded by the kinds of aid proposed by Western countries. Equally exacerbating was the fact that African states did not have sufficient time to develop an agreed program or strategy of development that aid could effectively support in its implementation. There was no coherent or efficient state machinery for scrutinizing aid, accepting it and channeling it through the most productive

fields. Then added to that state of affairs was the total absence of management values and principles to promote efficiency in aid disbursement. In this
situation, aid in Africa, became in effect, the most potential denial of
whatever modernization had connoted in the experience of other countries.

Lessons of history have clearly established the fact that although
political and economic factors are important considerations in nation
building and therefore have to be tackled simultaneously as a unified
process, it is most obvious that *political consensus* in nation building and
modernization is primary. Jack Greene has argued in a recent lecture on
"The American Revolution and Modern Revolutions" that the 1776
Constitution of the American people was "a modern instrument, the expression of the modern society out of which it came."[7] Consequently, the
American Revolution did not have to contend with socio-economic problems, hence its overiding concern and preoccupation with political issues.
Thus, a central concern of these political issues, what he terms as an
"unfinished agenda" was the "continuing movement toward an expanding
conception of citizenship, of who should be included in the political
category of people."[8] This problem led to a civil war to determine whether a
nation such as America could afford to remain, in the words of Abraham
Lincoln, "half-free, half-slave." The historicity of that civil war did not only
lie in the will towards complete nationhood but in its principled drive
towards a consensus of values of nationhood, of what ought to constitute an
ideal modern society in which considerations of race and colour will not
determine social relations and the pursuit of life and liberty. Indeed, it was
the resolution of this central issue, and perhaps more important, the creation
of a consensus based on the constitutional document of the American
Revolution which really enabled America to release its energies towards effective modernization in terms of industrial, scientific and technological development.

Similarly, the historical experience of Britain in this respect is equally
instructive. By the time of Queen Elizabeth I, a single and powerful
monarchy supported by a disciplined Aristocracy had become the basis of a
strong, united and stable country, whose successful maritime ventures
instilled added confidence in her people. Yet, soon afterwards, it became
obvious by the time of Charles I in 1625 that there was need for a civil war
to resolve the political question concerning the values and institutions which
should symbolize and represent, without reservation, the popular will of the
people of the United Kingdom. The turmoil of that struggle is now history.[9]
But its resolution enabled the Victorian era to undertake massive imperial
ventures, radical social transformations and industrialization at home. Thus,
as we find in the American situation, the struggle to elevate and establish
'popular representation' as a framework for national consensus on

everything became the most important political decision for true development to emerge in Britain.

The Japanese experience is even more telling. After the consolidation of
the shogunate, the Imperial Monarchy felt powerful enough to cut Japan off
from the rest of the country by 1630. For over two hundred years, Japan
became "the closed country." It sought to control all factors that might
threaten political stability, while it consolidated and defined its primary
political values and institutions. One result of this isolation, wrote
Reischauer and Craig in 1981, was Japan's ability to develop its "native
characteristics" and "native Japanese traits."[10] Further, as a consequence of
this isolation, the Japanese "have developed a large proportion of their
culture themselves than have most nations."[11] By the time of Meiji
Restoration in the 19th Century, Japan had made up its mind on the effective
values and institutions to promote its development. A favourite slogan at that
time was "Western Science, Japanese Mind." Thus, as Gregory Clarke has
observed, the miracle of the Japanese economic growth "is the mystery of its
value system . . . . It allowed the sophisticated sense of consensus, the
human relations values such as *giri* and so on. Combined with outside
rationalism, it resulted in rapid growth."[12] For Japan therefore, 'cultural
consensus' became the most important factor for development.

From the experiences of the countries we have alluded to so far, it
seems that a historical paradigm emerges. There is first a situation of
instability and chaos, when the fragmented realms or estates within the
country have to be forced into a central direction or identity. This is
followed by a phase of stability in which the collective inner forces of
strength within the society are released towards national unity. Side by side
with this is a search for a 'national ethic' or a body of ideals and aspirations
and values which clearly define the country's collective urges towards progress and development. It is a situation of commonly agreed principles and
assumptions of state which are intended to motivate and define the society's
sense of development. An enunciation of consensual values, in all spheres of
life, that invigorate collective behaviour and guide the conduct of state
institutions.

We in Africa have not been able to determine whether this kind of
consensus should be built around cultural political or economic necessity.
Historically it must be emphasized that the colonial intervention put an end
to the effective and systematic establishment of nation states in Africa and
disrupted its people's sense of values. Consequently, the postwar Revolution
in Africa and its urgent nationalism had to deal with political, cultural and
socio-economic problems at the same time. Not only did the individual
African states have to be ushered into the scientific, industrial and
technological age, but they also had to develop corresponding values and

institutions that will make such a transformation permanent and meaningful and constitute for Africans a way of life. In the face of the fairly obvious complexity of Africa's historical past, including the need to come to terms with modern systems of advanced economies and market forces, the only choice open to Africa was to develop quickly a consensus on *all* fronts at once *within a given framework of priorities*. Nkrumah's dictum for Ghana's Independence struggle, "seek ye first the political Kingdom, and all other things shall be added unto it" was a profound metaphor for such a framework. His subsequent attempts at Continental Unity through the pursuit of political goals were all profound expressions of the need to establish politics as the 'framework of priorities' for Africa, a framework through which Africa can build up its consensus on all fronts. Paradoxically, after his death, African leaders in their collective wisdom decided that national and continental economies of Africa should be the framework for such a consensus. Thus, even as recent as 1985, *West Africa* magazine, in its editorial of 15th July 1985 asserted that indeed Africa needs "political clout to deal with the challenges of the modern world . . . . And that begins with economics."[13]

This view reflects a mood in Africa since the 1970's, which perceived Africa's problems exclusively in the economic mould. Accordingly, that period witnessed a marked concentration on economics and the establishment of economic institutions and groupings, particularly at the level of O.A.U. forums.[14] Coincidentally, it also marked a period when development aid became a craze on the continent, an essential commodity that every country and government in Africa needed in order to exist or survive. Multi-national banks and their collaterals such as the World Bank and the IMF became the central agencies of 'aid for development' in Africa. In the words of one commentator, they cashed in on the African situation with a 'vengeance'.[15] They established conditionalities for loans which very often trespassed "into the exercise of (state) sovereignty."[16] They created situations which raised disturbing arguments about 'the unjust economic system in which (African states) are mere appendages of the rich countries."[17] And worse still, even under such difficult conditions, aid was offered and utilized without any real effect, impact or result on African societies. As Edward Hirabayashi *et al.* observed in 1976, International development aid in Africa has suffered 'reversions' whose reasons are in most cases 'unclear.'[18] Some have attributed the ineffectiveness of aid to 'a lack of understanding of the local population's socio-cultural systems along with a lack of local participation.'[19] People have pointed to the evidence of massive corruption in the body-politic of African countries from the governmental level to the level of implementation bureaucrats, a situation that has led to the misappropriation or misdirection of aid funds. Political instability in the form of chronic coup d'etats and frequent changes of government has also led to the abandonment of development projects and lack of zeal or consistency in the prosecution of agreed development programs. Others have drawn attention to inefficiency in administrative and bureaucratic structures owing primarily to a lack of infrastructural development and the non-existence of a sharp business-like attitude and management expertise among African program implimentors.

In my view, a more telling reason is the use of aid as a *manipulative* device by donor countries and multinational banks to maintain economic, political and diplomatic leverage in African countries. "Aid without strings" either in the form of securing raw materials or sustaining a sphere of political and military influence is completely unknown in African's post-Independence history. Under this category may also be mentioned the kinds of aid, whose cumulative effect in terms of bank interest rates, has tended to cripple the ability of African countries not only to develop but to pay for their original loan components. Thus, it is not unusual, at the change of government in African countries, for the new leaders to 're-assure' donor and creditor countries of their willingness to fulfill repayment schedules and obligations as the first act of winning international acclaim and support. In this very act, the Western mass media and their diplomatic channels have always responded most favourably and most encouragingly even where suspicious of the ultimate political allegiance or ideology of the in-coming regime are obvious in their reports and by-lines. A more recent scenario in the attitude of donor countries is the fact that contract awards under aid proposed by such countries are invariably 'won' or given to firms and contractors who originate from the donor country. The ritual of open tenders may be performed, but at the end of it, the receiving country has no say in who ultimately wins the contract at a lower or higher cost. The receiving country has no control on *where* to order a particular equipment, even if it wishes to do so for purposes of standardization. Indeed, the attitude here is that firms and contractors from donor countries must be made to keep a firm grip on spare parts supply as a definite avenue of continued economic dependence.[20]

Also, a more fundamental issue is the fact, already suggested, that aid has been concentrated in sectors of life that completely exclude development in terms of building up ideas and institutions that can integrate the country on a more continuous, stable and permanent basis. It has taken Africans themselves more than two decades to realize that they have no cultural consensus, no social consensus on anything within their modern independent boundaries. It has taken them the same period of agonizing experiences to realize that they have been promoting, through emphasis on trade and import habituation, and artificial *divorce* of political and institutional development from economic development. They have tended, in fact, to give *primacy* to economic development — notwithstanding the manipulations and constraints in that sector — when they should first and foremost give priority to the creation, establishment and perpetuation of political consensus as a condition for economic development.

Fortunately, the nineteen-eighties has seen a determined effort on the continent to reverse this trend with a concentration on *political* development, particularly in the area of consensus politics. If Ghana's example can be cited here, there have been fundamental attempts to re-structure economic relations to correspond with reforms in the educational, cultural and political sectors. Indeed, African countries are now faced with the search for a grand 'national ethic,' a hard core of permanent values that define a collective temperament or a national spirit and vision of goals and aspirations that can support systematic development. This search has involved mental and psychological changes, the introduction and acceptance of concepts such as 'self-reliance', 'social justice', 'mass participation in the decision-making process', 'grassroots democracy' and 'decentralization'. It has also involved the mobilization of development initiatives at village, town and district administrative levels in terms of providing new skills and new forms of knowledge that can lead to the physical transformation of the environment. Quite clearly, then, Africa is on the verge of releasing her peoples' inner forces for real development.

The attempt to lay emphasis on political development now or at least complement economic initiatives with a new framework of political action does not, in my view, seek to project the white man, his culture and money as centres of emulation or excellence. It does not encourage development initiatives that do not originate from African traditional thought and practice. It is an inner search for strength to forge a national consensus on a common image and identity for the continent while crating corresponding values that ought to give meaning to the concept of a self-reliant people. It is only in this context that development aid in Africa can become effective, meaningful and significant. Development aid that merely opens our eyes to possibilities in other lands and cultures to the total neglect of ours, a situation that creates 'dependence development' in the thinking and behaviour of our people is bound to end in failure. Development aid that recognizes the responsibility to promote a coherent strategy for national consensus and, in the end, motivates and mobilizes the collective energies of African people towards their *own* vision of positive transformations in the environment; development aid that opens a people's eyes to their inner strengths and makes it possible for them to exercise initiative and sense of responsibility towards themselves and others certainly constitutes development to mankind.

In effect therefore, African states today are caught up in the whirlpool of developing basic ideas, values and assumptions in the political, cultural, social and economic fields, that may unite all shades of opinion, and which in turn, may significantly shape the basis for collective national policies and development strategies. Consequently, although aid for development, particularly in the industrial, scientific and technological fields in Africa is important and desirable, it may nevertheless have no impact on African societies unless the primary question of consensus has been settled by Africans themselves. Development aid that is not designed to support such efforts towards institutional stability and ideological coherence based on consensual values, may prove to be futile in the end. This paper would therefore suggest that aid in Africa should recognize that the most important developmental issue in Africa today is the establishment of a national consensus. When development aid becomes a force of fusion, a point of integrating and translating both the political and economic aspirations of Africans into reality in their modernization process, only then will it be effective. Thus, unless development aid is emphasized along such lines, it will continue to fail in its obsession with manipulative designs.

NOTES

1. Similar views have been expressed in an editorial article on "The Changing role of the Bank," in West Africa. No. 3541 (July 8th), 1985, p. 1355.

2. According to a correspondent in West Africa. No. 3542 (July 15th), 1985, p. 1408, from 1980-84, the Continent's external debts reached an estimated $150bn in 1983 and $158bn in 1984 both of them representing about 190 percent of Africa's exports of goods and services. The debt service alone is estimated at about $12bn a year.

3. Interestingly, an editorial in West Africa. No. 3541 (July 8th), 1985 stated inter alia, "Under pressure from stagnating economics, mounting debts and creditors too anxious to reform them into their own image, the Africans began to discern a new imperialism . . . . And the IMF is seen as the main agent of this new imperialism."

4. The O.A.U. Conference of Heads of State in Addis Ababa held in July 1971 passed a resolution affirming the right of all African countries to exercise permanent sovereignty over their natural resources, specifically mentioning 'oil and other minerals'. The same resolution according to a correspondent in West Africa magazine No. 2822 (July 16th), 1971, also denounced the economic and political pressures which certain developed countries were "attempting to bring to bear on African countries with a view to threatening their development efforts and hampering them in the exercise of their sovereignty over their natural resources."

5. "The Lagos Plan of Action" adopted by the O.A.U. in 1980 was the first landmark in Africa of this attempt to fuse economic nationalism and political nationalism, for it recognized the fact that the only hope for the continents development lay in greater cooperation and self-reliance in the economic field.

6. Part of the inspiring speech delivered by Dr. Kwame Nkrumah at the Old Polo Grounds, Accra, Ghana at the birth of a New Nation — Ghana — at midnight before 6th March 1957.

7. This is a lecture presented on Martin Luther King Day, January 19th, 1987 at the King Library in Accra, Ghana and published by the U.S. Information Centre, Accra Ghana. The text was delivered by Jack P. Greene, an Andrew W. Mellon Professor in the Humanities at

Johns Hopkins University, U.S.A.

8. Greene, J.P., p. viii.

9. See Davies, G. *The Early Stuarts 1603-1660*. London: Oxford University Press, 1959.

10. Reischauer, E.O. and A.M. Craig. *Japan: Tradition and Transformation*. Tokyo: C.E. Tuttle Company Inc., 1981, p. 2.

11. Reischauer, E.O. and A.M. Craig, *ibid*, p. 2.

12. Clark, G. *The Japanese Economy*. (Orientation Seminars on Japan No. 3) Tokyo: Japan Foundation, 1981, p. 6.

13. *West Africa*. No. 3542 (July 15th), 1985, p. 1407.

14. This period saw the establishment of the Economic Commission for Africa (ECA), the African Development Bank (ADB), ECOWAS in 1975, the Economic Community of Central African States (CEEAC) in 1983 and the wide-ranging Preferential Tariff Area (PTA) which stretches from Southern Africa to Ethiopia and Somalia. Sub-groupings within these Regional Economic groups include C.E.A.O. and Mano River Union which exist within ECOWAS and the Southern African Development Co-ordination Conference (SADCC) which also exists within the P.T.A.

15. See, Moremi, C. "Poor Aid and the Poor," *West Africa* No. 3451 (July 8th), 1985, p. 1365.

16. *West Africa*. No. 3542 (July 15th), 1985, p. 1409.

17. *West Africa, ibid*, p. 1409.

18. Hirabayashi, E. and others. "The Focus on the 'Other 40%': A Myth of Development," in *The Third World Review*. Vol. 2, No. 1 (Spring), 1976, p. 61.

19. Hirabayashi, E. and others, p. 61.

20. See *West Africa*. No. 3541 (July 8th), 1985, p. 1355 where its editorial on "The Changing Role of the Bank" expressed the following related view, namely that "the World Bank's loans, for instance, are usually administered externally, and purchases are by international tender, which almost always means that all inputs are imported, even where local capacity to supply them exists."

Trilateral Aid: Portugal's Aid Relationship With Its Former African Colonies

Shirley Washington
Ohio University

The concept of trilateral cooperation with Africa represents a pragmatic approach to Portugal's limitations as an aid donor nation. Severely circumscribed by a weak industrial base and a fragile economic structure, Portugal cannot assume a comparable role to that of Britain or France with their former colonies. Yet, Portugal does seek to retain some important influences in its former African colonies beyond the use of Portuguese as a common official language. Britain and especially France have used their economic dominance in terms of aid and trade to retain close political links with their former colonies which some would label neo-colonialism. Using its long African colonial experience, Portugal seeks partnership with the richer nations of the West to promote joint development projects in its former colonies. The Portuguese recommend their own cheaper, less sophisticated technology as more commensurate with modern African needs, and their allies seem to have accepted the idea.

The purpose of this paper is to examine the implications of Lisbon's trilateral aid, the success or failure of its implementation, and the response of the potential recipients. Most of the former colonies seem to have quietly acquiesced to the concept as an immediate convenience, although Angola has vigorously rejected any pretensions on Portugal's part to act as interpreters of its national needs.

While Lisbon's view of the matter is one of "facilitator" in the relations between Africa and the West, ironically, it puts Portugal back in the same middleman role that it had assumed during the latter years of colonialism and the dictatorship.

Portuguese Main Lines of Foreign Policy Concerns

That it rest firmly in the camp of Western Europe which includes democratic parliamentary government and adhesion to the EEC and NATO.

To be accepted by the West as a valuable member capable of bringing much of its experience in parts of the world less known and can serve as a useful interlocutor.

To play a role as a valuable intermediary in the North-South debate. It too seeks a new international order.

To seek a close relationship with Africa, a re-engagement, rapproachment, that approximates mutually beneficial relations and even privileged relations with former colonies somehow mirroring those of their European former colonial counterparts.

To continue a valuable relationship with the U.S. in terms of trade, emigration and a variety of issues where there is broad agreement on such trilateral assistance with Africa.

Portugal's Fear of Being Replaced by Others in Africa

Portugal fears losing its presence and influence to others in their former African colonies, not only to the Soviets and the Cubans, but especially to the French whose experience with wooing African elites (i.e., the presence of Lusophone African nations at annual meetings of the French Community as observers), and the Brazilians, their linguistic rivals, the Italians, the Spaniards, the British and even the Americans. From the Far Right along the political spectrum to the Far Left, nothing pains Portuguese leaders more than the sight of other foreigners playing critically important roles in their former colonies. It is a consequence of the discontinuity in their decolonization process. Thus, trilateralism as a concept of cooperation as postulated by Mario Soares when he was Prime Minister, is viewed as a practical method for assisting the African nations for whom there is some Portuguese moral responsibility while retaining a presence despite Portugal's inability to deliver the massive aid required because of its own enduring economic crises. But while Lisbon views itself as one of "facilitator" in the relations between Africa and the West, ironically, it puts Portugal back in the same middleman role that it had assumed during the latter years of colonial rule and those of the dictatorship, as mentioned earlier.

The European Economic Community sees an important role for Portugal to play in its former colonies, and views that participation almost as a right in accordance with that of France which has asserted such rights for years. Such relations are expected and were almost a requirement for membership. Certainly, it was a motivating factor for Portugal's search for good relations with Africa, and now that it has entered the EEC, it is expected to deliver. The question is whether nations like Angola will cooperate with this notion. In any case, trilateral cooperation is especially appropriate within this context of wealthier, more industrialized partners.

Rational For Cooperation with Africa

As previously mentioned, Portugal accepts — within limits — moral responsibility for assisting the former colonies in their development. There are some potent economic benefits. Africa is the only area of the world with which Portugal has a favorable balance of trade. There is an even greater potential if Portugal has the capability. The limitations are the persistent lack of capital, and the ability of the smaller nations to repay their debts which have been up till now mainly in the form of lines of credit for items bought in Portugal.

The Role of Language

One cannot underestimate the role of language in this matter. It is the tie that binds. Language itself creates a kind of dependency even in self-proclaimed revolutionary nations. However, it is the language of the elites since one of the worst features of Portuguese colonialism was the extremely low level of educational opportunities for the colonized Africans. In their daily transactions, most still speak their native languages and some poor Portuguese. Nevertheless, all official business is conducted in the colonial language and this is a critical hook. With language often go imagery and ways of thinking despite the intended revolutionary discontinuity with the colonial past.

Rationale for Cooperation With Portugal by the Africans

Africans seek a positive role for democratic Portugal in their economic development, and consider a good working relation as very important. Moreover, they view their former colonizer as primarily responsible for the years of war, exploitation, and neglect that have left their nations underdeveloped. Moreover, Lisbon is a storehouse of knowledge about Africa. It contains vital navigational maps of each country, for example. It has a tropical medical center, an overseas museum of priceless archival material on each country, and is a natural source for education and training. For years they have had access to the services of *cooperantes* or skilled workers whose past experience in Africa make them more adaptable to the difficult living conditions there.

No African Fear of Neo-colonialism

Jaime Gama, the former Foreign Minister, noted that "Portugal is the only country which decolonized and did not maintain neo-colonial relations with its former colonies." The Africans, while agreeing, would attribute it more to an historic fluke than a deliberate policy. It was really the result of the revolutionary nature of the decolonization process which led to the unusual discontinuity in administrative and economic structures. African leaders do not fear a neo-colonial relationship because they perceive Portugal as incapable of pursuing such a policy successfully due to its own political and economic weakness. Moreover, the Africans take very seriously their own ideological commitments to non-exploitation and continued vigilance against neo-colonialism developed during their long armed struggle. However, a leading theorist, the late Amilcar Cabral, noted that they never lost sight of the fact that they had fought against the machinery of oppression and not against the Portuguese people whom they regarded as fellow victims of the dictatorship. They were well aware that many Portuguese democrats had been either exiled, imprisoned, killed, or bullied into silence. In the post-independence era, they were careful to maintain good relations with democratic forces in Portugal with whom there was a natural empathy and remembering that it was only with a revolutionary and democratic Portugal that independence negotiations were possible. They recognize Portugal's usefulness in persuading its Western allies to support some of their foreign policy concerns. For example, while Prime Minister, Mario Soares wrote a letter of protest to Jesse Helms in trying to dissuade him from pushing his amendment in U.S. Congress to impose mandatory and unreasonable restrictions on Mozambique in order to qualify for foreign aid.

The Africans realize the limitations of cooperation with Portugal in terms of its frequent government changes and its inability to supply massive capital for aid and investment due to the relatively low levels of their former colonizer's own development. What is a more unforgiveable source of frustration is Lisbon's almost legendary bureaucratic inertia which is centered in the Department of Cooperation, a part of the Ministry of Foreign Affairs.

Governmental Institutions of Portugal's Foreign Policy Establishment

The General Direction of the Department of Cooperation handles the daily administration of foreign aid programs and pays the salaries of the *cooperantes* in the field. These salaries are often in arrears causing unbelievable hardship for the workers abroad. The department is not only inefficient but steeped in the tradition of the stullifying bureaucratic practices of the Salazar regime. The Revolution never touched them. One could rather easily develop a great deal of sympathy for African students in training in Portugal in having to deal with them concerning the necessary paper work or receiving promised funds.

On the other hand, the Department of Economic Administration appeared to be run by more efficient staff who at least had some facts and figures readily at their disposal and could disseminate them in written fashion. They had generally good charts that give the volume of aid flows. If the figures were correct and actually took place, then the amount of aid to the former African colonies, with the exception of Angola, have been considerable and have grown over the years in broad areas of the economic sector. This whole bureaucratic structure is headed by the Secretary of State for Cooperation who is usually a career diplomat or high civil servant. One of the most colorful was Dr. Gaspar da Silva who was known as a militant for cooperation with Africa. He was a no-nonsense man who clashed with the minister over the ambiguous practices of the political regime and was quietly uprooted to the ambassadorship in Paris. No doubt, the uncertainty of the chief executive officers' longevity contributes mightily to the evasions of the bureaucratics within the Department. Continuity must suffer grievously in such a system. Thus, there is more dynamism outside the governmental structures proper in foreign aid.

Non-Governmental Institutions of Foreign Aid in Portugal

The most prominent and almost semi-governmental institution is the Calouste Gulbenkian Foundation, headed by Azevedo Perdigao, who was a close friend of the late founder who was born in Eastern Europe but found refuge and fortune in Iraqi oil under the auspices of the Portuguese. His gratitude resulted in an enduring institution of philanthropy that could rival the Ford Foundation in scope and diversity. Dr. Sa Machado, the Administrator, is a former Foreign Minister and former political leader of one of the rightist parties. The Foundation attracts the best and the brightest in and out of Portugal whose main objective is the proliferation and propagation of Portuguese language and culture.

Gulbenkian figures regularly into any foreign assistance that the Portuguese government may offer to new nations. The foundation has a specific department devoted to the former African colonies headed — until his recent death — by an Angolan emigré, Dr. Mario Antonio de Oliveira. Gulbenkian has a myriad of functions such as scholarships, research fellowships, grants to institutions of health, education and general welfare and even publishing. Its annual giving runs in the millions of dollars. The Lusophone African nations respect it and have come to rely on it in many of their social development projects. Gulbenkian hosts many conferences, cultural exhibitions and other events in Lisbon and abroad and has a magnificent library and public garden.

Another very prominent organization which has grown up since the revolution is the Amilcar Cabral Information and Documentation Center or CIDAC. No comparison to Gulbenkian in wealth, but CIDAC more than makes up for it in dedication and solidarity with the peoples of the former colonies. Though Luis Moita, a former Catholic priest, Left-wing radical, and member of earlier revolutionary military governments, is its chief spokesman, CIDAC is a cooperative of equals. The membership consists of volunteers who contribute their time after their regular job to run the center. It acts as a clearing house for information, interviewing *cooperantes* for the various countries, holding seminars on issues involving the Third World and especially Africa. CIDAC provides such services as language training and orientation sessions of foreign *cooperantes* on their way to their assignments in Africa. It too has an excellent library of periodicals from all the former colonies since independence. It now publishes its own thought-provoking monthly magazine, *Terra Solidaria* on Third World political and economic matters.

Trends in Portuguese Foreign Assistance to Africa

Foreign assistance modalities reflect the political character of the regime. In the earlier revolutionary period immediately after the 25th of April, 1974 through to the adoption of the post-revolutionary constitution in 1982, much of the aid was actively initiated by the government to the recipient governments. There was a period of confusion during those years reflecting the moderating nature of the trends in politics as the standard liberal democratic parliamentary system took hold, and with it a move toward the important entrepreneurial sector. This was the period of anxious maneuvering to enter the EEC and the search for a role for Portugal within Europe and away from the earlier flirtation with being part of the Third World. It was within this context that the idea of trilateralism surfaced. It was clear that Portugal could not play the powerful benefactor of massive aid to its former colonies and yet those new nations desperately needed such assistance. The idea arose of Portugal, the facilitator between Europe and Africa as proffered by Soares while still retaining some dignity and presence for Lisbon on the world stage.

While the idea was generally accepted as pragmatic, Portugal exhibited no intention of relinquishing its cultural patrimony in Africa. The Portuguese appear to have gone on the offensive in defense of their language and culture. This offensive has been especially taken up by the Northern region and particularly the industrial center of Oporto. The private sector has been actively engaged in promoting business interests and instituting new cultural ties with Africa. It should be stated from the outset that underlying these activities are a set of assumptions about the alleged values of Portuguese culture that the Africans may or may not share and has yet to be proven that these have any real intrinsic purpose for them unless it is closely bound up with tangible forms of development assistance. Beside the very important aspect of sharing a common official language, the idea of certain shared common interests may indeed be resting on very shaky foundations for the Portuguese and Africans. Yet there is a certain effort to create a new myth in order to promote a deeper form of cooperation that perhaps can overcome a rather sad historic past and current ideological reality.

In any case, the Portuguese seemed to have embarked on a rather helter-skelter institution-creation binge. Only time will tell whether these will bear fruit or be paper phantoms. The Afro-Lusitanian Foundation was created in Oporto in March 1986 as an outgrowth of a forum held there chiefly concerned with the development of the Northern region, and the related cooperation with the former African colonies grew out of it. It has business origins. Its stated objective is to motivate the creation of a broad community of nations which speak Portuguese and have common interests to protect. Inspired by the election of Mario Soares to the Presidency and the new government of Cavaco Silva, favorable conditions were deemed to have been created to have non-ideological cooperation and dialogue for future relations. Early analysis would suggest an implicit Soares project with neo-colonial pretensions which are bound to have little impact on the reality of those extremely poor nations, two of them (Mozambique and Angola) are in the throes of civil war. Nevertheless, the press conference announced a new foundation created for cultural, social and economic relations with those nations. But it also went beyond the former colonies to any African country where there is an important Portuguese presence like the 8,000 or so who reside in Zaïre.[1]

A less dubious and more thought-provoking entity was created in 1985 with the long title of the Luso-African Institute for the Development and Activities of the Population. It is a private, non-profit, non-partisan, secular institution with an international vocation. It proposes to give technical and scientific assistance in the areas of social-economic development of the peoples of the Third World either through national or international organizations, private or government. Probable areas of interests are the environment, public health, education, agriculture, housing and industrial development. The stated objective is to place Portugal's considerable cultural, scientific and technological knowledge at the service of Africa. The President of the new institute is a university professor of Physics and also President of the National Institute of Meteorology and Geophysics. Mendes Vitor had collected data during the colonial era. His major complaint, "In the past ten years of African independence, we have allowed ourselves to be overtaken by others." He stated that his proof was that international agencies routinely ignore the role of the Portuguese reflected by the small number of them present in them or working in the field for them. Yet some 80,000 Northern European technical experts are working and absorbing great quantities of funds earmarked for Africa. He implored his nation to rethink the importance of the Portuguese presence in Africa.[2] It was a clear expression of Portuguese sensitivity on the subject.

Portugal's Trilateral Strategy — a Partial Success

Lisbon has enjoyed partial success with various Western partners in providing the intermediate personnel in a number of development projects in the former African colonies. The most successful has been with the Germans and the Americans.[3] A new foundation has been created to do development projects in Portugal, but it has freed funds for Portugal to play a greater role in Africa in joint projects. A development bank has been set up in Lisbon in which capital from the United States, Canada, and West Germany would be channeled to African projects where Portuguese workers have a major role. Britain was studying supplying credit to the bank. The United States has already started work in Guinea-Bissau and Cape Verde under these arrangements. Holland, Italy and France have already been working on specific projects in Africa jointly with Portugal for some time now. Portuguese as intermediate personnel are often at the insistence of the African nations. A decidedly non-cooperative nation in this philosophical approach is Brazil which views itself as a linguistic, rival. Gaspar da Silva, the former Cooperation Secretary minimized Brazil by stating that if it didn't want trilateral cooperation, Portugal had other partners.[4] Of more importance, has been the new opportunities for Portuguese businessmen in Africa under the Lome Convention since their country's entrance in the EEC.[5]

The Persistent Problem

For the most part, despite the grand strategy, Portugal has failed rather badly in the overall effort to aid Africa and gain some benefit from it for Lisbon as well. The same fundamental problem exists. The lack of adequate financing has caused the Portuguese consultants and experts to have been beaten by the competition outside with regard to Africa. In the first place, the general demand for consultants has dropped in recent years, probably reflecting the effects of the world economic crisis which has had an even more devastating effect on Africa. As resources for even the wealthier donor countries dries up, there is greater pressure to use their own personnel. Jose Araujo Coutinho, the President of the Portuguese Association of Consultants and Planners lamented the inability of his members to successfully compete with their counterparts of other nations with development proposals that they could finance. He could not blame the Africans who must consider proposals most likely to be sponsored by donor nations with the financial ability to back them up.[6]

A report by the prestigious Institute of Development Studies was even more pessimistic in concluding that within the institutional framework of Portuguese cooperation with Africa, the situation posed a very poor model. That despite the rather rosy assessment made by the experts of certain organizations, the reality is that Portuguese efforts had failed principally for one reason and that wasthat they were severely limited by the admitted scarcity of financial resources. That depending on a third party is extremely hazardous and unreliable and deprived Lisbon of its own initiative.[7]

Conclusions

I have adopted a saying for some time now which still unfortunately holds true even in the present situation, Portugal, the first into Africa, the last out and the least to show for it. If one accepts Walter Rodney's theories that much of European trade and the Industrial Revolution was fueled by its contact with Africa and Asia, and I do, then, it stands self-evident that though Portugal had a critical historic role as having discovered much of the world for Europe centuries ago, and for better or worse, brought diverse peoples together in the most systematic way during the era of the great discoveries, enjoyed a brief moment of glory, and then was overtaken by other European imperialists.

In the current situation in which Portugal could play a much more beneficial role mainly due to the near symmetry in relationship with Africa, it stands to be overtaken again because of its own poverty and underdevelopment. Perhaps its membership in the EEC will help but that remains a long way off. In the meantime, there is a tremendous amount of goodwill and sincere interest in mutual cooperation between the Africans and Portugal. Unfortunately, the real problems seem to be outside of the control of all concerned.

My tentative conclusion is that Portugal and its former colonies can have exemplary relations and be a model in Euro-African relations if Portugal avoids any neo-colonial pretensions and maximizes those traits that have permitted that nation to live relatively harmoniously with diverse peoples over the past centuries and if Portugal's Western partners care to assist in that endeavor.

NOTES

1. "Fundação Afro-Lusitana Vai Nascer no Porto," *Diário de Lisboa*. (March 4th), 1986, p. 5.

2. "ILADAP Vai Estimular Cooperação em Africa," *Diário de Lisboa*. (July 31st), 1985, p. 4.

3. "Genscher Vai Analisar Cooperação Tripartida," *Diário de Notícias*. (October 16th), 1984, p. 5, and "Fundação Luso-Americana: Seis Milhoës de Contos por Ano," *o Jornal*. (January 1st), 1985, p. 38.

4. "Se o Brasil Não Quiser Cooperação da Portugal Tem Outros Parceiros para Africa," *Diário de Lisboa*. (September 28th), 1984, p. 5.

5. "Empresarios Associam-se para Cooperar com a Africa," *Diário de Lisboa*. (October 21th), 1986.

6. "Consultores Portugueses Batidos Pela Concorrência em Africa," *Diário de Lisboa.* (October 29th), 1985, p. 14.

7. "Esgotou-se Modélo de Cooperação com Africa," *o Jornal.* (April 18th), 1986, p. 16.

Social Paediatrics: Child Survival Strategies in the New Curriculum for the Developing World

Donald A. Hillman and Elizabeth Hillman
Memorial University of Newfoundland,
Makerere University and UNICEF,
Kampala, Uganda

During the past 20 years a great deal of our personal and academic effort has been devoted to the promotion, development, and participation in medical AID to African children. Friends and colleagues have been skeptical about our activities, pointing out that the Governments of the countries we are trying to help are unstable and sometimes corrupt, and that the seemingly uncontrollable population explosion will only be increased by our efforts to reduce infant and childhood mortality and morbidity. They also remind us of unmet medical needs in Canada particularly in remote areas including the North, and our responsibilities to Canadian children and to our own families.

We feel that a critical assessment of these projects justifies the personal and financial investment made by the Canadian Government, the participating Canadian Universities, and the participants themselves.

In support of this, we would like to review two completed programs in which we have been involved — one in Kenya and one in Uganda and, based on the successes and failures of these 2 programs, describe our plan to initiate a third program in Africa later this year.

The Kenya Program

The CIDA — McGill medical education program in Kenya was developed in the 60's at the request of the newly independent Republic of Kenya to establish its own medical school. Prior to this, all East African physicians were trained at Makerere University in Uganda. Canada, through McGill University, was responsible for the departments of Paediatrics and Medicine.

The medical school grew rapidly from its initial intake of 30 students in 1967 to 110 per year in 1973.

In 1973 postgraduate programs, three years in length, were started. The Paediatric program was based on the model established by the Royal College of Physicians and Surgeons of Canada. Previously, Kenyan doctors wishing to specialize went overseas, mainly to Great Britain.

The rationale for developing postgraduate training in Kenya included the following:

• Much larger numbers of trainees could be trained locally for the same cost as sending one or two students overseas.

• During training, the postgraduates would provide the essential elements of clinical service, teaching, and research that are features in Canadian teaching services.

• The knowledge, skills, and attitudes gained by students during their training would be appropriate and relevant to the medical, socio-economic and political conditions of their future practice as specialists in Kenya.

• The very real possibility of "brain drain" might be avoided.

The thorough and extensive evaluation of this program by Dr. Eva Rathgeber was disappointing to the participants and to McGill, for the western medical school model appeared to have failed to produce the physicians appropriate for the health care needs of Kenya. The evaluation revealed that many of the early graduates were planning further training or academic appointments outside of Kenya.

However, a follow-up of the paediatric and child health trainees of this Kenyan program (reported last year at the annual meeting of the Canadian Paediatric Society) provided a much more favourable view of the long term impact of the program.

TABLE 1
CIDA/McGILL/UNIVERSITY OF NAIROBI
67 McGILL MEDICAL PAEDIATRIC GRADUATES (KENYAN)
PRESENT EMPLOYMENT

Ministry of Health	28	
University of Nairobi		
i) Teaching	11	
ii) Health Services	3	
City Council	2	— 80%
Armed Forces	4	
Mission Hospitals	1	
Research Institute	3	
Private Practice	11	15%
Left the Country	4	5%
Total	**67**	

Up to the end of 1986, 78 physicians had successfully completed the 3 year paediatric training program at the University of Nairobi. Sixty eight of these (see Table 1) were Kenyans, and the remainder came from other East African countries.

Fifty three physicians (80%) remain in the public sector working for the Ministry, the University, City Council, Missions, or the Research Institute. Only eleven (15%) are in private practice and four (5%) have left the country.

The findings of the paediatric program indicate that the Canadian input into Kenyan medical education was successful and laid the foundation for an effective paediatric and child health service.

The Ugandan Program

The Ugandan program, completed in April 1987, was developed at the request of Makerere University in Kampala, to provide teaching support for the Department of Paediatrics and Child Health. The Makerere faculty had been decimated by the brutal Amin years and the disastrous sequence of unsuccessful Governments that followed. The major difference from the Kenya programme was that in Uganda the Canadian teachers were supporting an existing training program, while in Kenya they were developing a new program. The Kenyan program was entirely a McGill operation. The Ugandan program, administered by Memorial University of Newfoundland, enlisted senior paediatric teachers from most of the Canadian Medical Schools, with the strongest participation from Edmonton (8 participants) and Newfoundland (7 participants).

Although the Uganda program achieved its broad objectives of providing immediate teaching support and reinforcement of the Governments commitment to Primary Health Care by development of undergraduate and postgraduate training in social paediatrics, the country's political instability, and the financial insecurity of our Ugandan counterparts limited our achievement of outreach programs and faculty development. In spite of these problems our program has been effectively transferred to Ugandan colleagues. Process and impact evaluation, to be conducted in a few years, will judge its long term success or failure. One clearly successful aspect of this program has been its effect on the more than 50 Canadians whose Ugandan experience has provided new insights and skills strengthening their performance in Canada and their recognition of international health problems.

Primary Health Care: The Child in the Family

The third program which has been funded by CIDA to start in September 1987, builds on our experience with the previous two East African programs. This program will involve a paediatric/child health faculty from four East African countries in developing a Primary Health Care (PHC) curriculum focused on the child in the family. The training of Faculty will take place in Africa, with an African program manager. Our role at Memorial University will be to coordinate the program, facilitate the establishment of an appropriate curriculum, and manage the overall funding, reporting and evaluation.

The participating African Universities will select the trainees who will become their PHC teachers and who will be assured faculty appointments during and after their nine-month training. Teaching and training will take place in each of the participating African Universities with each trainee rotating to two countries outside their own University.

The design of the curriculum and the strategies to be used will be decided by the participating Universities during an initial workshop in which the Chairmen and trainees of the African Universities will meet with Canadian educators. A second workshop will provide an opportunity to modify the initial design if necessary, assess progress, and make ongoing plans. The recognition of the need for management skills, and improved communication will be a major part of this new program.

In reviewing these programs and planning for the future, we feel it is important to stress the following:

- We must establish a partnership, not a charity, in which both partners know all the details of the program including commitments of time and finances. Any changes in the program should be understood and agreed upon by all participants.

- The major objective should be the transfer of skills, knowledge and attitudes, when appropriate. The success of such a transfer should make the Canadian input redundant.

- On-site training should be practiced whenever possible. Bringing students or trainees to Canada for long periods weakens the African programs, it is extremely expensive and probably not cost effective, and it may not strengthen local centres of excellence in Africa.

- Modern communication techniques using tele-conferencing and/or computers will be essential in the support of the African programs and will strengthen the link with the sponsoring University.

In a truly successful program the objectives of all parties must be clearly defined, understood, and achieved.

Socio-Economic Development and Mental Health in Ghana

Angela M. Lamensdorf
University of British Columbia

This paper is meant to provoke reactions, thought, and research into several assumptions and hypotheses posed about the mental health system in Ghana. The system has not kept up with the general pace of social and economic development. Some of the reasons for its stagnation are discussed, and some suggestions towards improvement are made.

Social Change

Neuroses and psychoses have always existed in Africa. Although there are few African studies available concerning the prevalence of these problems in the past and present, epidemiological studies in North America have shown that substantial correlations exist between forms of psychopathology and poverty, feelings of powerlessness, low self-esteem, loneliness, social isolation, and social marginality (Albee, 1986). These feelings are known to occur among people who have removed themselves from traditional social support networks such as would occur in a move from rural to urban environments (Frank, 1973). Such feelings would also occur among people whose standards of living are low, thus making them unable to support themselves or their families financially. Finally feelings such as these can arise in people whose belief and value systems are riddled with conflicts.

Many Africans have experienced these feelings as a direct result of social change. Often changes have themselves been a result of the centralization of governments, changes in the old belief systems, industrialization and its associated economic restructuring (e.g. Lucieer, 1984-85).

Conflicts in Belief Systems

Perhaps the biggest crisis in the mental health area in Africa concerns conflicts in belief systems. Frank suggested (1973) that when people's ideas are not in consensus with those of their group members, they experience conflicts which they try to resolve with whatever skills they have at their disposal. Frank also argued that if help is sought for such conflict, the seeker would need to share many of the same values as the healer from whom help is sought, would need to believe in the same universe, the same reality.

To illustrate this, picture a person who has been educated in accordance with Christian values and beliefs, and yet has been brought up to believe in the traditional African lore. Again picture this person under a great deal of stress, who consequently complains of feeling unwell. In search of relief, this person first seeks help from the hospital. Mental health patients often first consult a physician. If the physician fails to provide relief, patients often turn to the church for prayers, and if that offers no help, they then go to a traditional healer. If traditional healers fail, the final stop is usually the Mental hospital (Danquah, 1983). In most cases, the church (usually non-conventional and evangelical) ascribes the causes of the mental impairment to demonic influences. On the other hand, a traditional healer's diagnosis often lies along the lines of an ancestor requiring pacification for wrong-doing by the patient or his family members, and on rare occasions, the symptoms may be deemed a call to serve the gods. Having come this far, trouble begins if the patient cannot accept this formulation of the problem because it violates Christian principles, or because he or she simply does not hold the same world view as the traditional healer. If healing can proceed only if the patient and healer share the same beliefs, then eventually the battle of values has to be resolved by the patient.

There may be more and more people who have to face this crisis now because of the increased proportion of literate or educated people. Often with education comes Christianity because schools teach "religious knowledge," and hold prayers at assembly. Given that this is the case in Ghana, why do some and not all Ghanaians who live in such a system develop a conflict of values? Is it the conflict of values that leads to the development of psychological problems, or do already existent problems compound the dilemma of which belief system to follow? It is hypothesized that unless one is challenged to choose a value system, one does not recognize the existence of a conflict in oneself. One would also be forced to choose "sides" if faced with therapy based on a religious set of beliefs, or even on a mechanistic world view. What avenues for therapy exist in Ghana to help in the resolution of such conflicts? This will be discussed in the last section below.

Economic change

What economic phenomena mediate mental health patterns in Africa, and Ghana in particular? African countries have suffered economic decline as the world economic growth slowed during the past two decades. As a result of this, and successive coup d'etats, there were mass emigrations from Ghana, especially of men of the low and middle income-earning classes.

Between 1969 and 1975, 40% of 85 patients who had sought "divine protection" from a traditional healer were female (Lamensdorf, 1985). This trend increased dramatically so that between 1979 and 1985, about 60% were now women. What accounted for this increase? It has been suggested that in the second period reported, the mass emigration of the men had led to women taking on the sole responsibility of heading families. To make this easier, to ward off illness, to ensure success in business ventures (these were reasons given by patients in the healer's case book), they now sought divine protection in ever increasing numbers. Lamensdorf postulated that those people who seek protection may do so because they feel insecure or because they feel the onset of a mood disturbance which is inexplicable in somatic terms. Thus the increase in the proportion of women seeking help for mild mental health concerns was possibly due to the increased stress and responsibilities they had to bear. This came about as a result of economic changes which led to the exodus of the male partners, leaving women to bear sole responsibility for their families.

Ghana's solutions: Past and present

The colonial administration established a Western-type psychiatric hospital in Accra, the capital city. Initially, this asylum was basically custodial in function and was brought into being by a legislative instrument signed by the Governor of the Gold Coast in 1886. In 1961, the hospital was expanded and moved into newer quarters. During the late 1950s and 1960s, it finally assumed the role of a truly therapeutic community. Sadly, however, the acute shortage of trained personnel and equipment has returned the hospital to its initial custodial role. Two other psychiatric hospitals in the country are in similar conditions.

The Ministry of Health in Ghana continues to use a psychiatric approach to mental health problems. The model followed is a bio-medical one in which the patient is kept in hospital for long-term drug treatment or, if possible, stays at home and visits the hospital periodically for more medication and case review; a kind of revolving door approach to psychiatry with no psychotherapy involved. Mental illness is therefore regarded almost solely from a physiological perspective.

With rapid population growth and lack of expansion in the health care system, the result has been over-crowding in the psychiatric institutions without enough staff to cater to the needs of patients. These factors, coupled with the fact that the psychiatric institutions are more custodial than therapeutic, have rapidly led to the development of symptoms of institutionalization in the patients. Many patients, unable to readjust to living in society, were therefore forced to return to the institution following discharge, making worse the vicious cycle of institutional congestion and over-stretched facilities. In response to this problem the Government designated to the Department of Social Welfare the job of rehabilitating patients after treatment. Although this was a shift to a more social outlook, it did not solve the problem because the logistical support needed to implement it thoroughly was not available. The reasons will be discussed below.

In the early 1980's, faced with a weak economy, with a famine caused by the failure of rains, and with the return of approximately two million Ghanaians who had been expelled from Nigeria, the Government turned in desperation to the public to ask for help in the mental health arena. The Medical School began a public mental health project in which psychiatric and public health nurses administered drugs to patients at home and visited them regularly to ensure that they were cared for. Although there were psychological benefits from these home visits, they were made essentially for medical and pharmacological reasons and no psychotherapy was offered. To its credit, however, the project was fairly decentralized and thus available to the inhabitants of rural areas.

At the community level, help also came from churches and business corporations, which adopted wards within the Accra psychiatric hospital. Members of these institutions provided simple logistic (e.g. cleaning detergents, curtains, books, vitamin tablets, and wall paint) and social support by visiting the ward and establishing relationships with the patients.

Evaluation of the efforts undertaken by the Health Ministry

Like many of the schemes undertaken by Governments of other African Countries in the past, the reasons for the failure of programs are not too difficult to find. Firstly the programs tend to be very large in scope and hence difficult to manage efficiently. Secondly, the state bears almost all of the health care costs of most of its citizens. As De Ferranti noted (1985), health services account for approximately five percent of total expenditure in developing countries and for approximately two to four percent of the GNP on average. As per capita incomes rise, health spending typically rises faster. For example, de Ferranti reported that in Ghana, approximately seven percent of the total expenditure of the government is allocated to health services and this cost is not recovered from those who use the services. This system favours urban over rural dwellers in that the health centers with the most facilities are often in or around urban areas and therefore more easily accessible to those who live there. There are also chronic financing crises in which funds available to Government officials fall far short of planned expenditure.

Thirdly, de Jong, de Klien, and ten Horn (1986) observed that health workers have hardly any knowledge of mental disorders, and on average recognize only about a third of patients with psychiatric disorders. Obviously, dependence upon untrained workers to provide care with the community is not very efficient or reliable. Clearly, more efforts should be made to make mental health an important part of public health training. At present, this is not the case, and the situation is further exacerbated by the chronic shortage of experienced psychiatrists and psychologists.

Fourthly, the problem of the conflicts of values is not unique to the patient alone but also affects the health workers. It is quite common to find health workers who are medically trained, yet believe in the traditional African interpretations of psychological disorders. Such a health worker is strategically placed to adapt the psychiatric model to the cultural beliefs and practices of patients in order to promote and facilitate therapeutic processes such as "expectant faith" (Rappaport and Rappaport, 1981). This can happen if training procedures encourage initiative in students, and instruction in ways to integrate traditional thinking into the mechanistic world view that psychiatry adopts.

The conflict of values is an endemic problem juxtaposed with our very rapidly changing social values and norms. It is the price we pay for the imposition of totally different value systems without regard for adaptability or understanding of the traditional explanations of health and disease.

Suggestions and Conclusions

The most discussed option open to African countries is the adoption of a system that integrates or blends the positive elements of traditional beliefs with modern medical knowledge. Such attempts have been made previously in Africa. For instance, in Nigeria, Lambo (1978) established a center which utilized traditional healers as consultants. In Ghana the Center for Research into Plant and Traditional Medicines also employs traditional herbalists as consultants. These are two very special and very rare cases. Rappaport et al. (1981) suggest that the reason that an integrated model has not been widely accepted may be attributed to scarcity of resources, mistrust of social scientific research, and a lack of respect for traditional healers on the part of classically trained psychiatrists.

What other models can be utilized which do not require a lot of money and which can incorporate already existing institutions? In Ghana, there is a national association of traditional healers. Although its members refuse to share knowledge, which they deem to be family secrets handed down from generations of ancestors, they are prepared to treat patients and to act as consultants if they will be paid as such. If psychiatrists and physicians are given a list of competent healers to whom they could refer patients who would benefit more from the traditional approach, then several goals could be accomplished. First, patients would deal with people who hold the same world view as they do. They would also receive care within their communities and not have to travel far if there is a competent healer close by. This would allow increased support by relatives. A list of competent healers could be assembled by the association of traditional healers and validated by the Ministry of Health at very little cost. Third, it would encourage the development of relations between the psychiatric/ medical communities and the traditional healers, and facilitate the exchange of knowledge and the building of mutual trust and respect.

As mentioned above, health workers, such as nurses, are often trained in medical and public health procedures. Training centers are therefore already in existence. Special instructions could be provided for specialization in psychological disorders which would emphasize the early detection of psychopathology. Of equal importance is training in alternative ways of diffusing the onset of pathology, for example by the creation of social support networks within the community, and showing patients how some of the current life stresses can be reduced with the resources available to them. Some simple, but very powerful, intervention tools such as relaxation through meditation — a concept which is not at odds with traditional thinking — could be encouraged, and ways could be found to integrate psychotherapeutic techniques into a cultural context. Because a form of cognitive restructuring (or guidance and counselling) is practiced by the elders of communities, health workers could set up a volunteer system of elders who could engage in consultation with troubled community members. Such health care workers would specialize in the mobilization of each community's human resources for the psychological good of each patient. Continuing in the same vein, it is time that African universities and medical schools incorporated courses in traditional health practices and beliefs into their health related curricula, as Tanzania has done (Rappaport et al., 1981).

Finally, African governments must look seriously at what seems to be the emergence of a culture of poverty. With the cost of living becoming higher and higher, and the standards of living dropping for most Africans, Albee's (1986) words offer was a challenge:

> Mental illness patterns are often learned patterns of socially deviant behavior of idiosyncratic thought that result from stress, powerlessness, and exploitation. Prevention efforts aimed at reducing psychopathology will often require social change and a redistribution of power.

And this challenge goes to every African Government: is it not possible to redistribute power by making the vast majority of people believe that they can change things and make things better? Changes in attitude do come with increased control and participation in both political and economic infrastructures, where the economic structure promotes growth and private incentive, while at the same time, incorporating sufficient social support systems and safety valves; a difficult but not impossible task and dream to accomplish! Increased participation in the economic and social development by the majority should give us a sense of self-confidence, and greater pride in being African. A strong sense of self-identity defeats the urge to always need to depend solely on external sources — be it a supreme being or the developed world — for help. Self-confidence will allow us to overcome the tendency to blame misfortunes on colonialism (and all other 'isms'), no matter how guilty such external powers have in fact been in the past. Quo vadis Africa?

REFERENCES

Albee G. (1986). Toward a just society: Lessons from observations on the primary prevention of psychopathology. *American Psychologist, 8,* 891-898.

Danquah, S. A. (1982). The practice of behavior therapy in West Africa: The case of Ghana. *Journal of Behaviour Therapy and Experimental Psychiatry, 1,* 1-13.

De Ferranti, D. (1985). Paying for health services in developing countries: An overview. *World Bank Staff Working Papers,* No. 721.

de Jong, J.T.; de G.A. Klien, and S.G. ten Horn. (1986). A baseline study on mental disorders in Guinee-Bissau. *British Journal of Psychiatry,* Jan., 148: 27-32.

Frank, J.D. (1973). *Persuasion and Healing.* Baltimore: Johns Hopkins.

Lambo, T.A. (1974). Psychotherapy in Africa. *Psychotherapy and Psychosomatics, 24,* 311-326.

Lamensdorf, A. (1985). *Psychotherapy, a Glimpse Into The Old Ways.* Unpublished Manuscript, Department of Psychology, University of Ghana, Legon.

Lucieer, W.M. (1984-85). The bitter taste of liberty: A study in ethnopsychiatry. *Psychopathologie Africaine, 1,* 17-40.

Rappaport, H. and M. Rappaport. (1981). The integration of scientific and traditional healing. A proposed model. *American Psychologist, 7,* 774-778.

Introduction of Income Tax in Nigeria 1927-1936: The Historical Legacy

Rina Okonkwo
University of Nigeria

More than 5,000 teachers serving in Jos local government area in Plateau state have now become tax collectors in an effort to generate revenue for the sate government to pay their salary arrears. Teachers, mostly in primary schools, were posted to strategic points on major roads, throughout the motor parks, in order to collect the arrears of community tax from eligible tax payers in the council.[1]

The non-payment of income tax in Nigeria is a persistent problem which has not been solved since the introduction of income tax in 1927. In studying the history of the problem, one gains insight into cultural differences which may necessitate adapting the tax laws to local conditions. As a colonial import, Nigerian income tax laws still follow the 1927 law. There is the possibility that if the whole conception and machinery were Nigerianized, there would be more ready acceptance and compliance with taxation.

The history of taxation in Southern Nigeria was a succession of protests. In 1897, the installation of electric lights in Lagos was to be accompanied by the introduction of a house tax to pay for it. The united opposition of the three unofficial Nigerian members of the Legislative Council, the official law-making body for Lagos, was sufficient to end the tax idea.

The building of a pipe-born water system for Lagos, 1908 to 1916, was contingent upon the payment of a house tax.[2] The Lagosians preferred to do without pipe-born water if it entailed a tax. The Governor dismissed the petitions opposing the water rate. "The people of Lagos have invariably succeeded in escaping from paying for benefits conferred upon them and are not likely to relax their efforts." Past success in the case of electric lights inspired the Lagosians to persist in their protest. The governor advised the Colonial Office to proceed with the scheme. "Once the water rate is accepted, the task of introducing municipal reforms and improvements involving further rates will be lightened.[3]

The arguments against the property tax were similar to those voiced against income tax in 1927. With the large revenue from import and export taxes, the government should provide free services.

> considering the large sums spent for palatial residences and providing comfort and conveniences for officials, to say nothing of the large salaries provided for them . . . and all contributed by the people, water should be free. Monkey work, baboon eat.[4]

The Nigerians also repeated the cry from the American colonists in 1776, "No taxation without representation!" African representation in the government would ensure that tax money was spent for the public welfare. The alienation of the people from the government is a legacy of colonialism and continues in the military regime where there is no popular voice in taxation policy or government spending.

As the water rate protest continued, the educated elite withdrew and the uneducated elite and masses fought on. The white cap chiefs of Lagos declared, "We would rather die than admit taxation among us. Taxation is against our national tradition."[5] The people launched a campaign of civil disobedience, boycott of the water and boycott of outside markets to cripple the supply of produce to Lagos. When two Muslims were arrested for failure to pay the rate, a crowd rioted. The water rate protest ended in the arrests of the demonstrators and the suspension of the Eleko, the traditional ruler of Lagos and his white cap chiefs for failing to secure popular acceptance of the tax.

The Lagosians were cowered, but unconverted to the principle of taxation. Ever alert to the danger of new taxes, the Lagos press warned, "people will not submit tamely to any scheme of direct taxation without representation and a measure of financial control."[6] Despite such fears, there were no new taxes during Sir Hugh Clifford's term, 1919 to 1925. Clifford used delaying tactics, but could not convince the government to abandon the idea. He proposed a long period of education before the extension of taxation.[7]

Clifford's successor, Sir Graeme Thomson, proceeded with great haste to extend direct taxation to the five untaxed provinces in Eastern Nigeria and to Lagos. A few days after arriving in Nigeria, in November, 1925, Thomson circulated a proposal to all Residents in the untaxed provinces. There was no mention of educated Lagosians being consulted. Thomson forwarded his proposals to the Colonial Office in November, 1926 and asked for a speedy reply since he wanted the measures to be enacted before he went on leave in April.

Thomson's reasons for extending taxation to Lagos were not financial. The new governor, a disciple of Lord Frederick Lugard, extolled the moral benefits of taxation. Taxation was a concomitant of civilization, and the duty of the colonial rulers was to lead the Nigerians along the path of development. "There can be no true advance without taxation."[8]

Thomson conceded that there was no need for additional revenue. For the sake of uniformity and equity, he sought to tax all provinces. Lagos could not be left out. The colonial office gave Thomson its full support. "Your proposal marks a definite step in the advancement of the peoples of the Southern province."[9]

Thomson suggested a poll tax, a flat rate of ten shillings for all adult males in Lagos over sixteen years of age. The printing of the bill in the gazette occasioned a storm of protest. All the Lagos newpapers, all the civic groups, including the Women's League, the People's Union, and the Nigerian National Democratic party (NNDP) rallied to defeat the poll tax. When the bill came up in the special session of Legislative Council, in April, 1927, both Europeans and Africans, elected and nominated unofficial members were unanimous in their rejection of the tax. They considered the poll tax to be medieval, degrading, and unfair to the poor, a throwback to Northern Nigerian oppression. By opposing the poll tax, the African elected members of the Legislative Council, were fighting against *any* tax. In the face of strong opposition, the governor decided to refer the matter to a select committee.

The press hailed the defeat of the poll tax as a great victory. "The 4 and 5 April, 1927 will go down as red letter days in which unofficial members of the Legislative Council put up a very stubborn fight in defense of the rights and liberties of the people."[10] The select committee replaced the poll tax with a graduate income tax. The vote was seventeen to ten in the Legislative Council. Although the Liverpool Chamber of Commerce, Kitoyi Ajasa, nominated member from Lagos, and the traditional chiefs called for a return to the poll tax, no such action was taken. It was a pyrrhic victory indeed for the opposition.

The income tax ordinance came under immediate criticism from the Colonial Office in London. H.B. Bushe, a tax expert in the Colonial Office, noted that the Attorney General in Lagos had ignored the model income tax ordinance of 1922 which had been framed by Bushe and others to aid colonial governments in formulating their own income tax laws. The Lagos ordinance departed from the model law in taxing only males, when the recommended procedure was to tax combined income of husband and wife. The Lagos law inexplicably did not tax companies as provided for in the model law. Also no deductions were allowed for wife and children.

As an income tax ordinance, this is quite inadequate and unsatisfactory. I think
it is regrettable that they were ever allowed to put it in this form . . . I feel it is
about as difficult to criticize this as an Income Tax Ordinance as it would be,
shall I say, to criticize Tit Bits as a literary production.[11]

The Board of Internal Revenue in England also attacked the measure.
Section five provided for taking the average income of each trade to serve as
a taxable income for all members of the trade. The London group preferred
that each individual be assessed separately. They also objected to the tax
schedule which contained large jumps of one pound tax for each one
hundred pounds. The Board wondered why they were consulted after the
passage of the law.[12]

J.W.E. Flood of the Nigerian department of the Colonial Office explained to the Board of Internal Revenue that, "the ordinance had to be
enacted speedily to synchronize with the extension of direct taxation
throughout the Protectorate." They considered the income tax law,
"experimental."[13]

Curtis Crispin Adeniyi Jones (1876-1957), elected member of the
Legislative Council, led the fight against the tax in the Council. He spoke for
three-quarters of an hour in the final hearing before the bill was passed in
August, 1927. His main argument was that increased representation should
precede taxation. Although only males earning one hundred pounds per
annum were eligible to vote in the Legislative Council elections, the minimum chargeable income for income tax purposes was thirty pounds per
annum.[14] If the government contends we are not ripe enough for changes in
the constitution, we contend we are not ripe enough for payment of income
taxes."[15]

Samuel Herbert Pearse, Nigerian nominated member for Egba objected
to the failure to tax banks, corporations, and limited liability companies.[16]
The unofficial member for banking complained, "We should be able to
produce a better measure than this."[17] The Acting Attorney General
defended the bill. "The immediate object of the bill is to establish a
principle."[18]

Contrary to expectations, the enactment of the income tax law did not
result in violent demonstrations against the government. The peaceful nature
of the protest can be credited to the leadership of the Nigerian National
Democratic Party (NNDP). Organized in 1923 to contest elections to the
Legislative Council, the NNDP was a coalition of chiefs, imams, market
women, the non-literate, with a few wealthy merchants dominating the party
executive and controlling the selection of candidates."[19] The leader of the
party was Herbert Macaulay (1864-1946), often called "the father of
Nigerian nationalism." "Macaulay's position was unique, he identified

himself wholly with traditional groups and enjoyed their absolute confidence."[20]

Despite Macaulay's reputation for radicalism, he did not embrace violent solutions. In the case of the water rate protest, he appealed to the magistrate court, but when the judgement was against him, he paid the tax.

Now he counselled Lagosians to pay the income tax. "Any stubborn resistance of 'nothing doing' by way of payment would only end in 'payment on protest' one day. The water rate agitation is a living evidence of that probability."[21]

The NNDP sent a petition detailing their objections to the ordinance in January, 1928. The bill was judged "superfluous and unnecessary." With the large surplus in government treasury, there was no reason for new taxes. The NNDP judged that Lagosians were already paying taxes, the water rate and improvement rate, which were equivalent to taxes in the other parts of Nigeria. The petition also called for provision for deductions for wife and children such as existed in English tax law. They spoke of the need to distinguish between gross and net incomes. Finally they proposed a three year period of preparation before the law went into effect. The NNDP argued that African culture with its extended family system already made so many financial demands on its members that income tax was too great a financial hardship. "The individual has not yet been able to dry up the milk of human kindness in the nation with regard to family relationships."[22]

Instead of confrontation over taxation, the Lagosians may have adopted a stance of passive resistance. The Commissioner of Taxation reported in 1933 that although the collection of taxes from Europeans and Africans in regular employment was relatively easy, "considerable ingenuity is sometimes required in obtaining payment from the large floating population. The uneducated African is still unwilling to fulfill his statutory obligation and without legal coercion as a civil debt, a certain amount of litigation is inevitable."[23]

The *Lagos Daily News*, organ of the NNDP was outraged at the high-handed methods of the tax collectors. They accused the tax collectors of "beating illiterate taxpayers and . . . hand-cuffing them." "Instances are not wanting where women and their children were turned out of their living rooms and their rooms sealed in the absence of the breadwinner, who it was discovered after, had already paid his income tax for which he holds a receipt."[24]

When the beloved Sir Donald Cameron left Lagos, the new Governor, Sir Bernard Henry Bourdillon, with renewed vigor, sought to insure compliance by introducing harsher penalties to the income tax law. He waived the usual publication of the amendment in the gazette and gave only one week's notice before the vote came up the Legislative Council. The situation was urgent. "The law is being brought into contempt and disrepute by wholesale attempts at evasion which, in a great many cases, are successful." In the previous year, 1935, 11,000 persons were assessed to tax and 11,000 summonses were issued.[25]

The amendment called for fine or imprisonment if anyone failed to pay his tax within three months of assessment. The elected members of the Legislative Council and the NNDP objected that the measure was an infringement of personal and civil liberties.[26]

As the first income tax law in Nigeria, the Lagos law of 1927, amended in 1940 and 1943 became the model law for the other regions when they introduced their own laws in 1956. "The Lagos law reflected the social customs of expatriate taxpayers. The present Nigerian system of domestic circumstances is entirely of foreign origin."[27] Thus the law takes no account of polygamous status of many Nigerians. Children are often the responsibility of their mothers and yet it is fathers who claim them for income tax purposes. R.H. Whittam, a British tax expert who spent twenty years in Nigeria, who recommended the abolition of all tax exemptions as unsuited to Nigerian conditions. The simplification of the system would improve assessment.[28]

In an effort to adapt the tax machinery to Nigerian society, emphasis should be on the community, rather than the individual. The community tax establishes a lump sum payment for the community. Payment is proportional to individual income. The community tax is closer to what is already obtained in many communities in Eastern Nigeria. The members of a particular town tax themselves to build schools, roads, markets and other desired amenities. There is strong compliance because the villagers themselves do the collection and enforcement. The force of public opinion is brought to bear to insure that everyone pays his share.[29]

Decentralization of taxation to the local level and involvement of the community in tax assessment and collection are two ways to combat the problem of evasion. The remoteness of the state tax authority and its projects is a major factor in non-payment of taxes in Nigeria. It is important for the community to retain the greater share of the revenue collected and to use the money for visible desired development.

Another major problem which has defied solution is inability to secure compliance from wealthy Nigerians. As Governor Bourdillon admonished in 1938,

The great majority of well-to-do African unofficials grossly understate their incomes. This is not very creditable state of affairs. It is scarcely an encouragement to the poor taxpayer to pay even a small sum demanded of him when he knows perfectly well that the majority of his wealthier brethren are paying very much less than is really due from them.[30]

As in the early days of income tax, so today, the bulk of tax revenue comes from employees in the PAYE, pay as you earn system. Until the wealthy bear a greater share of the burden, many will be unwilling to comply and the tax revenue will remain inadequate.

Suggestions for insuring greater payment of tax among the wealthy include introduction of more taxes at source. A recent tax conference in Kano suggested taxation of interest rates directly from the banks. Taxes could also be levied on dividends directly from companies before they are paid to investors. The conference proposed a tax on wealth, but details were not disclosed.[31]

Although voluntary compliance is the key to a successful tax system,[32] prosecution of tax evaders may be useful. One handicap in litigation is that the courts are already over-burdened and thus slow to handle the tax cases. It has been suggested that special state revenue courts be created to deal with tax evaders and defaulters. "When a violation is effectively prosecuted and penalties are assessed, public confidence in the tax system is strengthened and potential evaders are discouraged."[33]

Other suggestions for increasing compliance among the self-employed are instrumental tax payment and advanced payment based on the previous year's income. The chronic problem of insufficient tax records is being aided by the attempt to computerize the data.

Sixty years after the introduction of income tax in Nigeria, the legacy of resistance is still very strong. As the community gains increased representation in collection and spending of tax money, compliance will increase. Decentralization of government will improve popular support and build appreciation for the necessity for payment of taxes. The process will take time, but the community-spirit of African society should be an asset if properly harnessed.

NOTES

The writer would like to acknowledge the financial assistance of a University of Nigeria Senate Research grant for aiding the research for this paper.

1. Ilelaboye, Jare. "Teachers Redeployed as Revenue Collectors," *National Concord.* (Nigeria), (April, 20), 1987, p. 1.

2. Okonkwo, R.L. "The Lagos Water Rate Protest, 1980-1916," *Eko Akete Journal of Lagos Studies.* (University of Lagos) Vol. 1, No. 1. In press.

3. Acting Governor of Nigeria to Secretary of State of the Colonies. London. (January 7), 1909, CO 520 77 46282.

4. Demesne. Letter, *Lagos Weekly Record.* (December 5), 1908.

5. Report of the Proceedings of Interview on Water Rate, quoted in Raymond Buell, *The Native Problem in Africa.* New York: Macmillan, Vol. 1, 1928, p. 662.

6. "Taxation and Finance in West Africa," *Lagos Weekly Record.* Editorial. (October 8), 1921.

7. Gailey, Harry A. "Sir Hugh Clifford," in *African Pro-Consuls.* L.H. Gann and Peter Duignan (Eds.). New York: Free Press, 1978, p. 282.

8. Thomson, Graeme. Governor of Nigeria to Secretary of State for the Colonies. Nigeria Confidential, CO 583 141, (November 18), 1926.

9. Secretary of State for the Colonies, London to Governor of Nigeria. Incoming Correspondence, Nigerian National Archives, Ibadan, Nigeria, CO 34 (January 24), 1927.

10. ..... "A Great Achievement," *Weekly Record.* Editorial. (April 9), 1927, p. 5.

11. Bushe, H.B. Minute. Nigeria Confidential, CO 583 152 (October 10), 1927.

12. Board of Internal Revenue, London to Secretary of State. (December 13), 1927, *Ibid.*

13. Flood, J.W.E. To Board of Internal Revenue, London. (November 8), 1927, *Ibid.*

14. Legislative Council Debates. (August 23), 1927, p. 50.

15. *Ibid.,* p. 53.

16. *Ibid.,* p. 58.

17. *Ibid.*

18. *Ibid.,* p. 46.

19. Sklar, Richard. L. *Nigerian Political Parties, Power in an Emergent African Nation.* Princeton: Princeton University Press, 1963, p. 47.

20. *Ibid.*

21. Report of the Proceedings of Magistrate's Court, Municipal Secretary v. Herbert Macaulay, September 5, 1916 in *Lagos Standard.* (September 13), 1916.

22. "Our Administrator," in *Lagos Daily News.* Editorial. (September 16), 1927, p. 2.

23. Nigerian National Democratic Party, Petition Against General Tax (Colony) Bill, 14 January, 1928, Macaulay Papers, Box 33, File 7, Manuscript Division, University Library, University of Ibadan, Ibadan, Nigeria.

24. Report of Commissioner of Taxation 1933, Macaulay Papers, box 33, File 8.

25. "The Brutality of Tax Collectors in the Colony," in *Lagos Daily News.* (September 13), 1932, p. 8.

26. Governor's Annual Report, Legislative Council Debates, Nigeria, (May 18), 1936, p. 42.

27. Legislative Council Debates, (May 19), 1936.

28. Whittam, R.H. "A Case for Uniform Tax," in *Daily Times.* (Lagos) (June 27), 1974, p. 7.

29. *Ibid.*

30. Whittam, R.H. "Personal Income Tax Administration," in *Ife Essays in Administration.* Colin Baker and M.J. Balogun (Eds.) Ife: University of Ife Press, 1975, pp. 119-123.

31. Governor's Report, Legislative Council Debates. (March 7), 1938.

32. "Seminar Calls for Tax on Individual Wealth," in *The Guardian.* (Lagos). (April 21), 1987.

33. National Tax Association. "Reconstruction of Foreign Tax Systems," *Proceedings of the Forty-Fourth Annual Conference on Taxation,* Sacramento, 1952, pp. 221-22, quoted in Milton C. Taylor, "The Relationship between Income Tax Administrations and Income Tax Policy in Nigeria," *Taxation for African Economic Development.* Milton C. Taylor (Ed.) London: Hutchison Educational, 1970, p. 521.

34. Rabiu, S.A. *Personal Income Tax in Nigeria: Procedures and Problems.* Lagos: John West Pub., 1981, p. 59.

Méthodologie pour l'évaluation des besoins des habitants à Lubumbashi (Zaïre)

Lelo Nzuzi
Université de Paris IV

[Les Tableaux et Graphiques se trouvent à la fin de cet essai, avant les Annexes — ED.]

Pour établir l'échelle de désirabilité des voeux jugés prioritaires par les usagers en prévision d'un aménagement de la ville de Lubumbashi, une nouvelle démarche méthodologique (jumelage des méthodes) fut conçue.

D'abord, un questionnaire ouvert évaluant les pratiques urbaines de la population fut administré à un échantillon de 600 habitants. Les résultats de cette enquête permit d'élaborer ensuite un questionnaire fermé sur les préférences-choix soumis à titre expérimental à 72 habitants.

L'Analyse en Composantes Principales (ACP) donna des résultats révélateurs. Pour la restructuration des quartiers spontanés et l'auto-construction guidée, contrairement à ce que l'on pourrait imaginer, la population préfère de loin les équipements de superstructures aux équipements d'infrastructures. Quant à la rénovation, inversement à ce que pensent les urbanistes, les zones qui méritent le bulldozer correspondent aux camps militaires et non aux quartiers spontanés. En matière de matériaux de construction, contrairement aux attentes, les usagers préfèrent de loin la brique adobe ou encore la brique cuite à la brique ciment.

a) Bref Regard sur la Ville de Lubumbashi

Par sa population et son rôle économique, la ville industrielle de Lubumbashi occupe la deuxième position en ordre d'importance après Kinshasa, la capitale du Zaïre. Située au Sud-Sud-Est du pays, elle est distante d'environ 3000 km de Kinshasa. Elle occupe donc une position excentrique à la fois par rapport au pays et à la province du Shaba dont elle joue le rôle de capitale provinciale *(fig. 1)* [*N.B.: Les figures, tableaux et graphiques se trouvent à la fin de cet article, avant les annexes.*]

Lubumbashi doit sa naissance en 1910 à la présence et à l'exploitation du cuivre par la société Générales des Carrières et des Mines (Gécamines). Alors qu'il n'y avait que la forêt claire au début du siècle à cet endroit, au fur et à mesure que s'implantèrent les usines de la Gécamines et les industries connexes, Lubumbashi draïna une population de plus en plus

219

importante malgré un hinterland peu peuplé. Il s'y est développé avec la présence de la Gécamines et des industries (société des chemins de fer, par exemple) qui sont venues s'y implanter une classe ouvrière bénéficiant d'importants avantages sociaux: camps des ouvriers, écoles, hôpitaux, cantines, etc . . . Une autre partie de la classe ouvrière fait par contre figure de sous-prolétariat urbain avec des salaires de misère, logée dans des vastes et précaires quartiers populaires que l'administration coloniale belge avait construite.

En 1921, Lubumbashi comptait 15000 habitants sur 600 ha. En 1950, la ville hébergeait déjà 100 000 habitants sur 17 000 ha dans des quartiers planifiés populaires comme Kamalondo, Kenya, Katuba. Depuis 1957, date de la construction du quartier Rwashi, aucun nouveau quartier n'a été construit par l'Etat. Le stock des logements sociaux est par conséquent insuffisant par rapport à la croissance démographique. Le cadre et la qualité de vie ne cesse de se dégrader depuis l'indépendance en 1960. La carence en logements sociaux est palliée par le développement en périphérie urbaine des quartiers spontanés (*fig. 2*): 2691 ha avec 243.220 habitants.

Ces quartiers spontanés (Kikalabuamba, Tumbototo, Tabazaïre, Bongonga, etc. . .) sont dépourvus de tout équipement d'infrastructure et de superstructure. En 1975, Lubumbashi concentrait sur 5000 ha, 430 000 habitants. Dix ans plus tard, cette ville qui continue à dévorer environ 200 ha chaque année, abrite environ 800 000 habitants sur une étendue de 7100 hectares. L'Etat est donc désarmé devant la dynamique effrénée de la ville et la crise urbaine ne cesse de s'accentuer.

Depuis une dizaine d'années, beaucoup de projets d'aménagement urbain furent mis sur pied pour amortir la crise urbaine. Certains furent pourtant réalistes comme par exemple celui du Bureau d'Etudes et d'Aménagement Urbain (BEAU) en 1975, mais ils n'ont pas abouti, à cause de la crise économique, à des réalisations concrètes. Lubumbashi, certes, est devenue un objet de réflexion par la richesse et la diversité d'études qui lui sont consacrées. Cependant, de tous ces travaux, aucun n'a à notre connaissance cherché à appréhender la manière dont le lushois perçoit sa ville et souhaite l'aménager. C'est pour cette raison que Lubumbashi fut sélectionné par nous pour servir de champ d'expérimentation sur une méthodologie de la recherche urbaine fondée sur le jumelage d'enquêtes: questionnaire ouvert et fermé.

II) Proposition d'une Methodologie D'Enquête

La pratique urbanistique lushoise est caractérisée par un urbanisme "descendant" comportant des déficiences méthodologiques qui l'invalident totalement. C'est pourquoi, cet article préconise une politique urbaine fondée sur le dialogue entre les urbanistes et les citadins d'autant plus qu'elle permettrait au gouvernement et aux urbanistes d'évaluer les voeux jugés prioritaires par les habitants.

Pour ce faire, l'article poursuit deux objectifs: proposition d'une démarche méthodologique fondée sur la consultation populaire, expérimentation de cette méthodologie sur la ville de Lubumbashi et présentation des résultats. L'hypothèse qui les sous-tend est que le jumelage d'enquêtes ouverte et fermée constitue l'un des moyens efficaces pour évaluer et hiérarchiser les besoins jugés prioritaires parceque l'enquête ouverte ou l'enquête fermée conduite séparément ne donne que des résultats généraux difficilement hiérarchisables.

En effet, les transformations socio-économico-politiques que connaît Lubumbashi ont déclenché une série de profondes mutations de son espace. Conscients de ces changements, beaucoup de chercheurs zaïrois proposent des modèles de développement urbain malheureusement limités parce qu'ils excluent les futurs usagers de leurs études. Par contre, lorsqu'ils les associent la déficience méthodologique se situe au niveau des techniques d'enquête utilisées, incapables de définir l'échelle de désirabilité des besoins jugés prioritaires par la population.

Par exemple pour évaluer les besoins des habitants, ils recourent séparément, tantôt aux techniques d'enquêtes ouvertes, tantôt aux techniques d'enquêtes fermées.

Avec des questions ouvertes, ils demandent à la population de porter un jugement sur la ville. En fonction des réponses, ils classent ces jugements et élaborent un projet d'aménagement. Or, il s'avère que ces jugements ou souhaits populaires récoltés pendant les enquêtes ouvertes sont d'habitude généraux, imprécis et ne permettant pas de brosser un tableau fidèle des besoins populaires selon une classification hiérarchique décroissante.

Par exemple, savoir que l'eau constitue un besoin populaire ne permet pas de comprendre si les habitants préfèrent l'eau courante domestique à la place de l'eau des puits ou des fontaines communautaires.

De même, quand les chercheurs zaïrois font usage des questions fermées, ils imposent leur perception et orientent les choix des usagers dans un cadre prédéterminé.

Il découle de cette défaillance méthodolgique une divergence entre les projets d'urbanisme et les besoins des citadins. C'est la raison pour laquelle nous préconisons le jumelage des enquêtes ouvertes et fermées réparties en dix étapes (*cf. Tableau 1*).

La première phase consistera à élaborer un questionnaire ouvert (1) destiné à un grand échantillon d'individus représentatifs de la population concernée. Ce qui suppose qu'il faudra définir au préalable une méthodologie d'échantillonnage rigoureuse car le nombre de répondants doit être important pour obtenir des résultats fiables et assurer l'exhaustivité de l'information

(2). La conduite de cette enquête se fera auprès de cet échantillon dans leur quartiers respectifs (3). Après les enquêtes, il faudra effectuer le comptage des fréquences pour définir les indicateurs fondamentaux en fonction des réponses les plus fournies (4), ce qui pourra faciliter la tâche des enquêteurs pour regrouper par item les réponses après le comptage fréquentiel (5).

Contrairement à certaines études antérieures, la consultation populaire ne s'arrêtera pas au seul comptage fréquentiel parce que le questionnaire ouvert ne servira qu'à évaluer les besoins généraux. Il faudra cependant restructurer les réponses de la première enquête. Le principe consistera à subdiviser ces items du premier questionnaire en choix alternatifs qui seront placés sur une liste à choix multiples que le répondant sera invité à classer en ordre de priorité lors de la deuxième phase (5).

Cette deuxième phase consistera à élaborer un deuxième questionnaire fermé, destiné à la seconde enquête (6) auprès d'un échantillon sélectif (7) dans différents quartiers (8) pour arriver à hiérarchiser et à interpréter ces besoins généraux. Les enquêteurs devront élaborer enfin un tableau à partir des réponses codifiées qu'ils soumettront à un processus de compilation croisée pour donner des tableaux de synthèse (9) et qui seront soumises ensuite à une autre compilation d'analyses factorielles destinée à définir les besoins jugés prioritaires par la population (10).

III) Experimentation Methodologique

3.1) L'Enquête ouverte

a) La séléction des quartiers d'étude

Comme les besoins populaires varient selon les quartiers, l'enquête avait séléctionné six quartiers correspondant à une coupe longitudinale de la ville de Lubumbashi: le centre-ville, le quartier industriel, le quartier populaire planifié des ouvriers de la Gécamines, le quartier populaire planifié de Kamalondo, le quartier spontané Kalebuka et le quartier sub-spontané Taba-zaïre.

b) La subdivision de chaque quartier d'études en 10 îlots d'enquêtes
Etant donné que les besoins populaires varient selon les îlots dans un quartier, l'enquête subdivisa chaque quartier en dix îlots de superficie égale.

c) L'échantillon-cible de 600 personnes
Puisque les besoins spécifiques sont fonction du sexe, de l'âge, de l'état-civil, etc. . . l'enquête avait reparti l'échantillon cible dans les proportions suivantes. Elle avait touché dans chaque îlot du quartier d'étude un(e) adolescent(e) de 12 ans et plus, un jeune garçon et une jeune fille célibataire,

un homme et une femme mariés, un homme et une femme célibataires, un homme et une femme âgés de 45 ans et plus. La compagne avait donc atteint dix personnes dans chaque îlot du quartier d'étude. Il y a eu au total 100 usagers enquêtés par quartier. L'échantillonnage avait donc permis de récolter au total 600 fiches pour l'ensemble des six quartiers d'étude.

d) Le questionnaire ouvert

Au questionnaire ouvert (*Annexe 1*) étaient ajoutés deux tableaux sémantiques des valeurs. Elles étaient attribuées à des éléments fixes de l'espace urbain. Les tableaux étaient centrés sur l'évaluation de la qualité de la vie et sur le degré de satisfaction des citadins face à la ville. Ils avaient pour objectif de comprendre les attitudes des citadins face aux éléments qui constituent leur espace urbain. Pour atteindre cet objectif, les citadins furent conviés donc à spécifier les éléments qu'ils jugeaient agréables ou désagréables, suffisants ou insuffisants.

e) La méthode de dépouillement

Il fallait compiler les questionnaires par comptage fréquentiel d'apparition des éléments recurrents de la liste dans chacune des réponses individuelles. Au terme de ce comptage des fréquences, les évaluations de la ville par type de rubriques furent regroupées en neuf thèmes: habitat et éléments de comfort, santé, voisinage, transport, espace vert, économie, culture et loisir, organisation-administration-Etat, lieux précis.

f) Les résultats

Le *Graphique 1* présente le degré de satisfaction des citadins face à la ville et les grands souhaits pour cette ville, le nombre de fois qu'ils furent évoqués et leur poids dans le total des réponses. L'analyse de ce graphique permet de retenir quatre catégories de réponses à travers lesquelles s'étaient dessinées les images des citadins sur leur ville. Elles furent resumées de la manière suivante: une attitude positive vis-à-vis la ville, une qualité de vie déficiente, un espace urbain agréable et attractif en dépit de la dégradation du cadre de vie, les grands souhaits pour la ville.

— La majorité des lushois aiment leur ville.

D'une manière générale, les lushois apprécient leur ville: 80% avaient déclaré l'aimer alors que 5,5% seulement avaient répondu ne pas l'aimer; 4,6% des enquêtés étaient sans opinion alors qu'une proportion de 9,7% avaient déclaré avoir une position mitigée.

Ces chiffres révèlent deux attitudes caractéristiques du lushois. D'abord, il aime bien sa ville bien que celle-ci soit dépourvue de certaines commodités urbaines. Ensuite, il fait fi des critères objectifs pour apprécier son cadre de vie, et pour en porter un jugement de valeur. Les deux attitudes observées auprès du lushois s'expliquent par le fait que sa ville possède une forte image symbolique au sein du pays. C'est cette vision gratifiante de s'identifier comme citadin de Lubumbashi qui lui tient à coeur. Sa ville, en effet, occupe le second rang en ordre d'importance, après Kinshasa, dans l'armature urbaine zaïroise. L'image symbolique de Lubumbashi est enivrante pour le lushois, même s'il déambule dans la crasse, même s'il n'arrive pas à échapper à une vie quotidienne médiocre. Le seul fait de participer à l'aventure urbaine le fait vivre.

— Une qualité de la vie qui se dégrade.

En règle générale, une ville doit fournir divers équipements d'usage quotidien à ses habitants. Or, il s'avère que pour Lubumbashi, la ville est loin de satisfaire aux besoins majeurs des usagers.

Les résultats montrent que le qualificatif "insuffisant" domine largement son antonyme "suffisant" avec 3654 réponses en regard de 1196 soit 75% contre 25%. Cela est dû au fait que Lubumbashi souffre d'une insuffisance notoire en équipements entraînant de ce fait le dégradation de la qualité de la vie des citadins. Ainsi par exemple, si le centre-ville et les quartiers planifiés populaires sont pourvus d'équipements, bien que surchargés, d'infrastructure et de superstructure; à l'opposé ce n'est pas du tout le cas pour les quartiers spontanés périphériques qui en manquent.

A la question de savoir s'ils étaient bien désservis par les équipements sanitaires, 77% des réponses les ont jugés insuffisants. A propos des tranports en commun, 90% ont exprimé un avis les jugeant également insuffisants. En ce qui concerne les lieux d'approvisionnement, ils sont aussi perçus comme insuffisants dans 69% des réponses données. Quant aux équipements culturels et de loisirs, 73% notent que les équipements scolaires au niveau primaire étaient largement débordés par la croissance démographique et migratoire, ce qui se traduisit par une évaluation globale de 73% pour l'ensemble. Qu'observe-t-on sur le terrain?

Devant cette crise urbaine, le pouvoir public à désarmé et abandonné la ville à son sort. Il s'y est par conséquent développé un urbanisme de débrouillardise populaire. Les équipements modestes se développent et se branchent à travers la ville par initiative populaire. Ainsi, voit-on se développer des dizaines des marchés spontanés populaires, s'organiser un réseau informel de transports en commun, se brancher des équipements scolaires, culturels et sanitaires. La ville voit aussi son habitat s'améliorer.

— Une ville agréable et attractive malgré la détérioration du cadre de vie.

Les réponses en faveur des éléments agréables dominent celles relatives aux éléments désagreables avec une fréquence de 4184 contre 1817, soit 70% de satisfaction pour 30% d'insatisfaction. même si dans les quartiers populaires planifiés, les logements sont éxigus, souvent jointifs, alignés en chapelet, coincés sur des parcelles minuscules, même si dans les quartiers spontanés les équipements font défaut, les enquêtes montrent qu'en régle générale, l'habitat est apprecié par 77% des répondants.

A la question de savoir si la population était sympathique, 65% des répondants trouvent qu'elle est conviviale. Le sens de la communauté lié à l'hospitalité explique bien les résultats. A Lubumbashi, personne ne peut souffrir de la solitude. Loin de déplorer le sens de l'hospitalité poussé à l'extrême, le lushois au contraire en tire un sentiment de solidarité, d'unité et de fierté. La permanente unité se manifeste aussi dans les associations qu'ils créent.

Les enquêtés (75%) apprécient également les places commerçantes parce qu'elles crèent de l'ambiance, du spectacle dans la ville. Le marché: lieu de cohue (l' "agora", le "forum"), était beaucoup apprécié par la population. Les équipements culturels et des loisirs contribuent aux aussi à entretenir l'ambiance urbaine. Dès que la nuit tombe les hauts-parleurs sortent sur la terrasse des night-clubs, diffusent une musique saccadée et ne s'arrêtent qu'au lever du jour. Pendant la journée, ce sont plutôt les disquaires qui prennent la rélève des tapages. Loin de souffrir des tapages quotidiens, des bagarres et des bruits dont les bistrots et les disquaires sont responsable, 71% des répondants tolèrent cependant la présence de ces équipements. Ils sont habitués à la nuit tombée de voir les hauts-parleurs sortir sur la terasse des night-clubs (*nganda*) pour diffuser une musique saccadée jusqu'au lever du jour.

Bien que Lubumbashi traverse une des pires crises urbaines depuis sa création, le score de celui qui est le principal responsable (l'Etat) n'atteint qu'un niveau désapprobation de 53% dans la faveur populaire. Toutefois, le chiffre ne réflète pas la réalité parce qu'en Afrique la libérté de parole n'existe point quand il s'agit d'émettre une opinion sur les pouvoirs publics. En réalité, plus nombreux furent les lushois qui désavouaient la politique urbaine gouvernementale.

En ce qui concerne l'animation dans la ville, nombreux trouvent qu'elle est attractive: 67% contre 33% ce qui veut dire qu'elle ne paraît pas attractive à l'unamimité. En effet, elle est repulsive, selon 55% des répondants, pendant la nuit. Ainsi par exemple, les espaces verts, les carrefours routiers et les emprises ferroviaires obtinrent respectivement 100% et 65% de jugements négatifs parce qu'ils ne sont pas éclairés la nuit. C'est dans ces endroits obscurs qu'opèrent les brigands désavoués par 67% des répondants.

— Les grands souhaits pour la ville.

Les propositions d'aménagement concernent l'habitat et les éléments de confort, équipements de transport, équipements publics et de loisirs, équipements sanitaires et de commerce.

Les citadins souhaitent que le gouvernement améliore l'habitat et y apporte des éléments du confort. Ils se soucient souvent de leurs conditions de logement. Ils vivent entassés dans des pièces surchauffées sous un toit de tôle ondulée qui craque dans la fraîcheur de la nuit. Ils déplorent aussi l'insalubrité des voies publiques dont les caniveaux sont bouchés par les ordures ménagères qui ne cessant de s'entasser. Ils souhaitent vivement que l'Etat crée à travers la ville les pôles d'attraction afin de désengorger le centre-ville.

— Les leçons tirées de l'enquête ouverte.

Les résultats prouvent que l'enquête ouverte offre un avantage, celui de rassembler et d'inventorier toutes les informations concernant les aspirations populaires. En revanche, elle pose des problèmes au niveau de l'interprétation en terme de priorités. Ainsi donc, le souhait le plus évoqué ne signifie pas qu'il est nécessairement le plus prioritaire des réponses.

C'est le cas notamment des besoins populaires à propos des écoles. Savoir que celles-ci sont reclamées par la population ne permet pas de déterminer si les préférences des habitants vont aux écoles primaires, secondaires, techniques ou aux écoles élémentaires.

En conclusion, bien qu'avec l'enquête ouverte on puisse explorer et énumérer les différents problèmes urbains qui tiennent les citadins à coeur, il est imprudent de s'arrêter à ces résultats qui sont loin de déboucher sur un projet urbain compatible avec les besoins populaires. Par conséquent, il fut donc nécessaire de compléter l'enquête ouverte par une seconde enquête à questionnaire fermé sur les préférences choisies.

A cet effet, l'*Annexe 2* présente la restructuration des réponses récueillies lors de la première enquête qui ont servi à confectionner le questionnaire ferme é de la seconde enquête. Le principe consiste à diviser les rubriques de la première enquête en choix alternatifs ou complémentaires qui furent placés dans une liste à choix multiples que le répondant fut invité à classer par ordre de priorité lors de l'enquête fermée.

3.2) L'Enquête fermée

a) L'objectif de l'enquête

Le but poursuivi est de déterminer une échelle de désirabilité des besoins jugés prioritaires par les usagers.

b) Le questionnaire

Il comprend quatre questions (*annexe 3*). Pour les deux premières questions, il était demandé aux habitants de choisir les équipements par ordre de préférence, pour un éventuel programme de restructuration des quartiers spontanés et pour un autre des trames assainies. Dans la troisième question, il leur était demandé de choisir sur une liste, par ordre de préférence, les lieux à démolir pour un éventuel programme de rénovation. Enfin, dans la dernière question, ils devaient choisir, par ordre de priorité, les matériaux de construction des clôtures, des toitures et les dispositifs de sécurité pour habitat.

c) La technique du questionnaire

Pour une question donnée, il était demandé aux répondants de classer leur préférence sur une échelle ordinale du plas désiré au moins désiré. Ce qui allait permettre, en se prononçant dans un cadre structuré au préalable et en s'exprimant à l'intérieur des limites imposées par les questionnaire, de mesurer la force de leur goût et de leurs aversions sur une échelle ordinale.

Cependant, la liste des choix n'était pas limitative. Au cas où le répondant manifestait le désir d'aller au-delà des choix offerts, il était prévu au bas de la question une rubrique d'ajout appelée "autres à préciser" réservée aux éventuelles préférences-choix. C'est de cette façon que l'enquête a réussi à la fois à maintenir les enquêtés dans un cadre prédéterminé et à faciliter le traitement des données en limitant au maximum l'interprétation subjective des réponses par l'enquêteur.

d) L'échantillon cible de 72 étudiants.

Comme l'objectif de la démarche était une expérimentation méthodologique, l'enquête se contenta d'un échantillon réduit en vue de minimiser les problémes logistiques de traitement des données. Ainsi donc, les étudiants de l'Université de Lubumbashi furent choisis comme échantillon cible parce que non seulement ils constituent le groupe facile à aborder, à motiver par le canal de l'université, mais aussi qu'ils comprennent l'utilité du questionnaire parce qu'il se développe au sein de ce groupe, représentant une société mutante, une culture et une conscience urbaine qui manque chez leurs parents.

e) Le traitement des données

— La codification et la compilation du tableau des réponses.

Toutes les préférences-choix, pour une question donnée, étaient codifiées par une lettre de A à Z. Ces codes ne se trouvaient pas dans le questionnaire initial. Ils furent ajoutés au moment de la saisie des données sur support informatique. Il aurait été préférable d'imprimer ces codes sur les questionnaires initiaux, ce qui aurait permis d'économiser une part appréciable du temps de saisie et de limiter les risques d'erreurs à la transcription.

Pour compiler le questionnaire et compter les fréquences, l'usage de l'ordinateur et du logiciel STATPACK (Statistical Analysis Package) s'avérèrent important. Ce qui permit d'appréhender le poids de chaque observation et d'obtenir des tableaux de fréquence présentant une compilation intégrée des quatre premiers choix et une colonne des fréquences totales déduites de la somme des colonnes précédentes.

La classification des fréquences dans l'ordre décroissant des fréquences totales permit de lire rapidement des échelles en priorité. Même si cette addition des fréquences individuelles donna des indications intéressantes, il fallait se méfier de cette simple addition qui accordait un poids égal à chaque mention quelque fut son rang. Il a fallu donc pondérer mais nous ne disposions pas de règles ou de critères de pondération valable. Cette lacune fut corrigée par l'Analyse en Composantes Principales (ACP).

Mais avant d'exploiter l'ensemble des résultats compilés avec l'ACP, nous mesurâmes leur degré de fiabilité par un test de consistance, de fidélitié, de précision et de stabilité selon les formules statistiques tirées de l'ouvrage de Hammond et McCullag (1978).

— Les quatre tests de fiabilité.

Premièrement, le calcul des tableaux croisés effectué sur l'ensemble des réponses et sur IBM/PC avec le logiciel STATPAC démontra que les réponses des enquêtés furent en général cohérentes. Les répondants rangèrent leurs choix selon un ordre consistant en tenant compte de la séquence normale des opérations d'aménagement. Ainsi par exemple, le répondants cochèrent la rubrique "tracer les routes" en premier choix et "asphalter les routes" en deuxième choix. Aucun des répondants n'éffectua ces deux choix en ordre inverse, ce qui serait la manifestation d'un manque de cohérence. Ce qui permit également d'exclure l'hypothèse d'une séléction aléatoire des préférences-choix.

Deuxièmement, le test de chi-carré prouva que la distribution des fréquences-choix exprimées sur les quatre premiers choix était significativement différente d'une distribution uniforme parmi les préférences-choix possibles. Il montra de concentrations de fréquences ne résultant pas d'une classification aléatoire. Ce qui signifia que la distribution des fréquences exprimées n'était pas uniforme et n'était pas due au hasard. Ceci, manifeste l'exercice d'un raisonnement logique. De même la concentration des préférences autour de certains thèmes était réelle et correspondait à une convergence manifeste des opinions des répondants.

Troisièment, le calcul d'un coéfficient de corrélation de rang de Spearman révéla qu'en général les corrélations calculées n'étaient pas significatives, c'est à dire que l'ordre d'apparition des préférences-choix dans le questionnaire n'avait pas influencé l'order de priorité des répondants. Ce qui permit de rejeter l'hypothèse d'une dépendance des deux séries données.

Quatrièmement, l'analyse de la fréquence des ajouts dans la rubrique "autres à préciser" démontra que sur les 100% (13 questions x 72 répondants = 936) des réponses attendues, il y a eu seulement une participation de 10.8% (101 réponses). La même rubrique fut rangée six fois seulement parmi les quatre premiers choix, ce qui représentait 0.6% du total. Quant aux points de vue réalistes des réponses dans la même rubrique, contrairement à toute attente, 30% de préférences ajoutées étaient satisfaisantes, 16% répétaient une rubrique déjà existante, 19% acceptable, 7% furent passables, et enfin 28% irréalistes.

En resumé, les quatre tests effectués montrèrent que le degré de fiabilité des résultats et des comptages fréquentiels était acceptable vu les circonstances, ce qui a permis le traitement des données.

— Les résultats obtenus avec l'Analyse en Compsante Principale.

L'ACP, calculée à l'aide du logiciel SAS avec le système VM/CS sur un ordinateur central IBM4341, permit de saisir l'échelle de désirabilité des souhaits jugés prioritaires par la population en les hiérarchisant un à un, en commençant par celui pour lequel la faveur populaire était la plus grande, s'arrêtant sur le voeu supplémentaire dont l'influence n'était pas significative. Les graphiques obtenus définirent une classification hiérarchique décroissante des voeux en trois classes: les plus préférés, les moyennement préférés et les peu préférés en présentant également pour chaque Préférence, sa position parmi les faveurs populaires.

— Les voeux populaires en prévision d'un projet de restructuration des quartiers spontanés.

Les équipements et les éléments les plus préférés

Il est à remarquer dans le *graphique 2* la priorité que la population accorde aux équipements publics, notamment le dispensaire, l'école primaire mixte, la maternité, l'hôpital. Un seul équipement d'infrastructure est préférés, c'est "tracer les routes."

Les équipements et les éléments moyennement préférés

Ce sont les éléments que les habitants ont rélégué au second rang en ordre des priorités. Dans cette classe, nous dénombrons trois équipements d'infrastructures (égout, robinet dans chaque parcelle, éclairage public) et deux noms des maîtres d'ouvrages les moins fiables (gouvernement, entrepreneur zaïrois).

Les équipements et les éléments peu préférés
Ils n'ont pas obtenu l'audience populaire. Il s'agit des équipements comme les latrines dans chaque parcelle, les puits collectifs, les bornes fontaines, la gendarmerie, le centre commercial, les écoles secondaires mixtes, l'église, l'école technique pour les filles, etc.

Il existe un lien entre ces préférences populaires et les réalités quotidiennes dans la ville. La raison est simple.

Contrairement à toute attente, les habitants ont besoin en priorité d'infrastructure et de superstructure. Curieusement, en l'absence de toute intervention des pouvoirs publics qui les "ignorent" d'ailleurs, ces habitants réussissent seuls à organiser leur habitat en prenant en charge la voirie et les réseaux divers.

Poussés par les événements, ils tirent parfois frauduleusement de l'eau et de l'éléctricité par de petits branchements discrets sur les conduites qui passent à quelques mètres de leurs maisons. C'est comme cela qu'ils amènent l'eau et l'éctricité par ramification et connexion; or ils ne peuvent pas, compte tenu du coût d'investissement, prendre eux-mêmes en charge les équipements publics. C'est ce qui explique les résultats-surprises des enquêtes.

La carence en équipements publics revêt une acuité particulièrement dramatique, nécessitant parfois l'intervention dans les quartiers spontanés des seuls organismes humanitaires non gouvernementaux étrangers et religieux. Ils y interviennent sous diverses formes, notamment en construisant des dispensaires, des écoles primaires, des centres sociaux, etc. Ces réalisations apparemment modestes, augmentent la côte de popularité de ces organismes. Voilà qui explique la faveur populaire que ces organismes ont pu recueillir et que les enquêtes révèlent.

— Les voeux populaires en prévision d'un projet de parcelles assainies.

Les équipements et les éléments les plus préférés
Le *graphique 3* fait apparaître une préférence prédominante pour des équipements publics comme le dispensaire, l'hôpital, l'école primaire mixte et la maternité. Ici également, la rubrique "tracer les routes" est la plus préféré par les habitants. Pour ce qui est des maîtres d'ouvrages appelés à réaliser cette opération, les voix furent vont par ordre de priorité aux religieux, aux organismes internationaux, aux coopératives des habitants et aux entrepreneurs privés étrangers.

Les équipements et les éléments moyennement préférés

Les équipements d'infrastructure comme les égouts, les robinets, les puits, les latrines par parcelle, etc. recoivent encore des faveurs moins immédiates auprès de l'opinion publique. Les maîtres d'ouvrage les moins favoris, comme le gouvernement et les entrepreneurs zaïrois, ne sont pas plus aimeés par la population.

Les équipements et les éléments peu préférés

Il s'agit des équipements, comme les latrines collectives, l'éclairage par parcelle, le ramassage d'ordures, les fontaines, l'église, l'école technique pour les garçons et pour les filles avec toutes les options, les écoles techniques pour les filles et pour les garçons, etc.

Ces résultats correspondent aux réalités quotidiennes. La raison qui justifie la grande préférence que la population accorde encore aux équipements publics est simple. A titre d'exemple, les enfants font des kilomètres à pied pour aller à l'école et sont souvent cinquante par classe, trois ou quatre par banc, si les bancs existent seulement. Il y a donc carence d'équipements scolaires. Il y a donc insuffisance d'équipements scolaires.

De plus, il n'y a même pas d'autobus qui entrent dans les quartiers populaires périphériques parce que les routes sont impraticables. C'est la raison pour laquelle ils souhaitent que l'on trace les routes. De même, pour se rendre au centre-ville, il y a des autobus à peu près toutes les trentes minutes à l'intersection des grandes avenues. Mais il faut se bagarrer pour les prendre. Ce qui fait que ce sont les plus aptes physiquement qui arrivent à être desservis. Ainsi, les femmes qui vont avec leurs enfants en consultation médicale au centre-ville et tous ceux qui veulent aller ailleurs sont obligés de faire de longues et épuisantes marches à pied. Voilà pourquoi, ils préfèrent que l'on construise des hôpitaux, des écoles primaires et des maternités dans leur quartiers.

Ceci dit les réclamations populaires ne sont pas un simple fait d'imagination, elles réflètent l'état de manque dans lequel la population se trouve. Voilà la raison pour laquelle leur réclamations opposent une fois de plus les équipements de superstructure jugés prioritaires aux équipements d'infrastructure qui furent relégués au second plan.

Force est de constater également la différence de côte de popularité entre les intervenants fiables et ceux qui brillent par leur inéfficacité (gouvernement et entrepreneur zaïrois). Une raison explique cette mauvaise perception que la population a du gouvernement: la lourdeur administrative et la corruption des fonctionnaires.

Donc pour un projet de trames assainies, la population souhaite en priorité que les religieux ou les organismes internationaux se mettent à construire un dispensaire ou un hôpital avant toute autre réalisation. Elle souhaite également qu'ils tracent des routes. Ce n'est qu'après avoir édifié des équipements sanitaires comme l'hôpital et le dispensaire que les maîtres d'ouvrages pourront alors entreprendre la construction de l'école primaire ou d'une maternité étant que les résultats de l'ACP montrent une forte corrélation entre les deux choix.

En résumé, les résultats démentent également les allégations selon lesquelles les habitants des quartiers démunis ont grandement besoin d'équipements d'infrastructures que d'équipements publics.

— Les voeux populaires en prévision d'un programme de rénovation urbaine.

Les équipements et les éléments les plus préférés

Les habitants n'ont pas su choisir les bâtiments à raser en priorité parce qu'ils ne sont pas partisans de la politique du bulldozer et parce que la rénovation urbaine ne paraît pas à leurs yeux comme une solution aux problèmes urbains (*graphique 4*). Toutes fois au cas il y aurait rénovation, ils préfèrent confier l'opération aux organismes internationaux et aux entrepreneurs privés (éfficacité oblige) et non aux réligieux, comme il fut le cas pour les programmes de restructuration et de trames assainies.

Les équipements et les éléments moyennement préférés

Certains quartiers spontanés cependant et surtout les camps militaires sont perçus comme nuisibles, mais il ne s'agit pas de les raser dans l'immédiat. En effet, beaucoup de répondants rêvent d'une ville où les camps militaires et les quartiers comme Katuba extension et Zaïre seraient démolis. Nous ignorons cependant les raisons qui ont poussé les répondants à préféré uniquement la démolition de ces deux quartiers spontanés.

De plus, la population préféré que les organismes internationaux et les entrepreneurs construisent des logements pavillonnaires à la place qu'auront libéré les camps militaires démolis. Préférences certes réalistes qui traduisent surtout les rêves des habitants voulant avoir de vastes terrains pour mieux vivre à l'Africaine.

Les équipements et les éléments peu préférés

Ce sont tous les quartiers d'habitation spontané comme Kigoma, Kampemba, Kasungami, Tabazaïre, Tumbototo, etc.

Si l'on se fie aux voeux populaires rien en génénral n'est voué à la destruction. Les habitants préférent garder leur patrimoine immobilier. Au contraire ils souhaitent la construction de nouveaux logements sociaux.

Un retour dans le passé aide à mieux comprendre les raisons qui poussent les lushois à refuser l'opération de rénovation en souhaitant néanmoins la démolition des camps militaires.

En effet, à l'époque coloniale, les camps militaires furent construits et intégrés dans le tissu urbain pour prévenir tout soulevement de la population africaine. Contrairement à toute attente, la cohabitation entre la population civile et les militaires tend ces dernières années vers un échec total parce que ces derniers se permettent toutes les bévues, faisant la loi dans les rues en "rançonnant" les paisibles citoyens. C'est une force armée détestée qui se sert plus qu'elle ne sert; une force armée qui, de plus, estime qu'elle n'a pas de compte à rendre à personne puisque le pays est sous la présidence militaire.

Les résultats *infirment* donc des mythes qui, jusque-là, avaient caracterisé la pensée urbanistique négro-africaine: lesquels prétendent que les quartiers spontanés sont répulsifs, dangereux et mal aimés par les populations. Ils viennent d'être *démentis* parce que ce sont au contraire les camps militaires qui sont perçus à la fois comme des endroits privilégiés de pathologie sociale et de prédilection pour l'agitation politique. En effet, jusqu'à ce jour, les 216 coups d'état ou tentatives de coups d'état réalisés en Afrique entre 1945 et 1987, ont souvent impliqué de loin ou de près les militaires.

Nous pouvons *affirmer* dans ce cas que les quartiers spontanés, du moins pour l'instant, ne posent pas encore des problèmes graves de sécurité publique. Force est de constater d'ailleurs que parmi la dizaine des quartiers spontanés qui pullulent à Lubumbashi, seuls le quartier Katuba extension et le quartier Zaïre qui n'ont pas obtenu l'audience populaire et sont susceptibles d'être démolis.

En définitive, les enquêtés ont defini avec une extrême rationalité les problèmes cruciaux de la ville. L'accent est mis sur les problèmes sociaux, nous croyons cependant que la population va orienter ses préférences vers les réalisations prestigieuses et gigantesques qui exigent de gros investissements financiers. A Lubumbashi, là où les problèmes financiers semblent les plus aïgus, le lushois a fait preuve d'une grande rationalité, il propose de confier les réalisations urbanistiques aux organismes internationaux et aux entrepreneurs privés étrangers parce qu'à ses yeux, ces derniers sont conscients de leurs responsabilités.

— Les voeux populaires pour les matériaux de construction, de toiture, de clôture et les dispositifs de sécurité dans l'habitat.

Au total, les nuages qui définirent les trois classes furent parfaitement catégorisés par le *Graphique 5*.

Les matériaux et les dispositifs les plus préférés.

Ils furent par ordre d'importance les briques adobes (banco), les parpaings (brique ciment), les briques cuites. Par ailleurs, le matériau de clôture le plus fréquemment préféré fut la brique ciment. L'éloignement de briques adobes sur le vecteur choix 4, de parpaings (2 et 9) et briques cuites sur le vecteur choix 1 signifia qu'ils furent des materiaux les plus fréquemment préférés par la population.

Les matériaux et les dispositifs moyennement préférés.

Ils furent concentrés nettement aux abords de l'origine dans le cadran positif. C'étaient des matériaux comme pierre de taille, tuiles, murs avec tessons de bouteille, sonnerie, éternit, et des dispositifs comme chiens et sentinelle etc . . .

Les matériaux et les dispositifs les moins préférés.

Ils se retrouvèrent dans le cadran négatif tels les planches, le toit plat, le grillage, la clôture éléctrocutante, les fûts déroulés, les euphorbes, les ardoises, etc . . .

D'une manière générale, la population préféra la brique adobe compactée, stabiliseée pour construire la maison. En ce qui concerne le matériau pour clôturer la maison, la préférence alla tout naturellement aux parpaings. Cette préférence s'explique par le fait qu'il est moins coûteux pour le lushois de clôturer sa maison avec la brique ciment que de la construire avec le même matériau. L'urbaniste peut aussi être étonné par l'importance accordée par le lushois à la brique adobe et à la brique ciment pour construire une maison. Une interprétation possible d'une telle importance peut être que la production du parpaing côute plus cher tant en capitaux qu'en énergie. Il résulte de cette situation que même un fonctionnaire et moins encore un ouvrier moyen, n'a les moyens de s'offrir la plus humble maison en ciment. La terre compactée permet de construire des maisons économiques et durables assurant une bonne protection contre la chaleur.

Remarquons dans *le graphique* l'intérêt que la population porte aux matériaux de construction. L'intérêt traduit bien le réalisme des lushois qui savent qu'il est primordial de resoudre le problème de logement avant de penser à resoudre le problème de toiture et de securité.

Pareillement, aucun dispositif de securité ne figura dans la classe des éléments des plus préférés si ce ne fut que dans la classe des moyennement préférés. Encore là, la population fit preuve de réalisme. Elle préféra le dispositif de securité le moins coûteux comme par exemple les murs avec les tessons de bouteilles et les chiens.

Conclusion

1) Retour sur l'hypothèse

Après les analyses, une vérification s'impose. Les résultats de l'enquête vérifient l'hypothèse de départ. Hypothèse selon laquelle les enquêtes ouvertes donnent des réponses trop générales et ne permettent pas de comprendre l'échelle de désirabilité des voeux jugés prioritaitres par la population. D'où la nécéssité d'un jumélage d'enquêtes fermées et ouvertes et où l'ACP va hiérarchiser les préférences populaires.

Dans le cadre d'un article, il est impossible de rendre compte de manière détaillée de toutes les étapes d'analyse et de la masse d'informations recueillies au cours du traitement. Mais nous pouvons maintenant, à partir de cette méthodologie expérimentale et aidé par notre étude sur l' "acceptabilité" à Lubumbashi faire un portrait de l'echelle de désirabilité des voeux jugés prioritaires par la population (*tableau 2*). Cependant, l'expérimentation que nous avons conduite à Lubumbashi, aussi révélatrice qu'elle soit, ne peut être considérée comme un "modèle" qu'il suffirait de réproduire parce qu'elle renferme des limites. Des recherches et d'expérimentations nouvelles sont encore nécessaires pour mettre au point une méthodologie de participation plus efficace.

2) Les limites de l'expérimentation

Bien que l'avantage de notre meilleure démarche méthodologique soit donc une meilleure repartition en classe avec de plus grandes interclasses entre les voeux populaires, elle présente toutefois des limites. Deux limites principales peuvent être formulés à l'endroit de la taille et de la représentativité de notre échantillion — test de la deuxième enquête. L'effectif restreint de soixante douze étudiants ne permet pas de tirer des conclusions définitives, mais permet néanmoins de dégager certaines lignes directrices pour une étude ultérieure. La constitution de notre échantillion — test aussi présente des lacunes. Les étudiantes n'étaient pas soumises à l'enquête en raison de leur nombre très restreint à l'université. Toutefois nous déplorons cette défaillance puisqu'elle nousa empêchés d'appréhender leurs voeux qui auraient sans doute présenté des caractères spécifiques face à ceux de leur confrères.

3) Avertissement

Que la participation populaire indirecte ne soit pas perçue par les urbanistes, ni par les citoyens, ni même par les pouvoirs publics comme une arme ou comme une voix des "sans voix"; qu'elle ne soit pas non plus considérée comme une finalité ni comme un vecteur d'une idéologie, mais plutôt comme une technique au service du développpment urbain. Ainsi délimitée, la concertation en urbanisme sera un objectif réalisable et les urbanistes pourront vérifier cette démarche méthodologique par touches successives. Néanmoins, nous avons la ferme conviction que la méthodologie que nous avons proposée aidera à bâtir des villes qui s'adapteront aux besoins et aux ressources des pays négro-africains, lesquelles villes que nous baptiserons avec fierté AFRIKAVILLE.

 Figure 1

LOCALISATION DE LA VILLE DE LUBUMBASHI

Figure 2

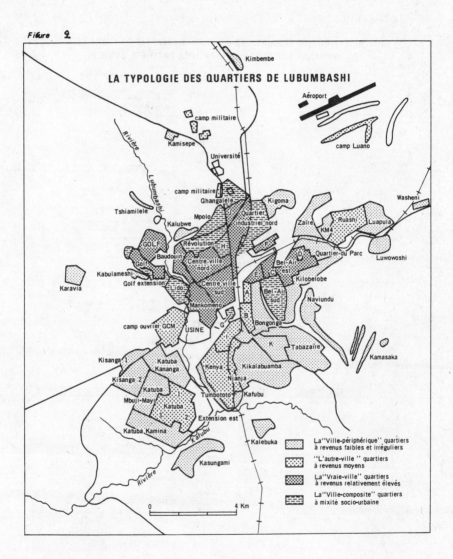

LA TYPOLOGIE DES QUARTIERS DE LUBUMBASHI

Graphique 1

LA COMPILATION DES ÉVALUATIONS DE LA VILLE CLASSÉES PAR TYPE DE RUBRIQUE PORTANT SUR LES RÉSULTATS DE LA PREMIÈRE ENQUÊTE

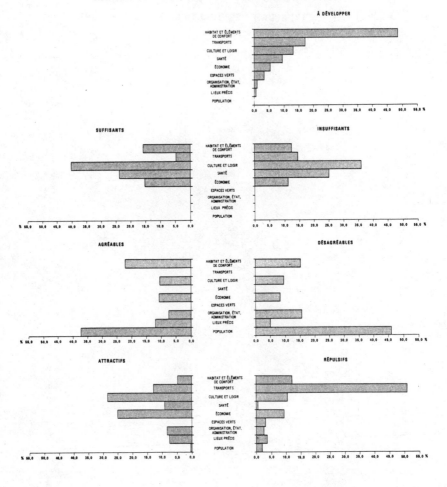

Graphique 2

LA HIÉRARCHISATION DE L'ACP EN TROIS CLASSES DES VOEUX JUGÉS PRIORITAIRES PAR LA POPULATION LORS DE LA RESTRUCTURATION DES QUARTIERS SPONTANÉS

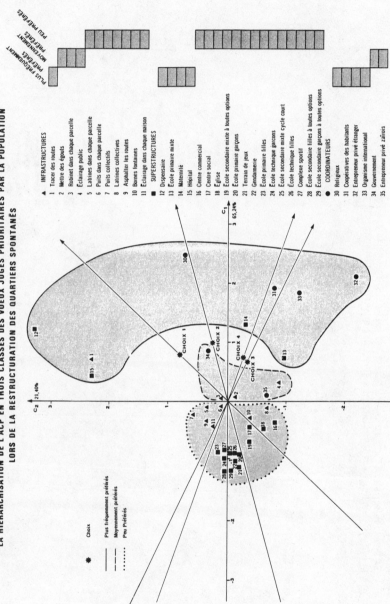

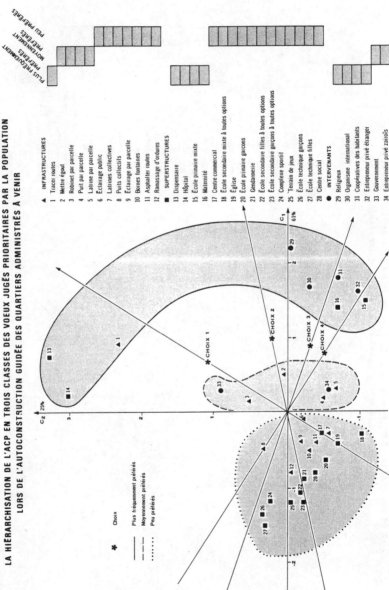

Graphique 3

LA HIÉRARCHISATION DE L'ACP EN TROIS CLASSES DES VOEUX JUGÉS PRIORITAIRES PAR LA POPULATION LORS DE L'AUTOCONSTRUCTION GUIDÉE DES QUARTIERS ADMINISTRÉS À VENIR

Graphique 4

LA HIÉRARCHISATION DE L'ACP EN TROIS CLASSES DES VOEUX JUGÉS PRIORITAIRES PAR LA POPULATION
LORS DE LA RÉNOVATION À LUBUMBASHI

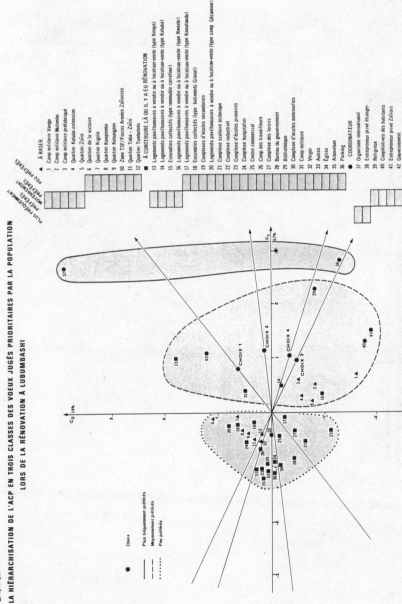

▲ À RASER
1 Camp militaire Vangu
2 Camp militaire Mulombo
3 Camp militaire préfabriqué
4 Quartier Kataba extension
5 Quartier Zaïre
6 Quartier de la victoire
7 Quartier Kigola
8 Quartier Kampemba
9 Quartier Kasungami
10 Zone TSF/Forces Armées Zaïroises
11 Quartier Taba - Zaïre
12 Quartier Tumbolobo

■ À CONSTRUIRE LÀ OÙ IL Y A EU RÉNOVATION
13 Logements pavillonnaires à vendre ou à location-vente (type Kenya)
14 Logements pavillonnaires à vendre ou à location-vente (type Katuba)
15 Ensembles collectifs (type immeuble carrefour)
16 Logements pavillonnaires à vendre ou à location-vente (type Rwashi)
17 Logements pavillonnaires à vendre ou à location-vente (type Kamalondo)
18 Ensembles collectifs (type bâtiments Gisasi)
19 Complexes d'écoles secondaires
20 Logements pavillonnaires à vendre ou à location-vente (type camp Gécamine)
21 Complexe scolaire technique
22 Complexe industriel
23 Complexe d'écoles primaires
24 Complexe hospitalier
25 Centre commercial
26 Camp des travailleurs
27 Complexe des loisirs
28 Bureau du gouvernement
29 Bibliothèque
30 Complexe d'écoles maternelles
31 Camp militaire
32 Verger
33 Autres
34 Église
35 Arboretum
36 Parking

● COORDONATEUR
37 Organisme international
38 Entrepreneur privé étranger
39 Religieux
40 Coopératives des habitants
41 Entrepreneur privé Zaïrois
42 Gouvernement

PLUS FRÉQUEMMENT PRÉFÉRÉS
MOYENNEMENT PRÉFÉRÉS
PEU PRÉFÉRÉS

Choix
Plus fréquemment préférés
Moyennement préférés
Peu préférés

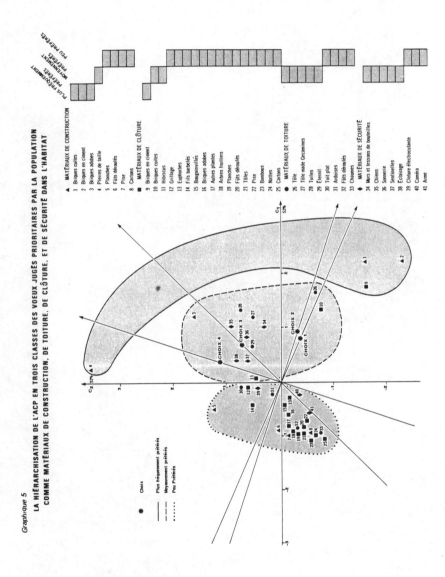

Graphique 5

LA HIÉRARCHISATION DE L'ACP EN TROIS CLASSES DES VOEUX JUGÉS PRIORITAIRES PAR LA POPULATION COMME MATÉRIAUX DE CONSTRUCTION, DE TOITURE, DE CLÔTURE, ET DE SÉCURITÉ DANS L'HABITAT

PLUS PRÉCEDEMENT PRÉFÉRÉS

MOYENNEMENT PRÉFÉRÉS

PEU PRÉFÉRÉS

▲ MATÉRIAUX DE CONSTRUCTION
1 Briques cuites
2 Briques en ciment
3 Briques adobes
4 Pierres de taille
5 Planches
6 Fûts déroulés
7 Pisé
8 Cartons

■ MATÉRIAUX DE CLÔTURE
9 Briques en ciment
10 Briques cuites
11 Hibiscus
12 Grillage
13 Euphorbes
14 Fils barbelés
15 Bougainvillées
16 Briques adobes
17 Autres plantes
18 Arbres fruitiers
19 Planches
20 Fûts déroulés
21 Tôles
22 Pisé
23 Bambous
24 Nattes
25 Cartons

● MATÉRIAUX DE TOITURE
26 Tôle
27 Tôle made Gécamines
28 Tuiles
29 Éternit
30 Toit plat
31 Ardoises
32 Fûts déroulés
33 Chaumes

◆ MATÉRIAUX DE SÉCURITÉ
34 Murs et tessons de bouteilles
35 Chiens
36 Sonnerie
37 Sentinelles
38 Éclairage
39 Clôture électrocutante
40 Caméra
41 Arme

✳ Choix

—— Plus fréquemment préférés

– – – Moyennement préférés

········ Peu Préférés

TABLEAU : 1

SCHÉMA DE LA DÉMARCHE MÉTHODOLOGIQUE POUR LE CLASSEMENT DES PRÉFÉRENCES D'AMÉNAGEMENT

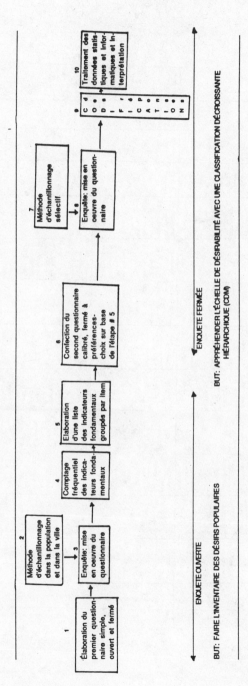

BUT: FAIRE L'INVENTAIRE DES DÉSIRS POPULAIRES

BUT: APPRÉHENDER L'ÉCHELLE DE DÉSIRABILITÉ AVEC UNE CLASSIFICATION DÉCROISSANTE HIÉRARCHIQUE (CDM)

TABLEAU 2

L'ECHELLE DE DESIRABILITE DES VOEUX JUGES PRIORITAIRES PAR LA POPULATION PENDANT LE REAMENAGEMENT DE LUBUMBASHI
TEL QUE DONNE PAR L'ANALYSE EN COMPOSANTES PRINCIPALES

Priorités / Classe	QUESTION A — La restructuration des quartiers spontanés			QUESTION B — L'auto-construction guidée			QUESTION C — La rénovation			QUESTION D — Les matériaux de l'habitat			
	A_1 Infrastr.	A_2 Superstr.	A_3 Coordonat.	B_1 Infrastr.	B_2 Superstr.	B_3 Coordonat.	C_1 A raser	C_2 A construire	C_3 Coordonat.	D_1 Constr.	D_2 Clôture	D_3 Toiture	D_4 Sécurité
Priorités / Classe	Tracer les routes	Priorité 1: Dispensaire, Hôpital; Priorité 2: *Ecole primaire mixte, *Maternité	Priorité 1: Religieux; Priorité 2: Entrepreneur étranger; Priorité 3: *Coopérative des hab., Organisme intern.	Tracer les routes	Priorité 1: *Dispensaire, Hôpital; Priorité 2: *Ecole primaire mixte, *Maternité	Priorité 1: Religieux, Organisme intern.; Priorité 2: Entrepreneur privé étranger, Coopératives	A raser	A construire	Organisme intern., Entrepreneur étranger	Briques adobes, Briques ciment, Briques cuites	Briques ciment	Tole	Sécurité
Plus fréquemment préférées / Première classe	Eclairage public, Egout, Robinet par parcelle			Robinet par parcelle, Egout, Puits par parcelle, Latrine par parcelle			Camp militaire Vange, Camp militaire Mutombo, Camp militaire préfabriqué Katuba ext., Quartier Zaïre	Logements pavillon. type Kenya, Logements pavill. type Katuba, Ens. coll. type carrefous, Logements pavill. type Ruashi	Gouvernement, Religieux, Entrepreneurs zaïrois, Cooperative des hab.	Pierre de taille	Briques cuites	Tole, Tole moderne, Tuiles, Eternit.	Murs avec tessons, Gecanines bouteilles, Chiens, Sonnette, Sentinelle, Eclairage
Moyennement préférées / Deuxième classe			Gouvernement, Entrepreneur zaïrois			Gouvernement, Entrepreneur zaïrois							
Peu préférées / Troisième classe	Latrines par parc., Puits par parcelle, Puits coll., Latrines collectives, Asphalte, Eclairage dans ch. maison	Centre com., Compl. sportif, Centre soc., Terr. jeux, Eglise, Ecole prim. garçons, Ecole sec. mixte, Ecole sec. mixte ttes options, Gendarmerie, Ecole primaire filles, Ecole tech. garçons		Puits coll., Eclairage public, Latrine coll., Asphalte, Borne font., Eclairage par parc., Ramassage d'ordures	Eglise, Centre com. mixte, Ecole sec. tech. garçons, Ecole tech. filles, Compl. sportif, Terr. jeux, Gendarmerie, Ecole sec. garçons		Quartier de la victoire, Kigoma, Kampemba, Kasungami, Zone TSF des FAZ	Compl. écoles primaires, Bur. gouv., Camp trav., Compl. indust., Compl. écoles maternelles, Centre com., Comp. hospit., Camp militaire, Vanger, Eglise, Arboretum, Bibliothèque		Planches, Pisé, Cartons, Futs déroulés	Grillage, Nattes, Fils barbelés, Cartons, Bougainvillés, Arbres fruitiers, Planches, Toles, Bambous, Autres plantes, Briques adobes, Futs déroulés, Tole, Pisé	Toit plat, Ardoises, Futs déroulés, Chaumes	Cloture électrocutante, Caméra, Arme

*Complémentaire à cause d'une forte corrélation observée entre les deux choix.

ANNEXE 1

Questionnaire de la première enquête

1) Que feriez-vous visiter à un ami étranger dans votre quartier? En d'autres termes, quels sont, à votre avis, les éléments qui caractérisent votre quartier et que vous préféréz?

2) Quels sont les lieux, d'après vous, les plus ternes, les plus mornes les plus maussades dans votre quartier? En d'autres mots, qu'est-ce que vous détestez dans votre quartier?

3) Quelles sont vos réflexions et vos propositions sur votre quartier et votre ville? C'est à dire qu'est-ce que vous voulez créer, développer ou supprimer?

	ilot1.	ilot2.	ilot3.	ilot4.	ilot5.	ilot6.	ilot7.	ilot8.	ilot9.	ilot10.
	S/I	S/I	S/I	S/I	S/I	S/I	S/I	S/I	S/I	S/I
Transp. publics										
Dispen. Hôpit.										
Ecoles prim.										
Ecoles secon.										
Equip. cultur.										
Assaini-ssement.										

S=suffisant   I=Insuffisant

	ilot1.	ilot2.	ilot3.	ilot4.	ilot5.	ilot6.	ilot7.	ilot8.	ilot9.	ilot10.
	A/D	A/D	A/D	A/D	A/D	A/D	A/D	A/D	A/D	A/D
Tapages noct.										
Bars/ Disquaires.										
Quartier										
Ambiance.										

Maisons.

Voisinage.

Jeunes.

Gendarmes.

Présence
industries.

A=Agréable   D=Désagréable

ilot1. ilot2. ilot3. ilot4. ilot5. ilot6. ilot7. ilot8. ilot9. ilot10.

Aime
la ville.

Aime
moins.

N'aime
pas.

Sans
opinion

ANNEXE 2

Restructuration des éléments de la premiere enquête en préférence-choix pour la seconde enquête et typologie des équipements requis

Elements de la 1ère Enquête	Choix Proposes pour la 11ème enquête	Typologie d'équipements
I) Habitat et élémentsde confort		
Eclairage	Eclairage public, éclairage individuel	Infrastructures
Latrines	Latrines collectives, latrines individuelles	Infrastructures
Matériaux de construction	Briques cuites, briques adobes, pierre de taille, briques ciment, fûts, déroulés, pisé, planches, cartons, etc.	Construction

Toiture	Tôle, tuiles, éternit, toit plat, ardoises, fûts déroulés, chaume	Construction
Sécurité	Murs avec tessons de bouteilles, chiens, sonnerie, sentinelles, éclairage, clôture électrocutante, caméra, arme	Infrastructures
Clôture	Briques ciment, briques cuites, plantes, planches, pisé, bambou, nattes, cartons, briques adobes, fils barbelés, grillage, etc.	Infrastructures
Assainissement	Système d'égout, ramassage d'ordures	Infrastructures
Maisons	Maisons individuelles, Habitat collectif Camp ouvriers, Camps militaires	Superstructures
Eau	Robinet individuel, fontaines, puits individuels, puits collectifs	Infrastructures

II) <u>Santé</u>

Dispensaire	Dispensaire, protection maternelle infantile, centre social	Superstructures
Hôpital	Hôpital, maternité	Superstructures

III) <u>Espaces verts</u>

Arbres	Verger, arboretum	Nature

IV) <u>Transports</u>

Routes	Tracer les routes, asphaltage des routes, parc automobile	Infrastructures

V) <u>Economie</u>

Lieux d'approvisionnement	Centre Commerical, marché	Superstructures

VI) <u>Culture et Loisirs</u>

Ecole primaire	Ecole primaire mixte, école primaire pour filles, école primaire pour garçons	Superstructures

Ecole secondaire	Ecole secondaire pour filles, école secondaire pour garçons, école mixte à cycle court, école secondaire mixte à cycle long, école secondaire pour filles ou pour garçons à toutes options	Superstructures
VII) <u>Administration</u>	Gendarmerie, bureaux, services	Superstructures

ANNEXE 3

Le questionnaire de la deuxième enquête

QUESTION A: LA RESTRUCTURATION DES QUARTIERS SPONTANES

A1) Si on doit restructurer les quartiers spontanés, placez près de chaque action un numéro de 1 à 11 pour ces Infrastructures, selon l'ordre de préférence. Ajoutez les équipements non mentionnés si possible.

a) aménager des puits conformes aux normes d'hygiène dans chaque parcelle;
b) construire des latrines conformes aux normes d'hygiène dans chaque parcelle;
c) brancher beaucoup de bornes fontaines;
d) mettre un système d'égout;
e) tracer les routes;
f) construire des puits collectifs conformes aux normes d'hygiène et équipés de pompes aspirantes;
g) construire des latrines collectives conformes aux normes d'hygiène;
h) brancher des robinets dans chaque parcelle;
i) asphalter les routes;
j) éclairage dans chaque maison;
k) autres à préciser.

A2) S'il faut équiper les mêmes quartiers spontanés, placez près de chaque équipement public un numéro de 1 à 18, selon l'ordre de préférence. Ajoutez les équipements non mentionnés si possible.

a) église;
b) maternité;
c) dispensaire;
d) école primaire mixte;
e) école primaire pour filles;
f) école primaire pour garçons;
g) aménager un terrain de jeux;
h) construire un complexe de loisir;
i) centre social;
j) école secondaires pour garçons à toutes options;
k) école technique pour filles;
l) gendarmarie;
m) centre commercial;

n) école secondaire pour filles à toutes options;
o) école secondaire mixte à toutes options;
p) école secondaire mixte à cycle court;
q) école technique pour garçon;
r) hôpital;
s) autres à préciser

A3) Placez près de chaque maître d'ouvrage un numéro de 1 à 6 selon l'ordre de préférence. A qui confierez-vous la réalisation de ces équipements? Ajoutez s'il y en a les maîtres d'ouvrages non mentionnés.

a) gouvernement ou autorités urbaines;
b) coppératives des habitants;
c) entrepreneur privé zaïrois;
d) religieux
e) organisme international;
f) entrepreneur privé étranger;
g) autres à préciser

QUESTION B: LES TRAMES ASSAINIES

B1) De toutes ces propopositions, que choisirez-vous comme projet prioritaire à mettre en oeuvre avant ou pendant l'installation de la population? Placez près de chaque proposition un numéro de 1 à 12 selon l'ordre de priorité. Ajoutez, si possible, d'autres équipements non mentionnés.

a) aménager des puits conformes aux normes d'hygiène dans toutes les parcelles;
b) construire des latrines conformes aux normes d'hygiène dans toutes les parcelles;
c) brancher beaucoup de bornes fontaines;
d) mettre un système d'égout;
e) tracer des routes;
f) construire des puits collectifs conformes aux normes d'hygiène, et équipés de pompes aspirantes;
g) construire des latrines collectives conformes aux normes d'hygiène;
h) brancher des robinets dans toutes les parcelles;
i) asphalter les routes;
j) ramassage d'ordures;
k) éclairage public;
l) éclairage dans toutes les maisons;
m) autres à préciser.

B2) S'il faut équiper les mêmes quartiers, placez près de chaque équipement public un numéro de 1 à 16 selon l'ordere de préférence. Ajoutex si possible les équipements non mentionnés.

a) église;
b) maternité
c) dispensaire;
d) école primaire mixte;
e) construire un complexe sportif;

f) école secondaire pour filles avec toutes options;
g) gendarmerie;
h) aménager un terrain de jeux;
i) école mixte avec toutes options;
j) école technique pour garçons;
k) hôpital;
l) école technique pour filles;
m) centre commericial;
n) école secondaires pour garçons à toutes options;
o) centre social;
p) autres à préciser.

B3) A qui confierez-vous la réalisation de ces projets? Placez près de chaque réalisateur un numéro de 1 a 6 selon l'ordre de préférence. Ajoutez s'il en manque des réalisateurs potentiels non mentionnés.

a) gouvernement ou autorités urbaines;
b) organisme international;
c) coopératives d'habitants;
d) religieux:
e) entrepreneur privé zaïrois;
f) entrepreneur privé étranger;
g) autres à préciser.

QUESTION C: LA RENOVATION URBAINE

C1) S'il faut raser des quartiers, des camps, des lieux, des bâtiments, des maisons, quels sont ceux qui méritent d'être immédiatment rasés? Numérotez de 1 à 12 par ordre de préférence. Ajoutez en d'autres s'il y a lieu.

a) quartier Taba-Zaïre;
b) zone de TSF des forces Armées Zaïroises;
c) quartier Kasungami;
d) quartier Kampemba;
e) quartier de la victoire;
f) quartier Kigoma;
g) camp militaire Yangu;
h) quartier Zaïre;
i) quartier Katuba extension;
j) quartier Tumbototo;
k) camp militaire préfabriqué;
l) camp militaire Mutombo;
m) autres à préciser.

C2) Que faut-il installer à la place? Placez près de chaque équipement un numéro de 1 à 23 par ordre de préférence. Ajoutez en d'autres s'il y en a.

a) bibliothèque;
b) logements pavillonnaires (type Kenya) ou à donner en location-vente;
c) logements pavillonnaires (type Rwashi) ou à donner en location-vente;

d) logements pavillonnaires (type Katuba) ou à donner en location-vente;

e) logements pavillonnaires (type Kamalondo) ou à donner en location-vente;

f) logements pavillonnaires (type camp ouvriers Gécamines) ou à location-vente;

g) ensembles collectifs (type immeubles carrefour);

h) ensembles collectifs (type batiment Granat);

i) complexe hospitalier;

j) complexe scolaire technique;

k) complexe d'école secondaires;

l) complexe d'écoles primaires;

m) complexes d'écoles maternelles;

n) camp militaire;

o) camp de travailleurs;

p) bureaux de la fonction publique;

q) parc automobile;

r) centre commercial;

s) complexe de loisir;

t) complexe industriel;

u) église;

v) arboretum;

w) verger.

C3) Placez près de chaque réalisateur du projet un numéro de 1 à 6 par ordre de préférence. A qui confierez-vous l'exécution de ces travaux de rénovation? Ajoutez s'il en a les maîtres d'ouvrage non mentionnés.

a) gouvernement ou autorités urbaines;

b) organisme international:

c) entrepreneur privé zaïrois;

d) entrepreneur privé étranger;

e) religieux;

f) coopératives des habitants;

g) autres à préciser.

QUESTION D: A PROPOS DE L'HABITAT

D1) Les matériaux de construction

De tous ces matériaux, que préféréz-vous utiliser comme matériaux de construction des logements? Placez près de chaque matériau un numéro de 1 à 8 selon l'ordre de préférence. Ajoutez des matériaux non mentionnés que vous préféréz aussi.

a) briques adobes (banco);

b) pisé;

c) briques cuites;

d) planches ou bois;

e) briques ciments (parpings);

f) fûts déroulés;

g) cartons;

h) pierre de taille;

i) autres à préciser.

D2) Les matériaux de clôture

Que préféréiez-vous utiliser comme matériaux de clôture des parcelles? Placez près de chaque matériau un numéro de 1 à 17 par ordre de préférence. Ajoutez des matériaux non mentionnés qui vous semblent utiles.

a) euphorbes;
b) briques adobes;
c) hibiscus;
d) autres plantes;
e) fûts déroulés;
f) grillages (treillis ou grilles);
g) nattes;
h) tôles;
i) briques ciment;
j) bougainvilliés;
k) arbres fruitiers;
l) bambous;
m) planches ou bois;
n) cartons;
o) briques cuites
p) fils barbélés;
q) pisé;
r) autres à préciser.

D3) Les matériaux de toiture

Pour vos maisons, que préféréz-vous avoir comme matériaux de toiture? Placez près de chaque matériau de 1 à 8 par ordre de préférence. Ajoutez des matériaux non mentionnés que vous jugez utiles aussi.

a) tôle ondulée;
b) éternit;
c) chaume;
d) ardoises;
e) tôle plate en cuivre fabriquée par la Gécamines;
f) fûts déroulés;
g) tuiles;
h) toit en terrasse, en dur (toit plat);
i) autres à préciser.

D4) Les matériaux de sécurité

Pour vos maisons, placez prés de chaque type de sécurité un numéro de 1 à 7 par ordre de souhait du type de sécurité que vous souhaiteriez. Ajoutez un ou d'autres types non mentionnés.

a) clôture avec tessons de bouteilles;
b) sonnerie d'alarme;
c) caméra;
d) sentinelles;
e) éclairage nocture;

f) clôture électrocutante;
g) armes;
h) autres à préciser.

The Cultural Factor in the Development of Rural Small Scale Industries: A Case Study from Bendel State of Nigeria

Albert A. Segynola
Bendel State University

Introduction

Small industrial establishments in the Nigerian rural areas can be broadly divided into four groups. In the first group are the industrial establishments that get their raw materials which are products of farming and other related activities. The industrial establishments which are agrobased involve grinding mills, food processing units, saw mills, weaving of cloths and baskets and the brewing of wine from oil palm trees and guinea corn respectively. In the second class we have industrial establishments that bring into the rural areas some raw materials from the medium-sized and urban settlements. The raw materials are obviously nonagricultural and the industries that use the raw materials are bakeries, blacksmithery, gold-smithery, tailoring welding, photo/printing works, bicycle and motor repair works. The industries in the third group use mainly nonmetallic or non-iron minerals such as clay and gravel/sandstones; in this group are pottery, brick and block moulding industrial units. Finally we have tertiary organizations that render some services which make the rural economy function properly. Some of the services are commercial, medical educational and transportational. In recent times in the various parts of Nigeria and Bendel State in particular the industries have become a vital part of the rural economy. In fact in northern Bendel alone the available evidence shows that about 44.2% of the surveyed industries were established in the eighties (Segynola, 1986). The industries thus form the off-farm sector of the rural economy and so provide off-farm employment for the rural population especially where farming is considerably seasonal and not particularly remunerative. Other factors which have helped tremendously to explain the development of small scale industries in rural areas include scarcity or shortage of cultivable land, the imbalance between population size and the extent of available cultivable land, availability of raw materials, presence of utilities such as water, electricity and roads and lastly the presence of large manufacturing plants in rural areas (Melvin, 1982; Segynola, 1986; Cawley, 1979; Buttel, 1982). Researchers particularly in Nigeria are yet to examine quantitatively or empirically the cultural factor in the development of the industries in the rural areas.

Culture has been defined in several ways (Piddington, 1950; Ayisi, 1979). Rather than engage in semantics about the definition of culture, the component parts of culture which are relevant to this study are denoted. Culture pertains to (i) the ways of life and the means of livelihood of a people including the products the tools and the techniques of production in use in the people's communities; (ii) the values of a people; (iii) the peoples' mode of dressing and worship (religion); and (iv) the prevailing laws of inheritance of property. An important feature of culture is that apart from the fact that it can evolve on its own and then subsequently change, as a result of some internal factors, change in the cultural system of a people can also be caused by external factors. Culture is therefore dynamic and the nature and rate of change is due to the diffusion (spread and adoption) of innovations and the resourcefulness of the people under consideration. In the process of change, the prevailing culture in a place becomes an amalgam of two cultures. The first is indigenous while the second is exotic. Whatever form it takes, culture has some relationship with the pattern of development which small scale industries in the rural environs are not an exception, although for rural Nigeria it is only the relationship between agriculture and culture that has been extensively documented (Famoriyo, 1979; Abogunje, 1981).

It is the above consideration that has motivated this study. The substantive objective of the paper therefore is to examine the role of culture in the development of some rural small scale industries located in northern Bendel, Nigeria. The remaining portion of this study is divided into three sections. In the first section, the study area is examined with a view to providing background information for the study. In this same section the research methodology is discussed. The second section deals with the findings of the study. The third section is brief and is the conclusion and the policy implications of the study.

The Study Area and Research Methodology

The area of study is northern Bendel. The region consists of five local government areas (LGAS), viz Akoko Edo, Agbazilo, Etsake, Okpevbo and Owan. Fig. 1 [see map at end of this article] which shows the location of the LGAS reveals further that they are situated in one of the 19 States of the Nigerian Federation. Longitudinally and latitudinally the area is between Long 5°.75' and Long 6°.45' east of Greenwich line and Lat. 6°.45' and Lat. 7°.75' north of the equator. Obviously the LGAS are far from the coastal portions of the country. Furthermore the prevailing geologic geomorphic, climatic and vegetative conditions are significantly different from the conditions in the coastal areas. While mangrove/swamp conditions predominate the coastal areas, guinea savana and rain forest conditions prevail in northern Bendel. In fact in Agbazilo and Okpebho rainforest conditions constitute the general rule while in the remaining three LGAS, guinea savana conditions prevail.

Generally the indigenes of the region are Edo speaking. The region in fact presently constitutes the northern part of the then old Benin Kingdom. Today the indigenous inhabitants based on lingual affinities can be divided into three main groups, viz the Ishans in Agbazilo and Okpebho LGAS, the Afenmais in Owan and Etsake LGAS, and the Yorubas in Akoko Edo. As a result of migrations into the area other ethnic groups like the Ibos from east of the Niger, the Yorubas from Southwestern Nigeria, the Hausas/Fulanis from northern Nigeria and the Igbirras from the Middlebelt of the country now live in the study region. To a considerable extent and in cultural or ethnic terms, the study region typifies the Federal Republic of Nigeria.

Apart from the Igbirras that live in scattered farmsteads in northern Bendel, all the other ethnic groups live with the indigenes in the existing settlements. This pattern of settlement notwithstanding the current ethnic composition is significant for the development of rural small scale industries. Because the rural small scale industries are deep rooted in the culture of the people and because this group of industries abound in all the states of the federation, the current rural small scale industrial landscape of the study region typifies that of the entire country. This observation is due to the fact a majority of the immigrants on getting to the study region practice some of the arts; furthermore, the presence of the nonindigenes creates a viable market for the continued functioning of the industries. On the part of the indigenes however, there is need to emphasize that apart from inheriting some of the techniques of producing the items of the industries from their predecessors, in recent times the industries help in "baiting out" some of the farmers, especially the small holders, from the undesirable consequences of seasonal farming due to the seasonal pattern of rain fall in northern Bendel. It is also important to stress that the two major external influences northern Bendel was exposed to beginning from the late 18th century A.D. (Bradbury, 1959) have some influences on the development of the industries. The first influence was Muslim-oriented, the perpetrators being the Hausa and the Fulani muslims or jihadists. The attempts were really to Islamize the indigenes. The adherents of Islam religion plus the Hausas and the Fulanis resident in the study region today provide the market for basket and mat weaving, tailoring and goldsmithing, the products of which are used to satisfy the demands of the Islamic faith. The second aspect of the influence

was the restoration of peace in the study region due to the British influence
(colonization). Many settlers who were forced uphill for the purposes of
shelter during the jihadic raids were again forced downhill partly to
minimize the problems of administration the hill settlements posed to the
British imperialists. Through the consequent diffusion of innovation
(entrepreneurial and consumer), modern small scale industries diffused into
the region thus transforming the rural landscape functionally. With the exit
of the colonial masters and the implementation of various rural development
strategies (government and individual) the development of modern small
scale industries has become intensified in the study region.

In summary the contemporary small scale industrial landscape of the
study region is therefore expected to reflect some of the aspects of culture
(indigenous and exotic) discussed above. The aspects of the development of
the industries examined pertains to type of industries, products, factors of
location, capital invested and sources of finance for investment and impact
of the industries on rural development. The data used in the study were
collected between January 1983 and September 1984 (Segynola, 1986). The
main source of information was extensive fieldwork which involves the
administration of questionnaires. The questionnaire which was administered
by trained field assistants sought for information on entrepreneurs' personal
information, type of industrial establishment, age of the the industrial
establishments, size and source of establishments, capital for the industrial
units and reasons for establishing the units in the rural areas (Segynola,
1986; Chapter I for the details on the sampling techniques employed). On
the whole 172 rural settlements were randomly selected from the existing
380 rural settlements in the study region for the questionnaire administration.

The Findings

Table 1 contains information on the number of industrial establishments covered in the survey.

Table 1: Small Industries in Rural Bendel North According to Type and Origin of Entrepreneurs.

No.	Type of Industry	No. of Establishments	Origin of Entrepreneurs Indigenes	Non-Indigenes
1.	Bakery	24	21	3
2.	Blacksmithing/Goldsmithing	38	33	5
3.	Blockmoulding	14	10	4
4.	Bicycle repairing	46	41	5
5.	Brewing	9	9	–
6.	Cassava processing	43	43	–
7.	Carpentry/Furniture	73	65	8
8.	Carving	2	1	1
9.	Cutlass/Knife repairs	2	2	–
10.	Commercial enterprises	19	11	8
11.	Drum making	1	1	–
12.	Electrical works	22	19	3
13.	Fishery	2	–	2
14.	Grinding mills	94	84	10
15.	Motor works	77	67	10
16.	Oil/Soap making	20	16	4
17.	Pottery	12	10	2
18.	Photography/Printing	15	12	3
19.	Weaving	21	21	–
20.	Welding/Panel beating	44	41	3
21.	Wristwatch repairing	15	11	4
22.	Poultry	5	5	–
23.	Tailoring	102	94	8
24.	Transportation	4	4	–
25.	Shoe making/Repairs	34	30	4
26.	Sawmilling	17	14	3
27.	Miscellaneous	7	5	2
	TOTAL	762	670	92
	Percent	100.00	87.93	12.07

Source: Field Survey.

Also shown is information relating to the number of indigenous and nonindigenous entrepreneurs. Seven hundred and sixty-two (762) establishments were covered while about 88% of the entrepreneurs are indigenes of the study region. The nonindigenes therefore form roughly 12% of the entrepreneurs operating the industries in the study region. The source regions of the non-indigenes as well as their ethnic composition has been discussed above.

The industries in Table 1 on cultural basis are divided into two broad groups. In the first group we have industries whose products are among others things used for dancing, decoration, tradomedical issue and entertainment all of which are highly valued by the indigenes. The industries in this class are blacksmithery/goldsmithery, brewing of wine, wood carving, drum making, oil/soap making, pottery and the weaving of cloths, ropes and baskets. The industrial units here number 103, i.e. about 13.52% of all the surveyed units. The activities are carried out largely by the indigenes who are resident in the study region. The blacksmiths produce hoes, cutlasses, axes, spears and arrows that are used by peasant farmers; these same products serve as gifts and ornaments for decoration of houses. The products of gold-smiths are earrings, necklaces and rings of different types, these are used mainly by women and girls for dressing and self-beautification. In the carving industry the products are carved doors, stools, wooden drums, walking sticks, mortars, etc. The wood is derived from the guinea savana and forest belts of the study area. As for the oil/soap processing industrial units, the products are palm oil and soaps which are used for domestic consumption and tradomedical works. In the weaving industry, cotton lint is converted into threads which are dyed and woven into cloths of different types; there are also works based on palm fronds and leaves, the products of which include ropes, fans, baskets, hats, bags and sleeping mats. The pottery industry in the study region depends on clay soils and pots of various types and uses are produced. The pots are used for storing water, cooking food, and decoration, i.e. as flower vases especially as flowers are planted in the pots.

Field inquiries reveal that the above industrial activities are practiced on part-time basis. The entrepreneurs who are farmers therefore engage in part-time farming and so during the slack period when farming activities are slowed down the farmers take to these off-farm activities. In the main the severity of unemployment is reduced in the study region as the farmers engage in the industries. The second major group constitutes 86.48% of the surveyed industries and can be said to be exotic to the region to a large extent. The industries can be subdivided into food processing (bakery, cassava/garri, and grinding mills), transportation (bicycle and motor repairs), apparel (tailoring), welding/panel beating and electrical and wrist-watch repairs. Others are photo-printing, cutlass/knife repairs, wood based industries (carpentry/furniture works and sawmills), shoe making/repairs and blockmoulding industries. All the industries in this group have been "imported" into the study region especially in terms of raw materials, the tools and the techniques of production.

There are two stages in the process of the diffusion or importation of the industrial activities into the area of study. The first stage involves the arrival of the industries, tools and techniques from the advanced countries to the major urban centres of Nigeria such as Lagos, Enugu, Ibadan, Port Harcourt, Benin, Kano and Kaduna to name just a few centres. This phenomenon can be ascribed to the contact Nigeria had with the advanced countries during the colonial period (Adegbola, 1983; Onyemelukwe, 1983) and thereafter. The second stage has to do with the "importation" into the rural areas from the Nigerian urban centres. For our study area the urban centres of Benin City, Onitsha and even distant centres like Lagos and Ibadan do play a major role in this regard. Raw materials in particular that have been known to have come from urban centres to the rural areas include flour, milk, sugar, threads, buttons, cement, foam, etc. (Segynola, in press).

The successful "importation" can be perceived in the form of an advanced culture diffusing or spreading into an area that has a less advanced culture especially in terms of the tools of production and the durability of goods. Many factors underlie the successful importation, the most important of which is the rural residents' acceptance of the new culture of production as a panacea to some for the existing causes of low production, low income and unemployment. In addition to the availability of raw materials and a ready market for the products in the rural areas, another important factor from the cultural point of view is the smallness and the sources of the capital (in monetary terms) needed to start and keep running the industries. More than sixty-two per cent of entrepreneurs indicated that they spent between N1.00 and N4,000 each. The sources of finance as shown on Table 2 are mainly four, with personal savings, and gifts from friends and relatives as the most important sources. The frequencies on Table 2 reveal some important factors about the culture of the Africans generally. The high frequencies for personal savings and relatives/friends portray on one hand, reveal the individual's indomitable will to eke out a living on his own and on the other hand the African's philosophy that people should help their friends and relatives in various forms depending on the work that has to be done. In the building of houses for instance, relatives and friends of the would be landlord do contribute in terms of personal labour and food items required to feed the workers. Also in burial ceremonies food items and money are contributed to the bereaved. It is not therefore surprising to find that even in starting and running the rural small industries, this agent of rural development has played a very vital role.

The Table shows further that the culture of borrowing cash with interest from modern financial institutions has not been completely imbibed by the inhabitants of the study area. Hence the small percentage that derived their establishment or investment finance from cooperatives, money lenders and bank loans. However, illiteracy and scarcity of modern financial institutions are responsible too. With particular reference to money lenders the terms of lending are very stringent. The interest rate for money borrowed for instance is 50K on every two naira per month. People who go to this source for money are those who do not have, in most cases, reliable or well-to-do friends and relatives who will not be happy to see their loved ones suffer in the hands of the money lenders. The procurement of bank loans nevertheless shows that the area is opening up to one of the modern means of acquiring credit for business development. The analysis of data shows that the majority of those who borrowed money from the banks are in the modern small scale industries such as sawmills, bakeries, motor works and blockmoulding.

Table 2: Sources of Investment Finance for the Small Industries Surveyed in Bendel North.

Source	No. of Responses	Percent of Total Responses
Personal Savings	660	67.55
Relatives/Friends	161	16.48
Cooperatives	71	7.27
Bank Loan	48	4.91
Money Lenders	37	3.39
Government	Nil	Nil
TOTAL	977	100.00

Source: Field Survey

Over all, the role of the industries in promoting rural development with specific reference to the boosting of the production of the raw materials and the creation of employment opportunities has been widely discussed by Segynola (in press, 1986). What can be added to the findings in these two studies is the items of wealth (goods) purchased by those engaged in the industries. This line of investigation is in order because no precise figures of the income and the profits generated are available. This is due to the fact that the income and the profits are not recorded as they come in irregular flows. Secondly the goods purchased from the income and the profits generated from the industries have some cultural significance. First, through the industries, items which contribute to rural recreation and to some nontraditional sources of information, are being introduced into the rural environs; the items are radios and television sets (28.98% of the responses). This is diverting people from traditional recreation like dancing, fighting, etc. The second area is transportational; the motor cycles and bicycles (12.66%) purchased are helping to reduce the incidence of human porterage in the study region. The third dimension is the monetisation of land for the diversification of the rural economy. Land that used to be individually or communally owned and not meant to be sold has eventually become an item that can be purchased; the buying of animals for domestication also shows some marked deviation from the traditional giving of animals free of charge to relatives for rearing. Finally are the items under miscellaneous. They include beds, various clothing materials, cooking utensils like stoves and furniture (chairs, tables, cupboards, etc); the items reveal considerable diffusion of consumer innovations into the rural environs. The innovations have helped in modifying part of the cultural landscape of the study region.

Table 3: Items of Wealth Acquired from the Income Earned by the Labour Employed in the Industries in the Study Region.

Items	Frequency	Percent of Total
Radios	110	23.61
Children's Education	68	14.59
Motor Cycles	42	9.01
Acquisition of Land	40	8.58
Rearing of Animals	40	8.58
Contribution to Development Fund	40	8.58
Houses	25	5.37
Television Sets	25	5.37
Bicycles	17	3.65
Electric Fans	17	3.65
Miscellaneous	42	9.01
Total	466	100.00

Source: Field Survey.

Synopsis

In this study the positive relationship between rural small scale industries, rural development and cultural issues has been demonstrated. The aspects of culture that have caused this relationship to exist need to be encouraged. Fundamental in the analysis is the cultural permissiveness of absorptiveness of the people living in the study region. This cultural feature has partly led to the location and the functioning of the industries. In addition is the impact of the industries on the development of the rural areas.

The first aspect that has to be encouraged is the provision of investment finance by relatives especially now that the Nigerian government financial resources are dwindling. Another alternative is for the government to encourage modern financial institutions to grant loans to the industrialists liberally. The second issue is the encouragement of consumers, especially those in the urban areas, to patronize the products of the industrialists; government patronage is also needed here. Finally the disposing of the income generated, thus diversifying the rural economy, should be encouraged.

BIBLIOGRAPHY

Adegbola, O. "Manufacturing Industries," in *A Geography of Nigerian Development* (2nd ed). J.S. Oguntoyinbo, O.O. Areola, and M. Filani (Eds). Ibadan: Heinemann Educational Books, Chpt 19, 1983, pp. 326-338.

Ayisi, E.O. *An Introduction to the Study of African Culture.* (2nd ed) London: Heinemann Educational Books, 1979, pp. 1-5.

Bradbury, R.E. *The Benin Kingdom and Edo Speaking Peoples of Southwestern Nigeria.* London: International African Institute, 1957.

Buttel, F.H. "The Political Economy of Part-time Farming," *Geojournal.* Vol. 6, No. 4, 1982, pp. 293-300.

Cawley, M.E. "Rural Industrialization and Social Change in Western Ireland," *Sociologica Ruralis.* Vol. 19, No. 1, 1979, pp. 43-59.

Famoriyo, S. *Land Tenure and Agricultural Development in Nigeria.* Ibadan: The Nigerian Institute of Social and Economic Research, 1979.

Mabogunje, A.L. *The Developmental Process: A Spatial Perspective.* London: Hutchinson, 1981.

Melvin, B.L. "The Place of Part-time Farmer," *Rural Sociology.* Vol. 19, 1983, pp. 281-286.

Onyemelukwe, J.O.C. "Structural and Locational Characteristics of Manufacturing," in *A Geography of Nigerian Development* (2nd ed). J.S. Oguntoyinbo, O.O. Areola, and M. Filani (Eds), Ibadan: Heinemann Educational Books, Chpt 17, 1983, pp. 296-310.

Piddington, R. *Introduction of Social Anthropology.* London: Oliver and Boyd, 1950, p. 3.

Segynola, A.A. "Rural Small Scale Industries in Bendel North and Their role in Rural Development," Unpublished Ph.D. dissertation, Department of Geography and Regional Planning, University of Benin, Benin City, Nigeria, 1986.

Segynola, A.A. "Rural Small Scale Industries in Bendel North, Nigeria: Their Role in the Production of Raw Materials," *Aman, Journal of Society, Culture and Environment* Vol. 5, Nos. 1 and 2, in press.

Location map of
Northern Bendel, Nigeria

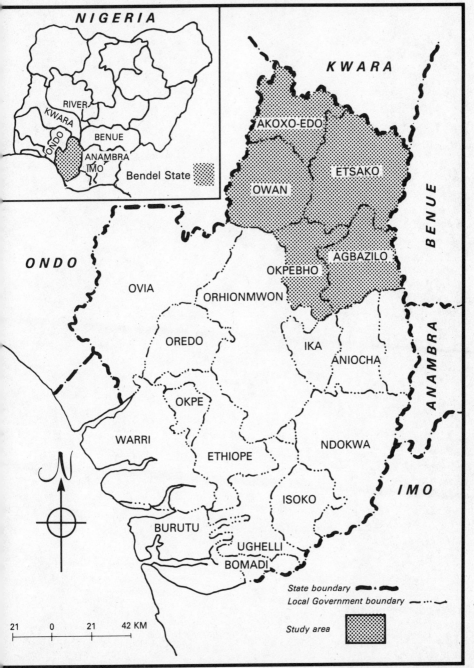

NIGERIA

RIVER

KWARA

ONDO

BENUE

ANAMBRA
IMO

Bendel State

KWARA

AKOXO-EDO

ETSAKO

OWAN

ONDO

OVIA

OKPEBHO

AGBAZILO

ORHIONMWON

OREDO

IKA

ANIOCHA

BENUE

ANAMBRA

OKPE

WARRI

ETHIOPE

NDOKWA

ISOKO

IMO

BURUTU

UGHELLI

BOMADI

State boundary
Local Government boundary

Study area

21   0   21   42 KM

Swaziland: The Vagaries of Geopolitics, Subordination, and Collaboration

Joshua B. Mugyenyi
Dalhousie University

I. Introduction

After an impressive degree of research activity and creativity during the 1960s and 1970s, the comparative study of foreign policy, just like the wider field of comparative politics, has since lost momentum and stature. It has become something of a degenerating research agenda, marked by the absence of any organizing macro theory or any agreed set of assumptions.[1] Foreign policy, for example, continues to be variously perceived as output, process or behaviour without any overall attempt to link these three types of perceptions into a coherent comparative framework;[2] i.e. there is not yet an agreed paradigm.

If, in general terms, comparative studies of foreign policy have not faired well, the study of small and peripheral states' foreign policies has been even more deficient. The dominance of "power politics" and "balance of power" approaches in orthodox versions of international relations has perpetuated the view of nation-states as motivated and preoccupied only by power maximization and strategies of self-help in an international system dominated by security concerns and anarchy.[3] This implied association between power and foreign policy necessarily defines the latter as a process of exercising influence in international relations. Thus, third world small states have been footnoted casually as inactive system "takers," characterized by reactive foreign policies in which information and substantive decision-making are controlled by external interests.[4] This perception was reinforced by the classical dependency analysis which dismissed the "satellite states" and ruling classes in such small "neo-colonial" states as simply auxiliary functionaries of the global capitalist system, with no independent domestic and foreign policies of their own.

The new realities of the 1980s, however, defy such blanket assertions. First, the "Third World" as an analytic category has had to give way to a more differentiated "periphery" resulting in "Fourth" (even "Fifth" worlds at the edge of the international division of labour. And second, these increasingly marginal states have responded to the contemporary socio-economic crises with strikingly different domestic and foreign policies even though they are similarly constrained by systemic variables emanating from the current international order. Therefore, the evident divergencies in foreign policy orientations among these states cannot be fully explained by their structural weaknesses and dependencies within the world economy because those attributes are a common denominator to all of them. Thus, there is a growing realization that external constraints need to be examined alongside the internal socio-economic and political dynamics of these (peripheral) societies, such as the nature and role of the state and of social structures, in order to understand the imperatives of, as well as differences in, foreign policy processes there.

Nowhere is this argument and debate more pertinent than in the Southern African region. Botswana, Lesotho and Swaziland (BLS) are small states whose landlocked economies are overwhelmingly dependent on South Africa. They are constantly living under the shadow of Pretoria's "total strategy" of regional destabilization. They have all been victims of South African political and economic pressure, as well as commando raids purportedly in pursuit of African National Congress (ANC) operatives and bases. Fore example, on 30 December 1985 South Africa imposed an economic blockade against Lesotho until the latter, in the face of starvation, yielded to the removal of ANC operatives from its territory.[5]

BLS countries are almost similarly vulnerable to South African military economic and political threats. Yet, within those tight regional parameters, the BLS countries' foreign policies exhibit markedly different orientations, attitudes and behaviours. Botswana and Lesotho have tended to keep their cooperation with the South African regime to a pragmatic minimum; quite often they have engaged in defiant opposition against apartheid policies and intimidation. On the other hand, Swaziland's policy has been characterized by warm, even enthusiastic, cooperation and collaboration with South Africa; it has diplomatic relations and a security agreement with Pretoria and opposes economic sanctions against South Africa, and its security forces routinely help their South African counterparts to hunt down ANC operatives in the kingdom. Although South Africa's economic dominance and destabilization strategy constitute the parameters within which BLS decision-making occurs, they cannot explain the qualitative differences among BLS foreign policies. The task of this study is to locate and explain domestic and external factors that have, over time, shaped Swazi foreign policy and to account for the evident policy differences among the BLS countries.

Swaziland's foreign policy processes: competing frameworks

Swaziland, stretching over 17,000 square kilometres, with a population of approximately 670,000, is the second smallest country on the African continent. Its diminutive size is exacerbated by its land-locked location between South African and Mozambique, two big yet unequal neighbours that are hostile to each other and are locked in civil wars that regularly spill over into the kingdom. Until the late 1970s, it was no more than an anthropological curiosity known to the rest of the world through the works of Hilda Kuper who also doubled as King Sobhuza's official biographer.[6] With heightened conflicts, confrontations, and contradictions in the region, Swaziland has gradually attracted more attention from political observers.

Largely inspired by the dependency school, most studies on Swaziland have focused almost entirely on the impact of the world economy, the pauperising nature of capitalism, and the subsequent formation of a dependent (labour reserve) economy totally subordinated to South African and British capital. These external forces were also presumed to have been largely responsible for Swazi political, social and power structures.[7] As dependency analysis came increasingly under attack so did the purely external logic explanation that ignored Swazi domestic social relations as an important factor in understanding the operations of the state. The interests, perceptions and ideologies of the ruling class — themselves crucial elements — together with the external parameters, seem to offer a more comprehensive explanation of Swaziland's foreign relations. The widening scope of the debate about Swaziland's foreign policy can be categorized into three loose frameworks.

The first framework is an "articulation" of the traditional power theory of international relations and the ideology of homogeneity. The former associates power with foreign policy. Thus Swaziland is simply assumed to be dependent upon, and threatened by, the more powerful South Africa, and its foreign policy necessarily reactive, inactive and submissive.[8] This traditional power approach is beefed up by what has been referred to as an "anthropological (state) ideology of homogeneity" which assumes that Swaziland is "somehow unique in the world in that inequalities in general and social classes in particular are absent, as the attributes of a traditional African redistribution system ensure an overall social equalization under the paternal guidance of a benign monarchy."[9] Thus this framework posits that the Swazi society can be understood outside southern African regional dynamics and contradictions. It also follows that the kingdom's foreign policy is viewed as a reactive process that, through diplomacy, negotiation and "good" behaviour, seeks to enhance the security of a homogeneous country and its romanticized "Swazi way of life."

The second framework, based on starker versions of underdevelopment theory, posits that the Swazi political economy is so structurally subordinated to international (and particularly South African) interests that the resultant internal political structures have no choice but to conduct a foreign policy that reflects this dependency.[10] In addition, the logic of external capital conceptualises Swaziland as a "comprador" state with a ruling class that is no more than a stooge of imperialism, and in which the external relationship with Britain and South Africa is seen as *the* all-determining relation for the Swazi economy and socio-political structures.[11] This framework, it has been argued, does not distinguish between economic and political forms of domination. Thus by denying it any measure of real as opposed to formal political independence, Swaziland is put on more or less the same footing as South Africa's bantustans.[12]

The third, and most recent, framework dismisses the preceding formulations essentially as follows: the first as descriptive and a reformulation of state ideology; the second as nefarious, linear, mechanical and incomplete. It suggests, instead, that Swaziland's foreign policy can be more adequately explained by the contradictory nature of Swazi social relations within which the ruling class and the state are situated; i.e. that the policy has its dominant imperatives inside, rather than outside, the country.[13] It is further posited that South Africa's economic domination and military coercion only establish wide parameters within which Swaziland and the other two BLS countries exercise a variety of foreign policy options.[14] The ideology, in tandem with foreign capital penetration and domination, offers the most complete explanation of Swaziland's foreign policy behaviour. This contention then opens the radical intra-paradigmic disagreements between instrumentalist and structuralist positions regarding the problematic of state autonomy. The "instrumentalists" conceive of the state as an instrument of domination and coercion at the hands of the ruling classes,[15] while "structuralists" contend that the functions and behaviours of the state are broadly determined by the structure of society rather than by particular individuals who occupy positions of power.[16]

By analyzing the conjuncture between international, regional and domestic factors this study hopes to be able to test the hypotheses and assumptions of the three frameworks already abstracted and throw further light on Swazi foreign policy-making and its points of departure from that of Botswana and Lesotho. Three factors have consistently had a profound influence on the Swazi foreign policy-making process:

1. penetration and incorporation of Swaziland into the global and regional (South African) economic structures;

2. South Africa's strategy of regional destabilization;

3. domestic structures, conflicts and struggles.

The Penetration and Incorporation Process

The penetration of Swaziland by British and Boer capital, dating back to the late nineteenth century, has been adequately documented and analyzed elsewhere.[17] Suffice it to note here that, by 1907, the Swazi colonial state had transferred two-thirds of the kingdom's land to settler concessionaires and foreign investors. The Swazi population was pushed into the remaining, and the poorest, one-third which was barely able to sustain the most elementary form of subsistence farming. This land alienation not only marginalized the Swazis but also created a huge reserve of cheap labour readily available for foreign-owned mines and sugar, pineapple and timber plantations.

It may be an oversimplification to impute a complete identity of interest among the colonial state, foreign and settler interests in Swaziland. While, for example, owners of capital were all for total land dispossession, the colonial state backed down on the issue in the face of sustained Swazi protest. Also foreign and settler interests disagreed intensely over the issue of labour supply.[18] The point, however, is that capital interests, with the help of the colonial state, and later with the collaboration of the local ruling class, were able to secure control over land and conditions under which plantation production took place. To date, twenty years after independence, 44% of arable land is owned by foreign companies.[19]

Over the years Swaziland's links with international and South African capital have deepened. Britain dominates the banking sector through Barclay's and Standard Chartered; it also controls sugar production, which accounts for 40% of Swaziland's foreign earnings. Between 1978 and 1982 the net outflow of repatriated profits and salary remittances on the services account was 40% of Swaziland's annual export receipts. These and other outflows left the country with only 50% of export value to finance imports.[20]

South African capital now controls almost all the commanding heights of the Swazi economy, particularly the agro-industrial sector. For example, the Anglo-American Corporation controls 90% of citrus production and has controlling shares in mineral extraction, timber production and meat processing; Zululand Food Producers have recently taken over the pineapple and grapefruit industries; Sun International controls tourism while Cencor dominates the coal and iron-ore industries; and South African Breweries, Barlow Rand and Natie Kirsh control manufacturing and commercial sectors.[21]

Swaziland imports all of its oil and 65% of its electric power from South Africa. The latter supplies 95% of the kingdom's imports, which include basic staple foods such as maize, potatoes and milk, and 18% of Swaziland's active labour force works in the Republic. Funds transferred to the kingdom as a member of the South African Customs Union (SACU) account for 61.4% of total government revenue.[22] Being a member of the Rand Monetary Authority (RMA), Swaziland's fiscal and monetary policies are effectively controlled from Pretoria. In any case, it relies entirely on the South African transportation system for its exports, a dependence that has deepened as Mozambique's transport infrastructure continues to be disrupted by South African and Mozambican National Resistance (MNR or Renamo) sabotage.

In 1964 Verwoerd, then prime minister of South Africa, was so satisfied with the economic subordination of Swaziland to South Africa that he did not even bother to resist the proposed independence of the kingdom. In his own words,

[I]f this is their [Swazi] place of employment, if this is the source of their revenue, if our cooperation in connection with the customs union is in their interest, then any individual government that is established there must maintain friendship with its neighbour in the interests of its people.[23]

Thus, in terms of physical outlay and investment, South African and international capitals historically have had far greater stakes and interests in Swaziland than in either Botswana or Lesotho. In order, therefore, to secure control of the conditions under which plantation production took place, capital owners needed a firmer grip on Swazi domestic and foreign policy processes than in the other BLS countries. This rather obvious factor is part of the complex jig-saw puzzle that needs to be put together in order to explain the Swazi brand of foreign policy as well as differences between its policy and those of Botswana and Lesotho.

South Africa's "total strategy" of regional destabilization

If the subordination of Swaziland to the needs of foreign capital has profoundly circumscribed the conditions within which its foreign policy operates, South Africa's belligerent strategy of regional destabilization constitutes a further complication. The collapse of the Portuguese empire in the 1970s, Zimbabwe's independence in 1980, and relentless internal resistance in the Republic, as well as external political and economic pressures, combined to throw South Africa's long-standing strategic assumptions and thinking off their hinges. Fresh from their own liberation struggles, the newly independent countries in the region were expected to give sanctuary and material help to the ANC. These new possibilities, construed by Pretoria as "total onslaught," prompted South Africa's so-called total strategy in which Swaziland has become a crucial player.

South Africa's regional strategy has several components: a drive towards a constellation of dependable "anti-marxist" (first line of defense) states that are structurally tied to its Unity (OAU); destabilization of hostile states' economic and military infrastructures; and mobilization of economic, political and military resources to defend the apartheid state.[24] South Africa has deployed a combination of (i) economic incentives (e.g. SACU revenue), (ii) economic threats such as restrictions on migrant labour from neighbouring black states, (iii) disruption of SADCC's transport system and deliberate delays in handling goods destined to its neighbours, and (iv) military action and harassment of established governments along with support of puppet groups (e.g. UNITA in Angola, Renamo, and the Lesotho Liberation Army). The main objectives are (i) to deny sanctuary to ANC operatives in the neighbouring states, (ii) to frustrate the latter's efforts aimed at reducing structural dependence on South Africa, (iii) to create conditions that sustain the perception that black majority rule invariably leads to chaos; and (iv) to drum up internal support from the white constituency.

In its apparent selective use of "carrots and sticks," the South African regime divides the independent states in the region into three broad categories: (i) conservative states which are seen as real or potential collaborators; (ii) states considered most vulnerable; and (iii) states whose political systems, ideologies and development strategies are seen as constituting the most fundamental challenge to the apartheid system.[25] Viewed on a single continuum, Swaziland remains a striking example of the first category to which South Africa offers "carrots" in return for collaboration and cooperation, while Angola and Mozambique have been subjected to a relentless "stick" in the hopes that "total strategy" might transform them from category (iii) countries to category (ii) and perhaps eventually to category (i). Thus Swaziland's foreign policy is in part a function of the broader South African "carrot-and-stick" regional policy.

The domestic structures, conflicts and struggles

While the impact of foreign capital in and South Africa's regional destabilization on Swaziland's foreign policy can be easily demonstrated, the role of internal factors remains underestimated, under-researched and rather problematic.

Although it is not readily admitted by many analysis of Swazi society (or of the other predominantly agrarian societies in Africa), there are considerable problems regarding the identification of domestic (incipient) classes and the precise nature and functions of the state.[26] The tip of this problem shows in Levin's treatment of relations and "coordination between *Tibiyo* and the *State*," a separation that points to a real difficulty (and potential confusion) in determining where the state begins and ends in Swaziland.[27] This enterprise is not made any easier by the complex power structures in which the "traditional" and "modern" institutions run into each other in such a way as to confound attempts at explicating the essentials of the state. Bearing those caveats in mind, there still remains the task of identifying methods by which the ruling class has secured political power and entrenched its economic interests that have in turn shaped its perceptions, ideology, and foreign policy.

During the colonial period, Swazi traditional rulers had a weak economic base. They were excluded from direct control of the productive process and accumulation by the colonial state. This was partly intended to protect the settler community from competition. Land alienation also reduced their political and economic control over the peasantry. Since the 1970s, however, this situation has changed substantially. At independence the Swazi monarchy won two important concessions from the colonial state: control over mineral rights and authority over the allocation of land on Swazi National Land (SNL). These two instruments, together with joint ventures with foreign capital, have consolidated the hold of the ruling class on the state machinery and, therefore, established its dominance. As the following foreign policy analysis will show, this process has enabled the ruling class to develop fairly independent interests and agendas that are not necessarily identical to those of foreign capital. In order to situate these assertions in the Swazi political reality, and to see how these ultimately enter the overall foreign policy equation, it is necessary to examine in some detail two related processes: (i) state accumulation, principally through *Tibiyo*; and (ii) the use of the state to preserve the *status quo*, i.e. "the Swazi way of life."

State accumulation: the role of Tibiyo TakaNgwane

As already noted, one of the most important concessions the Swazi aristocracy won at independence was control over mineral rights and the revenue accruing therefrom. In 1968 the king formed *Tibiyo TakaNgwane* as a depository for the income derived from mineral royalties. In theory, *Tibiyo* belonged to all Swazis who, "as of right," owned nominal shares in the fund. In practice, however, *Tibiyo* benefited the royal family and a few chosen members of the emergent middle class.[28] From its inception *Tibiyo*'s operations have been shrouded in mystery: its board is appointed by the king and its revenue is neither taxable nor subject to public accountability. Meanwhile, through joint ventures with foreign capital, albeit as a junior partner, *Tibiyo*'s growth has been phenomenal. These partnerships with foreign-owned — agro-industrial, banks, service, insurance, manufacturing, newspaper and tourist — multinationals have been documented and analyzed elsewhere;[29] as have *Tibiyo*'s purchases of land from non-Swazis which have been converted into large, highly mechanized, agricultural enterprises. [30]

Tibiyo has thus been the single-most important vehicle for state accumulation as well as the centre-piece of the alliance between the Swazi ruling class and foreign capital. The two share ideological perceptions and interests in the preservation of the *status quo* in the region. But it has also heightened conflict and contradictions within the ruling class: with the death of Sobhuza in 1982, contending factions joined the race to gain access and control of *Tibiyo*'s enormous patronage, political power, and unaccountable investments and cash reserves. The tensions between "modern" and "traditional" arms of the state, between members of the royal families culminating in four palace coup attempts in 1984 alone, centred around control of this organization.[31] These factional fights were also characterized by varying positions regarding major foreign policy issues such as relations with South Africa, the ANC and the land "deal."

Use of the state as an instrument of control, repression and domination

The most potent state instrument used by the ruling class to secure political power has been control and distribution of "communally owned" land (SNL) supposedly held in trust by the king. Traditional institutions, principally the chiefs, have enormous leverage over the peasantry whose continued access to land is contingent upon their loyalty to the monarchy and the *status quo*. There have been numerous occasions when chiefs, acting on behalf of the king, have not hesitated to dispossess peasant households of their land, if the latter were deemed disloyal. As a result, thousands of peasants have been removed forcibly, banished, resettled or simply dumped by government trucks in the middle of nowhere. For example, between May and November 1984, three hundred and sixty-five families, involving about 1,700 people, were thrown off their land.[32] Although land allocation, as a political instrument, will continue to be eroded by increased education and urbanization, it still remains a major mechanism by which the state controls the fortunes of the peasantry.

There are several other state-directed methods which the ruling class has employed to secure political control and sustain the *status quo*. They include: (i) use of traditional courts which use unwritten "laws," dispensed by the king's nominees, to preside over land, marital, and civil cases; (ii) subversion of the labour movement through systematic harassment of trade unions and the use of the monarch's representatives (*Ndabazabantu*) as labour relations officers in industrial establishments; (iii) abrogation of the constitution and strengthening of the traditional administrative system (*Tinkundla*); (iv) manipulation of the electoral, rather selection, system that enables the king and the chiefs to pack the "modern" parliament with their cronies; and (v) perpetuation of feudal rituals and ceremonies that are intended to reinforce the Swazi "law and custom"[33] — i.e. a vague form of "mystification" intended to legitimize the *status quo*.

Thus, through *Tibiyo*, control over land allocation, and use of a host of state controls, the Swazi ruling class has acquired and consolidated economic and political power; these power structures have developed a base, interests, and logic that cannot be explained as the actions and behaviour of mere stooges of imperialism in a comprador stated. Rather, the full explication of Swaziland's foreign (and domestic) policies requires analysis of the confluence of global, regional and domestic imperatives, crises and discontinuities. A simple focus on structural subordination and the ruling class/capital alliance — valid and common attributes as these are — only tends to give a partial explanation which is incapable of accounting for differences in foreign policy behaviour among small players in the international system.

A profile of Swaziland's foreign policy

Having established the major parameters within which Swazi foreign policy operates, specific policies and behaviours gradually emerge into comprehensible patterns. At the general level Swaziland's foreign policy displays two apparently contradictory elements: on the one hand, it is South Africa's closest ally in the region and, on the other, a member of the OAU, SADCC, the Preferential Trade Area for Eastern and Southern Africa (PTA), and a signatory to the series of Lome Conventions with the European Community (EC). These contradictory allegiances have served the South African regime and Swazi ruling class interests well. It is known, for example, that South Africa uses part of Swaziland's Lome Convention quota to break into the European market: beef is bought cheaply from the neighbouring countries and South Africa's own production is sent to Europe. Nearer home, Swaziland is used as a gateway for South African industrial and other goods to several African countries. With galloping inflation and a scarcity of commodities (partly as a result of destabilization) most SADCC member-states routinely purchase South African consumer and durable goods which are conveniently available in Swaziland. In any case, it is common knowledge that planeloads of South African goods are airlifted from Swaziland to as far north as Tanzania on a regular basis. Official statistics, meanwhile, show that Tanzania has no trade with South Africa.[34] There is even a persistent rumour that some of the Frontline States' armed forces' uniforms are made in the Republic! Such are the contradictions in the region which tend to reinforce the perception of Swaziland's political leaders that their disposition towards South Africa is both realistic and beneficial.

The Swazi ruling class has also benefited from its close association with South Africa on several other grounds. The former has skillfully used socio-economic disintegration in some of the SADCC states, principally Mozambique, to remind the ordinary folks of hard times awaiting them in the event of change in the country's foreign policy orientation. Swaziland's leaders continue to argue that African rhetoric against South Africa is largely hypocritical — a luxury that can only be afforded by states further north.

In more immediate material terms, Swaziland's membership in SACU and RMA have sheltered it from foreign exchange and consumer good shortages.[35] This short-run stability, threatened by increasing regional conflict and confrontation, remains part of the legitimation of the Swazi state in general, and a lubricant to the alliance between the ruling class and the apartheid regime in particular.

Be that as it may, however, there is also evidence to suggest that on some occasions Swazi foreign policy has conflicted with South African regime interests in the region, thereby suggesting both more state autonomy and more independent self-interest of the ruling class in the kingdom than has hitherto been realized. For example, when liberation struggles in the former Portuguese colonies and Rhodesia gathered momentum in the 1970s and it appeared as though the dominos were due to fall all the way to the Cape, Swaziland's foreign policy shifted substantially to accommodate OAU and FLS positions. Swaziland refused the temptation of joining the Constellation of Southern African States (CONSAS) and, instead, joined SADCC; it also improved relations with Mozambique which resulted in the expulsion of Renamo and anti-Frelimo organizations from the kingdom. In April 1981 it joined Lesotho and Botswana in denouncing South Africa's destabilization in the region.[36] Further back, in 1977, King Sobhuza, following a meeting with Oliver Tambo, granted sanctuary to ANC operatives though fully aware that the latter would use this opportunity to stage guerrilla attacks inside South Africa.[37] More recently, in early February 1988, it was reported that Swaziland's two most senior policy officers were dismissed because they had handed over an ANC suspect to South African agents across the border.[38]

This series of foreign policy decisions indicates a certain degree of deliberate and independent calculation on the part of the Swazi state, in contrast to the commonly held view that BLS states are "helpless hostages" entirely subordinated to South African capital and strategic interests. In fact, it would seem that South Africa's destabilization policy was itself a response to decisions such as these in Swaziland, as well as others elsewhere in the region, the were perceived to run counter to its strategic interests.

Since 1982, however, Swaziland, under pressure from internal conflicts and South African destabilization, has shifted its policy toward more cooperation and collaboration with Pretoria. In that year a ferocious crackdown on suspected ANC members began in earnest. More than 200 alleged ANC cadres were deported to Zambia and Tanzania, five were killed in police operations, and another five were handed over to the South African police.[39] These actions were followed quickly by a spate of mysterious abductions of South Africans in Swazi jails. In June 1986, three ANC members were killed by what the Swazi police described as "foreign personnel," an oblique reference to South African agents.[40] Between August and October 1986 South African commandos attacked suspected ANC targets in the kingdom while the local police looked the other way.[41]

In 1984 the signing of the Lusaka and Nkomati accords, in which Angola and Mozambique were forced to enter what turned out to be hollow non-aggression pacts with South Africa, presented Swaziland with an unusual diplomatic windfall. Feeling vindicated about its own "realistic" relations with South Africa and no longer particularly stigmatized as a pariah state, Swaziland was confident enough to publicize its own secret dealings with South Africa by announcing the existence of a two-year security pact with Pretoria.[42] This pact was intended to:

> combat terrorism, insurgency and subversion individually and collectively as well as their right to call upon each other for such assistance and steps as may be deemed necessary or expedient to eliminate the evil.[43]

In January 1985 Swaziland/South African relations were cemented further with the opening of a South African consulate in the former's capital, Mbabane. This marked the first new South African diplomatic mission in any independent African state (Lesotho appears to have secretly followed suit in 1986) since relations were established with Malawi in 1966.[44] Despite Swaziland's insistence that the establishment is simply a trade mission, there are clear indications that this is a listening post for the South African intelligence services.[45]

IX. Economic sanctions against South Africa

One other foreign policy area in which Swaziland has fully collaborated with South Africa is on the issues of divestment, disinvestment, and economic sanctions against South Africa — instruments considered by FLS as the last peaceful means of resolving the regional conflict. While Swaziland is on record as being unequivocally against these measures, Botswana and Lesotho, admitting their inability to impose sanctions, have given tacit encouragement to others in the region and beyond to proceed with them. In the 1985 Nassau Heads of Commonwealth Conference, only Swaziland joined Britain in arguing against the imposition of such sanctions.[46] Its voting record at the United Nations is also consistently pro-South African.

The simple argument of BLS subordination to South African capital and the imperatives of the latter's regional policy cannot adequately explain the positions of the three neighbours' varying positions on the issue of sanctions. Rather, we have to look elsewhere for a fuller explanation. As the political crisis deepens in the Republic, there is likely to be an upsurge in the relocation of South African capital to Swaziland as a convenient if illicit, conduit to the outside world. There are also signs that international capital may follow this move. For example, Bata, a Canadian shoe company, closed down its factories in KwaZulu and relocated in Swaziland.[47] Thus as regional conflicts and contradictions continue to deepen, the Swazi ruling class hopes to reap short-term material benefits while publicly advancing familiar geopolitical and structural subordination arguments.

X. Incentives for collaboration

South Africa has given selected material incentives to Swaziland for such collaboration and cooperation. For example, the kingdom received material assistance from Pretoria to build a railway line through the country linking it to Eastern Transvaal and Richards Bay. South Africa also provided Swaziland with a short-term relief contribution of 50 million rands and helped in the expansion of the kingdom's main airport, Matsapa, a facility that could be used as a forward base for the South African airforce against SADCC member-states.[48]

Perhaps the biggest "carrot" Swaziland expected in return for collaboration and cooperation was the hope of a negotiated transfer of KaNgwane and Ingwavuma parts of South Africa to the kingdom, an official and long-standing dream of the Swazi ruling class. This transfer, apart from the more obvious irredentist considerations, would have afforded the kingdom direct access to the Indian Ocean while South Africa would have grabbed the opportunity to dump 750,000 blacks beyond its borders as part of its drive toward the establishment of a technical white "majority" in the Republic itself. As it turned out the South African government ran into severe resistance from white conservatives, liberal critics and bantustan leaders. In a rapid sequence the Rumpff Commission, which was handling the land deal inquiry, was dissolved. In a bizarre irony South Africa informed Swaziland that the transfer would not proceed without express consent of the relevant bantustan leaders.[49]

For all intents and purposes, then, the land deal issue is now as good as dead. By way of explanation, one speculation is that South Africa never really intended to implement the "deal." Rather, the idea was to expedite the ANC clampdown in Swaziland and then drop the issue.[50] In fact South Africa has since announced an economic package aimed at enabling KaNgwane to compete with Swaziland in attracting new investment. In addition South African fertilizer firms helped to drive Swaziland Chemical Industries, a local competitor, into bankruptcy and Pretoria did nothing to intervene.[51] Yet, despite these rebuffs, Swaziland remains strongly pro-South African, a trend which suggests that its foreign policy cannot be explained simply as responses to South African incentives.

As has been suggested elsewhere, there is a growing sense of mutuality between the Swazi ruling class and South African capital in their world view: shared beliefs in the superiority of the capitalist mode of production and fears of a "marxist threat" and revolutionary ideology in the region.[52] This threat, perceived to be represented by the ANC, is seen by the Swazi ruling class as having its parallels within the kingdom itself. So the harassment of the ANC in Swaziland in this interpretation goes beyond structural subordination to, and rewards and threats from, South Africa. Rather, this perspective points to more independent interests and calculations on the part of the Swazi ruling class which might be fulfilled within the context of the alliance with South African and international capital.

Post-Sobhuza foreign policy trends

King Sobhuza's reign, spanning six decades, provided an extraordinarily long thread of continuity in Swaziland's domestic and foreign policies. That longevity also created a false sense of homogeneity and cohesion at the levels of society, the state and the ruling class. Major conflicts at all these levels were to unfold in a complex drama after his death in 1982. Clearly in favour of close cooperation with South Africa in political, economic and security issues, Sobhuza was at the same time cautious about, and sensitive to, Swaziland's image among the independent Sub-Saharan states. As mentioned earlier, he opened Swaziland's doors to both South African capital and ANC refugees; he also maintained "correct" diplomatic relations with Mozambique. Although his intense desire for the land deal was widely known, Sobhuza's pragmatism went short of establishing diplomatic relations with South Africa, a decision that was taken only after his demise.

Sobhuza's death in 1982 did not, and could not, result in *fundamental* changes in Swaziland's foreign policy because it is structurally determined. It did, however, create a huge political void and a crisis within the ruling class. Intense factional in-fighting, palace coups and counter coups, and rival attempts to control the state machinery, including *Tibiyo*, revolved around two groups. First, the Mfanasibili-Msibi group which, often in total disregard of the traditional ground rules, advocated closer ties with South Africa. It stepped up the harassment of the ANC, and spent considerable diplomatic energy pursuing the land deal; it also took over the *Tibiyo* Fund, its leading members helping themselves to double salaries, and passing a decree declaring their actions to be above the law. Before the dust settled both the queen mother (a cornerstone of monarchical tradition) and the prime minister has been overthrown. The heads of *Tibiyo*, the army, and police were put in jail. This breath-taking whirlwind overwhelmed the second, Mabandla (then prime minister), group which was more cautious about dealings with South Africa, less enthusiastic about the land deal and more considerate towards the ANC. In time, however, the more pro-South African (Mfanasibili-Msibi) group, under relentless internal opposition by a large section of the royal family and other organs of the state, was dislodged from power. Its leaders have since taken their turns in jail, all without evidence of high profile interference from South Africa. These dramatic events do not lend themselves to easy analysis. Three interpretations are quite apparent, however, each with foreign policy implications:

1. The Mfanasibili-Msibi faction, by disorganizing the ANC network in the kingdom, fulfilled South Africa's immediate goal. The faction's recklessness and flair for "short cuts," however, were threatening the durability of the monarchy and traditionalism. South Africa's long-term interests lay with a stable traditional monarchical system, a preoccupation that far outweighed the advantages of a short-term alliance with the otherwise intensely pro-South Africa faction.

2. The other, Mabandla, faction included members of the royal family and powerful individuals who were well-connected with international capital. When the chips were down, this connection eventually carried the day. In any case, the two factions differed only in degree, not substance, in their dealings with South African and foreign capitals.

3. The structuralist imperative of the state triumphed: the eventual subordination of the Mfanasibili-Msibi faction was broadly determined by internal social and state power structures; i.e. the state, being above the interests of individual class factions, was reasserting and reorganizing the overall interests of the ruling class in Swaziland within the matrix imposed by external factors.

XII. Conclusion

To a very considerable extent Swaziland captures the dilemmas and constraints facing small players in the international system. Layers of global and, in the case of Southern Africa, regional structural linkages severely limit the capacity for independent domestic and foreign policy-making. Within these broad parameters, however, the ideologies, attitudes and aspirations of the local ruling classes (partly derived rom prevailing social relations and reflected in state actions) remain relatively important in not only contributing to a fuller explanation of the factors behind foreign policies but also in accounting for differences in policy orientation so evident among African states. Each state is located in specific circumstances — historical, geographical, economic, and strategic — that determine the precise character of the conjuncture of internal and external actors and factors in the policy-making process.

In the case of Swaziland, its size and geopolitical circumstances constitute severe limitations in foreign policy-making whether one views state decision-makers as collaborators, short-sighted, realistic or pragmatic. The above factors, however, do not fully bring to the fore all the crucial relations that have historically defined the role of Swaziland in the international division of labour. This paper argues that Swazi foreign policy can be located at the interface of four major factors: (i) international capital, largely emanating from South Africa, (ii) South Africa's regional policy of destabilization, (iii) settler community interests, and (iv) Swazi social relations within which state and ruling class interests and perceptions are situated.

The widening material base of the ruling class, largely through *Tibiyo TakaNgwane*, has established a considerable identity of interest with foreign and settler capitals and, therefore, relatively similar perceptions regarding domestic and foreign policies. And, as will be seen below, internal processes in Botswana and Lesotho have historically emerged differently from those in Swaziland.

Viewed from another angle, Swaziland's peculiar brand of foreign policy has been reinforced by regional contradictions in Southern Africa. Caught between South Africa's regional domination and attempts at delinkage by SADCC member-states, Swaziland remains a weak link in SADCC's chain.

Destabilization of SADCC states and escalating internal and external pressures on South Africa have turned Swaziland into a focal point in the region, a trend that may assume more importance in the (unlikely) event that comprehensive economic sanctions are imposed on South Africa. The latter has already increased the use of Swaziland as a conduit for its products to external markets and as an alternative target for capital investment relocation. On the other had, SADCC states, hard-pressed by inflation, shortage of foreign exchange and other results of destabilization, may have, ironically, increased their collective purchase of South African goods conveniently located in Swaziland. these enduring regional contradictions were given a new twist with the signing of Nkomati in 1984.

The experiences of post-revolutionary, perhaps socialist, states in Africa have demonstrated the impossibility of successful disengagement from the global economic system, suggesting that for sometime to come small players at the margin will have to be content with negotiations for better dependency terms. that message has struck home with the growing influence of Bretton Woods institutions on the African continent. This perplexing prospect, perhaps already a growing reality, raises a number of sobering questions: What constitutes successful foreign policy in small dependent states like Swaziland? What factors, and in what order of priority, measure and characterize success or failure: national survival, political stability, sustained economic growth, ideological direction and policy consistency?; or simple common sense ability to adjust to systemic variables? Is pragmatism, however defined, a necessary imperative in the face of the African crisis, IMF/World Bank conditionalities for structural adjustment, destabilization in Southern Africa, and the intensifying marginalization of the neo-colonial states in the global system? Moreover, is pragmatism a measure of success or failure? And, who judges failures and successes and by what measure?

Using different tools and levels of analysis, successive studies reveal the kaleidoscopic nature of Swaziland's foreign policy which cannot be adequately accounted for in any simple analysis or through a single paradigm. Thus while this study argues that exclusion of the abiding domestic dynamic in the study of Swaziland's foreign policy is willfully perverse, temptations to want to explain this policy exclusively in terms of developmentalist, dependency or class terms have their own analytical and logical validity as well as pitfalls.

Just as earlier anthropological studies saw too much bliss and homogeneity in the kingdom, there is now a real chance of seeing too much class confrontation and action through the more teleological and deterministic analyses. Potential disjuncture between concepts and reality notwithstanding, it is such intense inter-paradigmic "hostilities" and debates, however, that may usher in more innovative and imaginative analyses of the run-away African crisis in general, and Swaziland's foreign policy constraints in particular; both of which will persist long after South Africa has achieved majority rule. Such new initiatives are all the more needed in the comparative study of small (peripheral) states' foreign policies where event (rather than process) analysis is still predominant.

NOTES

1. Maria Papakadis and Harvey Starr, "Opportunity, Willingness and Small States: The Relationship Between Environment and Foreign Policy," in Charles Hermann, Charles Kegley and James Rosenau, eds., *New Directions in the Study of Foreign Policy*, Boston: Allen and Unwin, 409, 1987.

2. *Ibid*, 413.

3. See Kenneth Waltz, *Theory of International Politics*, New York: Random House, pp. 102-128, 1979.

4. Papakadis and Starr, "Opportunity, Willingness and Small States," p. 427.

5. John Daniel and Johnson Vilane, "Swaziland: political crisis, regional dilemma," *Review of African Political Economy*,35 (May 1986): 55.

6. Hilda Kuper's studies include: *An African Aristocracy* (London: Oxford University Press, 1947), *An African Aristocracy: rank among the Swazis* (London: Oxford University Press, 1969), and "Colour, Categories and Colonialism in the Swazi Case," in V. Turner, ed., *Colonialism in Africa: Vol. 3, 1870-1960*, (Cambridge: Cambridge University Press, 1971).

7. Michael Neocosmos, ed., *Social Relations in Swaziland: critical analyses*, Social Science Research Unit, University of Swaziland, p. 19, 1987.

8. See Papakadis' and Starr's theoretical framework in their "Opportunity, Willingness and Small States," pp. 421-429.

9. Neocosmos, ed., *Social Relations in Swaziland*, p. 10.

10. See John Daniel, "The Political Economy of Colonial and Post-Colonial Swaziland," *South African Labour Bulletin*, 7: 6, 1982; Jonathan Crush, "The Genesis of Colonial Policy in Swaziland," *South African Geographical Journal*, 62:1, 1980; I. Winter, "The Post-Colonial State and the Forces of and Relations of Production: Swaziland," *Review of African Political Economy*, no. 8, 1978.

11. Neocosmos, ed., *Social Relations in Swaziland*, p. 34.

12. *Ibid*, p. 36.

13. *Ibid*, p. 119.

14. Daniel and Vilane, "Swaziland: Political Crisis,", p. 55.

15. Ralph Miliband, *The State in Capitalist Society — the analysis of Western systems of power*. London: Quarterly books, 1969: p. 72.

16. R. Chilcote, *Theories of Comparative Politics: the search for a paradigm*, Boulder: Westview, p. 195, 1981.

17. John Daniel, "Swaziland," in *Africa South of the Sahara*. London: Europa Publications, p. 979, 1987. See also Michael Fransman, "The Colonial State and the Land Question in Swaziland, 1903-1907," in *The Societies of Southern Africa in the 19th and 20th Centuries*, 9: 24, 1979; G. Whittingham and John Daniel, "Problems of Land Tenure and Ownership in Swaziland," in Whittingham, ed., *Environment and Land Use in Africa*, 1969; and Jonathan Crush, "The Genesis of Colonial Policy in Swaziland," *South African Geographical Journal*, 62: 1, 1980.

18. For example, Allan Booth, *Swaziland: tradition and change in Southern African kingdom*, Boulder: Westview, 1984; *idem* in *Journal of Southern African Studies*, 13, p. 125-150, 1986; and Christian P. Pothlom, *Swaziland: the dynamics of political modernization*. Berkeley: University of California Press, 1972.

19. Paul Ares and Andrew Williams, "Food Security: The Basis of Global Security," Paper presented at the Conference of Peace, Food Security and Development, Carleton University, Ottawa, Canada, December 3, 1987.

20. Richard Levin, "Uneven Development in Swaziland: Tibiyo, Sugar Production and Rural Development Strategy," *Geoforum*, 17: 2, p. 245, 1986.

21. *Ibid*, p. 241. Also, for more details see I. Winter, "The Post-Colonial State and the

Forces of and Relations of Production: Swaziland."

22. Canadian International Development Agency (CIDA): *The Impact of Economic Sanctions against South Africa on the SADCC States.* p. 18, Ottawa, 1986.

23. H. Macmillan, "Swaziland: decolonization and the triumph of tradition," *Journal of Modern African Studies*, 23: 4, p. 662, 1985.

24. See analyses by R. Davies and Dan O'Meara "South Africa's Strategy in the Southern African Region: A Preliminary Analysis," paper presented at the Inaugural Congress and Workshop on Development and Destabilization in Southern Africa, at the Institute of Southern African Studies, National University of Lesotho, Roma, October 1983; and Timothy M. Shaw, *Southern Africa in Crisis: an analysis and bibliography.* Halifax: Centre for Foreign Policy Studies, 1986.

25. Davies and O'Meara, "South Africa's Strategy,", 16.

26. Neocosmos, ed., *Social Relations in Swaziland*, p. 35.

27. Levin, "Uneven Development in Swaziland," pp. 242-243.

28. Daniel and Vilane, "Swaziland: Regional Crisis," p. 58.

29. *Ibid.*

30. Levin, "Uneven Development in Swaziland," pp. 242-243.

31. *Africa Confidential*, 25: 13, p. 5, 1984.

32. Joshua Mugyenyi, "Popular Alliances and The State in Swaziland," in Peter Anyang Nyong, ed., *Popular Struggles For democracy in Africa*, London: Zed Press/United Nations University, pp. 278-279. 1987.

33. *Ibid*, pp. 280-282.

34. UNIDO Statistics, 1984.

35. Levin, "Uneven Development in Swaziland," p. 240.

36. Daniel and Vilane, "Swaziland: Regional Crisis," p. 62.

37. *Ibid*, p. 63.

38. B.B.C. News Bulletin, 3 February 1988.

39. Daniel, "Swaziland," p. 984.

40. *Ibid.*

41. *Africa Confidential*, 27:23, p. 7. 1986.

42. Rok Ajulu and Diana Cammack, "Lesotho, Botswana, Swaziland: captive states," in Phyllis Johnson and David Martin, eds., *Destructive Engagement: Southern Africa at War*, Harare: Zimbabwe Publishing House, p. 159. 1986.

43. *Ibid*, p. 60.

44. *Africa Confidential*, 26:6, p. 8. 1985.

45. Daniel, "Swaziland,", p. 984.

46. *Africa Confidential*, 27:23, p. 7. 1986.

47. "Swaziland," in Colin Legum, ed., *African contemporary Record*, London: Africana, B849. 1986.

48. Davies and O'Meara, "South Africa's Strategy."

49. "Swaziland," in Legum, ed., *Africa contemporary Record*. B849.

50. Daniel, "Swaziland,", p. 983.

51. Daniel and Vilane, "Swaziland: Regional Crisis," p. 65.

52. *Ibid*, p. 66.

Cooperation Ideology and the Realities of Cooperation in West Africa

Chaldeans A. Mensah
University of Alberta

Introduction

As the Economic Community of West African States (ECOWAS) inches along the tortuous road toward the end of realizing the objectives enshrined in the Treaty of Lagos, it is perhaps important to situate this cooperative effort within the context of wider attempts at South-South cooperation and also to indicate the linkages between the two levels. The ECOWAS scheme obviously helps, in a sub-regional sense, to engender joint endeavours that would otherwise not have developed spontaneously in a region with an unimpressive track record in cooperation and highly vulnerable to external influences. The orientation of West African states, as they focus on regionalism, is definitely geared toward strengthening collective self-reliance through joint policies of economic cooperation and coordination designed to accelerate the rate of development of both the member states and the sub-region. In concrete terms[1] the desire at the regional level to bring cooperation into fruition is expressed in the Treaty as a number of timetabled commitments with respect to a tariff standstill, trade liberalization, fiscal harmonisation and the introduction of a common external tariff. There is optimism in the sub-region that beyond conference rhetoric ECOWAS will depart markedly from externally-imposed basic needs approaches, that do not build on the self-reliance and self help of governments, and will instead contribute to ameliorating economic problems in consonance with the Development Strategy for Africa for the Third Development Decade.

ECOWAS is a pivotal element in Third World attempts to fully exploit the existing and potential complementarities in their economies and at the same time promote the rational and efficient use of human, material, financial and technological resources. For one thing, it must be realized that in terms of constituting members, ECOWAS is the largest multi-country economic community in the world. (See Table 1 for the comparative economic statistics on the size of the member countries of ECOWAS and their external positions.)

Table 1
ECOWAS: Comparative Basic Data

Country	1978 Population (In millions)	Area (In thousand square kilometers)	Gross National Product Total (In millions of U.S. dollars)	Gross National Product Per Capita (In U.S. dollars)	In millions of SDRs	As percentage of GDP #	Balance of payments and Current Account Overall balance (In millions of SDRs)	Gross official reserves (In months of imports)
Benin	3.3	113	759	230	-58.4	-9.9	-9.6	1.1
Burkina Fasso	5.6	274	896	160	-64.8	9.0	-28.0	1.7
Cape Verde	0.3	4	78	260	-6.2	–	-2.0	7.8
Gambia, The *	0.6	11	108	180	-93.9	-31.5	-28.2	1.2
Ghana	11.0	239	4,290	390	-38.5	-0.1	-88.5	4.4
Guinea	5.1	246	1,071	210	-148.0	-7.9	-101.5	1.2
Guinea-Bissau*	0.9	36	153	170	-40.8	–	-4.5	3.3
Ivory Coast	7.8	322	6,522	840	-756.3	-7.9	-200.0	1.1
Liberia	1.7	111	782	460	-103.8	-12.5	-25.2	0.6
Mali	6.3	1,241	756	120	-59.5	-4.8	-7.4	0.5
Mauritania	1.5	1.031	405	270	-179.0	-46.9	-7.4	0.5
Niger	5.0	1,267	1,100	220	-40.4	-2.8	13.6	5.8
Nigeria	80.6	924	45,136	560	149.0	-4.3	1,207.0	2.3
Senegal	5.4	196	1,836	340	-239.8	-10.2	-94.2	0.2
Sierra Leone	3.3	72	693	210	-87.0	-13.3	-32.2	1.4
Togo	2.4	56	768	320	-197.5	-17.1	-18.1	2.1
Total	140.8	6,143	65,383	494+				

Sources: World Bank, *World Development Report,* 1980; and IMF Staff estimates. Data represent 1977 figures for Guinea-Bissau and Niger; 1978 figures for Benin, Cape Verde, The Gambia, Ghana, Guinea, Liberia, Mali, Mauritania, Togo and Burkina Fasso; and 1979 figures for Ivory Coast, Nigeria, Senegal, and Sierra Leone.

\# Average of 1977-79 figures.
* Data on population and GNP represent 1979 figures.
+ Weighted average. Arithmetic average is 309.

The U.N. Economic Commission of Africa (ECA) which partly inspired the creation of ECOWAS recognizes not only the importance of strengthening regional cooperative schemes in a "willed future" of the African continent by the year 2008[2] but also places such activities firmly under the ambit of the need for greater South-South cooperation. Furthermore the ECA has clearly indicated that interregional cooperation in the South would be of great importance for the success of the development scenario since Africa could benefit largely from developmental experiences of other Third World regions.[3] It is also noteworthy that commitment by ECOWAS members to the principles of collective self-reliance and South-South cooperation makes the scheme essential for the setting up of an African Common Market by the year 2000 as envisaged under the Lagos Plan of Action. As African Heads of States and Government have highlighted: "efforts towards African economic integration must be pursued with renewed determination in order to create a continent-wide framework for the much needed economic cooperation for development based on collective self-reliance."[4]

Recognizing the linkages between ECOWAS and the global level attempts in the Third World to formulate a comprehensive and coherent strategy for economic cooperation among developing countries, this paper will deal briefly with the following issues:

1. A discussion of cooperation theory and its relevance for South-South cooperation.

2. Cooperation ideology and ECOWAS.

3. Possible incompatibility between policies pursued in the West African sub-region within ECOWAS and the global level ideology.

Cooperation Theory and South-South Cooperation

The whole area of cooperation and discord in the international political economy has recently triggered a stream of analyses. Unfortunately, unlike the regional integration literature, remarkable little work has been done to assess the theoretical utility and empirical validity of the assumptions of cooperation theory nor any attempt made to relate these to South-South cooperation. I undertake the overview in this section with few pretensions: my aim here is to simply point out some of the lapses in cooperation theory and also the failure of cooperation theorists to relate their work to economic cooperation among developing countries.

Cooperation theorists,[5] especially those working in the game-theoretic mold are concerned, at the global level, with what is known as the "anarchy problematic" — that is the problem of policy coordination given the absence of central rule. In Robert Axelrod's pathfinding work, *The Evolution of Cooperation*, which best exemplifies this group of theorists, he argues that cooperation can emerge in a world of egoists without central authority. It seems to me that the assumption in his book of self-interested actors developing effective rules or social conventions spontaneously does not aptly describe the ECOWAS situation. Applied to ECOWAS, Axelrod's analysis neglects the role of ideology in the perception of interests and thus the possibility that states may act not out of blind egoism but rather in conformity with the tenets of a shared ideology. This approach to the problem of explaining and promoting international cooperation seems to be narrowly bounded when applied to ECOWAS considering that the scheme did not develop spontaneously, as the game scenario would suggest, but instead through delicate negotiations during which countries took into account their individual vulnerability in the international system and the dictates of a shared global perspective.

Another contribution to the study of cooperation is offered by Robert Keohane in *After Hegemony: Cooperation and Discord in the World Political Economy*, albeit he does not deal expressly with cooperation among developing countries. To him intergovernmental cooperation takes place when the policies actually followed by one government are regarded by its partners as facilitating realization of their own objectives as a result of the process of policy coordination. It will certainly be interesting, as a side comment, to ascertain within the context of ECOWAS the extent to which Treaty members realize their economic and political objectives as a result of policies undertaken by their partners in the sub-region. Briefly, Keohane grapples with the question of how cooperation can take place in world politics in the absence of hegemony and argues that "despite the erosion of American hegemony, discord has not triumphed over cooperation; instead, they coexist."[6] Keohane's analysis should be seen against the background of the work of so-called hegemonic stability theorists who have posited that conventionally a hegemonic power can provide the "collective goods" of global stability (Charles Kindleberger, 1973) or create a stable international economic order and that the decline of the hegemon leads inexorably to global instability. In other words, according to hegemonic stability theorists, order is forged by a hegemonic state achieving multilateral cooperation through a combination of coercive threats and positive inducements.

The analysis offered in this paper for the understanding of the dynamics of cooperation in the Third World starts from the premise that there is the lack of a "hegemonic state"[7] in the South. How then, the question crops up, do we explain and account for South-South cooperation and even sub-regional cooperation of the ECOWAS kind, assuming that Keohane is right and hegemony and cooperation are not alternative.[8] My basic contention is that instead of the traditional association of the rise of economic cooperation with the rising power of hegemons, as in Victorian Britain and Bretton Woods under U.S. tutelage, the *leitmotif* of the strategy of South-South cooperation is marked by the absence of a hegemonic state or "patronal leadership" (Klaus Knorr, 1975) and by the inching toward "non-hegemonic interdependence" (Fishlow and Diaz, 1978) in the Third World context. Given this state of affairs, countries in the South including ECOWAS members, have emphasized the importance of greater economic interdependence among themselves by embracing what may crudely be termed a "cooperation ideology." This ideology is reflected in the set of principles and technical policy analyses on South-South cooperation embodied in programmes such as the Arusha Programme for Collective Self-reliance and Framework for Negotiations and the Lima Declaration and Plan of Action. Apart from serving as a focal point for shared expectations on cooperation, I also see cooperation ideology as counter-hegemonic to the prevailing liberal ideology underpinning the Bretton Woods system. This latter conception builds on Goran Therborn's contention that "all ideologies exist only in historical forms in historical degrees of salience and modes of articulation with other ideologies."[9]

Cooperation Ideology and ECOWAS

The global cooperation ideology emphasizes common attitudes and shared responses among developing countries rather than differences and also places high premium on shared problems of weakness and a sense of deprivation and the shared conviction that the rules of the international economic order are working against them. One scholar has correctly noted that "the unity of developing countries is a product of their objective situation and subjective self-understanding."[10] The subjective communality in the South is in a sense a movement of thought that stresses two key aspects of South-South cooperation, first as an instrument for the consolidation and effective use of the developing countries' combined power in international economic relations, and second as a valuable instrument for promoting the rational and efficient use of human, material, financial and technological resources available in developing countries for their individual and collective welfare. Indeed the Treaty of ECOWAS clearly captures the latter component of South-South cooperation when it states that:

It shall be the aim of the Community to promote cooperation and development in all fields of economic activity particularly in the fields of industry, transport, telecommunications, energy, agriculture, natural resources, commerce, monetary and financial questions and in social and cultural matters for the purpose of raising the standard of living of its peoples, of increasing and maintaining economic stability, of fostering closer relations among its members and of contributing to the progress and development of the African continent.[11]

My reflections on cooperation ideology is guided by Craig Murphy's discussion of the New International Economic Order (NIEO) ideology[12] and his explicit assumption that "the development of consciousness and ideology has an important, relatively autonomous role in world politics."[13] Essentially then, cooperation ideology should be seen as encompassing a set of principles and technical policy analyses, that is economic goals, factors affecting these goals, proposed economic policies designed to manipulate those factors and political strategies to overcome those impediments. This ideology asserts the "unity of the South based on a shared historical experience, a continuing dependence and a shared set of needs and aspirations." This view of the "unity" of the South is best stated in Julius Nyerere's oft-quoted statement:

. . . Our diversity exists in the context of one common and overriding experience. What we have in common is that we are all, in relation to the developed world, dependent not interdependent-nations. Each of our economies has developed as a by product and a subsidiary of development in the industrialized North, and is externally oriented; we are not the prime movers of our destiny; we are ashamed to admit it, but economically we are dependencies — semi-colonies at best — not sovereign states.[14]

As indicated earlier, the tenets of the cooperation ideology have been formulated around the theme of collective self-reliance adopted in various Nonaligned and Group of 77 programmes. The following principles, among others, have featured prominently in this ideology:

1. that the strategy of collective self-reliance embodies the potential for joint action by developing countries that will strengthen their capacity to negotiate with developed countries and reduce their dependency;

2. principle of solidarity of the South which makes it possible to harmonize diversity of interests;

3. sovereign equality and respect for different economic and social systems and the right of each state to exercise full and permanent control over its own resources; and,

4. that collective self-reliance is an instrument for structural changes based on the

principle of genuine mutuality of interests and accommodations.

Among the goals espoused by the South as part of this ideology are the restructuring of the international economic relations, the rational use of resources internally, the tapping of the vast markets, human resources, technical skills and manufacturing capacities in the South. The ideology also serves the function of unifying the interests of Southern countries and raising their consciousness to see cooperation as necessary for the transformation of the international economic order.

Some of the high-sounding principles like mutuality of interest and equity, which undergird the global-level Third World programmes, have been translated in the Treaty of Lagos. Perhaps reflecting the cooperation ideology, the Preamble asserts a commitment to "the need for a fair and *equitable* (italics mine) distribution of the benefits of cooperation among member states."[15] Article 25 reinforces the equity principle by indicating that compensation shall be paid to a member country suffering loss of import duties as a result of the application of the Charter. Other provisions relating to compensation include the annexed Protocol on Compensation for Revenue Loss and Decision 19/5/80 of the Authority (A/Dec 19/5/80)[16] and Article 50 which establishes the Fund for Cooperation, Compensation and Development. These provisions are designed to ensure equity and obviate the problem of the distribution of costs and benefit which partly accounted for the failure of the East African Community.

The principle of solidarity is enshrined in the ECOWAS Treaty through provisions relating to the establishment of a customs union. This is sought through the elimination of all tariffs and non-tariff barriers on goods of Community origin. In furtherance of this objective three stages are recognized in this process: i) the first consists of a two-year standstill period for tariffs that terminated in May 1981; ii) the second comprised the next eight years over which member states must reduce and ultimately eliminate their import duties on intra-Community trade; iii) finally, the succeeding years over which the common external tariff is to be established.

Solidarity is also effected through the "most favoured nation" principle, thereby ensuring the "any agreement between a member state and a third country under which tariff concessions are granted, shall not derogate from the obligations of that member state under this Treaty" (Article 20(3)). Like other regional schemes in incipient stages of Treaty implementation, ECOWAS makes a modest attempt[17] at permitting less developed member states to adopt a slower pace toward full trade liberalization than their relatively advanced partners. In fact the Community has agreed that in implementing its trade liberalization provisions, the former countries shall pursue a slower timetable — though they will still have to complete the process by the same terminal date, 1988, as the latter countries.

It seems to me that the commitment by member states to harmonise their industrial policies to ensure similarity of industrial climate and industrial incentives demonstrates the desire to utilize the power that accrues from joint action, especially in dealing with external actors and ultimately breaking away from the "neo-colonial mesh."[18] Thus far, in terms of the harmonisation of investment incentives, the most important formal initiative within the Scheme is the local participation provision that has been added to its rules of origin. A serious weakness[19] is the absence of specific provisions for bargaining with the North, as well as the lack of a common policy on foreign investment, technological controls and divestment.

A key element of the cooperation ideology is the reduction of dependency. This is in keeping with Andrew Axline's contention that "one of the salient consequences of integration among underdeveloped countries is a reduction of the degree of dependence with the rest of the World."[20] An important objective of ECOWAS is to alter 'centuries of extroverted development' for the sub-region; to this end Article 32 of the Treaty calls upon the Council of Ministers to "take steps to reduce gradually the Community's economic dependence on the outside world." It should also be noted that since ECOWAS is not a "political union" by any stretch of the imagination there is respect for sovereign equality and respect for different economic and social systems. This perhaps explains why ECOWAS exists side-by-side with the francophone dominated Communauté Economique de l'Afrique de l'Ouest (CEAO). The ECOWAS treaty provides that the rights and obligations of members deriving from previously signed contracts (including the CEAO) are not affected by the ECOWAS Treaty.[21]

Assessment of the Realities of Cooperation and the Global-Level Ideology

Drawing on the lines of the argument presented in this paper it is again important to note that there is lack of a hegemonic state in the South at the global level and that the role of "hegemonic leadership" (Hirsch and Doyle, 1977) in galvanising the process is undertaken through an ideology. Having noted the tenets of this ideology and how they are reflected in the Treaty of Lagos, we should now transcend mere Treaty provisions or even rhetoric and ascertain whether the Treaty is being implemented in conformity with the cooperation of ideological principles.

At the global level developing countries have de-emphasized the concepts of hegemony, dependence and domination and have rather emphasized equity and fairness. The immediate question that one has to grapple with in the ECOWAS context is whether Nigeria constitutes a hegemonic state at the sub-regional level? In other words is Nigeria supporting and maintaining a kind of asymmetrical cooperation? Supposedly, the fear of Nigerian hegemony[22] featured in the move by Senegal at the inception of ECOWAS to counter Nigerian influence by seeking to extend ECOWAS to include Cameroon and Zaïre. Certainly by virtue of its wealth, demographic advantage and physical size, Nigeria has a seemingly unchallenged status as "the bull in the regional china shop."[23] In 1980 Nigeria accounted for 75 percent of the Community's GNP, 55-60 percent of its population, 75 percent of its exports, including oil, and 55 percent of its manufacturing industry.[24]

There are no indications, however, that other countries in the sub-region have been willing to defer to hegemonic leadership on the part of Nigeria. In Wallersteinian terms Nigeria has not demonstrated any exercise of hegemony through a "combination of hierarchies of control and the operation of markets."[25] Hegemonic stability theorists indicate that hegemonic powers must have control over raw materials, control over sources of capital, control over markets and competitive advantages in the production of highly valued goods. The key word here is *control*; unlike Victorian Britain one cannot argue that Nigeria exercises any degree of control over the raw materials of the states in the West African sub-region, or that it has shown competitive superiority in the production of goods; nor can it exercise any real power by threatening to cut off any ECOWAS states' access to her market. As Keohane has correctly pointed out "to be considered hegemonic in the World political economy, therefore, a country must have access to crucial raw materials, control major sources of capital, maintain a large market for imports, and hold comparative advantage in goods with high value added, yielding relatively high wages and profits."[26] According to these criteria, Nigeria does not constitute a "hegemonic state" within the West African sub-regional setting and it is not unreasonable to conclude that there is lack of domination and hegemony within ECOWAS. There is no denying, however, in the forseeable future, that Nigeria will continue to play a decisive and positive role in the development of ECOWAS.

A possible incompatibility between cooperation ideology and the realities of cooperation relates to the definition of interest. the global-level ideology stresses "harmony of interest" whereas the assertion of national interest seems to be the rule in the Community. Indeed the former Nigerian Minister of External Affairs, Dr. Ibrahim Gambari, did not mince words when he stated at a speech given at Princeton University that:

> We are ready to contribute to promote the good neighbourly relations with our sister states in the region without however compromising on any issue of vital national interest to us nor hesitating in affirmatively protecting such interests.[27]

The principle of "harmony of interest" was definitely relegated to the background in favour of national interest in the Nigerian expulsion Orders of 1983 and 1985. While the Nigerian action did not violate any part of the ECOWAS Protocol on free movement of persons, the perception in the region was that it was "rash" and hardly compatible with the spirit of the Lagos Treaty, and for a while it raised regional friction. By no means, in Keohane's terms, can the Nigerian action be interpreted as constituting cooperation considering that the affected states did not see it as facilitating the realization of their objectives.

The area of trade liberalization *tout ensemble* does not convey any semblance of solidarity. Peter Robson points out "that the ECOWAS programme of trade liberalization is being undertaken against the background of national protective structures that are diverse but generally very high, but which in any case have not been constructed with the needs and opportunities of a regional market in mind."[28] The Community's trade liberalization programme is also hampered by the impact of the Community's rules of origin as well as currency restrictions and the lack of convertibility of the currencies of major members of ECOWAS. In addition the existence of the Communauté Financière Africaine (CFA) in the francophone countries with full convertibility to the French franc, does not help fulfill the ideological goal of reducing dependency.

The ECOWAS Protocol on the definition of the origin of the products from the Community leaves some loopholes as far as manufactured goods are concerned, albeit it is specific as to imported raw materials. It is noteworthy that product processed within the Community may use materials from "foreign or undetermined origin." The problem is that the Treaty does not specify the meaning of "undetermined origin." Also it gives two independent forms of calculation, by value and by quantity. In fact progress on the Trade Liberalization Programme (adopted in May 1980 in line with Articles 12 and 13) was slowed down considerably because of the interpretation of this provision. The Trade Programme prescribed the total elimination of all tariff barriers to unprocessed goods as from May 28, 1981, clearly behind the originally planned date of November 1978.

It is perhaps in the area of the payments problem that the West African Clearing House features prominently within the Third World programme of enhancing solidarity through monetary cooperation.[29] The West African Clearing House, whose establishment on March 14, 1975 preceded the adoption of the ECOWAS Treaty, involves a clearing of interregional payments on a multilateral basis by members' central banks. Its objectives are to promote the use of members' currencies for sub-regional trade and other transactions, to bring about economies in the use of foreign reserves; and to promote monetary cooperation and consultation among its members.

It is a positive step in the direction of easing payment difficulties to increase economic intercourse in the sub-region. However, it is beset by serious problems including those cited in an I.M.F. study[30] such as relative lack of interest by banks in the payments system due to the low level of intra-regional trade and the "relatively low priority given by many banks to transactions channeled, or to be channeled, through the Clearing House."

One further principle of the cooperation — equity — must be discussed at this point. In the first place the Fund conceived as a means of ameliorating inequity in the implementation of the Treaty has no resources of its own and therefore depends on members for prompt payment.[31] By 1983 it was estimated[32] that about $23.5 million was owed in delayed contributions, thereby seriously compromising the principle of equity. Another crucial factor likely to lead to the infringement of the equity principle relates to what Peter Robson calls "the lack of simultaneity in the obligations and benefits implied by the Community's Programmes."[33] His argument is that the industrially less developed countries are unlikely to benefit from the timetabled obligations of the Treaty on customs union and may likely suffer through the trade creation and the trade diversion that results.[34] Since the scheme does not compensate for the contingent losses from trade creation, it is not unreasonable again to expect the less developed countries in the Community to safeguard their interest by holding back from the implementation of formal commitments to trade liberalization.

Concluding Remarks

It would seem that as a concrete example, in the regional vein, of the desire of Third World countries to collectively facilitate the attainment of the objectives of self-reliance and self-sustainment, the ECOWAS Treaty derives ideas and principles from the global cooperation ideology which has provided a subjective identity to the Third World. The global programmes upon which this ideology is based are inspirational in character, lacking contractual commitments and often falter when their principles are applied at the regional level. Shridath Ramphal[35] is perhaps right, and past experience indicates, that often the Third World tends to be declamatory and not empirical enough, too generalized and not specific enough, too allembracing and not selective enough and too entrenched at the level of macro change.

A real test for a budding scheme such as ECOWAS and indeed for broader South-South cooperation is the extent to which principles such as equity, harmony of interest and solidarity can be operationalised at the regional setting to ensure continuity between the global and regional phases of South-South cooperation. There is no doubt that the consolidation of regional cooperative schemes will constitute a vital building block or perhaps a *sine qua non* for the promotion of South-South cooperation. In this regard efforts should be intensified by Third World countries not only to implement global programmes but also actively to take policy measures, at the regional level, conducive to maintaining genuine economic inter-dependence and complementarity between their economies.

BIBLIOGRAPHY

Asante, S.K.B. *The Political Economy of Regionalism in Africa: A Decade of the Economic Community of West African States*. New York: Praeger, 1986.

Axelrod, R. *The Evolution of Cooperation*. New York: Basic Books, 1984.

Axelrod, R. "The Emergence of Cooperation Among Egoists," *American Political Science Review*. Vol. 75 (June), 1981.

Axelrod, R and R. Keohane. "Achieving Cooperation under Anarchy: Strategies and Institutions," *World Politics*. Vol. 38, No. 1 (October), 1985.

Axline, A. "Underdevelopment, Dependence and Integration: The Politics of Regionalism in the Third World," *International Organization*. Vol. 31 (Winter), 1977.

Cox, R. "Ideologies and the NIEO: Reflections on Some Recent Literature," *International Organization*. Vol. 33, No. 3 (Spring), 1979.

ECA and Africa's Development 1983-2008: A Preliminary Perspective Study. Addis Ababa: ECA, 1983.

Hirsch, F. and M. Doyle. *Alternatives to Monetary Disorder*. New York: McGraw-Hill, 1977.

Jervis, R. "Cooperation under the Security Dilemma," *World Politics*. Vol. 30, No. 2 (January), 1978.

Keohane, R. *After Hegemony: Cooperation and Discord in the World Political Economy*. Princeton: P.U.P., 1984.

Kindleberger, C. *the world in Depression, 1929-39*. Berkeley: University of California Press, 1973.

Knorr, K. *The Power of Nations: the Political Economy of International Relations*. New York: Basic books, 1975.

McLenaghan, B.J. and others. *Currency Convertibility in the Economic Community of West African States*. Washington: I.M.F., 1982.

Murphy, C. *The Emergence of the NIEO Ideology*. Boulder, CO: Westview Press, 1984.

Murphy, C. "What the Third World Wants: An Interpretation of the Development and Meaning of the NIEO Ideology," *International Studies Quarterly*. Vol. 27, No. 1 (March), 1983.

Oye, K. "Explaining Cooperation under Anarchy: Hypotheses and Strategies," *World Politics*. Vol. 38, No. 1 (October), 1985.

Therborn, G. *The Ideology of Power and the Power of Ideology*. London: Verso, 1980.

Zartman, W. and C. Delgado. (Eds.) *The Political Economy of Ivory Coast*. New York: Praeger, 1984.

NOTES

1. See Peter Robson, "Regional Integration and the Crisis in Africa South of the Sahara: Performance and Priorities," paper presented at the conference on Rehabilitation and Recovery in Sub-Saharan Africa (Sussex: IDS, Nov. 1984), p. 7.

2. ECA and Africa's development 1983-2008: A preliminary perspective study (Addis Ababa: ECA, 1983), pp. 93-103.

3. *Ibid.*, p. 102

4. See Organization of African Unity Assembly of Heads of State and Government, Second Extraordinary Session, April 28-29, 1980 Lagos, Nigeria, "Plan of Action of the implementation of the Monrovia Strategy for the Economic Development of Africa," Section 14 (vi) of Preamble.

5. I am referring here to theorists such as Robert Keohane, Robert Axelrod, Kenneth Oye, Charles Lipson and Robert Jervis.

6. Robert Keohane, *After Hegemony: Cooperation and Discord in the World Political Economy* (Princeton: Princeton University Press, 1984), p. 184.

7. The concept of hegemony is used here as applied to world order by Robert Cox from the Gramscian notion. The use of the concept of hegemony in the Gramscian sense must be distinguished from the original Greek meaning, the predominance of one nation over another. In Gramsci's scheme of things, the starting-point of hegemony is that a class and its representatives exercise power over subordinate classes by means of a combination of coercion and persuasion. Borrowing from Machiavelli he evokes the image of power as the mythical Greek centaur, half man and half beast, a necessary combination of consent and coercion. Robert Cox has noted that hegemony at the international level is an order within a world with a dominant mode of production. For him, world hegemony is expressed in universal norms, institutions and mechanisms which lay down general rules of behaviour for states and for those forces of civil society that act across national boundaries — rules with support the dominance mode of production. For further elaboration of this position, See Robert Cox "Gramsci, Hegemony and International Relations: An essay in method," *Millenium*, vol. 12 no. 2 (Summer 1983), pp. 162-175., and John Hoffman, *The Gramsci Challenge: Coercion and Consent in Marxist Political Theory* (Oxford: Basil Blackwell, 1984).

8. Robert Keohane, *op. cit.*, p. 46.

9. Goran Therborn, *The ideology of Power and the Power of Ideology* (London: Verso, 1980), p. 32.

10. Stephen Krasner, *Structural Conflict: The Third World against Global Liberalism* (Berkeley: University of California Press, 1985), p. 308.

11. *Treaty of the Economic Community of West African States*, Article 2 (1).

12. See Craig Murphy, *The Emergence of the NIEO Ideology* (Boulder: Westview, 1984).

13. Craig Murphy, "What the Third World Wants: An Interpretation of the development and meaning of the NIEO ideology," *International Studies Quarterly*, vol. 27, no. 1 (March, 1983), p. 59.

14. Julius Nyerere, "Unity for a new order," in K. Haq (ed.), *Dialogue for a New Order* (New York: Pergamon, 1980), p. 5.

15. Preamble to ECOWAS Treaty.

16. ECOWAS, Official Journal (June 1980).

17. Peter Robson, *Integration, Development and Equity: Economic Integration in West Africa* (London: George Allen and Unwin, 1983), p. 25.

18. For a discussion of the trappings of neocolonialism in the ECOWAS region, see S.K.B. Asante, *The Political Economy of Regionalism: A decade of the Economic community of West African States (ECOWAS)* (New York: Praeger, 1986) pp. 35-42.

19. Olatunde J. Ojo, "Nigeria and the formation of ECOWAS," *International Organization*, vol. 34 no. 4 (Autumn, 1980), p. 60.

20. Andrew Axline, "Underdevelopment, Dependence and Integration: the politics of integration in the Third World, *International Organization*, Vol. 31, No. 1 (Winter, 1977). See Kuehn, R. and Seelow, F., "ECOWAS and CEAO: Regional cooperation in West Africa," *Development and Cooperation*, No. 3 (May/June, 1980), p. 12.

21. Achi Atsain, "Regionalism economic integration and foreign policy" in I.W. Zartman and C. Delgado (eds.), *The Political Economy of Ivory Coast* (New York: Praeger, 1984), p. 214.

22. S.K.B. Asante, *op. cit.*, p. 148.

23. World Bank (1982) Annex, *World Development indicators*.

24. Wallerstein, Immanuel., *The Modern World-System: Capitalist Agriculture and the origins of European World-Economy in the Sixteenth Century* (New York: Academic Press, 1974), pp. 15-17.

25. Robert Keohane, *op. cit.*, p. 33.

26. Excerpts of Dr. Gambari's speech are published in *West Africa*, 22 October, 1984, p. 2117.

27. Peter Robson, "Regional Integration and the Crisis in Africa South of the Sahara," *op. cit.*, p. 16.

28. For the present state of monetary cooperation among developing countries, see UNCTAD IV, Economic Cooperation among Developing Countries (TD/192/Supp.1), in *Proceedings of the U.N. Conference on Trade and Development, Fourth Session*, Vol. III Basic Documentation (TD/218).

29. John B. McLenaghn, *et al.*, *Currency convertibility in the Economic community of West African States*, I.M.F. Occasional Paper No. 13 (Washington: I.M.F., 1982), p. 27.

30. S.K.B. Asante, *op. cit.*, p. 103.

31. "Budget for ECOWAS" *West Africa*, January, 1984.

32. "Budget for ECOWAS" *West Africa* January, 1984.

33. Peter Robson, *Integration, Development and Equity: Economic Integration in West Africa, op. cit.*, p. 119.

34. *Ibid.*, p. 121.

35. Shridath Ramphal, "Unity alone is not strength," in K. Haq (ed.), *Dialogue for a New Order* (New York: Pergamon, 1980), p. 11.

African Women and Sex Role Studies: A Methodological Critique

Moji Ideh
University of Jos

Introduction

This paper focuses on sex role studies of African females of all ages. Sex role studies are those research efforts that have concerned themselves with sex role styles and sex stereotype characteristics attributed to an individual due to biological and social factors. Such studies of African women include those of Mbogowo (1984), Ugbabe (1985), Ware (1977), Novadonsk (1984), and Ntamere (1984). These and other studies demonstrate that an important influence on women in sex role studies is sex role stereotyping (SRS). SRS is the attribution of roles to persons or groups of persons based on their sex (Ekstrom, 1979). SRS has been found in occupational selection in situations where the majority of those in an occupation are of one sex and there is an associated normative expectation that this should be so (Epstein, 1970).

This paper will review and critique the literature of the past ten years which deals with sex role stereotyping of African women; in particular it will attempt to analyze how the methods used in such studies may provide results which do not portray African women as they actually are.

Clarification of Concepts and Antecedents of Sex Role Stereotypes

In this paper, the concepts "sex role," "work role" and "occupational role" are used interchangeably. This is because certain roles, work and occupations are often associated with a particular sex. From time immemorial certain roles have been expected to be played by women and, they have been exempted from others. Though things are changing and we now find some women in traditionally masculine jobs, these women and their male colleagues are still being affected by traditional sex role stereotypes.

The antecedent of sex role stereotyping has been explained to be the anatomical differences between males and females. Women have always been perceived biologically different from men. "Woman" as a concept means more than just a human female; the latter refers to the physical organism with primary consideration of the reproductive system. According to Freud, the female differs from the male because of her genitalia and because she carried a child in the womb. Biological differences become the basis for differences in privileges and role expectations.

Others have looked at cultural factors in explaining the emergence of sex role stereotyping, but this approach has been associated with biological characteristics or attributes. Based on these biological characteristics, each culture elaborates an entire configuration of values, attitudes and expectations. This has led some authors to claim that, how a woman is defined and what her roles are, are a cultural definition rather than resulting from biological facts. Motherhood is a consequence of being a female, but the maternal role may be interpreted in different ways. Here motherhood is not synonymous with femalehood. Zborowski and Herzog (1952) cite the example of what motherhood is to the Jews of Eastern Europe; motherhood was considered to be the central focus of a woman's life, and mothering behaviour was expected to stem from her selfless devotion. In contrast, the Aborsee subordinate the nurturing aspects of the maternal role to economic activities and do not expect the mother to be warmly cherishing or self-sacrificing (Dubois, 1944). For the African women, sex role identity is not different from gender role identity. Personality factors are associated with masculine and feminine roles and they too vary according to cultural definition. A study by Mead (1939) demonstrated that cultural definition of sex-typed personality may differ markedly even with a rather circumscribed geographical area. She studied three tribes in north eastern New Guinea and found that each had its own distinctive set of norms characterizing the temperaments of men and women.

Historically, women have been considered to be the weaker sex as is seen even in the Bible where Eve (a woman) was made out of the rib of Adam (a man).

Women's Studies in General

Oakeley (1981) claims that there is no definition of women's studies. However, according to her, it is a growing subject in its own right and with an approach to traditional subjects. However defined, women's studies depend upon a concept of female inequality (Bristol Women's Study Group, 1979). "Women's Studies" is perceived as an academic offshoot of the women's liberation movement. According to Oakeley (op cit), women's studies face problems such as:

such studies being considered as both academic and nonacademic, they are interdiscplinary or antidisciplinary, and

there is the question of whether it is a mode of academic consciousness-raising designed to produce feminists out of nonfeminists.

Feminism can be defined in many ways; how to define it is one of the tasks for women's studies at the moment (Oakeley, op cit). Generally, however, any feminism is about focusing on women and thus about judging women's interests, however defined, to be important and to be sufficiently represented and accommodated within mainstream politics or academia.

In developed parts of the world, women's centres have been founded in college campuses and in local communities and they are an accepted major. The role of women in society is acknowledged as a valid and significant field of investigation.

Studies on women in general have shown that women are more identified with roles related to domesticity, motherhood, selflessness, low temperament. Thus, it therefore appears that modern conceptions, such as those by Oakeley (op cit), run counter to universal perceptions of the role of women in society. Flowing from this therefore, is the notion of the paradigm of female studies that tends to overemphasize superiority of women as opposed to equality/complementarity may not be entirely accepted within the African context in particular and the world in general.

Methodological Critique

Considering issues of methodology, studies cited in this section are rather archival, for example, Mead and Dubois, and could be said to have been based on "arm chair ethnography." If this is the case, one can say that the methodology which allows researchers from one race to study members of another race leaves much to be desired. Such methodology is not likely to allow a deep rooted appreciation of the cultural, traditional, and oral history ramifications of cultures of the third world which too often are seen as primitive, tribal and negative by anthropologists from more developed countries. Thus much weight should not be attached to studies generalized across the globe. It is now being concluded that many studies done by Westerners of Africans and third world people must be questioned because of the cultural differences that are so deep rooted. The West approaches the study of Africa from their perspective. The use of positivism, which is Western scientific methodology, or traditional rationalism, to study non-scientific phenomena is like using a microscope to observe witchcraft. This situation is unfortunate methodologically. Positivism does not allow researchers (for example Jahooda's study of Ghana), to write about or explain findings to a superstitious and metaphysical group of people. Thus there is a great problem.

Associated with this problem of methodology is Ottenberg's study of the Afikpo people of Imo State, Nigeria between 1952 and 1957. As an anthropologist, Ottenberg claimed to study the Afikpo people, but he knows nothing about their tradition and culture. He lived with them and was initiated by them but this was during the day time and not at night time. This is a problem of some ethnographers who do not seek to know and understand the full range of behavior. Even with Afikpo interpreters, Ottenberg did not get to know anything about the people he claimed to study, for his findings cannot be validated. Angela Little studied Birom Women of Nigeria but there is evidence she never had direct contact with them. Such researchers stay in one place (sometimes, their own home) and write about a group they claim to study. The African traditions are mystical and superstitious — how can researchers, with their objectivity, study these *subjective* matters? For instance, the concept of fertility in Africa is tied to the concept of land, which is property. Land is even referred to as "mother earth." If the land is producing in abundance, the inhabitants believe that so would their women, and vice versa. These things however cannot be easily understood by Europeans or non-Africans. It is therefore this author's conclusion that positivism is thus not suitable as methodology for studying non-positivistic societies such as Africa.

Women's Studies in the West

Societies assign differential roles to men and women. This is usually based on physical differences. Masculinity and femininity denote complexes of attributes and behaviors, considered appropriate and desirable in a particular society and culture, to the personalities of the male and female sexes respectively (Ogbalu, 1982). Biological basis for sex roles have been supported by Nash (1970), Maccoby and Jacklin (1974. Without dismissing a biological basis for sex role assignments, the more logical basis is social in nature (Sears, 1970).

Studies on sex roles have demonstrated that women are usually portrayed in a "negative" light. Bardwick and Dovan (1972) showed that women were characterized as having qualities such as dependence, passivity, fragility and non-aggressiveness which were shown to be opposite to leadership qualities and effectiveness. Dominance and independence have been linked with the masculine role and submissiveness, passivity and nurturance with the feminine role (Broverman, et al., 1970). This also is nature-nurture issue. Is it natural for women to be passive, non-aggressive and nurturent or is it nurture (socialization) that makes them that way? Thus one could consider whether these feminine behaviour (roles) are ascribed (nature) or achieved (nurture). For convenience or by habit and tradition, certain traits are associated more with the male or described as masculine behaviour and some with the activities or reactions of the female, that is, feminine behaviour. In Nigeria, roles are ascribed. Females believe that they are girls and thus they cannot do anything about their circumstances. When nature says give birth, they do, and so have as many as 13 children. With the introduction of family planning, people do not understand it is changing the long-standing definition of being female — our society is therefore not like the West.

Studies in this area are those of Aswell (1982); Schiffer (1978); More and Rickel (1980); Forisha (1978); Massengill and Dimarco (1970); Sappenfield and Harris (1975); Valentine, et al. (1975); Miller (1980); Place (1979); Orlofsky and Stake (1981); Eze, et al. (1982); Gearty and Milner (1975); Stewart and Winter (1976); Rice and Vitters (1980); Terborg and Ilgen (1975). These studies used a variety of survey techniques.

Methodological Critique of Studies of Women in the West

From the studies on western women it can be concluded that the portrayal of women is more in the context of their roles (work) or careers that are male oriented (non-traditional roles) of management, occupations and professions. This gives the impression that women in the west do not consider domestic/ familiar roles as being as important. The net effect is a larger proportion of studies of women who are career women, have less/ fewer children, place less emphasis on husbands or on family associated privileges, for example, husband's protection.

In these studies, three broad categories of methodology are discerned:

Those who have used survey methods.

Those who have used laboratory experimental method, and,

Those who have used a combination of survey and laboratory experimental method.

It would appear that those researchers who used survey methods and laboratory experimental methods exclusively, arrive at conclusions that portray women in their studies as non-traditional and attracted into masculine fields in terms of occupational choice and role identity, and so tend to portray women in a negative perspective. Such methods also portray women as having the same achievement orientation as men (needing power and achievement) and so tend to neglect fundamental differences that may arise between males and females in terms of identity and perception. However, although studies based on a combination of methodologies are fewer in number, their results show that such a combination has more merits than demerits. A combination of methods allows researchers to compare the effectiveness of methods and so is likely to allow them to arrive at more objective and sounder conclusions.

Studies of Women in Africa

There has been an appreciable number of studies on women in Africa and in Nigeria in particular. They include: Ugbabe (1984); Makinwa-Adebusoye (1984); Egwu (1985); Ikonne (1985); Okonjo (1983); Ware (1977); Schildkrout (1983); Fapohunda (1984); Navodonsk (1984); Roberts (1984); Ottenberg (1983); Mbosowo (1984); and, Nweke (1984).

Ugbabe (1984) examined selected women writers and male critics in the African context and concludes that when women writers confine themselves to traditionally women's issues such as marriage, childbirth, divorce and gossip, and when women readers are being largely addressed, the resulting work is looked on with paternal approval. Makinwa-Adebusoye's (1984) findings suggest that the most important factors that account for lower school enrollment rates for girls than for boys include the deeply rooted entrenched social traditions and attitudes towards women's perceived roles in society. Egwu (1985) concluded that there have been radical changes in the roles of women in society all over the world and that educational and intercultural influences have made these, *great* changes. Ikonne (1985) used a theological perspective. He comes up with the finding that Christianity has done only little for the liberation of the Nigerian woman. He advocates a little dose of sexual revolution to maximize her contribution to nation building. Okonjo's (1983) study used impressionistic methods and concludes that the Hausa's, Igbo's and Yoruba's of Nigeria traditionally had certain specific roles for women and men. He also suggests that the current male dominated nature of national politics in Nigeria, which is a slight modification of the imported prototype of a western representative governmental model, continues to stifle Nigerian women's participation in politics.

Ware (1977), using a case study to analyze African women's fertility, found that women's workforce participation in Africa is extremely high, but it is not the type of employment that serves to reduce fertility. Schildkrout (1983), on the basis of a longitudinal study, studied female — male relationships in Kano with those in other parts of the Islamic world. He found that the strength and the particular form of the institution of purdah, the seclusion of women in northern Nigeria and, in particular, Kano City (which is economically stratified), has few married women that are not in seclusion. He also found that this seclusion in Kano was stricter than what appears in other parts of the Islamic world because in the former, women hardly go out at all during the day, not even to the market; however, in North Africa, specifically Morocco, women use veil to segregate themselves from men and from places in the public where there are men.

Fapohunda (1983) studied female/male work profiles in West Africa. The conclusions were that most women and men are employed in agriculture and yet the characteristics of male workers as compared to female counterparts are quite different. Men are self-employed farmers, while women are generally unpaid family workers. Furthermore, she found that as modem sector industrial and service employment is quite small in West Africa, relatively few women and men were wage earners and even fewer were technical, administrative, clerical or managerial personnel.

Roberts (1984) used both interviews and questionnaires to look at parental attitudes towards the education of female children in Bori Local Government Area of River State, Nigeria. The results showed that parents generally had higher educational aspirations for their male children than females. Parents with higher education were more disposed to educating their daughters than parents of lower education. Finally, girls from smaller families had a better chance of being educated than those from larger families.

Novadonsk (1984) used survey questionnaires to look at the possible factors and motivations that underlie the pursuit of higher education by married women in Bendel State of Nigeria. The factors include potential to achieve a higher economic status, prestige, emancipation, to remedy lost opportunity, and to avoid domestic problems, and were ranked as follows: economic status and prestige were ranked highest, remedy of lost opportunity and emancipation were grouped relatively lower on the scale, and domestic problems ranked lowest.

Ottenberg (1983) in survey found that the major sex roles he studied in the chiefdom in Sierra Leone had features/ characteristics of other West African societies in that formal political roles are almost entirely in the hands of males.

Nweke (1984), using survey methods in Nigeria, found that most media establishments (which are by and large partially or fully government owned), are male dominated. Furthermore, the media in Nigeria are male dominated, male owned and controlled, and thus when addressing issues related to women, information given is not actually how women are, but a reflection of male views and perceptions. She also found that women liked to be featured on programmes which had subject matters related to traditional women's concerns.

Mbosowo (1984), used literary criticism to show that sexual harassment of African women in the labour force is prevalent in post-independence African society as reflected in the book *Devil on the Cross* written by an African, Ngugi Wa Thiongo. Ugbabe (1984), using a similar approach, analyzed books of African writers to show how life circumstances weigh heavily on a woman and turn her into a victim. One example is Emecheta's book title *Second-class Citizen*.

Conclusions point to the fact that rural women in Africa seem to be different from urban women in terms of their aspirations, job roles, perceptions of the African world and in terms of achievement motives. Urban women in Africa are career oriented and educated and so more prone to nontraditional role stereotypes. The rural women are still perceived to be more susceptible and malleable, and they constitute the majority of women in Africa. In terms of leadership, studies show that in general African women have played a long historical role in leadership. Some studies tend to give the impression that there is hardly any difference in leadership role in terms of sexes.

Education and marriage are also issues raised in the studies reviewed. There is a likely relationship between these two concepts in the sense that with more education the less attractive marriage becomes for the African woman. One concludes that in terms of characteristics and personality, the educated African woman tends to look like her Western counterpart.

With regard to fertility, the studies cited seem to give the impression in general and with respect to Africa in particular, that the more educated a woman is the less fertile she is; however, this is an erroneous impression. Because the educated woman spends more years outside marriage, going first to a primary, then secondary, possibly a tertiary school/college, she is likely to have fewer children than her less educated counterpart who began child bearing earlier. Thus considering fertility in terms of the total number of children a woman has, the more educated woman will be less fertile.

Methodological Critique

In general, studies on African women have adopted methodologies that can be classified into three broad categories:

Survey methods: longitudinal and cross-sectional;

Desk research methods, including literary analysis and criticism;

Impressionistic methods.

It is this author's view that these methodologies do not allow enough scope for detailed study of the African woman in-situ, deriving as they are from Western oriented positivistic methodologies. It is unlikely that researchers who come to Africa will uncover the deep rooted ramifications of culture, traditions, mores, norms and religious dynamics of African women if they depend solely on these positivistic methodologies. Survey methods suffer methodological default based on the use of questionnaires which are written in English and are administered to illiterate or semi-literate sample populations. Even with local language and back translation, there is insufficient communication between the researcher and the researched which can contribute to a better understanding of the researched.

Africa in general is still a "shy" continent. People are not likely to be free to discuss private matters with strangers. In particular, when issues of fertility are being investigated using a survey method, the result may be what Alan Edward calls "metholdological default of social desirability." The African would provide the least amount of information possible in order to get rid of the experimenter as soon as possible. Thus results derived in this way are more likely interpretations and impressions of the researcher, and not the views of the researched, or, accurate data. Take for example, the practice of "purdah" in the moslem religion. The African mind nor the African environment can be penetrated through the use of questionnaires. The women in the purdah will not be seen by the researcher and if seen, an understanding of who she actually is and motives behind her seclusion in Africa, cannot be fully understood. When the positivistic methods are unfamiliar in terms of the African background and where the researcher, particularly those from developed nations, have found that going into the fields to gather data yields largely unreliable data, they may resort to sitting in their own libraries, or offices to write up their study without doing any actual field work. They come up with "armchair ethnographic results" like those of Simon and Ottenberg (1968) who could not understand the culture of Afikpo people in Imo State of Nigeria who would not talk of their mind (psyche). All of their findings are doubtful, though they lived among the Afikpos. Their survey method did not fit the cultural realities of the situation.

In the nineteen-fifties, sixties and seventies, there were various studies in African conducted by researchers from the West. Based on the findings of these studies, scholars in Europe and America created a view of Africa. Westerners are unlikely to cut through the jungle of the African mind no matter how sharp their intellect. Survey methods also tend to work "on" people rather than "with" people; they are non-participative methods. The African woman likes to feel she is being part of the research. This is a way to get her commitment and cooperation. However, many studies by organizations and agencies have not addressed the actual needs of the respondents.

On the basis of the above summaries and criticisms, this paper attempts the development of a methodological model which is presented as a paradigm or heuristic framework for future studies on African peoples in general and African women in particular.

Towards a Methodological Model for Studies on African Women

The salient features of the methodological model presented here will support the following objectives:

To present a strategy of research which can enable researchers to penetrate the African culture with all its complexities, thereby reaching the African minds to be surveyed and interviewed.

Given the largely illiterate, simple nature of the African society, the methodological model presented aims at simplicity in form and content.

Given the universal aspect of the African culture and people. Another salient aspect of the model is generalizeability, therefore the model is seen as useful all over African and possible in other Third World countries.

The model will be based on combining the relevant features of reviewed methodologies in combination with approaches.

The model will aim at working "with" the people and not "on" the people. From the design of the study to the end, people's needs, aspirations and so on will be addressed by the researcher.

Research based on the model will be directly relevant to African needs and problems. The studies should not merely be done to fulfill requirements for promotions in Universities and other organization.

Facets of the Model

Studies on African women should use a circular methodological model (C.M.M.) that incorporates a combination of the best aspects of positivistic approaches with epistemological, ethnomethodological and clinical/psychological approaches. An advantage of this circular methodological model is that any of the four methods can be chosen for a particular study or a combination of any of these for a particular study. The model appears as Figure 1, below.

Fig 1:

CIRCULAR METHODOLOGICAL MODEL (C.M.M.)

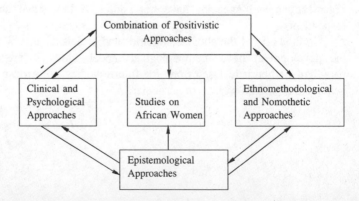

Positivistic Methods

Surveys and laboratory experimentation can be appropriate for studying educated African women.

Ethnomethodological Methods

These are recommended in cases where exploratory research work is needed to discover the features and characteristics of certain groups of women. Studies like those of Herbert Mead and Irvin Goffman (1960) use ethnological methods. They imply an effort to understand the process of life of the people rather than to impose your perceptions. The researcher should attempt to see issues from the perspective of those being studied. This may involve role playing, providing the researcher an opportunity to see and interpret issues.

Epistemological Methods

This is the studying of African societies using African methods. This implies that Africans have related knowledge to study themselves. Africans attach meanings to various African contexts: e.g. the name of a person has a meaning; streams and forests have names that are meaningful. In studying African women and their characteristics, there is a need to go back to African epistemological approaches which attach meaning to what we are doing. When the researcher seeks for meaning from the researched, the latter is committed, interested and participates because the relevance of the study is understood.

Clinical and Psychological Approaches

One can penetrate African Women's minds through "free association." This implies that researchers of African women should be African researchers who can use such clinical approaches. The psychological variable comes into the model, resulting from the author's own profession. Psychology, as a discipline, looks at the individual in a social setting.

Implications of Using the Model

1. Opportunity is provided to develop a research strategy which is more robust than previous methodological strategies used on African women. The circular nature allows future users a wider range for choice.

2. Being based on a thorough understanding of diverse cultural ramifications of the African society, the model reflects the African social reality.

3. In terms of cost, the proposed model would be more cost effective than question-naires. Once the research package is finalized, the people, being more

committed, will be more likely to cooperate because they can see benefits and relevance to themselves.

BIBLIOGRAPHY

Aswell, K.M. "Working Women in Transition: Changing Attitudes and Behaviours Regarding Work, Partnership and Family," *Dissertation Abstracts International* (April, 1983) 1982.

Bardwick, J.M. and E. Douvan. "Ambivalence: The Socialization of Women," in *Readings on Psychology of Women*. J.M. Bardwick (Ed.). New York: Harper and Row, 1972.

Bristols Women's Study Group. *Half The Sky: An Introduction to Women's Studies*. London: Virago, 1979.

Broverman, I., Broverman, D., Clarkson, F., Rosenkrantz, P., and Vogel, S. "Sex-role Stereotypes and Clinical Judgments of Mental Health," *Journal of Consulting and Clinical Psychology*. 1970.

Dubois, W.E. *Dusk of Dawn: An Essay Toward an Autobiography of a Race Concept*. New York: Schocken books, 1944.

Egwu, E.U. "Women and Leadership Role in Contemporary Nigeria: Some emerging Issues," paper presented at the P.W.P.A. Seminar, Port Harcourt, Nigeria. (May), 1985.

Epstein, C.F. *Woman's Place*. Berkeley: University of California Press, 1970.

Ezel et al. "Women Entering Management: Differences in Factors Influencing Integration," *Group and Organization Studies*, pp. 243-253, 1982.

Fapohunda, E.R. "Female and Male Work Profiles," in *Female and Male in West Africa*. C., Oppong (Ed). George Allen & Urwin Limited: pp. 32, 1983.

Forisha. "Creativity and Imagery in Men and Women." *Perceptual and Motor Skills*. 1978.

Gearty and Milner. "Academic Major, Gender of Examiner and the Motives to Avoid Success in Women." *Journal of Clinical Psychology*, pp. 13-14, 1975.

Goffman, I. *The Presentation of Self in Everyday Life*. 1960.

Ikonne, C. "The Myth of the Weaker Vessel and Female Leadership in Nation Building," paper presented at the Seminar of Professors World Peace Academy. Port Harcourt. 1985.

Makinwa-Adebusoye, P.K. "The Role of Women in Nigeria's Socio-economic Development," paper presented at the Seminar Organized by Women in Nigeria, (W.I.N.). Port Harcourt. 1984.

Massengill and Dimarco. "Sex-role Stereotypes and Requisite Management Characteristics: A Current Replication," in *Sex-Roles*. pp. 561-570, 1970.

Mbosowo, M.D. "Women in the Labour force and sexual harassment in Ngugi wa Thiongo's *Devil of the Cross*." Paper presented at the Nigerian Anthropological and Sociological Association, Unijos. 1984.

Mead, M. *Coming of Age in Samoa: A Study of Adolescence in Primitive Societies*. London: Cape, 1939.

Miller, J. "Relationship Between Fear of Success to Perceived Parental Attitudes Toward Success and Autonomy in Men and Women," *Psychology Reports*. Vol. 47 (i), pp.

79-86, 1980.

More and Rickel. "Characteristics of Women in Traditional and Non-traditional Managerial Roles," *Personnel Psychology*. Vol.33 (2), pp. 317-333, 1980.

Nash, J. *Developmental Psychology: A Psychology Approach*. 2nd Ed. New York: Prentice-Hall, 1978.

Novadonsk, J. "Motivations of Married Women to Higher Education in a Nigerian Setting," paper presented at Women in Nigeria Seminar. Port Harcourt, 1984.

Ntamere, C. "Choice of Career and the Effect on Income Differences Between Men and Women," paper presented at the W.I.N. Seminar. Port Harcourt. 1984.

Nweke, T. "Media Attitudes Towards Female Education," paper presented at the Third Annual Conference of Women in Nigeria (W.I.N.). Port Harcourt. 1984.

Oakeley, A. *Subject Women*. New York: Pantheon Books, 1981.

Ogbalu, E. "Psychological Androgeny and Sex Role Adaptability: A Case Study of Nigerian Undergraduates," unpublished B.Sc., thesis, Unijos. Nigeria. 1982.

Okonjo, K. "Sex Roles in Nigerian Politics," in *Female and Male in West Africa*. Oppong (Ed.). United Kingdom: George Allen & Urwin Limited, pp. 211, 1983.

Ottenberg, S. "Artistic and Sex Roles in a Limba Chiefdom," in *Female and Male in West Africa*. Oppong (Ed.) London: George Allen & Urwin Ltd., pp. 70, 1983.

Ottenberg, P. and S. Ottenberg. *Double Descent in an African Society: The Afikpo Village-Group*. Seattle: University of Washington Press, 1968.

Place, H. "A Biographical Profile of Women in Management." *Journal of Occupational Psychology* (1979), pp 267-76.

Rice, W.R., L.R. Bender, and A.G. Vitters. "Leadership, Sex Follower Attitudes Toward Women and Leadership Effectiveness: A Laboratory Experiment," *Organizational Behaviour and Human Performance*. No. 25, pp. 46-78, 1980.

Roberts, G. "Parental Attitude towards the Education of Female Children: A Survey of Gokanna in Bori Local Government Area," paper presented at the Women in Nigeria (W.I.N.) Conference. Port Harcourt. 1984.

Sappenfield and Harris. "Self-Report Masculinity-Femininity as Related to Self-Esteem," *Psychological Reports* Vol. 37 (2), pp. 669-670, 1975.

Schiffer, D. "The Inter-relationship of Sex Role Stereotyping, Locus of Control, and Psychological Success Among Women in Business," *Psychology Dissertation Abstracts*. 1977.

Schildkrout, E. "Dependence and Autonomy: The Economic Activities of Settled Hausa Women in Kano," in *Female and Male in West Africa*. Oppong (ed.). London: George Allen and Urwin Ltd., 1983.

Sears, R.R. "Relation of Early Socialization Experiences to Self-Concepts and Gender Role in Middle Childhood," *Child Development* (1970), pp. 34.

Stewart and Winters. "Arousal of the Power Motive in Women," *Journal of Counselling and Clinical Psychology* (1976), pp. 495-496.

Terborg and Ilgen. "A Theoretical Approach to Sex Discrimination in Traditional Masculine

Occupations," *Organizational Behaviour and Human Performance.* No. 13, pp. 352-376, 1975.

Ugbabe "The Muted Minority: Women Writers, Male Critics." Paper presented in a series of departmental seminars organized by the Faculty of Arts, Unijos, Nigeria. 1984.

Valentine et al. "Sex-role Attitudes and The Career Choices of Male Graduate Students," *Vocational Guidance Quarterly* (1975), pp. 48-53.

Ware, H. "Women's Work and Fertility in Africa," in *The Fertility of Working Women: A Synthesis of International Research.* S. Kupinsky (Ed.). New York: Praeger, 1977. Pp. 1-34.

Women and Development: The Tanzanian Case

David Gabba
Université de Montréal

Colonization and Social Change

Since 1500, well before the colonial conquest, even though the European presence was confined to short coastal tracts, it fostered profound political and economic changes in Africa. Slavery had either directly or indirectly caused the breakdown of the old societies; through slave trade the western economy had made itself felt in the remotest areas of Africa. One of the most frequent consequences was the breakdown of the family structure and the traditional kinship grouping, followed by a transformation of the social function of the family that inevitably affected the traditional sexual division of labour. Such transformation took place under the violent pressure of the forces of colonialism. The colonizing process included the introduction of cash economy and wage labour in the whole of Africa. The African farm labourer's response to the stimulus of taxes imposed by the colonial government and the replacement of local goods with European goods which could only be acquired by cash was the quest for wage labour.

The colonial administration opted for a family policy aimed at strengthening particular rules of the customary laws, twisting their original meaning to support the exigencies of the colonial economy, while purporting to comply with tradition. The colonial administration on the one hand intensified the customary female subordination, while making use of the dowry on the other. In the same way they enforced compulsory taxation, thus ensuring that people became more deeply enmeshed in the cash economy.

The colonial administration's marriage laws were carried out with the complicity of the native authorities. After independence, people were marrying according to the marriage ordinance, but the marriage can either be according to the marriage ordinance or the customary laws, thus introducing uncertainty about when a customary marriage may be regarded as definitive. Such uncertainty becomes very serious indeed in cases such as when a woman is, or is not, a widow, and consequently if she is entitled to social security benefits, pension, etc. Polygamy was tolerated by the colonialists, who did nothing but superimpose laws of the western type which, far from abolishing it, have simply lowered the status of the supplementary wives. Colonialism strengthened the patrilineal law, as it denied the matrilineal family structure of its positive significance, thereby depriving women of their customary rights.

Women in Rural Settlement Schemes

Soon after independence, the government set up a village settlement program. Most rural Tanzanians lived on small homesteads organized around the extended family or the lineage group. President Nyerere felt that the village was the minimum level of social organization necessary before the benefits of modern development could be brought to the people. Each village in the government's settlement program was to be run by a manager and his staff. The original plan for the villages had envisioned that work would be done collectively, but because of recruitment problems settlers tended to be the least effective farmers in the country.

Plans for the women on the settlement schemes were nonexistent. Each man chosen as a settler could only come if accompanied by a wife, rather as though a wife were a necessary piece of equipment. Women involved in the schemes were bitterly disgruntled to find that they were comparatively worse off than they had been before they joined the scheme, when they had their own crops apart from those raised jointly with their husbands.

In the settlement all rights in land use were vested in the husband and as a corollary all proceeds were handed over to him. In the planning of the settlements, it was assumed that a man and his wife were complementary units for farm labour, but the reality was whereas men were expected to carry out only farm work, the women were also expected to cook, care for the children and fetch water in addition to providing farm labour. Another feature of the settlement scheme showing a disregard for the rights of women involved the question of inheritance. Land was controlled by a descent group and allocated to its male members. A woman whose husband died could take advantage of the levirate by which one of her deceased husband's brothers would take her as one of his wives to continue to use the same land, or she could return to her own people. The government scheme was presumably based on the patrilineal notion that women are given land by their husbands, but made no provision at all in the event of the husband's death.

In 1967, Tanzania committed itself to a fully socialist economy in the Arusha Declaration. One of the new policies concerned villages. It was now proposed to abandon completely the original villages settlement plans, partly at least as a result of research findings about inequities. Instead, it was planned that encouragement should be given to people to form their own villages without expert supervision and without capital input. The idea and ideal was to establish UJAMAA villages. "Ujamaa" is a Swahili word meaning "familyhood."

Women in Ujamaa Villages

The establishment of Ujamaa villages held out special promise for rural women. By concentrating rural populations in planned villages, the government intended to foster the ideals of cooperation, familyhood, hard work, and social equality. The villages would also facilitate the kinds of investments in agricultural technology and water, power and educational facilities that are essential to rural development. Between 1974 and 1976, vast numbers of people were moved into villages. The potential of these villages to help rural women has only been partially realized. Women can be registered as Ujamaa members in their own right, and they are guaranteed access to land, capital, inputs and information. Provision of water at a central location is an example of an Ujamaa service that frees women from an arduous household task. But there are several barriers to realizing the full potential that the Ujamaa concept holds for women. The men's attitudes at the village level reflect traditional prejudices against women. Women have access to Ujamaa communal land, but it may not be very good land, and there is a tendency for people to put less effort into the Ujamaa farm than into their private plots. Sometimes Ujamaa increases the women's work load with little or no reward. Moreover, the government's rural development policy has provided a rationale for expanding the state bureaucracy in which women are poorly represented.

Ideological and Political Struggles of Working Class Women

The Right to a Decent Wage

One of the primary struggles of working women has been over security of employment, the length of the working day and the rate of pay. In 1975 for instance, a cashewnut factory forcibly retired women workers due to old age, lack of education and mechanization processes. However, the severance pay did not take into account their long years of work; therefore, they struggled to retain their jobs or else receive severance pay in line with their work experience. For many years large numbers of women had been employed on a temporary basis in the cashewnut industry, contrary to the relevant employment acts. Barmaids are another segment of the labour force which is highly exploited and unprotected by legislation with respect to the length of the working day, minimum wages, weekly days off and leave benefits. Employers use them for prostitution services for their clients. In 1971 a group of barmaids stopped work at a public institution in protest over wages which were far below the minimum wage. Domestic servants comprise another category of highly exploited women, including men as well. For many the wage is paid in kind, with provision of housing, meals and cast-off clothes. Often these workers are children brought from the villages as "ayahs." Working days extend to 12 hours or more for a seven day week without regular holidays and leave benefits. Domestic servant struggles take the form of absenteeism, absconding from one employer to another for better conditions, stealing subsistence needs to complement the new wages, a "go-slow" performance of tasks and eventual search for alternative forms of employment of subsistence including prostitution, concubinage or marriage. The domestic servant issue is complicated by the fact that it is working women who hire these working girls to take care of their infants. As most of the women are themselves minimum wage earners, they are unable to pay the servants the same minimum wage.

Control of Sexuality and Femininity

Struggles over maternity leave benefits have clarified the significance of the question of biological reproduction and how it is socially organized. Debates began in 1971 over whether or not to extend maternity leave pay to unmarried mothers. Unmarried mothers were labeled as prostitutes and provision of leave benefits was perceived to be tantamount to an encouragement of young girls to engage in sexual relations with men and conceive without marriage. Women workers themselves argued that they had the same right to be unmarried and bear children without being subjected to patriarchal relations of women's subordination, and that as workers they had the same right to maternity leave benefits as married women have. This line contradicts the way both precapitalist relations and capitalist relations have allocated women to the process of social reproduction as subordinated reproducers of the labour force. This was not the line initially adopted by United Women of Tanzania (UWT), the national women's organization, and the debates within over this issue classified the different class lines being taken in the organization at that time. Women workers accused the UWT of being an organization of "big-wives," wives of party and government bureaucrats, which did not represent their interests. Policies corresponding to the interests of the majority of working women were finally adopted by UWT at its annual conference at Mbeya in 1971.

Sexual Harrassment

This can take many forms. Bosses in factories or offices demand sexual services from women workers in exchange for employment, on-the-job training placements and consideration for a higher wage. Girls moving to towns in search of work are often faced with the problem of having pre-marital relations with men before they can be considered for employment.

The threat of sexual harassment or rape is extremely powerful in controlling women's movements and, even in defining what kind of work they are "safe" to do. A shoe worker noted that "Many a times the woman from her night duties has been rebuked, scandalized, chased and even assaulted."

Rejection of "Patriarchal" Marriage

A proportion of adult urban women are single and have never married or else have married and are now divorced. Some women divorcees have completely rejected the patriarchal form of marriage. Their explanations stress the costs of having a husband in terms of family maintenance expenses, which include his personal consumption of alcohol and women. In addition, there is maintenance of his relatives, and, oppressive family relations expressed in wife beating, expected subservience to the husband and his relatives, and constant ridicule or being put in one's place as an inferior member of the household despite the substantive contributions made of wages, other incomes and domestic labour.

Access to a wage or other source of income "frees" women, redefining marriage and other forms of sexual relations. These changes are a result of the 1971 Marriage Act which, on the whole, reconstituted patriarchal relations of marriage as the legitimate form of state organization forms. Women, thus, are dispossessed of their children as a result of divorce or death of spouse if the widow refuses to be inherited.

UWT has repeatedly protested against polygamy. Ultimately, through the legal system and the courts, the state has constructed the definition of woman as "motherhood," subordinate and dependent on males for existence and exchangeable as a commodity through the medium of bridewealth.

Struggles of Women Peasants

Peasants include both the rich and the poor. This is due to the differential ownership and control of the means of production, the market orientation, scale of production and the extent of exploitation of hired labourers. Some members of the poor peasant class hire out their labour on a temporary or permanent basis to a neighbouring state or parastatal enterprise, pastoralist and other villages. Women, particularly poor peasants, are among those economically compelled to hire out their labour to others. Often, their labour power is exploited by middle and rich class peasant women. Women and men migrate from villages in search of wage employment or other sources of income, despite state policies against migration. Women in some parts of the country complained that they are compelled to leave their husbands and children behind because farming provides them with inadequate food and cash income to maintain their children.

Relations of Distribution and Consumption

Male control over major cash flows in the household, and the way men engage in personal consumption, for example, drinking, paying bridewealth for additional wives, etc., is bitterly resented by women. They react to patriarchal consumption relations by refusing to work on their husbands' farms or by lowering the amount and quality of labour put in, by expanding production of food crops over whose sale they have more control, by hiding the amount produced and earned so as to avoid its being appropriated by the husband, and ultimately by rejecting the patriarchal form of marriage altogether.

Sexual Division of Labour

Labour time studies have documented the fact that the length of the working day for women is one and one half to two times that of men, including domestic labour activities (cooking, toting water and firewood) as well as directly productive activities. As a result, women peasants in some areas have refused to contribute labour for village self-help activities or to adopt new technologies requiring additional labour inputs.

Struggles Over Land and the Product of Labour

The village act requires each village member, male or female, to be allocated separate plots of land and to cultivate crops which are designated in local village by-laws. However, in many areas of the country, the practice of the village government is to allocate the land to male household heads, who then allocate land to wives and unmarried sons. Historically, peasant women struggled over the related questions of allocation of land and labour. Post-independence settlement schemes partly failed because women peasants resisted the transformation of matrilineal land tenure systems into patrilineal systems.

In some villages, women peasants have protested at village assemblies about the appropriation of their labour product by husbands and the village government.

Gender and Class Politics

Peasant women speak of their frustration over being excluded from village government and exclusion from decision making at village assembly level. Also fear of wife beating and public ridicule intimidates poor peasant women from speaking out at village assemblies.

During the early phase of Ujamaa villagisation, women and poor peasants were often the most enthusiastic to join Ujamaa villages and to work in collective production systems. The line taken by UWT, the prime minister's office and international agencies towards development of peasant womens' lives is the promotion of income-earning activities like cooperative shops, poultry raising, beer brewing and beer selling clubs. But these cooperative enterprises have been a failure due to lack of sufficient capital, skills, knowledge and material support. Women's cooperatives in rural and urban areas were often controlled by men, rich peasants and others who hired the labour of poor peasant women.

The usefulness of UWT includes learning family planning techniques and child care, providing women with the opportunity to express themselves, to fight shyness, learning household management skills, providing leadership training and helping women to organize themselves.

Education

There is ample documentation of the structural inequalities in provision of places at all levels of the formal schooling system: at primary, secondary and university levels. Rich peasants (Kulaks), traders, primary school teachers and other government functionaries enrolled all their children in school. Poor peasants in some areas tended to select one or two boys to go to school and usually girls were married off after a few years of elementary education.

Universal primary education (UPE), which began in 1974/75, has led to the massive enrollment of both girls and boys in primary school, offsetting earlier sex and class differences. Resistance to enrollment of girls remains among pastoralists. The drop-out rate is much higher for girls than for boys in urban and rural areas. One of the major reasons for this is expulsion of schoolgirls due to pregnancy. There are far more boarding school places for boys than for girls at secondary level.

Sex differentiation exists in subject specialization at secondary and post-secondary levels, which leads to diminished employment and educational opportunities for women. For example, lower access to math combinations has led to the lack of women graduate teachers to teach math. Domestic science, with fewer returns in higher education or employment, is taught only to girls. This can be interpreted as a mechanism to reinforce sex differentiation not only in education, but also, in work in the home. While men are taught agriculture, mechanics, carpentry etc., women are taught cookery, sewing and child care. Even radio education programs for women emphasize subject matter which reflects the sexual division of labour at home. Radio Tanzania has run special announcements encouraging women to attend adult literary classes and asking husbands to "allow" them to do so.

Many husbands are not happy about their wives leaving home to go to work, or to attend literacy classes.

Sex discrimination in hiring and promotions of teaching staff at the University of Dar-es-Salaam has recently been raised by women academics. Only 11% of the teaching faculty are women; the majority of them at junior levels of the professorial hierarchy. Sex differentiation and sex discrimination in education have been attributed to a combination of forces: patriarchal relations, the sexual division of labour in peasant production systems and in wage labour and structural inequalities in the number of opportunities offered to girls and women.

Legal Issues

Any legal system becomes ineffective when there is ambiguity or conflict. In Tanzania, ambiguity and conflict are facilitated by the existence of more than one code of law and by what appears to be an inordinate desire to maintain the customary law, even when it is seen to be unfair and unjust.

Law and Socio-economic Status of Women

Eight of the tribes in Tanzania are patrilineal and in these groups descent is almost exclusively through males. Even where changes have occurred to allow women to inherit, usually they get usufruct rights rather than outright ownership with full rights to dispose of the property by grant, will or sale. In cases of separation or divorce, the law, particularly customary law, ensures that the men will take the children. this is related to the traditional values of the children as a source of labour and the role of women as mere producers of these children. As an extension of this law, women have also been kept out of cooperative agricultural marketing societies and thus deprived of the right to participate in the sale of cash crops.

Law and the Changing Socio-economic Political Situation

The law has not kept pace with political/sociological changes taking place, resulting in contradictions that have not been resolved. These include the division of labour at the household level, the division of proceeds obtained from group labour on individual plots, the division of family income obtained from wages, the rights of widows and divorcees. The 1971 Marriage Act has some progressive measures, but it will remain ineffective as long as they are paralleled by provisions in the customary law and interpretation between the two is subjective. Some laws unintentionally penalize women; for example, legislation providing working women with 84 days paid maternity leave has resulted in some employers preferring males instead of female employees.

Political Participation

The participation of women in politics and leadership positions in Tanzania is very low, whether at national or local level. The 1979 Village Survey showed that 6.5% of the village managers were female while there was not a single female chairman or secretary. At the national level, out of over 200 members of parliament elected in 1980, less that 15 were women. The new policies of Ujamaa and villagisation have not made much difference.

A survey in Mwanza region showed women constituted less than 10% of the membership of all committees, with a ratio of 2:3 (women to men) in 55% of the villages surveyed. The low level of participation is rooted in the womens' role in production and reproduction. The sexual division of labour assures that women are tied to household activities while men have more mobility and leisure. One researcher noted that while the men enthusiastically debate, women fall asleep during Ujamaa meetings. They have worked so hard in the course of the day to make Ujamaa living a reality that they are too exhausted to stay awake.

The UWT has failed to mobilize women, especially in rural areas. A very small percentage of women in Tanzania are UWT members. Fuller mobilization is constrained in varying age groups and classes of women. The recent attempts to incorporate university women in joint research projects is breaking down barriers between the highly educated and the less educated.

Health and Nutrition Education

Out of over 8,000 villages only 1750 had maternal child health (MCH) centres in 1979. The rural areas were worse off due to lack of transportation. The distances involved, combined with transportation difficulties, effectively prevent women from attending these centres. A related constraint in seeking health services is the women's workload in productive and domestic labour.

Health and nutrition education are aimed entirely at mothers. Ignorance of adequate nutritional practices is considered the ignorance of women alone. Thus a woman is blamed if her children suffer malnutrition but a man is excused if he uses if he uses the cash obtained from sale of crops to buy non-food items including non-essentials, or if he neglects his share of work in food production.

Improved nutrition in Tanzania is usually interpreted to mean improved nutrition of children. Neglect of the care of pregnant women adversely affects the health of the fetus and newborn infant. The debate on infant feeding, in which women are blamed for not breastfeeding their babies for a "reasonable" length of time, also underlies the societal conception of women's primary roles as producers of children.

Summary

Colonial conquest in Tanzania caused a breakdown of the family structure and the traditional kinship grouping followed by a transformation of the social function of the family. Further, colonialism strengthened the patrilineal law to the disadvantage of women.

Post-independence settlement schemes partly failed because women peasants resisted the transformation of matrilineal land tenure systems into patrilineal systems. Women simply refused to cultivate as initially planned by the government; as a result, large numbers left the schemes and returned to their homes to retain matrilineal rights to land and the product of their labour.

Ujamaa would appear to have had little favorable effect on women's work. It has not been implemented in a way that lessens women's workload or makes them more productive. In some cases it has increased the workload. In general, it has not provided women with a reliable alternative to private production patterns, nor has it much improved women's status and power other than on paper.

Both working class and poor peasant women of all ages are rejecting patriarchal forms of family and employment and exploitative capitalistic relations. UWT, being a national mass organization, has had some minor achievements. For instance, its campaigns to obtain paid maternity leave for women workers and to allow female students to enter university directly after national service were both successful. However, the fact remains that UWT has failed to mobilize women, particularly in rural areas.

BIBLIOGRAPHY

Bay, Edna G. *Women and Work in Africa*. Westview Press Inc., 1982.

Charlton, Sue Ellen M. *Women in Third World Development*. Westview Press Inc., 1984.

Collier, Paul, Samir Radwan and Samuel Wangwe with Albert Wagner. *Labour and Poverty in Rural Tanzania — Ujamaa and Rural Development in the United Republic of Tanzania*.

Cutrufelli, Maria Rosa. *Women of Africa, Roots of Oppression*. Zed Press, 1983.

Hafkin, Nancy J. and Edna G. Bay. *Women in Africa*. Stanford: Stanford University Press, 1976.

Mascarenhas, Ophelia and Marjorie Mbilinyi. *Women in Tanzania*. Uppsala: Scandinavian Institute of African Studies, 1983.

Women in Development

Eloise Murray
University of Alberta

[This is a report of the 'WID' Workshop, delivered by its Director to the opening plenary session of CAAS '87.]

Women in development (WID) is a policy initiative of many national and international organizations. The policy stresses that women will be considered as both agents and beneficiaries in the development process. The major purpose of WID is to focus on the realities of the lives of women affected by the development process. This can be done from a wide range of discipline perspectives and program options.

The issues of women in Sub Saharan Africa have attracted considerable attention, if not sufficient action. Concern for WID was evident in many aspects of CAAS '87. The diversity of the four WID papers selected for inclusion in these proceedings — Gabba, Ideh, Lyons, Osborn — reflects the breadth of application of a WID perspective. These papers focus on issues of gender, class and politics in Tanzania, research methodology, agroforestry development and representation of women in television programming.

David Gabba, in a paper titled "Women and Development: The Tanzanian Case," traces changes in women's labor demands and opportunities from the pre-colonial period to the present time. The analysis includes examination of some unintended implications for women of both law and policy initiatives. His conclusion is that women's work demands have increased without related improvement in their income, status or power.

Moji Ideh's paper focuses on alternative research methodologies which have been used to study African women and is titled, "African Women and Sex Role Studies: A Methodological Critique." Based upon an analysis and critique of many studies of African women, she recommends that the most valid and reliable studies will be done by African researchers using a combination of research methodologies.

"Women and Trees" by Liz Osborn is a review of literature from sub-Saharan African countries which examines gender based divisions of labor and rights regarding agroforestry development. She concludes that there is a rich diversity of women's rights and activities regarding trees and these must be considered in related projects. The main recommendations are that the research initiatives must go beyond present levels of analysis to become inclusive of more forestry activities and to become more specific in delineation of which women and which trees are being studied.

The portrayal of women by the media has been a perennial concern of feminists. This concern is reflected in Harriet Lyons' paper, "Nigerian Television and the Problems of Urban African Women." This paper is based upon research conducted jointly with her spouse. The approach included media analysis and consumer interviews. The article concludes that while the television programs in Nigeria take women and their problems seriously, they do not provide sustained positive images of women (or men). The issue is raised as to whether or not Nigerian mass media can continue to be entertaining without merely duplicating North American models.

These four papers were not the only ones related to women and development. For example, Wanjiku Kironyo from Kenya was a participant in CAAS'87 funded by Alberta Change for Children. Her paper was titled, "Problems Facing Women and Children in African Countries with Reference to Kenya." Other relevant papers were presented by Achanfuo-Yeboah, Turrittin and Warkentin.

CANADIAN ASSOCIATION OF AFRICAN STUDIES

Women in Development Workshop — May 4 - 6, 1987

E. Murray, Workshop Coordinator

This workshop began with two guiding objectives. These objectives were:

1. To develop an understanding of women and development issues, with particular reference to Sub-Saharan Africa.

2. To consider program and policy initiatives to address effectively the needs of women and families in Africa.

There is considerable evidence with shows that African women have not been full participants in or beneficiaries of the development process, and further, that as a result of development initiatives they and their families have been made progressively more vulnerable to changing economic and social realities. This workshop focused upon selected factors which have placed women in a disadvantaged position. Particular attention was paid to the role of the policy maker and development planning process in addressing the needs of women and families.

Program

A. May 4

1. Introductions
2. Pretest
3. Women in Development as Focus and Policy
   a. Origins
   b. Events
   c. Alternative Paradigms for Women and Development
   d. Research, Policy, Practice

4. Women and Health
   a. The Issues
   b. Patients
   c. Caregivers
   d. Traditional/Clinical Approaches

B. May 5

1. Joint meeting with Theatre and Development workshop participants
2. Family economics issues and their impact on African women
3. Development of story lines based upon discussion
4. Presentation and discussion of five resulting stories

C. May 6

1. Women and Agriculture: Joint meeting with Agricultural
   Systems Research and Methodology Workshop
2. Review of case materials
3. Gender issues in agriculture
4. CIDA policy
5. Program Need Analysis and Policy Development
6. Special Guests: Edwin Lake, CIDA
   and Barbara McCann

Discussion

The workshop was approached as a flexible teaching/learning environment. The presence of both African and Canadian men and women enhanced the opportunity for participant centered instruction as well as coordinator structured sessions. An effort was made to provide data and articles which were current and in some cases unavailable through usual library resources.

Not all programs focusing upon women actually improve their situation either as persons or in families or in larger community systems. Three dominant approaches have been suggested to improve women's situation.

These are changes in household, economic initiatives and empowerment within the system. These three approaches were the subscores in the pretest used in the workshop.[1] The pretests were scored and returned to participants with interpretation. As Table I indicates, the most highly endorsed WID strategies were those which were empowerment oriented, while those addressing economic objectives were least supported by workshop participants. These results and implications were discussed in the workshop.

Table 1
Results of Pretest
(n=33)

	Total	% of Possible Total	Possible Total	Range
Household	47.1	73.5	64	38-62
Empowerment	44.7	85.9	52	29-52
Economic	27.8	63.2	44	17-37

The decision to work collaboratively with the Theatre and Development Workshop participants on economic and family issues was to reinforce knowledge that everyday life and statistical interpretation are often vastly different. Further, the process of discussing issues and developing story lines helps to note the differences in the generalizations developed by those who are part of a social system and those who are not. In retrospect, this process seems to have been as useful to the WID workshop participants as it was to the Theatre and Development group.

The cooperative effort with the Agricultural Systems Research and Methodology Workshop was to focus on policy issues impacting women as agriculturalists as well as family members in agricultural systems. An existing case study was provided; however, the guest speaker confined his remarks primarily to CIDA project policy and practices. Workshop participants attempted by their questions to raise WID issues which kept slipping out of focus. Perhaps the session was reality training.

The final session was designed to examine the project development process. Two discussion topics were the role of the expatriate as an administrator in development programs and consideration of the possible conflicting agendas of donors, recipients and intermediate personnel in the development process. It was a lively and useful session although many workshop participants were not available to attend.

A three day workshop is not sufficient time to address all possible WID issues. However, it is possible in that time frame to develop some ways of looking at WID policy, programs, research and practices. As workshop coordinator I am satisfied that was done. This view is reinforced by the correspondence received from some of the participants. It was an excellent opportunity to teach and to learn. Thank you.

NOTES
1. Prehm, M. "International Home Economics: Exploratory Study of the Interface of Home Economics Programming with Women and Development." Unpublished dissertation. The Pennsylvania State University, University Park, PA, 1985.

Economic Development and Management Development: CAAS Workshop

Workshop Director: Terry Mackey
University of Alberta

Main Contributors

James Campbell, Government of Alberta.

Allan Culham, Canadian International Development Agency (CIDA).

Wilbur Collins, Grant MacEwen College, Edmonton, Canada.

Naison Mawande, Government of Zimbabwe.

Gelase Mutahaba, African Association of Public Administration and Management (AAPAM), Addis Ababa.

Ven Mvano, Eastern and Southern Africa Management Institute (ESSAMI) Arusha, Tanzania.

The role and nature of management is currently under review around the world. Business theorists in North America are taking a broader, more culturally based approach to organizational analysis and are looking at what really happens in corporations, rather than whether business conforms to a particular model. New approaches to managerial decision-making are being explored in China and the Soviet Union. Management in the public and private sectors in the UK is being shaken up by the economic and political policies initiated by the Conservative Government and with the pending changes in the economic situation in Europe. Japanese management techniques are being scrutinized carefully to see how appropriate they are to other cultures. Structural adjustment policies are being introduced in many developing countries.

We have yet to see what the outcome of some of these experiments will be, whether they be structural adjustment, market forces or privatization. The long term impact of privatization on public services in the UK is far from clear and the implications of policy initiatives in other countries have yet to be seen. The political and social ramifications, in particular, of the new policies that are being adopted in Eastern Europe, South America or in Africa may be dramatic and there is no guarantee that these policies will

331

create a more secure economic order. So there is scope for caution. Nevertheless, it would be foolish to ignore the new ideas and the excitement that has been generated in the field of management on an international scale.

Africa has not been immune from this process. African policy makers, and the development agencies that work in Africa, are also experiencing a resurgence of interest in mangement, for a number of different reasons. Partly, this is because many projects that have been initiated by governments, the private sector or development agencies in Africa appear to have failed due to poor management. These errors have been costly and there is pressure on African Governments to improve managerial performance. The need to address managerial capability on the continent has been sharpened, also, by the dire economic situation faced by so many countries. Finally, there is a sense amongst Africans that they need to develop a managerial ideology and practice that is appropriate to the cultures of that continent, rather than importing wholesale the ideas of managerial thinkers and practitioners in Europe or North America. Consequently, a reappraisal is beginning in many African countries and there is a renewed focus on how management can play a role in the economic regeneration; on what problems African managers face; and on what sort of management development and training programmes should be made available in Africa. It was in this context that the Workshop on Economic Development and Management Development took place at the 1987 Canadian Association of African Studies Conference.

Economic Background

> "That Africa is facing an economic crisis of unprecedented magnitude is now an acknowledged fact."

These opening words from a key speaker set the tone for the discussion. The seriousness of the situation was taken as a given. The main concern of the Workshop was with the implications of the crisis — on what could be done about the situation. More precisely, we were concerned with the role that management could play in resolving the crisis. In the currently popular academic argot, we were concerned with "implementation," rather than policy issues. That is not to say that Workshop participants ignored the realities of the economic situation. A number of speakers opened their remarks by outlining some of the key economic problems, but went on to consider what this meant at an operational level for managers. In order to convey something of the background discussion, let us look at the contribution of Professor Mutahaba:

As Africa attained independence all countries had high hopes. The attainment of independence in and of itself was expected to release energies for development and the good life. Nkrumah's dictum of 'Seek you first the political kingdom and all else would be added unto you' seemed so valid. For a while the developments seemed to confirm these hopes. That, however, seemed to last only for awhile. The emerging picture is not as bright as was anticipated. Instead of rapid economic growth, Africa has witnessed economic decline. Poverty, destitution and hunger have been the norm in most countries. The continent today faces a plethora of crises — the food crisis, the energy crisis, the balance of trade crisis, the debt crisis.

The situation has especially become alarming since the late 1970s and early 1980s. The current crisis is reflected in sluggish economic growth, rising inflation rates and widening deficits in current accounts of the balance of payments of most countries. Thus economic growth which has averaged about 5 per cent during 1974-76 fell to about 2 per cent during 1977-79 and had fallen even further by 1983. Accordingly per capita real income actually declined during the period. The rate of inflation, which averaged an annual rate of about 16 per cent during 1974-76 continued to rise dramatically, averaging more than 18 per cent during 1977-79.

The gravity of the African condition can be illustrated even more when one compares economic conditions in African countries with those of the rest of the world. Thus although Africa is part of the developing world, if one focuses on Africa South of the Sahara, it seems to be developing far less rapidly than any other region in the same category. (. . .)

A few countries may have been exceptions to this general decline; thus the oil rich countries such as Nigeria experienced better times although this was a temporary phenomenon, because the foreign reserves which had been accumulated during the boom period were mostly invested in infrastructure which with the glut, which set in since the early 1980s, has made these countries resort to frantic austerity measures to cope with serious balance of payments problems resulting in serious declines in growth.

For most countries, development had to depend upon agriculture, since they had no other exportable commodity. Yet the agricultural section has, in most countries, gone into decline. Nigeria, which had previously met its food requirements, has now become a net importer of food. Figures released by FAO convey an alarming message on the state of African agriculture. Thus between 1970 and 1981 African countries imported a greater volume of agricultural products than they exported. This situation notwithstanding, there is also a tendency for imports to cost more than what the countries receive for their exports. Africa is fast becoming a net importer of food.

A final illustration of the crisis is data on Africa's external indebtedness. As the continent's economic problems have compounded, so has its external indebtedness. Whereas in 1973 external indebtedness stood at US $13.1 billion it had increased to $56 billion by 1981. As these developments were taking place at a time when GNP was growing sluggishly this meant that an increasing proportion of GNP and GDP had to go to debt servicing. Thus whereas the debt service ration stood at 8.00 per cent in 1974 it had increased to more that 25.00 per cent by 1983.

Implications of the Economic Crisis for Management in Africa

The Current State of Management in Africa:

In the light of such a gloomy economic picture, what is the state of management on the continent? Professor Mutahaba cautioned against trying to describe African management in monolithic terms and thereby oversimplifying the situation. Whilst recognizing variations from country to country depending upon colonial heritage, post-independence reorganization and restructuring, and local environments, he sought to draw some general conclusions about trends. He concentrated upon the critical role that public administration plays in Africa: "Typical amongst the features are: the central, if not dominant role of public administration in society, the relative inefficiency of the system, the increasing bureacratization of structures, norms and processes, coupled with social and ecological pressures directed at perverting the structures and norms."

Mutahaba went on to review briefly these points:

Big Government: Central Government bureacracies do not only collect taxes, ensure law and order as well as providing basic services, they are involved in banking and insurance, brew beer, refine oil and distribute cement.

Efficiency Levels: There have been outcries from many circles concerning the level of productivity of public organizations. This cry has been loudest in respect to public enterprises where calls for privatization have been heard in many countries, as well as at many international forums.

Bureaucratic Tendencies: Another major feature of African administration is the predominant role of "bureacracy," as transplanted from the metropolitan centres to what were then colonies. The possession by public service agencies of bureaucratic features in and of itself is not bad. What is bad is to adopt it for organizations where the features become dysfunctional and cause constraints. The increasing adoption of bureaucratic organization for public enterprises has, in the main, tended to make those organizations lose money and become dependent upon the public purse.

Socio-cultural Constraints and Rationality in Bureaucratic Organizations: Problems posed by the adoption of bureaucratic organizations seem to be less onerous than the problems of the effectiveness of African public administration which arise out of the fact that the bureaucratic organizations have to operate in a socio-cultural setting which is at variance with the very standards and norms upon which bureacracy is built. This has tended to place role incumbents in a dilemma. Either they stick to the demands of rationality, as per bureaucratic organizations and become social outcasts or they bend to social pressures and thereby become irrational. In either case, organizational effectiveness will be greatly constrained.

The above characterization is the state of public administration, with or without the economic crisis. It is not in the best shape to handle normal governance and developmental functions, let alone when a crisis of the magnitude faced by Africa at present sets in. Already some efforts were being made to streamline, restructure and reorient public administration in order for it to cope with the increased and expanded governance functions ushered in by independence and the needs of development. Much of the growth in scope, complexity and size of the administrative system was due to these developments. The state and centre expanded its scope, size and activities because nobody else — private enterprise, citizen groups — was doing anything about certain tasks. The contraction of the state has, in and of itself, not expanded the capacity and capability of the non-state sector. This does not mean that there are no activities that can be done by private groups, but the range of these activities is still very limited. Many of the calls for privatization and de-scaling should be heeded carefully and the choice of privatization strategy should be approached with care.

Operational Problems of African Managers:

Dr. Mvano also considered the situation of African managers, but from an operational perspective. One telling comment he made whilst introducing his paper illustrated the different environment faced by African managers. In all the years he had studied and worked in the USA, he had never heard managers mention foreign exchange. For many African managers, the problems associated with the lack of foreign exchange are a constant headache. They experience delays in achieving their goals, and frustration at receiving, perhaps, only a third of the foreign exchange required.

Dr. Mvano offered a framework of analysis for approaching African organizations that put them in the centre of a managerial web, with interaction taking place between the enterprise and the global environment, the domestic economic environment, the political system and the socio-cultural environment. Dr. Mvano supported the idea that analysis of African organizations needs to be placed into an African context, but cautioned about any wholesale jettisoning of management theories from western societies. He reviewed the weaknesses of public sector enterprises and went on to consider what this meant at the operational level:

What comes out clearly from all the studies of public enterprises in Africa is that their managerial problems are as a result of both the macroeconomic management policies of governments and internal (inherent) inefficiencies in the enterprise itself, and that perhaps external factors only help to exacerbate an already bad situation. This conclusion is shared, among others, by Hyden.

According to Hyden (G. Hyden — 'No Shortcuts to Progress: African Development Management in Perspective' — Heinemann: London, 1983), the causes of the poor performance of public enterprises are of four types: politicization of decisions and the decision-making structures; corruption; shortage of manpower; and lack of financial and other internal controls.

Hyden says,

> Politicization manifests itself both in the substance of decisions and the appointment of officials to make those decisions. Politicized decisions here refer to those instances when economic and financial feasibility considerations are deliberately ignored in the interest of pursuing a given political objective. . . . Politicalization tends to mean giving up managerial autonomy. A case in point is when parastatals in Tanzania in 1975 were called upon to engage in food production quite irrespective of opportunity cost of such assignment and its physical and economic feasibility. Another example is the inclination to let public enterprise borrow from the commercial banking system, irrespective of their chances to improve performance.

Hyden goes on to say that corruption manifests itself in many ways in public enterprises ranging from bribery and misappropriation of funds to favouritism in personnel activities, including political patronage in hiring of employees. He attributes the problem of shortage of manpower to the rapid proliferation of public enterprises in Africa, which was not accompanied by a correspondingly rapid increase in production of qualified and experienced staff to run these enterprises. Also the fact that the private sector on Africa often pays better salaries than the public sector means that qualified staff prefer to move into private sector employment at the expense of the public sector. One can go on with the long litany of problems in Africa; suffice it to say that problems of African managers are caused by a socio-political macroeconomic environment that, in the words of Hyden '[does not show] much interest in or concern with the fundamental principles of business management' as much as failure of the microeconomic management system of the enterprise to follow sound business practices.

The picture presented of the managerial problems in general and those of public enterprises in particular, does indicate that the African manager has a very difficult task indeed in trying to improve enterprise performance. Operational problems, in addition to the broad problems already discussed, complicate his job more. A lot of the latter problems tend to be sector or industry specific but others are more 'universal.' Some of these constraints will have been touched upon, but it may be useful to restate them here.

Enterprises in the transport and manufacturing sectors have been hit most severely by lack of spare parts and essential raw materials. One of the main reasons why a number of firms operate at less than 40% capacity in Tanzania, for example, is the failure to obtain spare parts for plant and equipment and imported raw materials. In several cases a factory has had to close down temporarily purely because an imported raw material (like hops used in the brewery or some chemical used in tire manufacturing) could not be obtained in time. The reason behind all this has often been, as mentioned before, inability of the organization to obtain from the Central

Bank all the foreign exchange it needs to import these materials. 'Export earnings retention' schemes devised by several African governments, including Tanzania and Kenya, have helped somewhat to ease the problem. In the case of Uganda, due to historical 'security' related reasons, several of the formerly very prosperous firms, like the sugar factories and cotton mills, have been closed down for a number of years, and only now is their rehabilitation and revival being seriously considered. Some of these plants will require sums of money in excess of perhaps one million dollars to make them operational again.

Managers of African enterprises, especially in the public and parastatal sectors are also faced with the problem of very low worker morale, especially as a result of wage scales which have no realistic relationship with the cost of living. This has been the case for many years in Uganda and Tanzania. Now the situation in Zambia too is becoming almost as bad as that in Uganda and Tanzania. And a similar situation prevails in many other African countries. This situation forces workers not to take their jobs seriously and instead to look to what Hyden calls 'the economy of affection' as the primary source of livelihood. This problem manifests itself in a high level of absenteeism, high labour turnover and, in general, very low productivity. But the problem of low productivity raises a more interesting and complex issue. This has to do with undercapacity utilization of the plant. Many firms in Tanzania, Uganda, Zambia and some other African countries operate at very low capacity levels and they tend to be generally overstaffed, and for various reasons managers are powerless to trim down the workforce. This means then that based on the marginal productivity theory of wage determination these workers are in fact being 'overpaid' even as their wages, both in absolute terms and relative to the cost of living, are low. In other words, given the low level of production and a high level of wage bill, the firm finds it difficulty to raise wages. The point needs to be made, however, that low productivity of workers is not entirely to be blamed on them. Their productivity is greatly affected by the availability and condition of other complementary factors such as equipment, raw materials, working environment etc., which in most cases are far from adequate.

Internal controls in most organizations, particularly as they relate to finances and stores, leave a lot to be desired. In some there are no established procedures for financial controls nor control of stores. Sometimes it is difficult for new and well intentioned managers to institute proper procedures either because some people in the organization would prefer to continue with the status quo or, more ominously, because some individuals may be benefiting materially from the 'confused' state of affairs and would not wish to see it changed.

Another serious constraint, especially to technically competent middle-level managers, is the quality of the top management team or the chief executive imposed on them by the political machinery. In the majority of African countries, heads of public enterprises are appointed by the government which happens to be in power at the time. In some countries the choice of even the second-level managers is influenced by political patronage. Given that it is now almost universally accepted that the success of an enterprise greatly depends on the abilities of the Chief Executive (C/E), political appointment of these executives raises a number of questions. Firstly, some of these appointments have neither the academic background nor the work experience necessary for the job. Secondly, because they lack tenure in that they can be fired any time they fall out of favour with their political benefactors, they feel insecure and therefore tend to employ 'survival' tactics, which are inconsistent with effective management of the enterprise. Because of their affiliation/loyalty to those who appointed them, these executives have no leeway to manage the organization in the most prudent business/entrepreneurial fashion. In addition, it is also true that there is a short supply of 'good' chief executives and as a result, turnover of top managers tends to be high and there is no continuity of leadership in the organization. And given the institutionalization of decision making in the C/E mentioned earlier, departure of the C/E can cause serious difficulties for the new Head of the organization.

Other operating problems have to do with not large enough markets for the products and services; poor management information systems; long procurement and tender procedures; difficulties in obtaining credit and working capital (the only source being commercial banks which tend to charge interest rates that are much higher than cost of equity capital); cultural influences; and low quality of products, especially where they are intended for export or where they are not protected from superior-quality products from abroad.

The contributions from Mutahaba and Mvano defined the scale of the problem and, in doing so, offered ways forward. Their ideas provoked considerable and thoughtful discussion in the Workshop. Similar lively discussion took place during the contributions of James Campbell and Wilbur Collins, who recounted their experiences in management training in Malawi and Botswana. Campbell, in a comparison between Canada and Africa, pointed to the risks associated with failure by managers in Africa. Not only are there problems associated with the loss of salary, but benefits such as housing and education for children are also lost. Consequently, managers act more cautiously. This lack of risk-taking in the public sector, whether in Canada or Africa, is a barrier to good management, according to Campbell.

Role of Development Agencies

The international agencies have been considering the problem of management in Africa. In 1986, a workshop was initiated by the Economic Commission for Africa concerning the need for improved managerial performance. Staff from the World Bank, the Commonwealth Secretariat and the International Labour Organization took part in the discussion and it was felt that technical assistance was not enough and that there should be more emphasis upon managerial effectiveness. Direct intervention by external funding agencies in management development was regarded as inadequate, in that it did not have a lasting effect. Nor was the policy of taking managers out of their own cultures and training them in North America or Europe regarded as satisfactory. Therefore the strategy to be adopted was that the project would seek to strengthen the capabilities of the major African Management Development Institutions (MDI). This, in turn would allow them to offer better services to their clients in the public and private sectors. This project, to be funded by the United Nations Development Fund and a number of other agencies will provide an interesting opportunity for new collaborative approaches to the questions raised in the workshop.

Allan Culham, representing the Canadian International Development Agency (CIDA), took a frank look at the way in which agencies approach management projects. In particular, he drew on a review CIDA had undertaken of projects dealing with public administration and management. A number of common themes had emerged from the evaluations of the projects:

a) Public administration projects must be culturally, linguistically and politically appropriate for the recipient country.

b) Involvement and support from the recipient leads to project success.

c) Recipient involvement in planning leads to ownership and commitment.

d) Critical assumptions/components need to be identified — there is a need for feasibility studies.

e) Project planning should identify areas within a country's public administration system that have the greatest potential for impact.

f) Recipient institutions need the capacity to benefit from and sustain the project's direction.

g) Personnel and wage policies need enhancement for projects to be sustained.

h) Efficient financial management is a constant need.

i) Quality of cooperants is a major determinant of project success.

j) Training and manpower needs assessment must be part of a Public Administration Project.

k) Materials and equipment supplied to Public Administration Projects must be technologically appropriate, arrive on time and be properly managed in order that they enhance project activities.

l) Effective communications is linked to the clarity of roles and responsibilities in the Terms of Reference.

Culham concluded that, overall,

... the review of past evaluation indicates that CIDA has done relatively well in providing helpful public administration projects. However, the problems encountered are not exotic or esoteric. The are relatively predictable but they continue to occur. Both CIDA and recipient countries need to take greater care in the design and implementation of projects with the above lessons learned in mind.

These points also need to be borne in mind by those launching the major funding initiatives for international and bilateral management programmes that are planned in the next few years. The concern by the agencies with new initiatives in management is welcome and reflects the general concern for the problem of management referred to at the outset. However, it remains to be seen whether these programmes will avoid replicating past mistakes.

Lessons for Management Educators

The need for culturally sensitive programmes mentioned by Culham is a critical point. Those working in the management field in Africa have to avoid importing models developed in a completely different culture. If consultants and business school staffs from North America and Europe do not adapt their ideas to local circumstances, and simply seek to run their standard programmes, albeit on African soil, then the initiatives that are being sponsored will be wasted. Indeed, the best hope is amongst those seeking to strengthen indigeneous capacities in Africa by working closely with African partners. African management educators need the time and resources to develop their own approaches. Researchers need to look closely at what makes a good African manager. Project staffs working in this way may have a slower and longer term project on their hands than those simply going into Africa with a "quick fix" solution, but the former is the only way in which real development can be sustained.

A key lesson emerged from the contribution to the Workshop of Naison Mawande, a Permanent Secretary in the Zimbabwean Civil Service. Space does not permit a discussion of the substance of his contribution on the managerial policies adopted by the Zimbabwean Government and, in particular, the process of indigenization of the Civil Service needs a full account elsewhere. However, his insights and guidance on how to operate managerially were an object lesson to all those in the Workshop.

Most of those attending the Workshop were African graduate students from a variety of disciplines, studying in Canada. Their stated aim in attending the Workshop was to gain some insight into the managerial process in Africa. Their problem, along with many students at this level, even those doing MBA courses, is that their programmes are wedded to technocratic and operational solutions to managerial problems. Rarely is the whole managerial picture painted for them. Managers do not face discrete problems of personnel, finance or operations. Usually all three gang up to make the manager's job difficult. Also, there is often little understanding by the faculty of their universities in North America of the environment in which such potential managers will operate. Partly this stems from ethnocentrism, partly because there is an urgent need for a body of research information on operating conditions of managers in Africa. This material is not just for academic purposes. Unless proper data is available on the exact strengths, weaknesses and constraints faced by African managers, then the danger of tilting at windmills is ever present.

What does the excellent African manager really do? How can many of the constraints on managers be lifted? What contribution do women managers make in Africa, in the formal and informal sectors? What are the proper spheres for politicians, civil servants, and business managers? Should there be a blitz on management development in critical sectors that might have a multiplier effect on the rest of the economy? These are some of the questions that need careful thought and substantive research. Some of the answers may not be comforting. This makes it all the more important to ask the questions in the first place.

The skills of the excellent African manager came through in Mawande's contribution. Questions of judgement, sensitivity, understanding of political pressures, recognizing limitations, obtaining good information and knowing when to move were all implicit or explicit in his approach to problems. How we convey such shrewdness in our management programmes is a challenge to all of us.

Seeking Sustainable Agriculture in Africa: Workshop and Conference Proceedings

E. Ann McDougall
University of Alberta

*[Dr. McDougall refers in her opening paragraph to "the second volume of these proceedings."
This book, titled* Sustainable Agriculture in Africa, *is also published by Africa World Press. Its
Table of Contents appears below as an appendix to this article. — Ed.]*

The second volume of these proceedings — *Sustainable Agriculture in
Africa* — is devoted to the problems of agriculture in Africa, a topic central
to the conference theme "Crises in Africa." It explores the "Achievements
and Failures of Aid, Academe and Governments" in this context, and
presents some fairly strong opinions about directions future action should
take. The volume is divided into three sections: the first examines the
three-day Workshop held prior to the conference on "Sustainable Agriculture
and Farming Systems Research"; the second includes an introduction to
selected conference papers, with an introductory essay; and the third
comprises an Annotated Bibliography prepared from suggestions by
Workshop participants (which will go without further comment here).

Part I: Agricultural Systems and Research Workshop, May 4-6

The workshop looked at agriculture in the context of rapidly changing
eco-systems, especially the widespread problems of desertification and soil
degradataion. Women's role as food producers and processors, fuel
gatherers, household managers and agents of change was given special
attention. And the definition of "agriculture" was broadened to integrate
activities such as forestry and pastoralism; hence the focus on farming
"Systems" research.

Monday May 4th we were pleased to have join us *Lee Holland* from the
United Church of Canada, Toronto. His experience drew on eighteen years
of work in Zambia, which included the organization of the indigenous NGO
"Family Farms" (in conjunction with the Zambian Government) which were
staffed by a number of CUSO volunteers. He focused on agricultural
systems with which he had personal experience, and the rapidly growing
problem of land degradation in most parts of Africa. Unfortunately, he could
spend only one day with the group but it was a day well spent.

Tuesday May 5th shifted specific emphasis but remained concerned with the same range of questions. In the morning *Roy Strang*, a specialist in agro-forestry with many years' work in Central and Southern Africa, discussed the problems of supplying fuelwood and providing adequate landcover for African agriculture in the future. He did a superb job of placing the issues — which all too often remain the preserve of scientists working in a vacuum — in the context of social and economic development. In the afternoon, *Roman Fodchuk*, a landscape architect and agricultural consultant from southern Alberta, discussed agricultural systems research with special reference to arid and semi-arid lands. He used his background in the Middle East, North Africa and the West African Sahel to explain components of systems analysis, and its potential for expanding our understanding of the wide variety of rural households emerging in Africa. This particular discussion was a lively one with considerable questioning of the 'pros and cons' of modelling for agricultural development.

Wednesday May 6th we met jointly with the "Women in Development Workshop," to benefit from the visit of a CIDA agricultural specialist, *Edwin Lake*. The question of the viability of agriculture remains central to the concerns of those interested in Women's Development, just as interest in women is central to those dealing with agriculture. Mr. Lake spoke to us about how CIDA views these intersecting interests, with particular reference to its recently created "WID" (Women in Development) component. Not surprisingly, this session drew a lot of critical comment from participants, especially about the issues of formulating and funding policy.

Evaluation, Conclusions and Recommendations

We moved on in the afternoon to evaluate the Workshop and to draw up some conclusions and recommendations. It was regretted that we had not had the opportunity to work through a "case study," as it would have been useful for us to apply our ideas to the process of policy recommendation in a 'real' situation. Several people also commented that not enough attention had been given to the subject of pastoralism and its relation to future agricultural development. What we had been hearing from people like Roy Strang and Roman Fodchuk about the increasing proportion of Africa which must be considered semi-arid and arid only reinforced the conclusion that pastoralism, as one of the few viable means of exploiting such environments, must become part of the discussion. It was further noted that we had begun the Workshop with the premise that agricultural development must be understood in historical context, and that an historical perspective must be integrated into systems analysis; yet we spent little time looking at why this was the case and how this was to be accomplished. Indeed, not one of our resource people had included an historian in the 'team' of analysts identified as necessary to implement the systems approach! Originally, a session dealing with political economy had been planned; some participants reminded us that many of the problems and solutions we were discussing could only have practical significance when examined within the reality of politics and national economic policy. While this was generally agreed, most felt that the Workshop had been wise to limit discussion more to the micro-level, and this sentiment was reflected strongly in the 'Conclusions' which emerged and which were part of the Plenary Report presented to the opening session of the CAAS meeting on May 7.

Conclusions:

1. An immediate concern expressed was the excess of generalized studies and the dearth of micro-level research. Following on this, more financing should be given to research on local conditions, crops and methods of production, with a view to basing programmes on existing, rather than imported, expertise. [The papers in Part II illustrate well the value of such research.]

2. More attention must be paid to what has been termed the 'holistic' approach, developing the tools and techniques for effective multi-disciplinary research, which will be respected at all levels — colleges, specialist institutions, universities, government and non-government agencies, and so on.

3. Several people felt strongly that we need to devise more effective means of project assessment, in terms of social, health and environmental consequences. In particular women, who are vital to almost all development programmes, must not only "be assessed," but must themselves be made part of the assessment process.

4. Finally, in the course of three days of meetings, one issue surfaced repeatedly: communication. Or, more specifically, lack of communication and dissemination of information pertinent to development programmes. Expensive "Learned Journals" are not the answer. It was pointed out that people have become wary of the researcher who collects over and over again information which seldom produces visible (let alone promised) results, and is almost never accessible to local practitioners. The danger here, already realized in some cases we were told, is that people's attitudes and declining expectations will become in themselves impediments to the successful implementation of even well-conceived projects.

Recommendations:

The question remains, of course — how to remedy this situation? In the first place, it seemed to us that much of this 'accessibility' problem stemmed from the policy of organizations like CIDA, IDRC, USAID, and even UN-affiliated groups monopolizing data collected by their researchers. These employees are usually prohibited by contract from making public any of the results of their work, except through authorized agency publications, in spite of the fact that these are publicly-funded. While acknowledging the present situation of inter-agency competition for influence and funding, still we urge that this policy be altered, and materials be made available to all those engaged in research and practical implementation of development projects.

It was also pointed out that we no longer live in the Dark Ages. Data management facilities exist involving the use of highly efficient computer systems. Micro-computers can now access huge data banks while operating autonomously, and they can function at all levels of project formulation and realization. Even in the local village where the computer itself is not a viable option, facilities in regional and national capitals can provide printouts of materials accessed from sources continents away. This should facilitate the work of international agencies, private researchers and most importantly, local practitioners.

Which brings us to a final consideration, one which was explored in both the Women in Development and the Theatre for Development workshops, as well as our own: the importance of involving local people not only in the implementation of a project but in its formulation. Our recommendation re: data accessibility is meant to provide those concerned at the local and regional levels with the information they need to identify and analyze their own problems, as well as to formulate solutions for them.

Part II: Seeking Sustainable Agriculture: Achievements and Failures

The papers in this section were grouped according to the issues they best reflected, although most of them cross-cut more than one category. [See attached list of contributions.] In "Development by Developers?", the Green Revolution of the 1950s and 1960s is revisited, both in order to raise questions about the validity of some of its assumptions, and to point out aspects of its programme which are continuing to shape contemporary development. Williams' "Developer's Viewpoint" contrasts interestingly with Thakur's more theoretical perspective and Parfitt's very illustrative case study. Issues looked at include the appropriateness or necessity of 'modernization' Western-style; the value of expensive technology and more training in its use; the possibility of avoiding 'dependency' on the West and its knowledge; the desirability of large-versus-small scale projects, of international and/or national versus local initiation; the viability of pastoralism in the future; and the role of history in understanding 'development.'

One of the critical questions to emerge from several papers is: can a developer really develop agriculture in Africa, or is this a job which belongs to Africans? And, more specifically, not to African politicians or businessmen, but to African farmers and herders — men, women and children. Is it possible that "aid, academe and government" alike have for too long overestimated what they can do to solve the problems and underestimated how much they have already done to bring them about?

The conclusion here, drawn largely from Parfitt's anatomy of a development project, is that "people's participation" is needed at every stage: to help identify projects in accordance with the needs of the community as the community perceives them, which may not always be those identified by aid agencies or governments; to help identify stumbling blocks likely to affect the implementation of a project; and ultimately, to help evaluate its effectiveness. It seems clear, he concludes, "that donors are undergoing a learning process through evaluating their projects and that the results appear to be a tentative move away from the 'top-down' philosophy of development to the 'Peoples' Participation' approach." In short, and in line with the suggestions of the Workshop, at every stage of the project better results are being obtained by drawing upon local knowledge, associations and participation.

All of the papers in the next section, "View from the Village," reject the 'top-down' approach and explore aspects of exactly what the 'local perspective' entails and how to employ it. They emphasize the important role anthropology must play in identifying the components of local social and cultural systems, political networks and labour organization. Specific information is needed in this context which reveals gender and age differentiation. It is noteworthy that in spite of the importance many people claim to be attaching to the gender (if not the age) factor in agriculture, only Ameyaw, Dei and Osborn really deal directly with the role of women in their contributions. They also discuss the flexibility and breadth we must bring to our definition of agriculture in Africa, which is to say looking at agro-forestry and agro-pastoralism. And lastly, in rejecting the 'top-down' approach, most authors agree that what is needed is not more western expertise, training or money *per se*, but more time spent at the local level, and more attention paid to integrating local, national and international systems.

How can the 'view from the village' be made compatible with the 'view from the capital'? This is the central theme of the section dealing specifically with the political economy perspective. One of the more interesting findings of some of the papers is the degree to which local action has been taking place outside the influence (and interference) of the state. This raises some very interesting questions about the feasibility of the African state playing any meaningful role in attaining sustainable agriculture. Both White's and Riddler's contributions deal specifically with this concern. White expresses the view common to most of the papers when he concludes; "it must be recognised that the government is limited in its ability to *deliver* rural development *to* the villagers. This is true even for a government with as good an administrative record as that of Senegal. For many reasons ... development must come *from* the villagers themselves. However, only if the government will use knowledge that is locally available and will *empower the peasantry* [my emphasis] can it reduce the risks in the face of climatic uncertainly and improve the chances of narrowing the food gap".

The fourth section deals with both the environmental and human dimensions of "the desert and the sown". Several papers look at the impact of "environmental tampering<drquote>, especially as it occurs in the wake of the kind of mega-irrigation projects so popular in the West African Sahel. Some interesting comments are also made about the different ways in which Westerners and Africans tend to approach so-called environmental 'problems', the former preferring to try to change the environment, the latter tending to adapt to it. Fodchuk's paper talks about the same issues in the context of trying to define exactly what is meant by 'semi-arid' and 'arid', and what can be done to prevent further deterioration from one to the other. In fact, it is the human resource which is often critical. The papers dealing with pastoralism remind us that pastoralists interacting with cultivators together make regions habitable which might otherwise be considered 'arid'; hence, it is the human dimension of the 'desert and the sown' which gives much of marginal Africa the potential for sustainable agriculture. The fact that most developers tend to 'write-off' pastoralists or turn them into ranchers and farmers, combined with the fact that many national governments actually see pastoralists as a threat to modernization, poses some very real economic and political dilemmas. The conclusion reached in this section notes that "given that so much of Africa is subject to semi-arid, potentially arid conditions, and that variable forms of agro-pastoralism are the only answers possible for developers, it is surely indisputable that national development policies which either ignore, or try to eradicate pastoralists, are destined to fail."

Finally, in "history and the future of African agriculture," an argument is made for looking to history both to understand the origins of development policy-making in Africa, and to uncover the dynamics of the societies being subjected to such policies. Gervais' and Giblin's papers on the colonial era are alarming in that both the 'development problems' and the solutions they discuss parallel those of the contemporary situation. Little has changed in that control of agricultural development, whether by a national or an international organization, remains a means of exercising political power. Present-day aid donors and national politicians appear no more willing to sacrifice the power this kind of patronage gives them than were colonial authorities and local chiefs. And refusal to recognize that man's political decisions can be more important than climatic change in producing droughts and famine remains as prominent a feature of dealing with 'disaster' today as it did in the 1930s. In terms of "understanding the local situation," which seems to be the key to success reiterated so often in these papers, we must remember that there is a history to the age, gender, ethnic, racial, and occupational relationships found in any given society.

Agricultural development, however it is defined, approached and implemented, cannot take place independently from societal 'development'. What we are doing today is no different from what colonial authorities were doing half a century ago; we are trying to "plan history" according to what we perceive to be desirable social, economic and political goals. But we must remember that what colonial authorities saw as "development," we now call "underdevelopment." In the quest for sustainable agriculture in Africa, history must not be planned to perpetuate itself.

Appendix: Table of Contents to *Sustainable Agriculture in Africa*, Volume II of the Selected Proceedings of CAAS '87

TABLE OF CONTENTS
Table des Matières